# 125 YEARS OF CANADIAN AERONAUTICS

## A CHRONOLOGY 1840 - 1965

CAHS

Canadian Aviation Historical Society

**Boeing Canada**
de Havilland Division

This Book

**125 YEARS OF CANADIAN AERONAUTICS**

is presented to
selected school libraries
on behalf of

THE CANADIAN AVIATION HISTORICAL SOCIETY,

BOEING CANADA
(DE HAVILLAND DIVISION),

&

PRATT & WHITNEY CANADA INC.

*November 1990*

# ABOUT THIS BOOK

## AUTHORS

**GEORGE A. FULLER** – George was born in Sherbrooke, Quebec, the son of Lieut. G.S.B. Fuller, Royal Flying Corps, WW I. The year was 1927 and George grew up with more than the average interest in aviation. He carried on the family tradition during WW II by joining the Air Cadets and took summer jobs at Canadian Vickers and Avro Canada. He served in the Auxilliary and his career took him into business with Noranda Metals.

Since then his enthusiasm for aviation has been directed toward researching the neglected early history of flight in Canada while enjoying every opportunity to fly and, in his words, "to look down on this wonderful country." He has contributed articles to the Canadian Aviation Historical Society Journal and is a Director of the Society.

**JOHN A. GRIFFIN** – John was born in Three Rivers, Quebec in 1922 and took his early education at Westmount, P.Q. He served with the RCAF in WW II and flew Liberators with the RAF in Africa and the Far East. After the war he attended Queen's University and joined Canadian General Electric in 1948.

He has been an active researcher into the history of aircraft and events associated with the RCAF. He was president of the Canadian Aviation Historical Society from 1965 to 1967 and contributed articles to the Society's quarterly JOURNAL. He is the author of "Canadian Military Aircraft, Serials and Photographs", published in 1969, and co-author, with Sam Kostenuk, of "RCAF Squadrons and Aircraft", published in 1977. Later he joined the Aerospace Industries Directorate of the Department of Industry, Trade and Commerce and is preparing a book on the colour and markings of RCAF aircraft.

**KENNETH M. MOLSON** – Ken Molson was born in Ottawa in 1916 and received his early education there. He attended McGill University and the Boeing School of Aeronautics in California and received his private pilot's licence in 1936. He worked his summers with Dominion Skyways Limited and joined the aircraft division of National Steel Car in 1941. He served through the periods of Victory Aircraft Limited and Avro Limited, and in 1960 became curator of the National Aviation Museum in Ottawa. He was responsible for putting together the present historic aircraft collection at Rockcliffe and left, following its absorption by the Museum of Science and Technology.

He has served as a Director of the Canadian Aviation Historical Society and written numerous historical articles which have appeared in aviation journals. In 1974 he wrote "Pioneering in Canadian Air Transport", a story of Western Canada Airways and Canadian Airways. In 1982 he collaborated with H.A. Taylor in the Putnam book "Canadian Aircraft Since 1909".

| | | |
|---|---|---|
| **EDITOR** | – | Fred W. Hotson |
| **GRAPHIC DESIGN** | – | John W. Phipps |
| **COVER PAINTING** | – | Robert W. Bradford |
| **REPRO ASSEMBLY** | – | Brad McLellan |
| **PHOTOGRAPHIC** | – | Ken M. Molson |
| **INDEX** | – | Donley Mogan |
| **FILM** | – | Alland Graphics Company Ltd. |
| **TYPESETTING** | – | Thomas Ng Graphics Ltd. |
| **JACKET PRINTING** | – | Swan Service Ltd. |
| **BOOK PRINTING** | – | T.H. Best Printing Co., Ltd. |

# 125 YEARS OF CANADIAN AERONAUTICS

## A CHRONOLOGY 1840 - 1965

BY

G.A. FULLER, J.A. GRIFFIN and K.M. MOLSON

PUBLISHED BY

THE CANADIAN AVIATION HISTORICAL SOCIETY

Printed and bound in Canada
by the T.H. Best Printing Co., Ltd.

Published by the Canadian Aviation Historical Society
P.O. Box 224, Station A
Willowdale, Ontario M2N 5S8

**Canadian Cataloguing in Publication Data**

125 years of Canadian aeronautics: a chronology 1840-1965

Bibliography: p.
Includes index.
ISBN 0-920610-02-1

1. Aeronautics – Canada – Chronology.
I. Fuller, G.A. (George A.), 1927-
II. Griffin, J.A. (John A.), 1922-
III. Molson, K.M.
IV. Canadian Aviation Historical Society

TL523.053 629.13'0971 C83-098462-3

# CONTENTS

# FOREWORD

I have followed the progress of the Canadian Aviation Historical Society since its formation in 1963 and have been pleased to take part in many of its meetings through the years. It was an honour to be made Patron of the Society in 1978 and I am proud to present their latest publication "125 Years of Canadian Aeronautics". I look on it as a major reference work on aviation that will be used for generations to come.

There is no publication in Canada giving such a complete listing of aviation events backed by so many photos. It could only have been achieved by the co-operation of many persons with a common bond of interest – a true "labour of love". The Society has proven itself again with this fine production. It is one more step in the Society's established goal of preserving Canadian aeronautical history.

I heartily recommend this book to all and look forward to seeing it in schools, libraries and universities across the country.

C.H. Punch Dickins.

C.H. "Punch" Dickins

# PREFACE

The aim of the Canadian Aviation Historical Society through twenty years has been to publish the research of its members and encourage further study into the early years of aviation. The need for a table of dates is essential to all historians and most prepare such a chronology relating to their own specialty. The thought of pooling this information was presented at a Directors' meeting back in 1973 and, after many years, has resulted in this publication.

The Society is proud that its members are contributing to a sound record of aviation history through articles in the quarterly CAHS Journal. A number of members have written highly valuable reference works of their own which have been well received. In this co-operative undertaking we have managed to combine their collective efforts in preparing a much-needed chronology of aeronautics in Canada.

Our thanks go to member Ken Molson who not only put his extensive aviation research at our disposal, but has been a major force in bringing this information together. The detailed work of arranging and checking proved time consuming but, even when it was completed, the problem of putting it into print became a major undertaking. It did not prove commercially attractive to the large publishers and the years went by until we could move forward on our own. We are indebted to CAHS members and friends with publishing experience who realized the importance of this venture and donated valuable assistance in the specialized production details.

The publication of "125 Years of Canadian Aeronautics" is our first major work outside the Journal and is presented in the hope that the aims and objectives of the CAHS will be truly served.

F.W. Hotson, President

# INTRODUCTION

This is the first complete chronology of Canadian aeronautics to be published although a number of abbreviated ones have appeared in serial publications. Foremost among these was an excellent RCAF chronology prepared by the late W/C F.H. Hitchins and published by the RCAF. It proved extremely useful in preparing the RCAF portion of this chronology – a fact that would undoubtedly please former CAHS member and frequent Journal contributor, Fred Hitchins, since death has made it impossible for him to contribute personally to this work.

Many previously unrecorded events are listed in this publication and some minor corrections are made to other incidents previously listed elsewhere. The chronology establishes a number of new Canadian 'firsts' in the field of aeronautics and we feel confident these well researched claims will stand the test of time. Nevertheless it is inevitable that additional items will be found in the future.

The following notes are provided to guide the reader in the use and understanding of the chronology:

1. Aeronautical events listed are those occurring within Canada or Newfoundland or achievements of Canadians in the field of aeronautics elsewhere.
2. Canadian aeronautics is considered to begin with the first manned balloon flight and this chronology is titled accordingly. Some unmanned experiments took place prior to the first manned flight and they are listed for completeness.
3. Each item is presented as briefly as possible consistent with the noting of relevant details. (e.g. – who did what, when, where and in what type of aircraft).
4. Canadian 'firsts' and world 'firsts' are shown in italics.
5. All known gas balloon ascensions between 1840 and 1914 in what is now Canada, are listed together with a representative number of the numerous hot air balloon ascensions.
6. All known demonstrations, exhibitions and constructions of heavier-than-air machines together with associated activities prior to 1915 are recorded.
7. Due to the many Canadians involved it is only possible to list a few of the many courageous or notable actions which took place during the two World Wars.
8. All long distance or record breaking flights that touched Canadian or Newfoundland soil are recorded. Those that overflew Canada or Newfoundland are not included.
9. The first flight dates of many Canadian-made aircraft are included but this listing is not comprehensive.
10. Many of the items listed have references to published material noted against them. This is intended to provide the interested reader with a source of further information or a starting point for further research. In some cases there have been several accounts of the events published – some good and some misleading – so in using reference material other than that listed, the reader should be guided accordingly.

The responsibility for preparing this chronology has been divided between the authors as noted below but, at the same time, they have felt free to contribute to each other's portion to ensure the end result would be as complete as possible.

| Author | Responsibility |
|---|---|
| G.A. Fuller | Pioneer aeronautics to the end of 1914 |
| J.A. Griffin | Canadian military and naval aeronautics 1920-1965 |
| K.M. Molson | Canadian military and naval aeronautics 1914-1919 |
| | Canadian civil aeronautics 1915-1965 |

# ACKNOWLEDGEMENTS

The CAHS and the authors are most grateful to our friends in Ottawa who have contributed to this chronology: W.A.B. Douglas, Directorate of History; R.V. Manning, Canadian War Museum, for permission to use certain RCAF chronological material prepared for the Museum by CAHS member, H.A. Halliday and published in 1975; Mrs. E. Collyer, Librarian, National Research Council; R.W. Bradford, Fred Shortt and Mrs. H. Jacob, Museum of Science & Technology, for their helpful cooperation in tracking down information and photographs. Our thanks, also, go to Peter Robertson, Public Archives Canada and Mel Lundy, Canadian Forces Photo Unit for their help with photographs.

Also, special thanks are due to Canada's pioneer aviation historian, the late Frank E. Ellis, for so helpfully pointing the way in this classic book 'Canada's Flying Heritage' and for his later fine work on transatlantic flying 'Atlantic Air Conquest' co-authored by his wife, Elsie.

On the subject of acknowledgements, it is important to recognize the work done within the Society. All members, from the authors who prepared the material to those who helped with the publication, contributed their services voluntarily. A number served on the chronology committee at various times and include: P. Allen, R.G. Batch, J.H. Ham, F.W. Hotson, H.R. Johns, A.A. McDermott, B. McLellan, K.M. Molson, D.F. Munro and J.W. Phipps.

Valued assistance was received from: R.M. Brass, D. Bromley, J.R. Ellis, W.D. Field, M.R. Hotson, N. Merrin, L. Milberry, P.D. Munro, K. Murray, M. Warner-Smith, W. Wheeler and A.G. Wingate.

Also gratefully acknowledged is the 1981 "99s Award" of $1,000 toward this publication.

The authors have a continuing deep interest in the history of Canadian aeronautics and consequently, additions, corrections or other comments on this chronology would be welcomed by them.

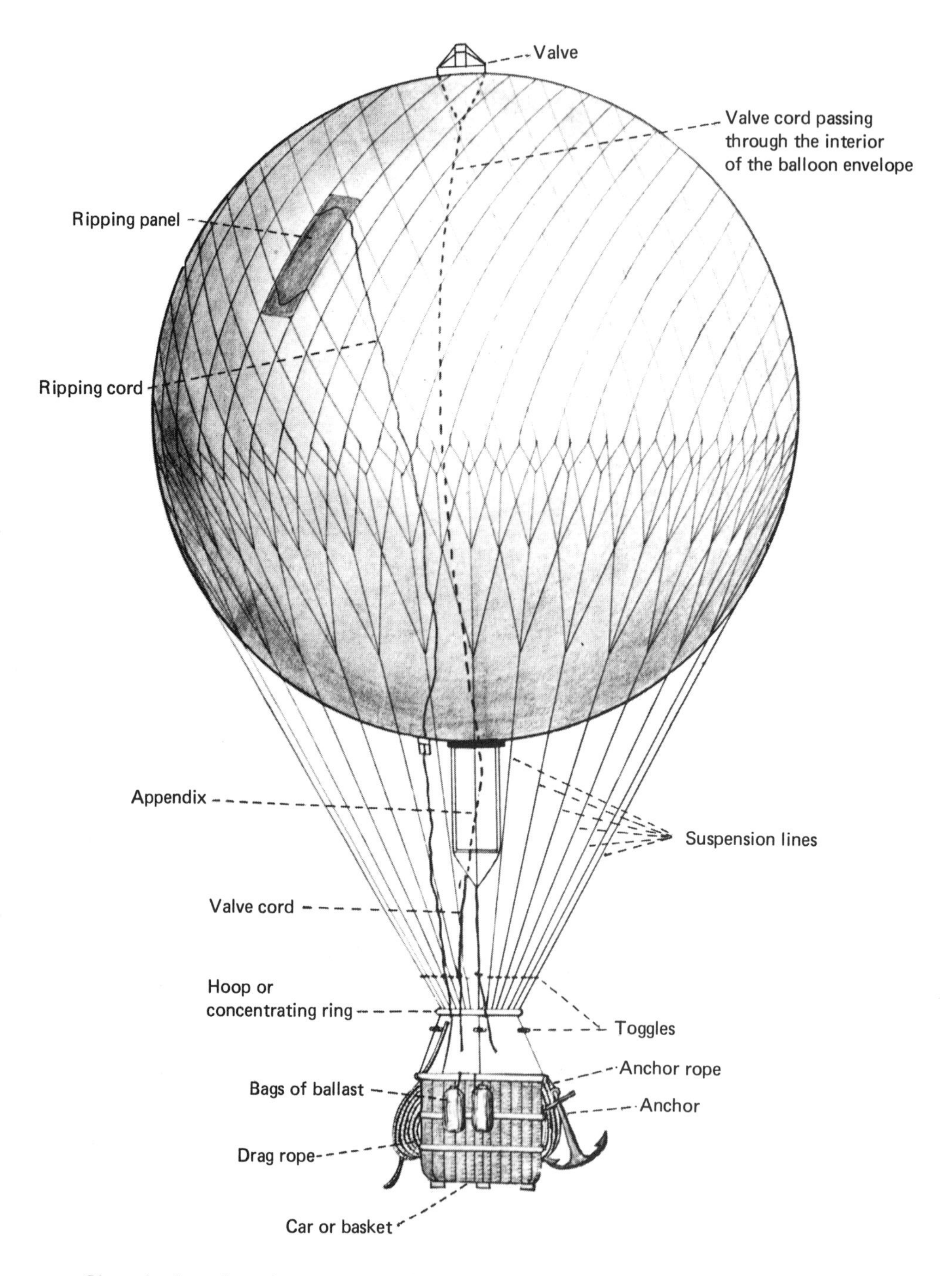


Sketch showing the construction and controls of a typical gas balloon. The ripping panel was used to collapse the envelope quickly on the ground or, in extreme emergency, to collapse the envelope in the air to form a parachute in the network of supporting cords. The drag rope was used to maintain a constant altitude at low heights without discharging gas or ballast. This was done by allowing it to drag along the ground.

# Pre - 1840

**16 OCTOBER, 1784.** *The first recorded eye-witness account of an aeronautical event by a Canadian* was written by William B. Jarvis, who later became Secretary and Registrar of Upper Canada. He wrote from London, England, to his brother in Parr Town (later Saint John), New Brunswick, describing the ascension of Vincent Lunardi's balloon on 15 September, 1784, beginning the first aerial voyage in England.

Ref: Jarvis Papers, Dept. of Can. History,Archives Section, New Brunswick Museum, Saint John, N.B.

**15 OCTOBER, 1834.** Three unmanned hot air balloons were to be sent up from the Champ de Mars, Montreal, Quebec, by W.M. MacGlashan. The exhibition was planned for the benefit of the Montreal General Hospital and the Orphan Asylum. A large and unmanageable crowd prevented the release of the balloons.

Ref. The Gazette, Montreal, L.C., 11-16 Oct. 1834.

**18 MAY, 1835.** An unmanned hot air balloon devised by F.E. Butterfield, a travelling comedian, ascended from the yard of the Farmer's Hotel, Kingston, Upper Canada.

Ref: The British Whig, Kingston, U.C., 19 May, 1835.

**24 AUGUST, 1835.** Three unmanned balloons provided by Joseph Donegani ascended during the grand fete at Guilbault's Botanic Garden amusement park, Montreal, Quebec.

Ref: La Minerve, Montreal, L.C., 31 August, 1835.

**10 APRIL, 1837.** *The earliest recorded aeronautical experiment in Canada* was devised by John Rae, headmaster of the Gore District Grammar School, Hamilton, Upper Canada. He successfully launched a weight-carrying paper balloon for which lift was provided by the heating, owing to its blackened surface, of the air within by the sun.

Ref: The American Journal of Science and Arts, New Haven, Conn., January, 1838.

**28 JUNE, 1838.** During celebrations for Queen Victoria's coronation, an unmanned balloon devised by E. Brown ascended fromThe Common, Halifax, Nova Scotia.

Ref: The Nova Scotian or Colonial Herald, Halifax, N.S., 5 July, 1838.

**22 JULY, 1839.** A celebration of the 27th anniversary of the Battle of Salamanca at Fredericton, New Brunswick, included the ascension of an unmanned hot air balloon devised by Benjamin Franklin Tibbitts.

Ref: Maxwell, L.M.B. The History of Central New Brunswick, Sackville, N.B., 1937.

**Louis Anselm Lauriat, the first aeronaut to ascend in Canada.**
**(via G.A. Fuller)**

**The site of Lauriat's ascension at Saint John, N.B. as it appeared in 1975.** **(G.A. Fuller photo)**

# 1840 - 1849

**10 AUGUST, 1840.** *First aerial voyage in what is now Canada.* Louis Anselm Lauriat of Boston, Massachusetts, ascended from Barrack Square, Saint John, New Brunswick, in his balloon "Star of the East" and landed at a point near the Quaco Road, 21 miles from the city.

Ref: New Brunswick Courier, Saint John, N.B., 15 August, 1840.

**EARLY SEPTEMBER, 1847.** A kite was flown fromThe Common, Halifax, Nova Scotia, to advertise Rockwell & Company's circus from New York City.

Ref: The Nova Scotian or Colonial Herald, Halifax, N.S., 6 September, 1847.

# 1850 -1859

**AUGUST-SEPTEMBER, 1850.** Small hydrogen-filled balloons carrying messages intended for the lost expedition of Sir John Franklin were released from the Royal Navy ship H.M.S. Assistance in Wellington Channel and Barrow Strait near Cornwallis Island, N.W.T. (within 50 nautical miles of the present airport at Resolute Bay).

Ref: Message copies in the collections of the Science Museum, London, England.

**15 JULY, 1851.** Three kites and a sail for auxiliary motive power were deployed by the Royal Navy sledge "Perseverance" (Lt F.L. McClintock) off Griffith's Island, west of Resolute Bay, Cornwallis Island, Northwest Territories while searching for the lost expedition of Sir John Franklin.

Ref: Additional Papers Relative to the Arctic Expedition Under the orders of Captain Austin and Mr. William Penny H.M.S.O., London, 1852.

**4 SEPTEMBER, 1856.** The balloon "Canada", which was constructed under the direction of M. and Mme. Eugène Godard in the Bonsecours Market building, Montreal, Canada East, was placed on public exhibition in the City Concert Hall in the same building.

Ref: Montreal Gazette, Montreal, C.E., 6 September, 1856.

**8 SEPTEMBER 1856.** *The first successful voyage of a balloon constructed in Canada was made and the first aerial passengers in Canada were carried.* The balloon "Canada" ascended from the yard of the Wesleyan Methodist Church in Griffintown, Montreal, Canada East, and landed at Pointe Olivier in St. Mathias parish, Rouville county, C.E. Accompanying French aeronaut Eugène Godard were: Alexandre Edouard Kierzkowski, civil engineer; Alfred Xavier Rambau, journalist, and Captain David S. Ramsay, advocate.

Ref: La Patrie, Montreal, C.E., 10 September, 1856.

A print depicting Professor Lowe's ascent at Ottawa on 17 July 1858.

(via Museum Sc. & Tech.)

**15 SEPTEMBER, 1856.** French aeronaut Eugène Godard and passengers L. Beaudry, G. Lamothe and J. Masson travelled with the balloon "Canada" from Griffintown, Montreal, to near St. Lambert, Chambly county, Canada East.

Ref: Montreal Pilot, Montreal, C.E., 16 September, 1856.

**22 SEPTEMBER, 1856.** The balloon "Canada" carried Eugène Godard and passengers A. Roy, L. Beaudry and M. Coursolles from Griffintown, Montreal, to Tanneries des Rollands (now St. Henri), Hochelaga county, Canada East.

Ref: Le Pays, Montreal, C.E., 23 September, 1856.

**OCTOBER, 1856.** *The first publication in Canada completely devoted to an aeronautical subject* was produced by Senécal et Daniel, printers of the newspaper La Patrie in Montreal. "Eugène Godard", a biographical sketch by Henri-Emile Chevalier, had already appeared in seven parts in La Patrie during the previous month while Godard was making balloon ascensions in Montreal, Canada East.

**11 OCTOBER, 1856.** Eugène Godard made the first of a series of ascensions from Philadelphia, Pennsylvania, with the balloon "Canada".

Ref: Public Ledger and Daily Transcript Philadelphia, Penna., 18 October, 1856.

**17 JUNE, 1858.** Thaddeus Sobieski Constantine Lowe, appearing as Monsieur Carlincourt, made his first public exhibition balloon ascension at Ottawa, Canada West. A previous attempt on 24 May had not been successful.

Ref: The Ottawa Tribune, 9 May & 19 June, 1858. Le Progres, Ottawa, C.W., 3 June & 8 September, 1858.

**1 SEPTEMBER, 1858.** Monsieur Carlincourt (T.S.C. Lowe) made his second successful balloon ascension at Ottawa, Canada West. The occasion was the completion (temporary) of the first trans-Atlantic telegraph cable.

Ref: Le Progres, Ottawa, C.W., 8 September, 1858.

**24 AUGUST, 1859.** The balloon "Europa" carried Professor John H. Steiner of Philadelphia, Pennsylvania, from Toronto across Lake Ontario to Minetto, Oswego county, New York.

Ref: The Globe, Toronto, C.W., 27 & 29 August, 1859.

**8 SEPTEMBER, 1859.** The balloon "Europa" carried Professor John H. Steiner and Captain Bob Moodie from beside the Revere House, Toronto, to near the Gates Tavern, Kingston Road, Canada West.

Ref: The Globe, Toronto, C.W., 9 September, 1859.

John La Mountain and John Haddock arriving in Canada during the night of 22-23 September, 1859, as depicted in a contemporary sketch by Scattergood.

**22-23 SEPTEMBER, 1859.** *First international air travellers arrive in Canada.* The balloon "Atlantic" carried Professor John LaMountain and John A. Haddock from Watertown, New York, to a landing in the wilderness more than 100 miles north of Ottawa, Canada West.

Ref: Haddock, John A., The Thousand Islands of the St. Lawrence River, Alexandria, N.Y., 1895.

# 1860 - 1869

**25 JUNE, 1860.** The balloon "Europa" carried Professor John H. Steiner and Joseph Simmons from Toronto to near Norway village, York county, Canada West.

Ref: The Daily Leader, Toronto, C.W., 27 June, 1860.

**25 JULY, 1860.** The balloon "Europa" carried Professor John H. Steiner from Tête du Pont Barracks, Kingston, Canada West, to near French Creek, Jefferson county, New York.

Ref: The Daily News, Kingston, C.W., 30 July, 1860.

**4 AUGUST. 1860.** The balloon "Europa" carried Professor John H. Steiner from Montreal to near St. Jean, Canada East.

Ref: Montreal Gazette, Montreal, C.E., 6 August, 1860.

**5 SEPTEMBER, 1860.** Professor John H. Steiner made his second successful balloon ascension from Tête du Pont Barracks, Kingston, Canada West.

Ref: The Daily News, Kingston, C.W., 6 September, 1860.

**29 MAY, 1861.** The balloon "Enterprise" carried Professor T.S.C. Lowe and R.C. Buscombe from the Crystal Palace grounds, Hamilton, to St. Anns, Monck county, Canada West.

Ref: The Evening Times, Hamilton, C.W., 30 May, 1861.

**30 MAY, 1861.** The balloon "Enterprise" carried Professor T.S.C. Lowe from St. Anns, Monck county to St. Catharines, Canada West.

Ref: The Evening Times, Hamilton, C.W., 31 May, 1861.

**22 JULY, 1862.** The balloon "Niagara"carried Professor and Mrs. M. Ayers from the James Street "pleasure grounds", Hamilton, Canada West, to Oaklands on Burlington Bay north of the city.

Ref: The Evening Times, Hamilton, 23 July, 1862.

**19 AUGUST, 1862.** The balloon "Niagara" carried Professor and Mrs. M. Ayers from Government House grounds, Toronto, to Scarborough township, Canada West.

Ref: The Daily Globe, Toronto, C.W., 20 August, 1862.

**21 AUGUST, 1862.** The balloon "Niagara" carried Professor M. Ayers from Dulmage's Square, London, Canada West, to near Thorndale Station, Middlesex county.

Ref: Free Press, London, C.W., 22 August, 1862.

**11 SEPTEMBER, 1862.** The balloon "Niagara" carried Professor M. Ayers from Victoria Gardens, Montreal, to St. Leonard, Canada East.

Ref: The Montreal Daily Transcript, 15 September 1862.

**25 SEPTEMBER, 1862.** The balloon "Niagara" carried Professor M. Ayers from Government House grounds, Toronto, Canada West, across Lake Ontario to near Gasport, Niagara county, New York.

Ref: The Daily Globe, Toronto, C.W., 26 September, 1862.

**16 OCTOBER, 1862.** Professor M. Ayers was carried in his balloon from Dulmage's Square, London, Canada West, to a point about 6 miles away on the outskirts of the city.

Ref: Free Press, London, C.W., 17 October, 1862.

**14 OCTOBER, 1863.** Professor Samuel Archer King and three passengers made a balloon voyage from Bangor, Maine, to Hartt's Mills, Sunbury county, New Brunswick.

Ref: New Brunswick Reporter, Fredericton, N.B., 30 October, 1863.

# 1870 - 1879

**4 JULY, 1871.** A balloon voyage by Charles C. Coe of Rome, New York, with a companion from Oswego, New York, ended at Irish Creek, Grenville county, Ontario.

Ref: The New York Times, N.Y., 8 July, 1871.

**8 JULY, 1871.** Appearing with Wootten & Haight's Empire City Circus, Professor Reno made a hot air balloon ascension at Woodstock, New Brunswick.

Ref: The Cartleton Sentinel, Woodstock, N.B., 15 July, 1871.

**12 JULY, 1871.** Professor Reno made a hot air balloon ascension from the Ballast Wharf, Saint John, New Brunswick.

Ref: The Daily Morning News, Saint John, N.B., 13 July, 1871.

**20 JULY, 1871.** The ascension of an unmanned hot air balloon devised by Mr. Howse was a feature of the British Columbia Confederation celebrations at Victoria.

Ref: Daily Standard, Victoria, B.C., 22 July, 1871.

**31 JULY, 1871.** Professor Reno made the first of three hot air balloon ascensions fromThe North Common, Halifax, Nova Scotia, during the engagement there of the Empire City Circus.

Ref: The British Colonist, Halifax, N.S., 1,3 & 5, August, 1871.

**8 AUGUST, 1871.** Professor Reno ascended with a hot air balloon from the Pottery Company grounds at New Glasgow, Nova Scotia.

Ref: The Eastern Chronicle, New Glasgow, N.S., 10 August, 1871.

**17 AUGUST, 1871.** A hot air balloon ascension was made by Professor Reno from Rochfort Square, Charlottetown, Prince Edward Island.

Ref: The Semi-Weekly Patriot, Charlottetown, P.E.I., 19 August, 1871.

**26-27 SEPTEMBER, 1872.** Professor S.A. King and L.L. Holden made a balloon voyage from Plymouth, New Hampshire, to near Sayabec, Rimouski county, Quebec.

Ref: The Public Ledger, St. John's, Newfoundland, 5 November, 1872.

**1 JULY, 1874.** Professor Herman D. Squire's attempted ascension from Court House square, Brockville, Ontario, ended when the balloon "Atlantic" collided and became entangled with a nearby church spire. The aeronaut, who was only slightly injured, was rescued with some difficulty.

Ref: The Recorder, Brockville, Ont., 9 July, 1874.

**23 SEPTEMBER, 1874.** Professor S.A. King ascended from the Toronto Cricket Ground with the balloon "Cloud Nymph".

Ref. The Mail, Toronto, Ont., 24 September, 1874.

**24 MAY, 1875.** Professor Justin Buislay performed acrobatics on a trapeze suspended beneath his ascending hot air balloon "Meteor" at the Toronto Cricket Ground.

Ref: The Mail, Toronto, Ont., 24 May, 1875.

**JUNE, 1875.** Professor Eliedon performed acrobatics on a trapeze suspended beneath his ascending balloon "Mercury" at the Great Forepaugh Show at St. Thomas, Ontario.

Ref: Weekly Dispatch, St. Thomas, Ont., 24 June, 1875.

**17 JUNE, 1875.** The balloon "P.T. Barnum" carried Professor Washington Harrison Donaldson and three passengers from Buffalo, New York, to Port Colborne, Ontario.

Ref: Amick, M.L. History of Donaldson's Balloon Ascensions, Cincinnati, Ohio, 1875.

**21 JUNE, 1875.** The balloon "P.T. Barnum" carried Professor W.H. Donaldson and three passengers from Hamilton, Ontario, to Nelson township, Halton county, Ont.

Ref: The Daily Globe, Toronto, Ont., 22 June, 1875.

**22 JUNE, 1875.** Professor W.H. Donaldson made a balloon ascension from Barnum's Hippodrome circus grounds, Toronto, Ontario.

Ref: The Daily Globe, Toronto, Ont., 23 June, 1875.

**23 JUNE, 1875.** The balloon "P.T. Barnum" carried Professor W.H. Donaldson and three passengers from Toronto to a landing in Lake Ontario near Long Point, Prince Edward county.

Ref: The Daily Globe, Toronto, Ont., 24 & 25 June, 1875.

Professor Grimley's ascension of 28 September 1878 at Montreal as depicted in the Canadian Illustrated News of 5 October, 1878.
(via Public Archives Canada)

**26 JUNE, 1875.** Professor W.H. Donaldson made his 128th balloon ascent at London, Ontario.

Ref: Amick, M.L., History of Donaldson's balloon ascensions, Cincinnati, Ohio, 1875.

**3 JULY, 1877.** The balloon "City of Worcester" carried Professor Charles H. Grimley of New York City from Cartier Square, Ottawa, Ontario, to near Chelsea, Ottawa county, Quebec.

Ref: The Free Press, Ottawa, Ont., 3 July, 1877.

**12 SEPTEMBER, 1877.** The balloon "City of Worcester" carried Professor Charles H. Grimley from the Ottawa Fair Grounds to near Cumberland, Russell county, Ontario.

Ref: The Daily Citizen, Ottawa, Ont., 13 September, 1877.

**31 MAY, 1878.** Richard W. Cowan and Charles Pagé of Montreal, Quebec, were granted Canadian patent 8860 covering "Improvements in Flying Machines".

Ref: Copy of patent in Museum of Science & Technology, Ottawa, Ont.

**1 JULY, 1878.** The balloon "City of Ottawa" carried Professor C.H. Grimley and George Fox from Ottawa, Ontario, to East Portland Township, Ottawa county, Quebec.

Ref: The Daily Citizen, Ottawa, Ont., 2 July, 1878.

**27 AUGUST, 1878.** The balloon "City of Ottawa" carried Professor C.H. Grimley and reporter Gibbons of "The Daily Citizen" from the Agricultural Show Grounds, Ottawa, to the edge of the Mer Bleue mire, Carleton county, Ontario.

Ref: The Daily Citizen, Ottawa, Ont., 28 & 29 August, 1878.

**28 SEPTEMBER, 1878.** The balloon "City of Ottawa" carried Professor C.H. Grimley and newspaper reporter Hiram Moulton from the Irish Protestant Benevolent Society picnic at Shamrock Lacrosse Grounds, Montreal, Quebec, over the city to land near the eastern entrance to the Lachine Canal.

Ref: The Gazette, Montreal, Que., 30 September, 1878.

**21 JUNE, 1879.** The balloon "Canada" carried Professor C.H. Grimley and reporter J. Creelman of the "New York Herald" from the Shamrock Lacrosse Grounds, Montreal, to St. Jude, St. Hyacinthe county, Quebec.

Ref: The Gazette, Montreal, Que., 24 June, 1879.

**28 MAY, 1879.** Richard W. Cowan and Charles Pagé of Montreal, Quebec, were granted U.S. patent 204,296 covering "Improvement in Aerial Paddle-Wheels".

Ref: Copy of patent in Museum of Science & Technology, Ottawa, Ont.

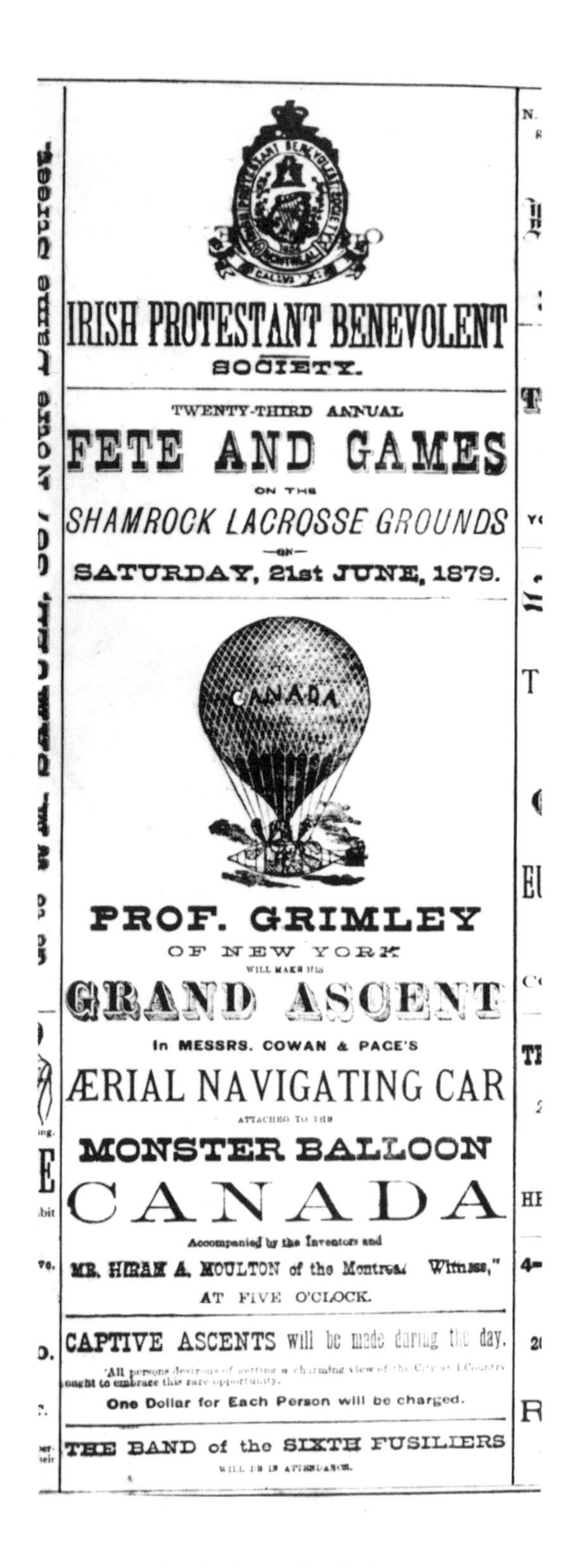


**Advertisement for Professor Grimley's ascent to test the propulsion system devised by Messrs. Cowan and Page.**
**(via Museum of Sc. & Tech.)**

**31 JULY, 1879.** In an unsuccessful attempt at powered, dirigible flight, the balloon "Canada" carried Professor Grimley and five passengers in a framework equipped with hand-cranked side propellers and a directional rudder. Those on board included the inventors of the apparatus, Richard V. Cowan and Charles Pagé of Montreal, and three newspaper reporters. They ascended from the Shamrock Lacrosse Grounds, Montreal and landed near Ste. Anne, Richelieu county, Quebec.

Ref: The Gazette, Montreal, Que., 1 & 2 August, 1879.

**29 AUGUST, 1879.** *First ascent in Canada by a female aeronaut.* The balloon "Lorne" carried Miss Nellie Thurston from McFarlane's Grove, Almonte, Lanark county, to near Merrickville, Grenville county, Ontario.

Ref: The Almonte Gazette, Almonte, Ont., 7 September, 1967.

# 1880 - 1889

**9 JUNE, 1880.** Professor LeClaire made a hot air balloon ascension from the Skinner Street show grounds, Nanaimo, British Columbia and landed in the harbour.

Ref: Free Press, Nanaimo, B.C., 12 June, 1880.

**11 JUNE, 1880.** Professor LeClaire ascended with a hot air balloon from Wellington, Vancouver Island, British Columbia.

Ref: Free Press, Nanaimo, B.C., 12 June, 1880.

**18 SEPTEMBER, 1880.** Professor C.H. Grimley ascended with the balloon "Canada" from the Grand Dominion Exhibition grounds, Montreal, Quebec, landing at the east end of the city.

Ref: The Gazette, Montreal, Que., 20 September, 1880.

**23 SEPTEMBER, 1880.** The balloon "Canada" carried Professor C.H. Grimley and J. H. Browning from the Grand Dominion Exhibition grounds, Montreal, to Marieville, Rouville county, Quebec.

Ref: The Gazette, Montreal, Que., 25 September, 1880.

**2 JULY, 1883.** Miss Carlotta Myers (Mrs. Mary H. Myers) of Mohawk, New York, ascended with the balloon "Flying Cloud" from the Exhibition Grounds, Ottawa, landing near Eastmans Springs, Russell County, Ontario.

Ref: The Ottawa Daily Free Press, Ottawa, Ont., 3 July, 1883.

**AUGUST, 1883.** Captain H. Elsdale, R.E., of the British Army, devised photography experiments from an unmanned captive balloon at Halifax, Nova Scotia.

Ref: Transactions of the Royal Institution of Chartered Surveyors, Vol. LVI, 1923-1924.

**15 SEPTEMBER, 1883.** Charles W. Williams of Cincinnati, Ohio, ascended with a balloon from the Toronto Exhibition, landing near Todmorden, York County, Ontario. Another such voyage by Williams on 17 September ended with a narrow escape from drowning in Lake Ontario.

Ref: The Toronto Mail, Toronto, Ont., 16-18 September, 1883.

**26 SEPTEMBER, 1884.** The balloon "The Queen of the Air" carried Madame Lowanda of White Haven, Pennsylvania, from the Exhibition Grounds, Ottawa, Ontario, to near East Templeton, Ottawa county, Quebec.

Ref: The Daily Citizen, Ottawa, Ont., 27 September, 1884.

**4-6 September, 1888.** *First parachute descents in Canada.* Canadian-born Edward D. Hogan, of Jackson, Michigan, performed hot air balloon ascensions and parachute descents at the Great Eastern Exhibition, Sherbrooke, Quebec.

Ref: Le Pionnier, Sherbrooke, Que., 6 September, 1888.

**22-28 SEPTEMBER, 1888.** Aeronauts Bready and Vandegrift of Cleveland, Ohio, performed hot air balloon ascensions and parachute jumps at the Western Fair, London, Ontario.

Ref: The London Advertiser, London, Ont., 24-29 September, 1888.

**26 SEPTEMBER, 1888.** *First aerial fatality in Canada* occurred during a balloon ascension by Professor C.W. Williams at the Ottawa Exhibition. Tom Wensley, one of a group of volunteer helpers, was carried into the air clinging to a rope hanging from the balloon. The aeronaut was unable to assist him and he fell to his death.

Ref: The Ottawa Free Press, Ottawa, Ont., 27 September, 1888.

**16 JULY, 1889.** *First Canadian-born aeronaut to die in an aerial mishap.* E.D. Hogan was lost at sea testing the Campbell "airship" balloon from Brooklyn, New York.

Ref: The New York Times, N.Y., 19 July, 1889.

**29 AUGUST, 1889.** *The first technical aeronautical paper in Canada* "Air Resistance of Inclined Planes" was presented at Toronto, Ontario by Octave Chanute at the annual meeting of the Association for the Advancement of Science.

Ref: The Globe, Toronto, Ontario 30 August 1889, page 2.

**19 JULY, 1889.** Professor W. Hogan parachuted from a hot air balloon at St. Thomas, Ontario.

Ref: Free Press, London, Ont., 20 July, 1889.

# 1890 - 1899

**27 JULY, 1891.** Professor Woodhall made a balloon ascension at Esquimault, British Columbia.

Ref: The Daily Colonist, Victoria, B.C., 28 July, 1891.

**2-3 SEPTEMBER, 1891.** *First parachute descent in Canada by a woman.* Professor W.W. McEwen and Miss Nellie Lamount performed hot air balloon ascensions and parachute descents at the Great Eastern Exhibition, Sherbrooke, Quebec. They returned for a similar engagement the following year.

Ref: Le Pionnier, Sherbrooke, Que., 31 August-4 September, 1891; 26 August - 9 September, 1892. Montreal Daily Herald, Montreal, Que., 8-9 September, 1892.

**22 SEPTEMBER, 1891.** Stanley Spencer of London, England, ascended with the balloon "Claymore" at the Provincial Exhibition, Montreal, Quebec.

Ref: The Gazette, Montreal, Que., 23 September, 1891.

**24 SEPTEMBER, 1891.** The balloon "Claymore" carried Stanley Spencer and Sgt A.F. Winfindale of the Victoria Rifles from the Provincial Exhibition grounds, Montreal, to near Beloeil, Verchères county, Quebec.

Ref: The Gazette, Montreal, Que., 25 September, 1891.

**2 OCTOBER, 1891.** Stanley Spencer parachuted from the balloon "Claymore" at the Exhibition, Halifax, Nova Scotia.

Ref: Morning Chronicle, Halifax, N.S., 3 October, 1891.

**7 OCTOBER, 1891.** Stanley Spencer parachuted from the balloon "Claymore" at Charlottetown, Prince Edward Island. A similar performance was given on 9 October.

Ref: The Daily Examiner, Charlottetown, P.E.I., 8-10 October, 1891.

**16 AUGUST, 1892.** Stanley Spencer parachuted from the balloon "Claymore" at the Parc Malone Trotting Races, Trois Rivières, Quebec.

Ref: Le Trifluvien, Trois Rivières, Que., 17 August, 1892.

**23 AUGUST, 1892.** Stanley Spencer parachuted from the balloon "Claymore" at the Trotting and Running Races, Parc Dery, Quebec City, Quebec. The performance was repeated the following day.

Ref: L'Evénement, Quebec, Que., 24-25 August, 1892.

**19 SEPTEMBER, 1892.** Stanley Spencer and a passenger ascended with the balloon "Claymore" from the Provincial Exhibition, Montreal. During an engagement there that lasted until 22 September, he made both captive and free ascensions and parachute descents.

Ref: Montreal Daily Herald, Montreal, Que., 20-23 September, 1892.

**21 JULY, 1893.** Miss Louisa Bates parachuted from a balloon at the Winnipeg Industrial Exhibition. She made two more successful jumps during the engagement.

Ref: Manitoba Free Press, Winnipeg, Man., 24 July, 1893.

**10 OCTOBER, 1894.** Charles Marble, from Washington State, drowned in the Fraser River after parachuting from a hot air balloon at New Westminister, British Columbia.

Ref: The Daily Colonist, Victoria, B.C., 11 October, 1894.

**20 FEBRUARY, 1895.** *First technical paper on aeronautics delivered in Canada by a Canadian.* C.H. Mitchell delivered a paper "Aerial Mechanical Flight" to the Engineering Society, School of Practical Science, U of T, Toronto, Ontario.

Ref: Original paper in Museum of Science & Technology library, Ottawa, Ontario.

**27 MAY, 1896.** Professor H. Menier parachuted from a hot air balloon at River Park, Winnipeg, Manitoba. Similar performances were given on 28, 29 and 30 May.

Ref: Manitoba Free Press, Winnipeg, Man., 28 May - 1 June, 1896.

**26 AUGUST, 1896.** Frank Miller parachuted from a hot air balloon at Oak Bay, Victoria, British Columbia.

Ref: The Colonist, Victoria, B.C., 27 August, 1896.

**2-5 SEPTEMBER, 1896.** Aeronauts Frank Stevens and Miss Nina Madison performed hot air balloon ascensions and parachute jumps at the Great Eastern Exhibition, Sherbrooke, Quebec.

Ref: Le Pionnier, Sherbrooke, Que., 4 September, 1896.

**8 SEPTEMBER, 1896.** Frank "Don Carlos" Stevens, of the Wolcott Balloon Company, was injured when his parachute did not fully open after jumping from a hot air balloon at the Huntingdon, Quebec Fair.

Ref: Canadian Gleaner, Huntingdon, Que., 10 September, 1896.

**1-3 SEPTEMBER, 1897.** Aeronauts Alexander Leo Stevens and Miss Cleo Carleton performed hot air balloon ascents and parachute descents at the Great Eastern Exhibition, Sherbrooke, Quebec.

Ref: Sherbrooke Daily Record, Sherbrooke, Que., 25 August - 4 September, 1897.

**29 AUGUST, 1899.** Professor John Leonard parachuted from a hot air balloon at Dawson, Yukon Territory, the first such performance in the Territory. The exhibition was repeated on 4 September.

Ref: Dawson Daily News, Dawson, Y.T., 30 August, 9 September, 1899.

**6 SEPTEMBER, 1899.** Miss May Juwel of Sherbrooke, Quebec, parachuted from a hot air balloon at the Sherbrooke Exhibition. She had made her first ascension and jump at Newport, Vermont, on 17 August, 1899.

Ref: Sherbrooke Daily Record, Sherbrooke, Que., 7 September, 1899.

# 1900 - 1905

**2 JUNE, 1900.** Professor Thompson parachuted from a hot air balloon at River Park, Winnipeg, Manitoba. The balloon carried advertisements on its surface.

Ref: Manitoba Free Press, Winnipeg, Man., 4 June, 1900.

**16 JUNE, 1900.** Miss Adela Thompson parachuted from a hot air balloon at River Park, Winnipeg, Manitoba. She narrowly escaped drowning when she parachuted on 29 June and dropped into the Red River.

Ref: Manitoba Free Press, Winnipeg, Man., 18 & 30 June, 1900.

**23 MAY, 1901.** Professor Earlston parachuted from a balloon at Oak Bay, Victoria, British Columbia.

Ref: The Daily Colonist, Victoria, B.C., 24 May, 1901.

**7 AUGUST, 1902.** Professor Frank Miller parachuted from a hot air balloon at Oak Bay, Victoria, British Columbia.

Ref: The Colonist, Victoria, B.C., 8 August, 1902.

**14 SEPTEMBER, 1902.** Frank Miller parachuted from a hot air balloon after ascending from the lawn in front of the North Vancouver Hotel, North Vancouver, British Columbia. He made a similar performance on 21 September.

Ref: The Province, Vancouver, B.C., 15 & 22 September, 1902.

**1902.** *First wind tunnel in Canada.* Wallace Rupert Turnbull completed a wind tunnel at Rothesay, New Brunswick.

Ref: Parkin, J.H. Wallace Rupert Turnbull 1870-1954. Can. Aero. Jour. Vol. 2, No. 1, January, 1956.

**25 MAY, 1903.** Professor John Leonard began his fourth visit to the Yukon with a parachute descent from the hot air balloon "Island Mail" at White Horse, Yukon Territory.

Ref. The Weekly Star, White Horse, Y.T., 30 May, 1903.

**28 DECEMBER, 1905.** Alexander Graham Bell's tetrahedral cell kite lifted Neil McDermid into the air on a rope ladder at Baddeck, Nova Scotia.

Ref: Parkin, J.H., Bell and Baldwin, Toronto, 1964.

# 1906

**1 JULY, 1906.** Professor R. Cross parachuted from a hot air balloon at Edmonton, Alberta.

Ref: The Edmonton Bulletin, Edmonton, Alta., 2 July, 1906.

L.J. Lesh's Montreal No. 1 glider, the first Canadian heavier-than-air aircraft, in which he made his over-water flight. (Scientific American)

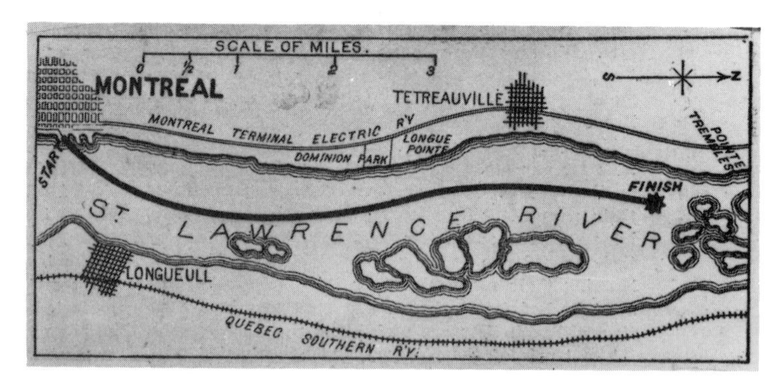


Map showing the route followed by Lesh in his long over-water flight in August 1907.

Lesh gliding in his Montreal No. 2 glider before adding ailerons. (Scientific American)

**11 JULY, 1906.** Professor Williams of Sturgis, Michigan, parachuted from a balloon at Victoria Park, Calgary, Alberta.

Ref: The Morning Albertan, Calgary, Alta., 12 July, 1906.

**13 JULY, 1906.** *The first engine-powered, directed flight on a lighter-than-air aircraft in Canada.* Charles Keeney Hamilton of New Britain, Connecticut, flew a Knabenshue dirigible at Dominion Park, Montreal, Quebec, after making a forced landing in attempted flight on the previous day. Further flights were made on 15 and 16 July.

Ref: The Montreal Gazette, Montreal, Que., 13-17 July, 1906.

# 1907

**MARCH, 1907.** *First Canadian technical paper on aeronautics was published in a technical journal.* W.R. Turnbull's paper "Research on the Forms and Stability of Aeroplanes" was published in the Physical Review.

Ref: Parkin, J.H. Wallace Rubert Turnbull, 1870-1954. Can. Aero. Jour. Vol. 2, No. 1, January, 1956.

**10 JULY, 1907.** Canadian-born Professor Thompson, of St. Paul, Minnesota, parachuted from a hot air balloon at the Industrial Fair, Portage la Prairie, Manitoba.

Ref: The Weekly Review, Portage la Prairie, Man., 11 July, 1907.

**10 AUGUST, 1907.** The Underwood brothers' flying machine/kite was tested in tethered flight carrying John Underwood at Krugerville, Alberta.

Ref: Ellis, Frank H. Canada's Flying Heritage, Toronto, 1954.

**AUGUST, 1907.** *First flight of a heavier-than-air machine in Canada.* Lawrence Jerome Lesh successfully tested his Montreal No. 1 glider at Montreal, Quebec. Precise date is uncertain, but is August 16, 17 or 18.

Ref: Molson, K.M. The Aileron Comes to North America - L.J. Lesh and his Aircraft. CAHS Jour., Vol. 12, No. 2.

**20 or 21 AUGUST, 1907.** *The longest overwater flight and longest towed glider flight on record was carried out at Montreal, Quebec.* L.J. Lesh completed a flight over the St. Lawrence River covering over 6 miles in about 24 minutes.

Ref: Molson, K.M. The Aileron Comes to North America - L.J. Lesh and his Aircraft. CAHS Jour. Vol. 12, No. 2.

**29 AUGUST, 1907.** Carl Robinson of Buffalo, New York, attempted to fly a Knabenshue dirigible at the Canadian National Exhibition at Toronto, Ontario. The airship was severely damaged in a crash landing due to engine failure and strong winds.

Ref: The Globe, Toronto, Ont., 30 August, 1907.

L.J. Lesh's Montreal No. 2 glider with ailerons added, September 1907. (Scientific American)

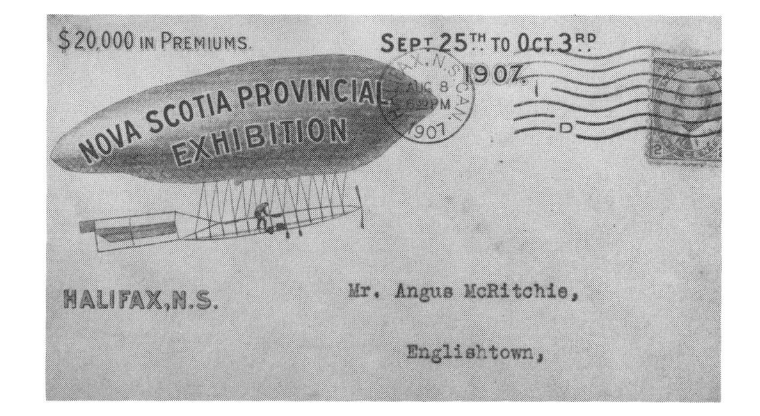


Envelope advertising Capt. T.S. Baldwin's flights at the 1907 Nova Scotia Provincial Exhibition. (via R.K. Malott)

The A.E.A. members L-R: F.W. (Casey) Baldwin, T.E. Selfridge, G.H. Curtiss, Dr. A.G. Bell, J.A.D. McCurdy, and Augustus Post, Sec., Aero Club of America May 1908 at Hammondsport, N.Y. (Bell family & Nat'l Geographic Soc.)

**31 AUGUST, 1907.** *First crash of a heavier-than-air machine in Canada.* L.J. Lesh crashed in his Montreal No. 1 glider at Montreal. He was uninjured, but his glider was demolished.

Ref: Molson, K.M. The Aileron Comes to North America - L.J. Lesh and his Aircraft. CAHS Jour. Vol. 12, No. 2.

**4 SEPTEMBER, 1907.** Lincoln Beachey flew his dirigible at the Dominion Exhibition, Sherbrooke, Quebec. Further flights were made on 5, 6, 8, and 13 September.

Ref: Sherbrooke Daily Record, Sherbrooke, Que., 31 August - 13 September, 1907.

**13 SEPTEMBER, 1907.** Charles Earl Hess of Toledo, Ohio, made a brief flight on a Knabenshue dirigible at the Western Fair, London, Ontario.

Ref: The Free Press, London, Ont., 14 September, 1907.

**26 SEPTEMBER, 1907.** Captain Thomas Scott Baldwin flew his dirigible "The California Arrow II" at the Nova Scotia Provincial Exhibition at Halifax, Nova Scotia. Another flight was made on 30 September.

Ref: The Halifax Herald, Halifax, N.S., 21 September - 1 October, 1907.

**SEPTEMBER, 1907.** *First photograph was taken from a heavier-than-air machine.* L.J. Lesh took a photograph from his Montreal No. 2 glider at Montreal, Quebec.

Ref: Molson, K.M. The Aileron Comes to North America - L.J. Lesh and his Aircraft. CAHS Vol. 12, No. 2.

**SEPTEMBER, 1907.** *First use of ailerons in North America and fifth in world.* L.J. Lesh fitted and used ailerons on his Montreal No. 2 glider at Montreal, Quebec.

Ref: Molson, K.M., The Aileron Comes to North America - L.J. Lesh and his Aircraft, CAHS Jour. Vol. 12, No. 2.

**1 OCTOBER, 1907.** The Aerial Experiment Association was inaugurated at Halifax, Nova Scotia. The officers were: Alexander Graham Bell, Fredrick Walker (Casey) Baldwin, John Alexander Douglas McCurdy, Lieut. Thomas Etholan Selfridge and Glenn Hammond Curtiss.

Ref: Parkin, J.H. Bell and Baldwin, Toronto, 1964.

**21 OCTOBER, 1907.** Henry Blanchard Hersey landed with the balloon "United States" at Tyneside, Haldimand county, Ontario, completing a voyage from St. Louis, Missouri, in the Gordon Bennett international balloon race.

Ref: Fly, Philadelphia, Vol. 1, No. 6, April, 1909.

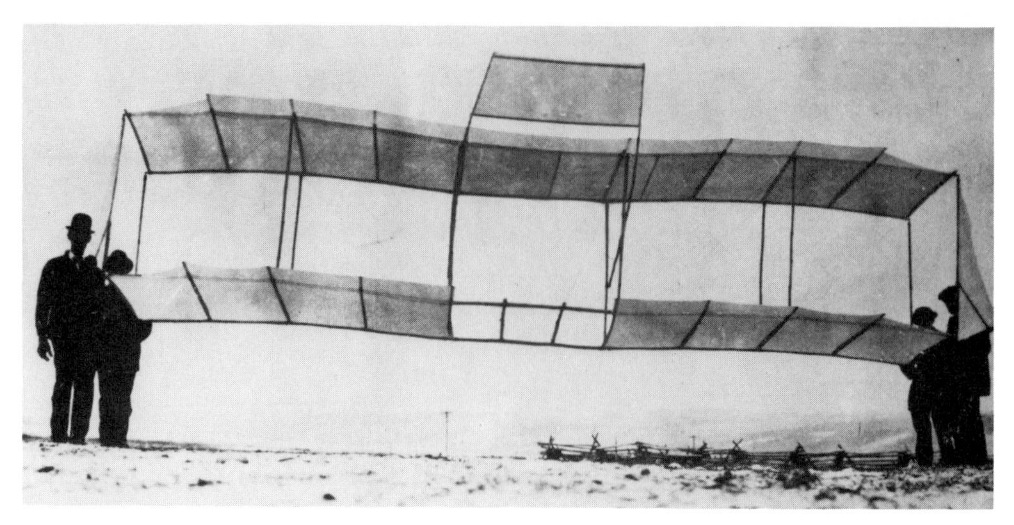

A.E.A. glider on which the association first became airborne.

A.E.A. Red Wing at Hammondsport, N.Y. March 1908, on which F.W. (Casey) Baldwin became the first Canadian to fly a powered heavier-than-air aircraft.

A.E.A. White Wing on which J.A.D. McCurdy made his first flight on a powered aircraft, 23 May 1908.
(all photos Bell Family & Nat'l Geographic Soc.)

**6 DECEMBER, 1907.** Lieut. T.E. Selfridge, U.S. Army, made a towed flight in the Aerial Experiment Association's tetrahedral cell glider/kite "Cygnet I" from Bras d'Or Lake, Nova Scotia.

Ref: Parkin, J.H. Bell and Baldwin, Toronto, 1964.

# 1908

**13 JANUARY, 1908.** F.W. Baldwin and Lieut. T.E. Selfridge began a series of flights with the Aerial Experiment Association Chanute-type hang glider at Hammondsport, New York.

Ref: Parkin, J.H. Bell and Baldwin, Toronto, 1964.

**12 MARCH, 1908.** *The first flight of a powered heavier-than-air machine piloted by a Canadian* was made by F.W. Baldwin on the Aerial Experiment Association's Red Wing biplane (40 hp Curtiss motor) at Hammondsport, New York.

Ref: Parkin, J.H. Bell and Baldwin, Toronto, 1964.

**17 MARCH, 1908.** The Aerial Experiment Association's Red Wing biplane, flown by F.W. Baldwin, was damaged beyond repair at Hammondsport, New York, at the end of its second flight.

Ref: Parkin, J.H. Bell and Baldwin, Toronto, 1964.

**18 MAY, 1908.** F.W. Baldwin made the first flight on the Aerial Experiment Association's White Wing biplane (40 hp Curtiss motor) at Hammondsport, New York.

Ref: Parkin, J.H. Bell and Baldwin, Toronto, 1964.

**23 MAY, 1908.** J.A.D. McCurdy made his first powered flight on the Aerial Experiment Association's White Wing biplane at Hammondsport, New York. It ended in a crash which damaged the airframe beyond complete repair.

Ref: Parkin, J.H. Bell and Baldwin, Toronto, 1964.

**20 JUNE, 1908.** G.H. Curtiss made the first flights on the Aerial Experiment Association's June Bug biplane (40 hp Curtiss motor) at Hammondsport, New York.

Ref: Parkin, J.H. Bell and Baldwin, Toronto, 1964.

**1 JULY, 1908.** Jack Dallas (Benjamin Parker) flew a Strobel dirigible at the Dominion Fair, Calgary, Alberta. It made several flights before being destroyed by fire on 4 July.

Ref: The Morning Albertan, Calgary, Alta., 1-6 July, 1908.

**5 JULY, 1908.** Dr. G.J. Fielding and Capt H.E. Honeywell descended near West Shefford, Shefford county, Quebec, completing a balloon voyage from Chicago, Illinois, and winning the Gordon Bennett Cup.

Ref: Sherbrooke Daily Record, Sherbrooke, Que., 6, 7 July, 1908.

A.E.A. Silver Dart in December 1908 at Hammondsport, N.Y., where it was first flown.
(Bell Family & Nat'l Geographic Soc.)

A.E.A. Silver Dart in flight at Baddeck, N.S. (H.M. Benner photo)

**8 JULY, 1908.** Walter Clark of Boston, Massachusetts, was forced to postpone the proposed flight of his pedal-power launched glider at Waterville, Quebec, due to the craft's structural weakness.

Ref: Sherbrooke Daily Record, Sherbrooke, Que., 6-8 July, 1908.

**13 JULY, 1908.** The first edition of the weekly "Bulletin of the Aerial Experiment Association", edited by A.G. Bell, appeared at Beinn Bhreagh, Baddeck, Nova Scotia.

Ref: Parkin, J.H. Bell and Baldwin, Toronto, 1964.

**8 AUGUST, 1908.** A hot air balloon ascension with a parachute descent took place at the Saskatoon, Saskatchewan, Exhibition.

Ref: The Daily Phoenix, Saskatoon, Sask., 10 August, 1908.

**6 DECEMBER, 1908.** J.A.D. McCurdy made the first flights on the Aerial Experiment Association's Silver Dart biplane (50 hp Curtiss motor) at Hammondsport, New York.

Ref: Parkin, J.H., Bell and Baldwin, Toronto, 1964.

# 1909

**28 JANUARY, 1909.** W.R. Turnbull of Rothesay, New Brunswick, was awarded the Bronze Medal by the Aeronautical Society of Great Britain for his paper "The Efficiency of Aeroplanes" which was considered the best presented in their Journal in 1908.

Ref: Parkin, J.H., Wallace Rupert Turnbull, 1870-1954, Canadian Aeronautical Journal, Vol. 2, Nos. 1 & 2, January & February, 1956.

**23 FEBRUARY, 1909.** *The first flight in Canada by a powered heavier-than-air machine* was made by J.A.D. McCurdy on the Aerial Experiment Association's Silver Dart biplane (50 hp Curtiss motor) at Baddeck, Nova Scotia. It was the first flight by a British subject in a powered heavier-than-air machine in the British Empire.

Ref: Parkin, J.H., Bell and Baldwin, Toronto, 1964.

**MARCH, 1909.** *First attempt to sell aircraft in Canada.* Franco-American Automobile Co. of Montreal, Quebec, advertised Voisin aircraft for sale and Chanute-type gliders.

Ref: A.E.A. Bulletin, 15 March, 1909.

**31 MARCH, 1909.** The Aerial Experiment Association was dissolved.

Ref: Parkin, J.H., Bell and Baldwin, Toronto, 1964.

**31 MARCH, 1909.** The Aero Club of Canada was formed at Winnipeg, Manitoba, "to assist and promote practical aeronautics by encouraging Canadian inventors".

Ref: The Winnipeg Telegram, Winnipeg, Man., 1 April, 1909.

**APRIL, 1909.** *The first Canadian aviation company was formed,* the Canadian Aerodrome Company, at Baddeck, Nova Scotia, by F.W. Baldwin and J.A.D. McCurdy, with the assistance of A.G. Bell.

Ref: Parkin, J.H., Bell and Baldwin, Univ. of Toronto Press, Toronto, 1964.

**18 MAY, 1909.** John Burton was injured in an attempted glider flight at Hamilton, Ontario.

Ref The Hamilton Times, Hamilton, Ont., 19 May, 1909.

**15 JULY, 1909.** The flying machine "Aerocar Canada", designed and built by William J. Robertson of Winnipeg, Manitoba, was put on display at the Happyland baseball park there. A planned flight was cancelled.

Ref: Manitoba Free Press, Winnipeg, Man., 15-16 July, 1909.

**2 AUGUST, 1909.** The first flight in the Province of Ontario was made by J.A.D. McCurdy in A.E.A.'s Silver Dart biplane (42 hp Kirkham motor) at Petawawa, Ontario. This was the first planned series of aircraft tests sponsored by the Canadian armed forces.

Ref: Parkin, J.H., Bell and Baldwin, Univ. of Toronto Press, Toronto, 1964.

**2 AUGUST, 1909.** *The first flight in Canada by a powered heavier-than-air machine carrying more than one person* was made at Petawawa, Ontario, by J.A.D. McCurdy with F.W. Baldwin as passenger on the A.E.A.'s Silver Dart biplane (42 hp Kirkham motor). The Silver Dart was damaged beyond repair at the end of its fourth flight that day.

Ref: Parkin, J.H., Bell and Baldwin, Univ. of Toronto Press, Toronto, 1964.

**9 AUGUST, 1909.** *The first night flight in Canada* was made by Jack Dallas (Benjamin Parker) on a Strobel dirigible, illuminated by spotlights from the ground, at Hanlan's Point amusement park, Toronto, Ontario.

Ref: The Globe, Toronto, Ont., 10 August, 1909.

**12 AUGUST, 1909.** *The first flight of a powered heavier-than-air machine built in Canada* was made by J.A.D. McCurdy in the Canadian Aeroplane Company's Baddeck No. 1 biplane at Petawawa, Ontario. The aircraft was powered by a U.S. - built 42 hp Kirkham motor.

Ref: Parkin, J.H., Bell and Baldwin, Univ. of Toronto Press, Toronto, 1964.

**2 SEPTEMBER, 1909.** The first aeroplane flight in Canada contracted for public exhibition was performed by Charles Foster Willard on the Curtiss pusher biplane "Golden Flyer" (20 hp Curtiss motor) at Scarborough Beach amusement park near Toronto, Ontario. The 300-yard flight ended in Lake Ontario without injury to Willard and with little damage to the aeroplane.

Ref: The Globe, Toronto, Ont., 3 September, 1909.

**2 SEPTEMBER, 1909.** The Aeronautical Society of Canada was formed at Toronto, Ontario, with F.B. Fetherstonhaugh as chairman, M.B. Logan, secretary.

Ref: The Globe, Toronto, Ont., 3 September, 1909.

**11 SEPTEMBER, 1909.** J.R. D'Almedia landed in Lake Ontario off Mimico, Ontario, after a flight attempt on a monoplane of his own design, apparently towed by a motor launch.

Ref: The News, Toronto, Ont., 13 September, 1909.
The Daily Mail and Empire, Toronto, Ont., 13 September, 1909.

**16 SEPTEMBER, 1909.** Anthony M. Nassr of Toledo, Ohio, made a dirigible flight at the Central Canada Exhibition, Ottawa, Ontario. The airship collided with electric wires on take-off and Edward Keating lost his life while attempting to assist Nassr. The airship was destroyed by fire after another flight attempt later that day.

Ref: Ottawa Journal, Ottawa, Ont., 17 September, 1909.

**21 SEPTEMBER, 1909.** W.R. Turnbull of Rothesay, New Brunswick, was granted U.S. patent number 934,771 for an "Aeroplane and Hydroplane".

Ref: Aeronautics, New York City, N.Y., Vol. 5, No. 5, Nov., 1909.

**22 SEPTEMBER, 1909.** James C. "Bud" Mars (J.D. McBride) flew a Strobel dirigible at the Victoria, B.C., Fair & Horse Show. Further flights were made on 23 and 24 September.

Ref: The Daily Colonist, Victoria, B.C., 18-26 September, 1909.

**25 SEPTEMBER, 1909.** The Canadian Aerodrome Co.'s Baddeck No. 2 biplane (40 hp Kirkham motor) made its first flights at Baddeck, Nova Scotia.

Ref: Parkin, J.H., Bell and Baldwin, Univ. of Toronto Press, Toronto, 1964.

**14 OCTOBER, 1909.** Harry Ginter flew a Strobel dirigible at the Provincial Exhibition, Queen's Park, New Westminister, British Columbia. The airship was badly damaged in a flight attempt the following day.

Ref: The Daily News-Advertiser, Vancouver, B.C., 15, 16 October, 1909.

# 1910

**7 MARCH, 1910.** The Canadian Aerodrome Co.'s Baddeck No. 2 biplane was flown by J.A.D. McCurdy with F.W. Baldwin as passenger at Baddeck, Nova Scotia.

Ref: Parkin, J.H., Bell and Baldwin, Univ. of Toronto Press.

**9 MARCH, 1910.** *The first serving member of the Canadian armed forces to take an aeroplane flight in Canada,* Major G.S. Maunsell, was J.A.D. McCurdy's passenger on two flights of the Canadian Aerodrome Company's Baddeck No. 2 biplane at Baddeck, N.S.

Ref: Parkin, J.H., Bell and Baldwin, Univ. of Toronto Press, 1964.

C.K. Hamilton on his Curtiss pusher at Vancouver, B.C., 25 March 1910. (unknown)

Canadian Aerodrome Hubbard monoplane. (Bell Family & Nat'l Geographic Soc.)

Canadian Aerodrome Baddeck No. 2 after its crash at Pointe Claire, Que., on 24 June 1910.
(via K.M. Molson)

**25 MARCH, 1910.** *The first aeroplane flight in* the Province of British Columbia was made by C.K. Hamilton of the Curtiss Exhibition flying team on a Curtiss pusher biplane at Minoru Park race track near Vancouver. A second flight was made later in the day.

Ref: The Daily News Advertiser, Vancouver, B.C., 26 March, 1910.

**26 MARCH, 1910.** *The first aeroplane flight over a Canadian city,* New Westminister, British Columbia, was part of a 26-mile trip made by C.K. Hamilton on a Curtiss pusher biplane from Minoru Park near Vancouver. He had made two short flights earlier that day.

Ref: The Daily News Advertiser, Vancouver, B.C., 27 March, 1910.

**26 MARCH, 1910.** Two monoplanes owned by Stanley Yale Beach of New York City, a Bleriot-type and an Antoinette-type, were exhibited at the 4th Annual Motor Show at the Coliseum in Montreal, Quebec.

Ref: The Montreal Daily Star, Montreal, Que., 25, 28, 29 March, 1910.

**28 MARCH, 1910.** During the final flight of his engagement at Minoru Park race track near Vancouver, British Columbia, C.K. Hamilton flew his Curtiss pusher biplane in a race against a race horse.

Ref: The Daily News Advertiser, Vancouver, B.C., 29 March, 1910.

**5 APRIL, 1910.** *The first aeroplane built in Canada to order and first for export,* the Canadian Aerodrome Company's Hubbard monoplane (40 hp Kirkham motor) made nine brief flights at Baddeck, Nova Scotia, piloted by its owner Gardiner Greene Hubbard II of Boston, Massachusetts.

Ref: Parkin, J.H., Bell and Baldwin, Univ. of Toronto Press, 1964.

**16 MAY, 1910.** A Bleriot XI monoplane, purchased in France by M. Jean Versailles, arrived at Montreal, Quebec, aboard the Allan Line steamer S.S. Sardinian.

Ref: The Gazette, Montreal, Que., 17 May, 1910.

**20-21 MAY, 1910.** The balloon "Cleveland" carried four persons from North Adams, Massachusetts, to St. Hyacinthe, Que.

Ref: The Montreal Gazette, Montreal, Que., 23 May, 1910.

**24 JUNE, 1910.** J.A.D. McCurdy crashed attempting a flight in the Canadian Aerodrome Company's Baddeck No. 2 biplane (40 hp Kirkham motor) at Lakeside (now Pointe Claire), Quebec.

Ref: The Montreal Gazette, Montreal, Que., 25 June, 1910.

**25 JUNE, 1910.** *The first successful aeroplane flight in the Province of Quebec* was made by Walter Richard Brookins of the Wright Brothers exhibition team in a Wright biplane (30 hp Wright motor) at Lakeside (now Pointe Claire), Quebec.

Ref: The Montreal Gazette, Montreal, Que., 27 June, 1910.

Montreal Aviation Meet. The near aircraft is Count J. de Lesseps' "Le Scarabée" and the far machine is probably his Anzani-powered Bleriot XI. (P.H. Reid)

Walter Brookins flying his Wright B at the Montreal Aviation Meet. (via K.M. Molson)

**25 JUNE, 1910.** *Canada's first aviation meet opened* at a specially prepared field at Lakeside (now Pointe Claire), Quebec. It was sponsored by the Automobile & Aero Club of Canada. That day successful flights were made by: W.R. Brookins (3) and Ralph Johnstone (1) on Wright biplanes (30 hp Wright motor) of the Wright Brothers exhibition team from the United States, Count Jacques de Lesseps from France on his Bleriot XI monoplane (25 hp Anzani motor) (3), and Cromwell Dixon from the United States on his dirigible (1). Balloon ascensions and parachute descents were performed by Jack Fanning and Benny Prinz.
An unsuccessful flight attempt was made by Paul Miltgen from France on the Bleriot XI monoplane (25 hp Anzani motor) owned by William Carruthers of Montreal.

Ref: The Montreal Herald, Montreal, Que., 27 June, 1910.

**26 JUNE, 1910.** At Lakeside, Quebec, successful flights were made by W.R. Brookins (1) on a Wright biplane and J. de Lesseps (1) on his Bleriot XI monoplane (25 hp Anzani motor). An unsuccessful flight attempt was made by J.A.D. McCurdy on the Canadian Aerodrome Baddeck No. 2 biplane.

Ref: The Montreal Daily Star, Montreal, Que., 27 June, 1910.

**27 JUNE, 1910.** At Lakeside, Quebec, successful flights were performed by W.R. Brookins (2), R. Johnstone (2), Duval LaChapelle (1) and Frank Trenholm Coffyn (1) on Wright biplanes, J. de Lesseps on his Bleriot XI monoplane (25 hp Anzani motor) (2), and Fred Owens (2) and C. Dixon on their dirigibles.
A balloon ascension and parachute jump was carried out by J. Fanning.
An unsuccessful flight attempt was made by J.A.D. McCurdy on the Canadian Aerodrome Baddeck No. 2 biplane and C. Dixon's dirigible was accidently destroyed during his second flight of the day.

Ref: The Montreal Herald, Montreal, Que., 28 June, 1910.

**28 JUNE, 1910.** At Lakeside, Quebec, successful flights were made by: W.R. Brookins (3), R. Johnstone (1), D. LaChapelle (1) and F.T. Coffyn (1, with W.R. Brookins as passenger) on Wright biplanes, J. de Lesseps (2) on his Bleriot XI monoplane (25 hp Anzani motor), and F. Owens (1) on his dirigible.
Two balloon ascensions with parachute jumps were performed.
J.A.D. McCurdy tried unsuccessfully to fly the Canadian Aerodrome Baddeck No. 2 biplane.

Ref: The Montreal Herald, Montreal, Que., 29 June, 1910.

F. Owens' dirigible at the Montreal Aviation Meet, 29 June 1910. (via K.M. Molson)

Count J. de Lesseps' "Le Scarabée" overflying the spectators at the Montreal Aviation Meet. (via K.M. Molson)

**29 JUNE, 1910.** At Lakeside, Quebec, successful flights were made by: W.R. Brookins (3, one with J. de Lesseps as passenger), R. Johnstone (1), and D. LaChapelle (2) on Wright biplanes, J. de Lesseps (2) on his Bleriot XI monoplane (25 hp Anzani motor), and F. Owens (1) on his dirigible. After completing three short flights, R. Baker Timberlake of Montreal crashed his Bleriot XI monoplane (25 hp Anzani motor) and J.A.D. McCurdy crashed while flying the Canadian Aerodrome Baddeck No. 2 biplane.

Ref: The Montreal Herald, Montreal, Que., 30 June, 1910.

**30 JUNE, 1910.** At Lakeside, Quebec, successful flights were carried out by: J. de Lesseps (2) on his Bleriot XI monoplane (Anzani motor), W.R. Brookins (3, including one with Bertrand de Lesseps as passenger), D. LaChapelle (3), F.T. Coffyn (1), and R. Johnstone (2) on Wright biplanes, and F. Owens on his dirigible.

Ref: The Montreal Herald, 1 July, 1910.

**1 JULY, 1910.** At Lakeside, Quebec, successful flights were made by: W.R. Brookins (4, one with F.T. Coffyn as passenger), F.T. Coffyn (1), R. Johnstone (1) and D. LaChapelle on Wright biplanes, J. de Lesseps (3) on his Bleriot XI monoplane (25 hp Anzani motor) and F. Owens on his dirigible.

Ref The Montreal Herald, Montreal, Que., 2 July, 1910.

**2 JULY, 1910.** At Lakeside, Quebec, successful flights were performed by: J. de Lesseps (2, one a 49-minute return flight to the centre of the City of Montreal) on the Bleriot XIbis monoplane 'Le Scarabée" (50 hp Gnome motor), W.R. Brookins (2), F.T. Coffyn (1) and D. LaChapelle (2) on Wright biplanes, and F. Owens on his dirigible.

Ref: The Montreal Herald, Montreal, Que., 4 July, 1910.

**3 JULY, 1910.** At Lakeside, Quebec, successful fights were made by: J. de Lesseps (1) on his Bleriot XIbis monoplane "Le Scarabée" and W.R. Brookins (2), F.T. Coffyn (1) and D. LaChapelle (1) on Wright biplanes.

Ref: The Montreal Herald, Montreal, Que., 4 July, 1910.

**4 JULY, 1910.** At Lakeside Quebec, successful flights were carried out by: J. de Lesseps (2), one on each of his Bleriot XI monoplanes, and D. LaChapelle (1) and W.R. Brookins (2, one with D. LaChapelle as passenger ended in a crash landing) on Wright biplanes. Cromwell Dixon made a short flight on the Carruthers Bleriot XI, landing outside the grounds and Gardiner G. Hubbard of Boston, Massachusetts, tried unsuccessfully to fly his "Mike" monoplane (40 h.p. Kirkham motor).

Ref: The Montreal Herald, 5 July, 1910.

Ralph Johnstone flying at Toronto in his Wright 1909 biplane.
(James Coll. Toronto City Archives)

Count J. de Lesseps about to start at Toronto in his Anzani-powered Bleriot XI. (Dr. Jewell photo)

**5 JULY, 1910.** On the last day of the Montreal aviation meet at Lakeside, Quebec, J. de Lesseps made two flights in his Bleriot XIbis monoplane "Le Scarabée".

Ref: The Montreal Daily Star, Montreal, Que., 6 July, 1910.

**7 JULY, 1910.** A Farman biplane (50 hp Gnome motor), bought in France solely for use as an educative exhibit by the T. Eaton Co. Ltd., was on display in their Toronto store.

Ref: The Toronto World, Toronto, Ont., 7 July, 1910.

**8 JULY, 1910.** An aviation meet, under the auspices of the Ontario Motor League, began at the Trethewey model farm at Weston, outside Toronto, Ontario. Single flights were made by Count Jacques de Lesseps on his Anzani-powered Bleriot XI monoplane and by Ralph Johnstone of the Wright Company exhibition team on a Wright biplane (30 hp Wright motor).

Ref: The Toronto World, Toronto, Ont., 9 July, 1910.

**9 JULY, 1910.** On the second day of the Toronto aviation meet, successful flights were made by J. de Lesseps on his Anzani-powered Bleriot XI monoplane and by Wright Co. aviators R. Johnstone (2) and D. LaChapelle on a Wright biplane.

Ref: The Toronto World, Toronto, Ont., 11 July, 1910.

**11 JULY, 1910.** At the Trethewey Farm aviation meet near Toronto, successful flights were accomplished by J. de Lesseps (1 each) on his Anzani-and Gnome-powered Bleriot XI monoplanes and by Wright Co. aviators R. Johnstone (2) and D. LaChapelle (1) on a Wright biplane.

Ref: The Toronto World, Toronto, Ont., 12 July, 1910.

**12 JULY, 1910.** A Curtiss-type pusher biplane was exhibited by Parker Brothers Shows at the Fair at Portage la Prairie, Manitoba. A report that it had been flown early that morning was not substantiated by subsequent reports.

Ref: The Weekly Review, Portage la Prairie, Man., 13, 20 July, 1910.
Weekly Manitoba Liberal, Portage la Prairie, Man., 16 May, 1912.

**12 JULY, 1910.** J. de Lesseps made the only successful flight of the 4th day of the Toronto aviation meet. John Stratton crashed attempting to fly a Bleriot XI monoplane belonging to William Carruthers of Montreal, Quebec.

Ref: The Toronto World, Toronto, Ont., 13 July, 1910.

**13 JULY, 1910.** J. de Lesseps flew his Bleriot XIbis monoplane "Le Scarabée" from Trethewey Farm over the city of Toronto and back, the first aeroplane flight over that city. He made an earlier flight that day on his Anzani-powered Bleriot XI.

Ref: The Toronto World, Toronto, Ont., 14 July, 1910.

Count J. de Lesseps' Gnome-powered Bleriot XI, "Le Scarabée" at Toronto in which he had flown the English Channel 21 May 1910.
(Dr. Jewell photo)

The 1909 Wright biplane flown by R. Johnstone and F.T. Coffyn at Toronto. Wheels are for ground handling only.
(Dr. Jewell photo)

Count Jacques de Lesseps in front of his Anzani-powered Bleriot XI.
(James Coll., Toronto City Archives)

**14 JULY, 1910.** There were brief flights on a Wright biplane by R. Johnstone and W.R. Brookins on the 6th day of the Toronto aviation meet.

Ref: The Toronto World, Toronto, Ont., 15 July, 1910.

**15 JULY, 1910.** Two successful flights were made by J. de Lesseps on his Anzani-powered Bleriot XI monoplane and the Wright biplane was flown by R. Johnstone (2) and F.T. Coffyn (1) at the Toronto Aviation meet.

Ref: The Toronto World, Toronto, Ont., 16 July, 1910.

**15 JULY, 1910.** *The first flight in the Province of Manitoba* was made by Eugene Burton Ely of San Francisco, California, on a Curtiss pusher biplane (30 hp Curtiss motor). Replacing another aviator, Ely found the aircraft underpowered for contracted flights from the grounds of the Winnipeg Industrial Exhibition. Moving to an open area on the western edge of the city, he made three flights, the last ending in a crash.

Ref: The Winnipeg Telegram, Winnipeg, Man., 15-23 July, 1910.

**16 JULY, 1910.** On the final day of the Toronto aviation meet at Trethewey Farm, J. de Lesseps made a flight with each of his two Bleriot XI monoplanes. The Wright biplane was used for flights by R. Johnstone (2) and F.T. Coffyn (1).

Ref: The Toronto World, Toronto, Ont., 18 July, 1910.

**22 JULY, 1910.** A glider, built by a group headed by a German mechanic, George Lohner, became airborne briefly while towed by an automobile at Lansdowne Park exhibition grounds, Ottawa, Ontario.

Ref: Ottawa Journal, Ottawa, Ont., 22 July, 1910.

**26 JULY, 1910.** J. de Lesseps flew his Bleriot XIbis monoplane 'Le Scarabée" on a 40-mile return trip over Montreal, Quebec, from King Edward Park on Ile Gros Bois in the St. Lawrence River.

Ref: The Montreal Gazette, Montreal, Que., 27 July, 1910.

**2 AUGUST, 1910.** Louis Prosper crashed attempting to fly a Bleriot XI monoplane at Ile Gros Bois near Montreal, Quebec.

Ref: The Montreal Daily Star, Montreal, Que., 3 August, 1910.

**27 AUGUST, 1910.** *The first successful radio communication between an aeroplane in flight and a ground station* was made by J.A.D. McCurdy on a Curtiss pusher biplane and H.M. Horton on the ground at Sheepshead Bay, New York.

Ref: La Presse, Montreal, Que., 30 August, 1910.
Aeronautics, New York City, N.Y., Vol. VII, No.4, October, 1910.

The two cycle Gibson engine developing 40 hp, was Canada's first aviation engine and is now in the National Aeronautical Collection at Ottawa.
(Museum of Science & Technology)

The Gibson Twin-plane. (via F.H. Ellis)

The start of the 1910 Gordon Bennett balloon race during which seven of the contestants landed in Canada.
(Aircraft)

**8 SEPTEMBER, 1910.** *First Canadian aircraft engine was tested.* William Wallace Gibson of Victoria, British Columbia, made a short test flight on his "Twin-plane" at Mount Tolmie, near Victoria. The aircraft was powered with an engine of Gibson's own design.

Ref: The Daily Colonist, Victoria, B.C., 10 September, 1910.

**24 SEPTEMBER, 1910.** W.W. Gibson made a short test flight on his "Twin-plane" at Mount Tolmie, British Columbia, which ended in a crash, seriously damaging the machine.

Ref: The Daily Colonist, Victoria, B.C., 25 September, 1910.

**27 SEPTEMBER, 1910.** Seven-year-old Fred Smith of Windsor, Ontario, was fatally injured by a falling pole which was being used to support a hot air balloon during inflation at Windsor.

Ref: The Montreal Daily Star, Montreal, Que., 27 September, 1910.

**17-19 OCTOBER, 1910.** Seven balloons taking part in the James Gordon Bennett Cup race from St. Louis, Missouri, landed in Canada, taking the first seven places in the race as follows:

1. "America II" (U.S.A.) with Allan R. Hawley and Augustus Post landed near Lac Blanc Sable, 58 miles north of Chicoutimi, Quebec.
2. "Dusseldorf II" (Germany) with Samuel F. Perkins and Hans Gericke landed 18 miles north of Kiskisink, Quebec.
3. "Germania" (Germany) with Baron Hugo von Abercron and August Blanckertz landed at Coocoocache Station, 60 miles north of La Tuque, Quebec.
4. "Helvetia" (Switzerland) with Theodore Schaeck and Paul Armbruster landed near Lac des Quinze, 6 miles from Lorainville, Quebec.
5. "Hamburg III" (Germany) with L. Vogt and William F. Assmann landed on Gull Island in Lake Nipissing, 10 miles north-east of North Bay, Ontario.
6. "Azurea" (Switzerland) with E. Messner and M. Givaudan landed in Lake Biscotasing, 40 miles north-west of Sudbury, Ontario.
7. 'Ile de France" (France) with Alfred Leblanc and Walter de Mumm landed 2 miles north of Pogamasing, Ontario (25 miles north of present Sudbury).

Ref: Aeronautics, New York City, N.Y., Vol. VII, Nos. 5 & 6, November & December, 1910.

**22 OCTOBER, 1910.** Achille Hanssens' monoplane "La Montréalaise" (30 hp Lair motor) was wrecked in an unsuccessful flight attempt at Parc Champlain near Montreal, Quebec. Both the airframe and engine were constructed in Montreal.

Ref: La Presse, Montreal, Que., 28 October, 1910.

J.A.D. McCurdy, Canada's first licensed pilot photographed at Toronto in August 1911.
(James Coll., Toronto City Archives)

J.A.D. McCurdy about to start from Key West for Havana in his Curtiss pusher. (unknown)

The McCowan glider being tested on a single float, probably in the summer of 1911.
(Gold Magazine)

**23 OCTOBER, 1910.** *First Canadian received a pilot's license.* J.A.D. McCurdy received Aero Club of America Certificate No. 18 after passing test on 5 October, 1910, at Hawthorne Race Track, Chicago, Illinois, in a Curtiss pusher biplane.

**13 DECEMBER, 1910.** W.W. Gibson of Victoria, British Columbia, was granted U.S. patent No. 978,732 for a "flying machine".

Ref: Aeronautics, New York City, N.Y., Vol. 8, No. 4.

**31 DECEMBER, 1910.** St. Croix Johnstone, who was born in Toronto, Ontario, qualified for Royal Aero Club Certificate No. 41 at the Bleriot School of Flying, Hendon, England, flying a Bleriot XI monoplane.

Ref: Brett, R. Dallas, History of British Aviation, The Aviation Book Club, London, n.d.

# 1911

**30 JANUARY, 1911.** Longest over-water flight to date was made by J.A.D. McCurdy on a Curtiss pusher biplane when he attempted to fly from Key West, Florida, to Havana, Cuba. After covering 96 miles, he was forced to land in the sea through loss of oil through a crankcase crack.

Ref: The Montreal Daily Star, Montreal, Que., 31 January, 1911.
Scientific American, 19 February, 1911.

**3 FEBRUARY, 1911.** The first hydrogen balloon for gathering meteorological data in Canada to be successfully recovered was sent up at Toronto, Ontario.

Ref: Patterson, J., Upper Air Investigations in Canada, Part 1, Observation by registering balloons, Ottawa, 1915.

**19-20 FEBRUARY, 1911.** The balloon "La Presse" carried Emile Barlatier and his wife, Simone Rivière Barlatier, from Ogdensburg, New York, to Tyotown, 4 miles east of Cornwall, Ontario.

Ref: The Cornwall Standard, Cornwall, Ont., 24 February, 1911.

**28 FEBRUARY, 1911.** The first kite flight for the gathering of meteorological data in Canada was made at Toronto, Ontario.

Ref: Patterson, J., Upper Air Investigations in Canada, Part 1, Observation by registering balloons, Ottawa, 1915.

**3 MARCH, 1911.** The balloon "La Presse" carried Mr. and Mrs. Emile Barlatier from Hochelaga, Montreal, to Ste. Julie de Verchères, Quebec.

Ref: The Montreal Daily Star, Montreal, Que., 4 March, 1911.

**15 MARCH, 1911.** Robert McCowan Jr. made a flight over the frozen harbour of Sydney, Nova Scotia, in a glider towed by an automobile.

Ref: The Halifax Herald, Halifax, N.S., 16 March, 1911.

Hugh Robinson flying at Edmonton in his Curtiss pusher. (via W.R. May)

The Templeton-McMullen biplane. (via F.H. Ellis)

R.C. 'Bob' St. Henry (C.W. Schaffer) in his Curtiss pusher. Note that an extra wing bay has been added to his aircraft. (via W.R. May)

**22 MARCH, 1911.** Toronto-born St. Croix Johnstone, on the Bleriot XIbis monoplane "Le Scarabée", now owned by H.A. Somerville of Montreal, Quebec, made the first flight over the city of Havana, Cuba.

Ref: Aircraft, New York City, N.Y., Vol. 2, No. 3, May, 1911.

**14 APRIL, 1911.** Jack DePries of Portland, Oregon, crashed attempting to take off on a Curtiss-type pusher biplane at Minoru Park race track, Vancouver, B.C. He managed to make a short flight on another Curtiss-type pusher biplane later that day. On April 15 he crashed and was injured in attempting to land after an otherwise successful flight.

Ref: The Daily News-Advertiser, Vancouver, B.C., 15-16 April, 1911.

**18 APRIL, 1911.** Browne Manning of Portland, Oregon, made two unsuccessful flight attempts on a Curtiss-type biplane at Minoru Park race track, Vancouver, British Columbia.

Ref: Ellis, Frank H., Canada's Flying Heritage, Univ. of Toronto Press, 1954.

**28 APRIL, 1911.** *The first aeroplane flight in the Province of Alberta* was made by Hugh A. Robinson of the Curtiss exhibition flying team at Edmonton. Using a Curtiss pusher biplane, he made two flights that day and three more on 29 April.

Ref: Edmonton Daily Bulletin, Edmonton, Alta., 29 April, 1 May, 1911.

**30 APRIL - 6 MAY, 1911.** During this week, the tractor biplane (35 hp Humber motor) built by William and Winston Templeton and William McMullen made a brief test flight at Minoru Park race track, near Vancouver, British Columbia.

Ref: The Daily News-Advertiser, Vancouver, B.C., 7 May, 1911.

**2 MAY, 1911.** Abel T. Newbury, of Vermilion, Alberta, was granted U.S. patent No. 990,897 for a "combination aeroplane, dirigible and helicopter".

Ref: Aero, St. Louis, Mo., 13 May, 1911.

**18 MAY, 1911.** After several flight attempts begun during the previous day, R.C. 'Bob' St. Henry (C.W. Shaffer) of the Curtiss exhibition flying team crashed at the Saskatoon, Saskatchewan, exhibition. He used a Curtiss pusher biplane (30 hp Curtiss motor).

Ref: The Daily Phoenix, Saskatoon, Sask., 18-19 May, 1911.

**30 MAY, 1911.** Charles Francis Walsh, of San Diego, California, made two flights on a Curtiss-Farman type biplane at Victoria, British Columbia. He made two more flights on 31 May.

Ref The Daily Colonist, Victoria, B.C., 31 May & 1 June, 1911.

**1 JUNE, 1911.** *The first successful aeroplane flight in the Province of Saskatchewan* was made at the Saskatoon exhibition grounds by R.C. 'Bob' St. Henry of Carrington, North Dakota. His Curtiss pusher biplane had a new 60 hp Curtiss motor. Other flights were made later that day and on 2 June.

Ref: The Daily Phoenix, Saskatoon, Sask., 2-3 June, 1911.

**6 JUNE, 1911.** William Boyd Alexander, Montreal, Quebec, was granted U.S. patent no. 994,106 for an "aeroplane".

Ref: Aeronautics, New York, Vol. 9, No. 1, July, 1911.

**20 JUNE, 1911.** McCurdy Aeroplane Co. was incorporated at Pittsburg, Pennsylvania, by J. A. D. McCurdy to manufacture aeroplanes and give exhibitions.

Ref: Aero (U.S.) Vol. II, NO. 14, July 8, 1911.

**20-22, 24 JUNE, 1911.** A successful aviation meet was held at the race track at Fort Erie, Ontario. Curtiss exhibition company aviators Lincoln Beachey, J.A.D. McCurdy and Charles C. Witmer flew Curtiss pusher biplanes.
McCurdy's flight on 21 June began the first professional exhibition flying engagement in Canada by a Canadian aviator.

Ref: Courier, Buffalo, N.Y., 21-25 June, 1911.

**23-24 JUNE, 1911.** The balloon "La Presse" carried Mr. and Mrs. Emile Barlatier from Montreal, Quebec, to Fairfax, Franklin county, Vermont.

Ref: The Montreal Daily Star, Montreal, Que., 24 June, 1911.

**24 JUNE, 1911.** Balloonist James Coakley descended into a river at Medicine Hat, Alberta, and was rescued by Boy Scout Norman Rossiter.

Ref: The Montreal Daily Star, Montreal, Que., 26 June, 1911.

**26 JUNE, 1911.** Lincoln Beachey flew from Fort Erie, Ontario, to Buffalo, New York, on a Curtiss pusher biplane.
On the following day, he flew through the Niagara Gorge and under the Upper Steel Arch Bridge.

Ref: Daily Record, Niagara Falls, Ont., 26-28 June, 1911.

**3 JULY, 1911.** Canadian-born St. Croix Johnstone, appearing with the International Aviators exhibition flying team at Detroit, Michigan, flew a Bleriot-type Moisant monoplane over the city of Windsor, Ontario.

Ref: Aero, St. Louis, Mo., Vol. 2, No. 14, 8 July, 1911.

**3 JULY, 1911.** Howard LeVan made the first aeroplane flight at Calgary, Alberta, in an engagement at the annual Fair. He used Charles J. Strobel's Curtiss-type pusher biplane and made subsequent flights on 5 and 7 July.

Ref: The Calgary Daily Herald, The Daily Albertan, Calgary, Alta. 3-8 July, 1911.

**8 JULY, 1911.** Joseph Richter, a German-born aviator, crashed and was injured attempting to take off on a Curtiss-type biplane from Hanlan's Point Stadium, Toronto, Ontario.

Ref: The Daily Mail and Empire, Toronto, Ont., 8 July, 1911.

**11 JULY, 1911.** Max Goehler, of Vancouver, British Columbia, was granted U.S. patent no. 997,804 for an aeroplane propulsion system.

Ref: Aero, St. Louis, Mo., Vol. 2, No. 16, 22 July, 1911.

**13 JULY, 1911.** Frank T. Coffyn made two flights on a Wright Model B biplane (35 hp Wright motor) at the Winnipeg, Manitoba, Industrial Exhibition. During a successful engagement ending on 22 July, he made a total of 18 flights.

Ref: Manitoba Free Press, Winnipeg, Man., 13-24 July, 1911.

**14 JULY, 1911.** Eugene Ely made two flights on a Curtiss pusher biplane (50 hp Curtiss motor) from the Lethbridge, Alberta, exhibition grounds.

Ref: The Lethbridge Daily Herald, Lethbridge, Alta., 15 July, 1911.

**20 JULY, 1911.** Professor Hi Henry's balloon caught fire and was damaged when he landed after an ascension at the Minnedosa, Manitoba, summer fair.

Ref: The Minnedosa Tribune, Minnedosa, Man., 27 July, 1911.

**22 JULY, 1911.** Frank T. Coffyn carried W.C. Power of Winnipeg, Manitoba, as a passenger on his Wright Model B biplane in the final flight of his engagement at the Winnipeg Industrial Exhibition.

Ref: The Winnipeg Telegram, Winnipeg, Man., 24 July, 1911.

**27 JULY, 1911.** C.F. Willard on his Gnome-powered, Curtiss-type biplane "Betsy" made the first flight at an aviation meet at Hamilton, Ontario. During the meet, which continued until 29 July, further flights were made by Willard and J.A.D. McCurdy on Gnome-powered McCurdy-Willard biplanes and by James V. Martin on a Farman biplane (50 hp Gnome motor).

Ref: Hamilton Herald, Hamilton, Ont., 24-31 July, 1911.

**1 AUGUST, 1911.** The Pepper brothers' biplane, operated by George Pepper, crashed during an attempted flight at Davidson, Saskatchewan.

Ref: Ellis, Frank H., Canada's Flying Heritage, Univ. of Toronto Press, 1954.

**2 AUGUST, 1911.** J.J. Jackson of Toronto, Ontario, crashed at Donlands Farm near Toronto attempting his initial flight in his Bleriot XI monoplane.

Ref: The Toronto World, Toronto, Ont., 3 August, 1911.

James V. Martin flying a Graham-White biplane at Hamilton, Ontario, 27 July, 1911. (James Coll.)

J.A.D. McCurdy in his McCurdy biplane at Toronto. (James Coll., Toronto City Archives)

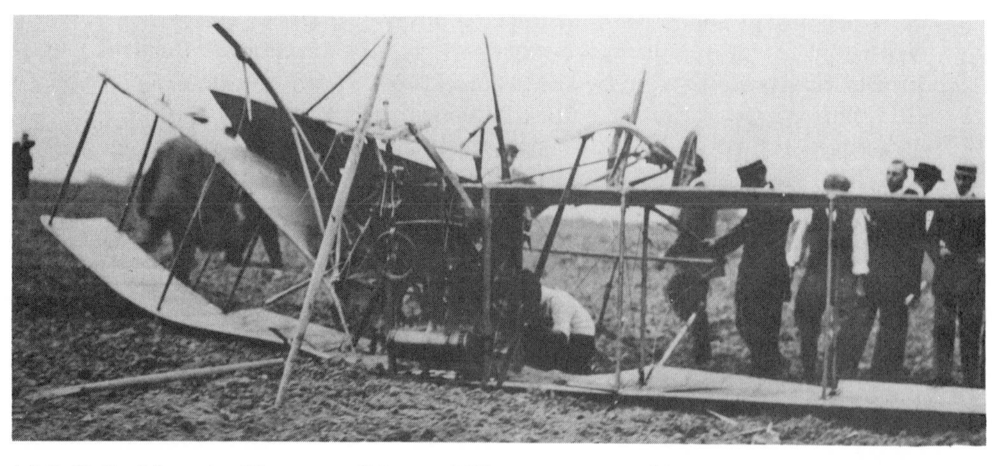

J.A.D. McCurdy's crash at Toronto on 3 August 1911. (James Coll., Toronto City Archives)

**2 AUGUST, 1911.** *The first inter-city aeroplane flights in Canada* were flown simultaneously between Hamilton and Toronto, Ontario. J.A.D. McCurdy landed his McCurdy/Willard racing biplane at Fisherman's Island in Toronto harbour and C.F. Willard landed his Curtiss-type pusher biplane "Betsy" at the Exhibition grounds. Both aircraft had 50 hp Gnome rotary engines.

Ref: Hamilton Herald, Hamilton, Ont., 3 August, 1911.

**3-5 AUGUST, 1911.** An aviation meet was held at Donlands Farm, Todmorden (near Toronto), Ontario, at which successful flights were made by J.A.D. McCurdy and C.F. Willard. Before the cancellation of the meet due to a dispute over the condition of the field, Willard made two flights carrying passengers on his Curtiss-type biplane, and McCurdy crashed on 3 August on a Gnome-powered biplane of his own design.

Ref: The Globe, Toronto, Ont., 3-8 August, 1911.

**5 AUGUST, 1911.** R.C. "Bob" St. Henry (C.W. Shaffer) of the Curtiss exhibition team made three flights on a Curtiss pusher biplane (60 hp Curtiss motor) at the Dominion Fair, Regina, Saskatchewan. Further flights were made on 8, 9, 10 and 11 August.

Ref: The Daily Standard, Regina, Sask., 5-12 August, 1911.

**9 AUGUST, 1911.** Canadian-born St. Croix Johnstone made the first aeroplane flight in the State of Maine, at Augusta, on a Moisant monoplane.

Ref: Aero, Vol. 2, No. 20, 19 August, 1911.

**12 AUGUST, 1911.** Alex Jaap, a native of Forest, Ontario, crashed during an attempted test flight of W.W. Gibson's Multiplane near Calgary, Alberta.

Ref: Edmonton Daily Bulletin, Edmonton, Alta., 15 August, 1911.

**15 AUGUST, 1911.** *The first Canadian to die piloting an aeroplane,* St. Croix Johnstone was killed flying a Moisant monoplane at the Grant Park aviation meet, Chicago, Illinois.

Ref: The Montreal Daily Star, Montreal, Que., 16 August, 1911.

**29 AUGUST, 1911.** French aviator Georges Mestach made the first aeroplane flight at Quebec City at the Provincial Fair in a Morane/Borel monoplane. Further flights, including two over the city centre, were made on 30 and 31 August and 1, 3 and 4 September.

Ref: The Quebec Chronicle, Quebec, Que., 28 August - 6 September, 1911.
L'Evénement, Quebec, Que., 28 August - 5 September, 1911.

**31 AUGUST, 1911.** Frank W. Goodale made the first of several flights on a small dirigible airship during an engagement at the Nova Scotia Provincial Exhibition in Halifax.

Ref: The Morning Chronicle, Halifax, N.S., 1 September, 1911.

**4 SEPTEMBER, 1911.** Alex McLeod, of Solsgirth, Manitoba, was seriously injured in an aeroplane crash during a training flight at West Pullman, near Chicago, Illinois.

Ref: Manitoba Free Press, Winnipeg, Man., 5, 7, 25 September, 1911.

**4 SEPTEMBER, 1911.** Edward C. Peterson, of Fort William, Ontario, failed to take off after several attempts in his Bleriot-type monoplane at the Labour Day sports program at Port Arthur, Ontario.

Ref: Manitoba Free Press, Winnipeg, Man., 5 September, 1911.

**11 SEPTEMBER, 1911.** The first aeroplane flight at Ottawa, Ontario, was made by Lee Hammond on Capt. T.S. Baldwin's "Red Devil" biplane. A second flight was made that day and two each day on 13 and 14 September. The engagement ended after a crash landing from a flight on 15 September.

Ref: The Ottawa Free Press, Ottawa, Ont., 11-16, September, 1911.

**19 SEPTEMBER, 1911.** Haden Herbert Bales, of Ashcroft, British Columbia, was granted U.S. patent no. 1,003,411 for an "Airship".

Ref: Aero, St. Louis, Mo., Vol. 3, No. 1, 7 October, 1911.

**19 SEPTEMBER, 1911.** John Jacob Day, of Montreal, Quebec, was granted U.S. patent no. 1,003,885 for an aircraft.

Ref: Aero, St. Louis, Mo., Vol. 3, No. 1, 7 October, 1911.

**6, 7, 14, 15 OCTOBER, 1911.** An aviation meet was held at Delorimier Park race track, Montreal, Quebec, Participants Albert Fileux, Romain Gressier and Charles G. King had come from New York City.

Ref: La Presse, Montreal, Que., 3-16 October, 1911.

**6 OCTOBER, 1911.** Charles G. King crashed his Curtiss-type biplane attempting to fly from Delorimier Park race track, Montreal, Quebec.

Ref: The Montreal Daily Herald, Montreal, Que., 7 October, 1911.

**6 OCTOBER, 1911.** The Maurice Vaux ornithopter-type aeroplane (35 hp Viale motor) was exhibited but not flown at the Delorimier Park aviation meet, Montreal, Quebec.

Ref: The Gazette, Montreal, Que., 7 October, 1911.

**6 OCTOBER, 1911.** Romain Gressier made two short flights on his "Farman-Curtis" biplane at Delorimier Park race track, Montreal Quebec. He crashed attempting to take off the following day.

Ref: Montreal Daily Herald, Montreal, Que., 3-9 October, 1911.
La Patrie, Montreal, Que., 3-9 October, 1911.

**9 OCTOBER, 1911.** Albert Fileux crashed in a Morane/Borel monoplane in attempting a flight from Bois Franc polo grounds to Delorimier Park, Montreal, Quebec.

Ref: La Patrie, Montreal, Que., 10 October, 1911.

**14 OCTOBER, 1911.** Romain Gressier made three flights from the Delorimier Park race track, Montreal, Quebec, over the city. He used his Anzani radial engine-powered "Farman-Curtis" biplane.

Ref. La Patrie, Montreal, Que., 16 October, 1911.
The Montreal Daily Star, Montreal, Que., 16 October, 1911.

**15 OCTOBER, 1911.** Romain Gressier was injured in a crash at Delorimier Park race track, Montreal, Quebec, attempting a flight on his "Farman-Curtis" biplane with his mechanic Jack Kirby as a passenger. He had already flown successfully once that day.

Ref: The Montreal Daily Star, Montreal, Que., 16 October, 1911.
La Patrie, Montreal, Que., 16 October, 1911.

**17 OCTOBER, 1911.** Didier Masson flew a Gnome-powered, Curtiss-type biplane at Calgary, Alberta. On 20 October, he made flights over the city centre.

Ref: Ellis, Frank H., Canada's Flying Heritage, Univ. of Toronto Press, 1954.

**5 DECEMBER, 1911.** F.W. Baldwin of Toronto, Ontario, was granted U.S. patent no. 1,010,842 for a "Flying Machine".

Ref: Aeronautics, New York City, Vol. 10, No. 1, January, 1912.

**5 DECEMBER, 1911.** A.G. Bell, F.W. Baldwin, J.A.D. McCurdy, G.H. Curtiss and T.E. Selfridge were granted U.S. patent no. 1,011,106 for a "flying machine".

Ref: Parkin, J.H., Bell and Baldwin, Toronto, 1964.

**28 DECEMBER, 1911.** P.H. Reid of Montreal, Quebec, made four flights on his Bleriot-type monoplane, the last ending in a crash.

Ref: The London Free Press, London, Ont., 29 December, 1911.

# 1912

**20 FEBRUARY, 1912.** L. Earle Sandt, of Erie, Pennsylvania, flew his Curtiss pusher biplane across Lake Erie from Erie, Pennsylvania, to Long Point, Ontario. The aircraft was lost after a crash landing on the lake ice while attempting to return to Erie.

Ref: The Montreal Daily Star, Montreal, Que., 21 February, 1912.

**10 APRIL, 1912.** William McIntosh Stark, of Vancouver, British Columbia, received Aero Club of America Certificate No. 110 after passing test on 22 March, 1912, at the Curtiss Flying School, San Diego, California, on a Curtiss headless pusher.

**13 APRIL, 1912.** W.M. Stark flew his Curtiss pusher biplane at Minoru Park race track, near Vancouver, British Columbia. Three exhibition flights were also made there on 20 April.

Ref: The Daily News-Advertiser, Vancouver, B.C., 14 April, 1912.

Within a week of his exhibition flights at Vancouver American aviator P.O. Parmelee died in a crash at North Yakima, Washington.
(Aero)

W.M. Stark's Curtiss pusher which he flew frequently on the Canadian west coast. A.H. Allardyce, a pupil of Stark's is at the controls.
(A.H. Allardyce photo)

**24 APRIL, 1912.** *The first woman aeroplane passenger in Canada,* Mrs. W.M. Stark, flew with her husband on his Curtiss pusher biplane from a field near Minoru Park, Vancouver, B.C. Stark carried a newspaper reporter on another flight that day.

Ref: Ellis, Frank H., Canada's Flying Heritage, Univ. of Toronto Press, 1954.

**4 MAY, 1912.** W.M. Stark made two flights from Hastings Park, Vancouver, British Columbia, the second ending in a crash landing.

Ref: Ellis, Frank H., Canada's Flying Heritage, Univ. of Toronto Press, 1954.

**9 MAY, 1912.** Samuel A. Tickell of New York City, New York, made a short test flight on a Curtiss-type pusher biplane at Winnipeg, Manitoba. He crashed during an attempted flight the following day.

Ref: Manitoba Free Press, Winnipeg, Man., 10-13 May 1912.

**22 MAY, 1912.** Hillery Beachey from St. Louis, Missouri, flew a Benoist biplane at Island Park race track, Portage la Prairie, Manitoba.

Ref: Manitoba Free Press, Winnipeg, Man., 23 May, 1912.

**23 MAY, 1912.** Phil O. Parmelee, from California, made the first aeroplane flight over the city of Vancouver, British Columbia. He flew a Gage tractor biplane from Hastings Park.

Ref: The Daily News-Advertiser, Vancouver, B.C., 24 May, 1912.

**24 MAY, 1912.** H. Beachey flew a Benoist biplane at River Park, Winnipeg, Manitoba. He crashed after a flight the following day.

Ref: The Winnipeg Tribune, Winnipeg, Man., 25 & 27 May, 1912.

**24 MAY, 1912.** *The first parachute jump from an aeroplane in flight over Canada* was made at Vancouver, British Columbia. by Charles Saunders from a Gage tractor biplane piloted by P.O. Parmelee. That day two flights each were made by Parmelee and J. Clifford Turpin. The complete program was repeated on the following day.

Ref: The Daily News-Advertiser, Vancouver, B.C., 25, 26 May, 1912.

**24 MAY, 1912.** W.M. Stark flew his Curtiss pusher biplane at Victoria, British Columbia. Although the aircraft was damaged in a landing accident, he was able to fly again the following day.

Ref: Victoria Daily Colonist, 25, 26 May, 1912.

**25 MAY, 1912.** Beckwith Havens from New York City, New York, flew a Curtiss pusher biplane at Carling's Farm, London, Ontario, the first aeroplane flight at that city.

Ref: London Advertiser, London, Ont., 25 & 27 May, 1912.

**3 JUNE, 1912.** Charles F. Walsh of the Curtiss Exhibition Co. made the first aeroplane flight at Kingston, Ontario. He flew a Curtiss pusher biplane (60 h.p. Curtiss motor) during the city's celebration of the King's birthday.

Ref: The Daily Standard, Kingston, Ont., 4 June 1912

The first seaplane flight in Canada was made by Fred Eells in his pusher, seen here at Hanlan's Point, Toronto Island.
(James Coll., Toronto City Archives)

**18 JUNE, 1912.** John R. Hendrickson, of Edmonton, Alberta, was granted U.S. patent no. 1,029,754 for an "Aeroplane".

Ref: Aeronautics, New York City, N.Y., Vol. 9, No. 3, September, 1912.

**19 JUNE, 1912.** Percival H. Reid, of Montreal, Quebec, flew his Bleriot-type monoplane at Bois Franc polo ground, Cartierville, Quebec.

Ref: The Montreal Herald, Montreal, Que., 20 June, 1912.

**19 JUNE, 1912.** Miss Ethel Davis, of Saint John, New Brunswick, made a 75-minute flight over the Boston, Massachusetts, area with George A. Gray in his Burgess-Wright biplane.

Ref. La Presse, Montreal, Que., 10 September, 1912.

**19 JUNE, 1912.** Robert B. Russell, of Toronto, Ontario, received Aero Club of America Certificate No. 132 after passing his test on 18 May, 1912, at the Curtiss Flying School, San Diego, California, on a Curtiss headless pusher biplane.

**1 JULY, 1912.** Charles Morok (Charles F. van dan Merrsche), of New York City, New York, crashed after a short flight on a rotary engine-powered Curtiss-type pusher biplane at the Fair Grounds, Chatham, Ontario.

Ref: Hitchins, F.H., Dominion Day, 1912, The CAHS Journal, Vol. 6, No. 3, Fall, 1968.

**1 JULY, 1912.** In an attempted flight at Sault Ste. Marie, Ontario, H. Beachey collided with a signboard. The Curtiss pusher biplane was wrecked, but the aviator escaped with minor injuries.

Ref: Hitchins, F.H., Dominion Day, 1912. The CAHS Journal, Vol.6, No. 3, Fall, 1968.

**1 JULY, 1912.** Beckwith Havens flew a Curtiss pusher biplane at Napanee, Ontario. He was only able to make one flight because of engine trouble.

Ref: The Daily British Whig, Kingston, Ont., 2 July, 1912, p. 3.
The Napanee Beaver, Napanee, Ont., 5 July, 1912.

**1 JULY, 1912.** James J. Ward of St. Hilaire, Minnesota, flew his Curtiss-type pusher biplane twice to open an engagement at Calgary, Alberta. He made three more flights on 3 July.

Ref: The Calgary Daily Herald, Calgary, Alta., 2-5 July, 1912.

**1 JULY, 1912.** W.M. Stark, of Vancouver, British Columbia, flew his Curtiss pusher biplane at Armstrong, British Columbia.

Ref: Ellis, Frank H., Canada's Flying Heritage. Univ. of Toronto Press, 1954.

**6 JULY, 1912.** *The first seaplane flight in Canada* was made by Fred G. Eells who took off and landed at Hanlan's Point in Toronto Harbour, Ontario. He flew a Rieflin pusher biplane with a Welles & Adams 50 hp motor.

Ref: The Toronto World, Toronto, Ont., 8 July, 1912.

J.J. Ward's Curtiss-type pusher at Winnipeg, 10 July, 1912. (WCAM)

The National Aeroplane Co.'s Nieuport monoplane which was flown at Brandon, Manitoba, by Marcel Tournier. (C.M. Vought Coll.)

**8 JULY, 1912.** Charles Morok, of New York City, New York, made an aeroplane flight at Ingersoll, Ontario.

Ref: London Advertiser, London, Ont., 9 July, 1912.

**10 JULY, 1912.** Georges Mestach crashed during an attempted exhibition flight at Winnipeg, Manitoba, on a Borel monoplane.

Ref. Manitoba Free Press, Winnipeg, Man., 11 July, 1912.

**10 JULY, 1912.** J.J. Ward flew his Curtiss-type pusher biplane "Shooting Star" at the Canadian Industrial Exhibition, Winnipeg, Manitoba. He made 18 flights during the engagement which ended on 20 July.

Ref. Manitoba Free Press, Winnipeg, 8-22 July, 1912.

**15 JULY, 1912.** Cecil Malcolm Peoli made the first aeroplane flight at Berlin (now Kitchener), Ontario, on a Baldwin "Red Devil" biplane.

Ref: Berlin News Record, Berlin, Ont., 15-16 July, 1912.

**17 JULY, 1912.** W.R. Brookins flew his Burgess-Wright hydroaeroplane from Lake Erie at Port Stanley, Ontario. On one of four flights, he carried Lorne Bradley of St. Thomas as a passenger. Further flights were made on 18, 19 and 20 July. On the last day, Miss Dora Labatt, of London, Ontario, made a flight with him.

Ref: The London Free Press, London, Ont., 18-22 July, 1912.

**18 JULY, 1912.** Miss Dorthy De Vonda parachuted from a hot air balloon at the Minnedosa, Manitoba, summer fair. The performance was repeated on 19 July.

Ref: The Minnedosa Tribune, Minnedosa, Man., 18 & 25 July, 1912.

**23 JULY, 1912.** French aviator Marcel Tournier, of the National Aeroplane Co., Cicero Field, Chicago, Illinois, flew a Nieuport monoplane at the Brandon, Manitoba, Fair. Further flights were made on the following three days.

Ref: Manitoba Free Press, Winnipeg, Man., 22-27 July, 1912.

**26 JULY, 1912.** R.C. "Bob" St. Henry made three flights on a Curtiss pusher biplane at the North Battleford, Saskatchewan, Exhibition.

Ref: The Daily Province, Regina, Sask., 29 July, 1912.

**27 JULY, 1912.** On the outskirts of Guelph, Ontario, a glider constructed by Harry Bond and Ben McConkey crashed during an attempted flight carrying the builders and a passenger. The glider was wrecked, but they escaped with bruises.

Ref: The Globe, Toronto, Ont., 29 July, 1912.

**30 JULY, 1912.** J.J. Ward made two flights on a Curtiss-type pusher biplane at the Dominion Fair, Regina, Saskatchewan. He made further flights, two each day on 31 July and 1 August.

Ref: The Daily Standard, Regina, Sask., 31 July - 2 August, 1912.

**JULY, 1912.** The Canadian Commissioner of Customs announced that aeroplanes imported to Canada would come under tariff item 453 and the following rates would apply: 15% British preferential, 25% Intermediate and 27% General. American and, apparently, most other aircraft would be subject to the 27% duty.

Ref: Aircraft, New York City, N.Y., July, 1912, P. 157.

**6 AUGUST, 1912.** Glen Luther Martin of Los Angeles, California, flew a biplane of his own design and construction at the exhibition at Saskatoon, Saskatchewan. He flew each day of the fair, which ended on 9 August, and in a flight on the last day he reached an altitude of 6,400 feet.

Ref: The Daily Phoenix, Saskatoon, Sask., 6-10 August, 1912.

**10 AUGUST, 1912.** James V. Martin crash-landed his Gage tractor biplane due to engine trouble during a flight from Minoru Park race track near Vancouver, British Columbia.

Ref: The Daily News Advertiser, Vancouver, B.C., 11 August, 1912.

**12 AUGUST, 1912.** The first aeroplane flight at Peterborough, Ontario, was made by William B. Hemstrought of the Curtiss exhibition team on a Curtiss pusher biplane.

Ref: The Peterborough Daily Evening Review, 13 August, 1912.

**21 AUGUST, 1912.** Fred Hoover crashed attempting to take off on a 50 hp Curtiss-type pusher biplane at the Fair Grounds, Chatham, Ontario.

Ref: Hitchins, F.H., Dominion Day, 1912. The CAHS Journal Vol. 6, No. 3, Fall, 1968.

**26 AUGUST, 1912.** Georges Mestach flew his Borel monoplane at the Provincial Exhibition, Quebec City, Quebec. At least two more flights were made during the Exhibition which ended on 3 September.

Ref: The Quebec Chronicle, Quebec, Que., 27-31 August, 1912.

**27 AUGUST, 1912.** Charles R. Haas of Brightwater, British Columbia, was granted U.S. Patent No. 1,036,834 for a "Propeller".

Ref: Aeronautics, New York, Vol. 11, No. 4, Oct, 1912.

**2 SEPTEMBER, 1912.** *The first aeroplane flight in the Province of New Brunswick,* was made by Cecil Peoli of New York City on a Baldwin "Red Devil" biplane. He made a total of 13 flights, two of these carrying a passenger during the six-day engagement. He flew from Courtenay Bay sands, Saint John.

Ref: The Daily Telegraph and The Sun, Saint John, N.B., 2-9 September, 1912.

**2 SEPTEMBER, 1912.** R.C. "Bob" St. Henry flew a Curtiss biplane at the Medicine Hat, Alberta, Trades & Labor Council sports program at the Fair Grounds.

Ref: Medicine Hat Daily News, Medicine Hat, Alta., 3 September, 1912.

**2 SEPTEMBER, 1912.** Georges Mestach made the first aeroplane flight at Sherbrooke, Quebec. He flew a Borel monoplane at the Great Eastern Exhibition there. Further flights took place before the Exhibition ended 7 September.

Ref: The Sherbrooke Daily Record, Sherbrooke, Que., 3, 5 September, 1912.

**4 SEPTEMBER, 1912.** William B. Hemstrought, of the Curtiss exhibition team, flew a Curtiss pusher biplane at the Brockville, Ontario, Fair & Horse Show. He made flights also on 5 and 6 September.

Ref: Brockville Recorder Weekly, Brockville, Ont., 6, 12 September, 1912.

**7-14 SEPTEMBER, 1912.** Professor E.R. Hutchinson's aeronauts, Howard LeVan and George Sewell, parachuted from hot air balloons at the Central Canada Exhibition, Ottawa, Ontario.

Ref: The Citizen, Ottawa, Ont., 9-13 September, 1912.

**12-14 SEPTEMBER, 1912.** Aeronaut Miss Dorothy De Vonda performed hot air balloon ascensions and parachute jumps at the Peterborough, Ontario, fair grounds.

Ref: Daily Evening Review, Peterborough, Ont., 4-16 September, 1912.

**14 SEPTEMBER, 1912.** George A. Gray, of Boston, Massachusetts, crashed attempting a flight on his Burgess-Wright biplane from Delorimier Park race course at Montreal, Quebec.

Ref: The Montreal Herald, Montreal, Que., 16 September, 1912.

**16 SEPTEMBER, 1912.** C.F. Walsh flew a Curtiss pusher biplane for the Curtiss exhibition team at the Provincial Exhibition, Halifax, Nova Scotia. The aeroplane had been damaged in an abandoned take-off attempt on 11 September. He made successful flights on 17, 18 and 19 September before crashing again on the last day.

Ref: The Morning Chronicle, Halifax, N.S., 9-20 September, 1912.

**21 SEPTEMBER, 1912.** James McGrath attempted a glider flight at Peterborough, Ontario.

Ref: The Peterborough Daily Evening Review, 23 September, 1912. McGrath says glider wrecked by wind before flight made.

**22 SEPTEMBER, 1912.** G.A. Gray needed police protection from angry spectators when he refused to fly his Burgess-Wright biplane for an engagement at Lafontaine Park, Montreal, Quebec, with a crowd of up to 100, 000 people on hand.

Ref: La Presse, (The sponsors), Montreal, Que., 23 September, 1912.

Cecil Peoli, one of the youngest American exhibition flyers made a number of flights in Canada, including the first in Prince Edward Island on 25 September 1912. (via K.M. Molson)

P.H. Reid of Montreal and fellow student, Miss Agnes Firth, at the Sloane Aviation School in October 1912. (NASM)

**24 SEPTEMBER, 1912.** Walter Edwards, of Portland, Oregon, flew a Curtiss-type pusher biplane at the Nelson, British Columbia, Exhibition. Further flights were made on the 25, 26 and 27 September.

Ref: Ellis, Frank H., Canada's Flying Heritage, Univ. of Toronto Press, 1954.

**25 SEPTEMBER, 1912.** *The first aeroplane flight in the Province of Prince Edward Island* was made by Cecil Peoli on a Baldwin "Red Devil" biplane at the Provincial Exhibition, Charlottetown.

Ref: The Island Patriot, Charlottetown, P.E.I., 26 September, 1912.

**26 SEPTEMBER, 1912.** *Photographs were taken from a powered aircraft in flight for the first time in Canada* by Cecil Peoli flying a Baldwin "Red Devil" biplane at Charlottetown, Prince Edward Island.

Ref: The Island Patriot, Charlottetown, P.E.I., 27, 28 September, 1912.

**6 OCTOBER, 1912.** Several short flights were made by Ernest Anctil and Gustave Pollien in their Caudron-type biplane at Bois Franc polo ground, Cartierville, Quebec.

Ref: The Montreal Daily Star, Montreal, Que., 7 October, 1912.
La Presse, Montreal, Que., 3, 7 October, 1912.

**9 OCTOBER, 1912.** Gustave Pollien flew a Caudron-type biplane from Bois Franc polo grounds, Cartierville, Quebec.

Ref: La Presse, Montreal, Que., 10 October, 1912.

**18 OCTOBER, 1912.** Short flights were made by Ernest Anctil and Gustave Pollien in their Caudron-type aircraft at Bois Franc polo grounds, Cartierville, Quebec.

Ref: La Presse, Montreal, Que., 19 October, 1912.

**20 OCTOBER, 1912.** Gustave Pollien crashed after a flight over Cartierville, Quebec, from the Bois Franc polo grounds in a Caudron-type biplane.

Ref: La Presse, Montreal, Que., 21 October, 1912.
The Montreal Daily Star, Montreal, Que., 21 October, 1912.

**22 OCTOBER, 1912.** Felix Gregoire, of St. Jean Baptiste, Manitoba, was granted U.S. patent No. 1,041,779 for a "Combination Aeroboat and Aeroplane".

Ref: Aero and Hydro, St. Louis, Mo., Vol. V., No. 9, 30 November, 1912.

**23 OCTOBER, 1912.** Percival Hall Reid, of Montreal, Quebec, received Aero Club of America Certificate No. 179 after passing his test on 18 October, 1912, at the Sloane Aviation School, Hempstead Plains, Long Island, New York, on a 35 hp Anzani-powered Deperdussin monoplane.

**28 OCTOBER, 1912.** William B. Hemstrought made the first aeroplane flight at Woodstock, Ontario, flying a Curtiss pusher biplane from the Athletic Association grounds.

Ref: The Montreal Daily Star, Montreal, Que., 29 October, 1912.

**5 NOVEMBER, 1912.** With Miss Isabella Patterson of Vancouver, British Columbia, as his passenger, Harry Bingham Brown set a new American altitude record for aeroplanes carrying pilot and passenger when he reached 5,300 feet in his Wright Model B biplane in a flight from Oakwood Heights, Staten Island, New York.

Ref Aeronautics, New York, Vol. 11, No. 5, November, 1912.

**26 NOVEMBER, 1912.** George M. Absalom, of Caistor Centre, Ontario, was granted U.S. patent No. 1,045,657 for a "flying machine".

Ref: Aero and Hydro. Chicago, Ill., Vol. 5, No. 14, 4 January, 1913.

**26 NOVEMBER, 1912.** Earl H. Kelsey, of Bawlf, Alberta, was granted U.S. patent No. 1,045,152 for a "Flying Machine".

Ref: Aero and Hydro, Chicago, Ill., Vol. V, No. 12, 21 December, 1912.

**10 DECEMBER, 1912.** Edgar L. Laur and George Florence, of Toronto, Ontario, were granted U.S. patent No. 1,046,814 for a "Propeller".

Ref: Aero and Hydro, Chicago, Ill., Vol. V, No. 12, 21 December, 1912.

**10 DECEMBER, 1912.** Charles W. Wolcott died in Edmonton, Alberta. His Balloon Company had performed hot air balloon ascensions and parachute jumps in many parts of Canada during two decades at the turn of the century.

Ref: The Edmonton Journal, Edmonton, Alta., 11 December, 1912.

**Victor Carlstrom at the Curtiss Aviation School at Long Branch, Ontario.**
**(photo Gilpatrick/NASM)**

# 1913

**28 JANUARY, 1913.** Stanley Drake, of Dunnville, Ontario, was granted U.S. patent No. 1,051,709 for a "Parachute safety device for use of the aviator".

Ref: Aeronautics, New York City, Vol. 12, No. 3, March, 1913.

**6 MARCH, 1913.** The formation of the First Saskatchewan Aviation Co. Ltd. to teach aviation was announced at Saskatoon, Sask.

Ref: The Saskatoon Daily Star, Saskatoon, Sask., 6 March, 1913.

**2 JUNE, 1913.** Raymond V. Morris of the Curtiss exhibition team made two flights on a Curtiss pusher biplane from the fair grounds at Kingston, Ontario.

Ref: Daily British Whig, Kingston, Ont., 3 June, 1913.

**3 JUNE, 1913.** Albert Sugden, of Stratford, Ontario, was granted U.S patent No. 1,063,843 for an "Aeroplane".

Ref: Aeronautics, New York City, Vol. 12, No. 6, June, 1913.

**3 JUNE, 1913.** William S. Luckey, of New York City, flying a Curtiss hydro-aeroplane from Lake Ontario at Kingston, Ontario, ran into a shore wall after landing and seriously injured two spectators.

Ref: Daily British Whig, Kingston, Ont., 2-6 June, 1913.

**9 JUNE 1913.** W.B. Hemstrought flying a Curtiss pusher biplane made the first aeroplane flight at Stratford, Ontario, from the agricultural park.

Ref: The Montreal Daily Star, Montreal, Que., 11 June, 1913.

**16 JUNE, 1913.** Victor Carlstrom, appearing with Colonel Ferari's Shows, flew a Rex biplane (70 hp Maximotor) at London, Ontario. Engine trouble caused a forced landing during a flight the following day, but he made further flights on 19 and 20 June.

Ref: The London Advertiser, London, Ont., 17-20 June, 1913.
The London Free Press, London, Ont., 21 June, 1913.

**23 JUNE, 1913.** W.S. Luckey abandoned an attempt to stage a flying exhibition at Trenton, Ontario, after a take-off accident.

Ref: The Montreal Daily Star, Montreal, Que., 24 June, 1913.

**23 JUNE, 1913.** Victor Carlstrom made the first successful aeroplane flights at Chatham, Ontario, on a Rex biplane from the fair grounds. He made two flights each day on 23 and 24 June.

Ref: The London Free Press, London, Ont., 24-26 June, 1913.

Arthur Smith who, after his appearance at Chatham, Ontario, became a leading aerobatic pilot.
(Gilpatric /NASM)

W.H. Blakeley, in his Curtiss-type pusher, carried out an exceptional exhibition tour in western Canada during July and August 1913 including some outstanding cross-country flights. (Aeronautics)

**26 JUNE, 1913.** Arthur Smith from Indiana damaged his biplane slightly in landing from a successful flight at Chatham, Ontario. He had crashed attempting a practice flight the previous day. On 27 June, another otherwise successful flight ended in a crash in which he was injured and the biplane was wrecked.

Ref: The London Free Press, London, Ont., 30 June, 1913.

**30 JUNE, 1913.** Cecil Peoli made two flights during the Barrie, Ontario, Diamond Jubilee program on the Baldwin "Red Devil" biplane. During a single flight on 1 July, he took photographs of the grounds with a fixed camera on the aircraft.

Ref: Northern Advance, Barrie, Ont., 3 July, 1913.

**1 JULY, 1913.** Curtiss exhibition flier, Charles Frank Niles, crashed after an aeroplane flight at the Napanee, Ontario, Driving Park grounds. The Curtiss pusher overturned in a forced landing and was wrecked, but Niles was only bruised.

Ref: The Globe, Toronto, Ont., 2 July, 1913.

**1 JULY, 1913.** R.V. Morris of the Curtiss exhibition team flew a Curtiss pusher biplane at Port Elgin, Ontario.

Ref: The Times, Port Elgin, Ont., 2 July, 1913.

**1 JULY, 1913.** William B. Hemstrought of the Curtiss Exhibition Company made a successful flight on a Curtiss pusher biplane at Bayview athletic park, Sarnia, Ontario.

Ref: Observer, Sarnia, Ont., 2 July, 1913.

**4 JULY, 1913.** Cecil Peoli made two flights on a Baldwin "Red Devil ' biplane at the Old Boys Reunion at Lanark, Ontario.

Ref: The Lanark Era, Lanark, Ont., 9 July, 1913.

**13 JULY, 1913.** Victor Carlstrom crashed near Oakville, Ontario, during an attempted flight from Brantford to Toronto on a Rex biplane.

Ref: Hamilton Daily Times, Hamilton, Ont., 14 July, 1913.

**15 JULY, 1913.** Lewis Hector Ray of Ottawa, Ontario, was granted patent no. 1,067,271 for a "control for aeroplanes".

Ref: Aeronautics, New York City, Vol. 13, No. 1, July, 1913.

**15 JULY, 1913.** Canadian-born Harold Wilton Blakeley flew a Curtiss-type biplane (60 hp 8 cyl. Hall-Scott motor) at the Dominion Livestock Show and Fair, Brandon, Manitoba. He made more than twenty flights during the engagement and on 17 July ascended to 5,500 feet.

Ref: Manitoba Free Press, Winnipeg, Man., 16-26 July, 1913.
Aero and Hydro, St. Louis, Mo., Vol. VI, No. 18, August, 1913.

**23 JULY 1913.** *The first night aeroplane flight in Canada* was made by H.W. Blakeley during his engagement at the Dominion Livestock Show and Fair at Brandon, Manitoba. His Hall-Scott-powered, Curtiss-type pusher biplane was fitted with small electric lights on the wing leading edges and an electric headlight. His landing area was outlined by fires.

Ref: Manitoba Free Press, Winnipeg, Man., 24 July, 1913.

**24 JULY, 1913.** Victor Carlstrom landed a Bleriot-type monoplane (Kirkham motor) at Hamilton, Ontario, en route to Woodstock, Ontario, from Savona, New York. After repairs were made, he continued on to Woodstock the following day.

Ref: Hamilton Daily Times, Hamilton, Ont., 24-26 July, 1913.

**25 JULY, 1913.** J.W. Marks narrowly escaped death at the Brandon, Manitoba, Fair when his arm became caught in a rope hanging from Howard Le Van's ascending balloon. The balloonist calmed him and brought them both down safely.

Ref: Brandon Weekly Sun, Brandon, Man., 31 July, 1913.

**28 JULY, 1913.** Victor Carlstrom flew a Bleriot-type monoplane at the Old Home Week celebration at Guelph, Ontario.

Ref: The London Free Press, London, Ont., 29 July, 1913.

**29 JULY - 1 AUGUST, 1913.** Aeronauts Howard LeVan and George Sewell of the E.R. Huchinson troupe performed hot air balloon ascensions and parachute jumps at the Provincial Exhibition, Regina, Saskatchewan.

Ref: The Daily Province, Regina, Sask., 28 July - 2 August, 1913.

**30 JULY, 1913.** Professor Stephen Allen parachuted from a balloon at Erie Beach, Welland county, Ontario.

Ref: Courier, Buffalo, New York, 31 July, 1913.
Tribune, Welland, Ont., 31 July, 1913.

**31 JULY, 1913.** *The first aeroplane flight by a woman pilot in Canada* was made by Alys McKay Bryant on a Curtiss-type pusher biplane at Minoru race track, Vancouver, British Columbia. Her husband, John Milton Bryant, made two flights that day.

Ref: The Daily News-Advertiser, Vancouver, B.C., 1 August, 1913.

**1 AUGUST, 1913.** H.W. Blakeley flew his Curtiss-type biplane from Brandon to Boissevain, Manitoba, a distance of 44 miles. He flew three times during theTurtle Mountain fair on 4 and 5 August.

Ref: The Saskatoon Daily Star, Saskatoon, Sask., 1 August, 1913.
Manitoba Free Press, Winnipeg, Man., 7 August, 1913.

**5 AUGUST, 1913.** Mrs. Alys McKay Bryant flew a Curtiss-type biplane from Willows polo grounds, Victoria, British Columbia.

Ref: Victoria Daily Times, Victoria, B.C., 5 August, 1913.

**5 AUGUST, 1913.** G.L. Martin began his second flying engagement at the Saskatoon Industrial Exhibition by a trial flight with his mechanic as passenger in his tractor biplane (80 hp Curtiss motor). On the last day, 8 August, he made three separate flights with single passengers.

Ref: The Saskatoon Daily Star, Saskatoon, Sask., 5-9 August, 1913.

**6 AUGUST, 1913.** H.W. Blakeley made two flights at the Virden, Manitoba, fair on his Curtiss-type pusher biplane. He had flown to Virden from Boissevain, a distance of 58 miles.

Ref: Manitoba Free Press, Winnipeg, Man., 7 August, 1913.

**6 AUGUST, 1913.** *The first fatal aeroplane accident in Canada* occurred when John M. Bryant was fatally injured in the crash of the Curtiss-type hydro-aeroplane he was flying at Victoria, British Columbia. He had flown successfully the previous day.

Ref: Victoria Daily Times, Victoria, B.C., 6,7 August, 1913.

**12 AUGUST, 1913.** Victor Carlstrom flew a Bleriot-type monoplane at the Hamilton, Ontario, Centennial celebrations. The engagement was terminated on the following day when the aeroplane was damaged by a heavy landing.

Ref: Hamilton Daily Times, Hamilton, Ont., 13-15 August, 1913.

**19 AUGUST, 1913.** H.W. Blakeley flew his Curtiss-type pusher at the North Battleford, Saskatchewan, exhibition. Several flights were made each day during the engagement which ended on 22 August.

Ref: Manitoba Free Press, Winnipeg, Man., 25 August, 1913.

**22 AUGUST, 1913.** During an exhibition engagement at North Battleford, Saskatchewan, H.W. Blakeley flew his Curtiss-type pusher biplane over the neighbouring town of Battleford.

Ref: Saskatchewan Herald, Battleford, Sask., 22 August, 1913.

**25-29 AUGUST, 1913.** Professor E.R. Hutchinson's troupe of aeronauts parachuted from hot air balloons at the Provincial Exhibition, Quebec City, Quebec.

Ref: The Quebec Chronicle, Quebec, Que., 23-30 August, 1913.

**30 AUGUST, 1913.** Professor E.R. Hutchinson's aeronaut troupe began an engagement at the Great Eastern Exhibition, Sherbrooke, Quebec, with a hot air balloon ascension and drop with six successive parachutes.

Ref: The Gazette, Montreal, Que., 1 September, 1913.

**4 SEPTEMBER, 1913.** Beginning an engagement at the Nova Scotia Provincial Exhibition at Halifax, Arthur C. Lapham parachuted from a Wright biplane (35 hp Wright motor) flown by Harry Bingham Brown. They were under the management of A. Leo Stevens, the inventor of the back-type "Life Pack" parachute used by Lapham.

Ref: The Halifax Herald, 5 September, 1913.

Walter Edwards on his Baldwin Red Devil biplane at Cornwall, Ontario, on 5 September 1913.
(N. McLeod photo)

The Pollien biplane at Cartierville, the building in the background was the first aircraft hangar in Canada, erected in 1912 on the site of the present Cartierville Airport. (P.H. Reid photo)

**5 SEPTEMBER, 1913.** Walter Edwards, of Portland, Oregon, flew a Baldwin "Red Devil" biplane at the Cornwall, Ontario, fair. Two flights daily were made on 5 and 6 September.

Ref: The Montreal Daily Star, Montreal, Que., 9 September, 1913.

**6 SEPTEMBER, 1913.** Gustave Pollien flew his Caudron-type biplane over Blue Bonnets race course, Montreal, Quebec, between races. He had made other flights from Bois Franc polo grounds, Cartierville, on 21, 28 and 31 August and 4 September. He flew from there again on 21 September.

Ref: The Montreal Daily Star, Montreal, Que., 22 August to 22 September, 1913.

**6 SEPTEMBER, 1913.** H.W. Blakeley flew his Curtiss-type pusher biplane from Brandon to Wawanesa, Manitoba, a distance of approximately 21 miles, where he gave a demonstration the following day.

Ref: The Independent, Wawanesa, Man., 12 September.

**10 SEPTEMBER, 1913.** *The first cross-country flight in Canada to exceed 100 miles.* H.W. Blakeley flew from Wawanesa to Morden, Manitoba, via Pilot Mound, Somerset, Miami and Manitou, a distance of about 115 miles. He gave a flying exhibition on his Curtiss-type pusher biplane at Morden that evening.

Ref: Brandon Weekly Sun, Brandon, Man., 18 September, 1913.

**11 SEPTEMBER, 1913.** Cecil Peoli on a Baldwin "Red Devil" biplane (80 hp Hall-Scott motor) circled the Parliament Buildings at Ottawa, Ontario. During his engagement at the Central Canada Exhibition, he made flights daily from 9 to 13 September inclusive.

Ref: The Citizen, Ottawa, Ont., 6-15 September, 1913.

**11 SEPTEMBER, 1913.** H.W. Blakeley flew his Curtiss-type pusher biplane from Morden to near Pilot Mound, Manitoba, via Manitou.

Ref: Pilot Mound Sentinel, Pilot Mound, Man., 18 September, 1913.

**12 SEPTEMBER, 1913.** H.W. Blakeley gave a flying demonstration at Pilot Mound, Manitoba. He had flown from Morden via Manitou the previous day. That evening he left for Wawanesa in his Curtiss-type pusher biplane, but was forced to land by a squall at Belmont.

Ref: Pilot Mound Sentinel, Pilot Mound, Man., 18 September, 1913.
The Independent, Wawanesa, Man., 19 September, 1913.

**13 SEPTEMBER, 1913.** H.W. Blakeley reached Wawanesa on his return from Morden, Manitoba, and gave his second exhibition flight there on his Curtiss-type pusher biplane in the evening.

Ref: Brandon Weekly Sun, Brandon, Man., 18 September, 1913.

**15 SEPTEMBER, 1913.** H.W. Blakeley, flying his Curtiss-type pusher biplane, returned to Brandon from Wawanesa, Manitoba, completing a nine-day, 220-mile exhibition flying circuit.

Ref. Brandon Weekly Sun, Brandon, Man., 18 September, 1913.

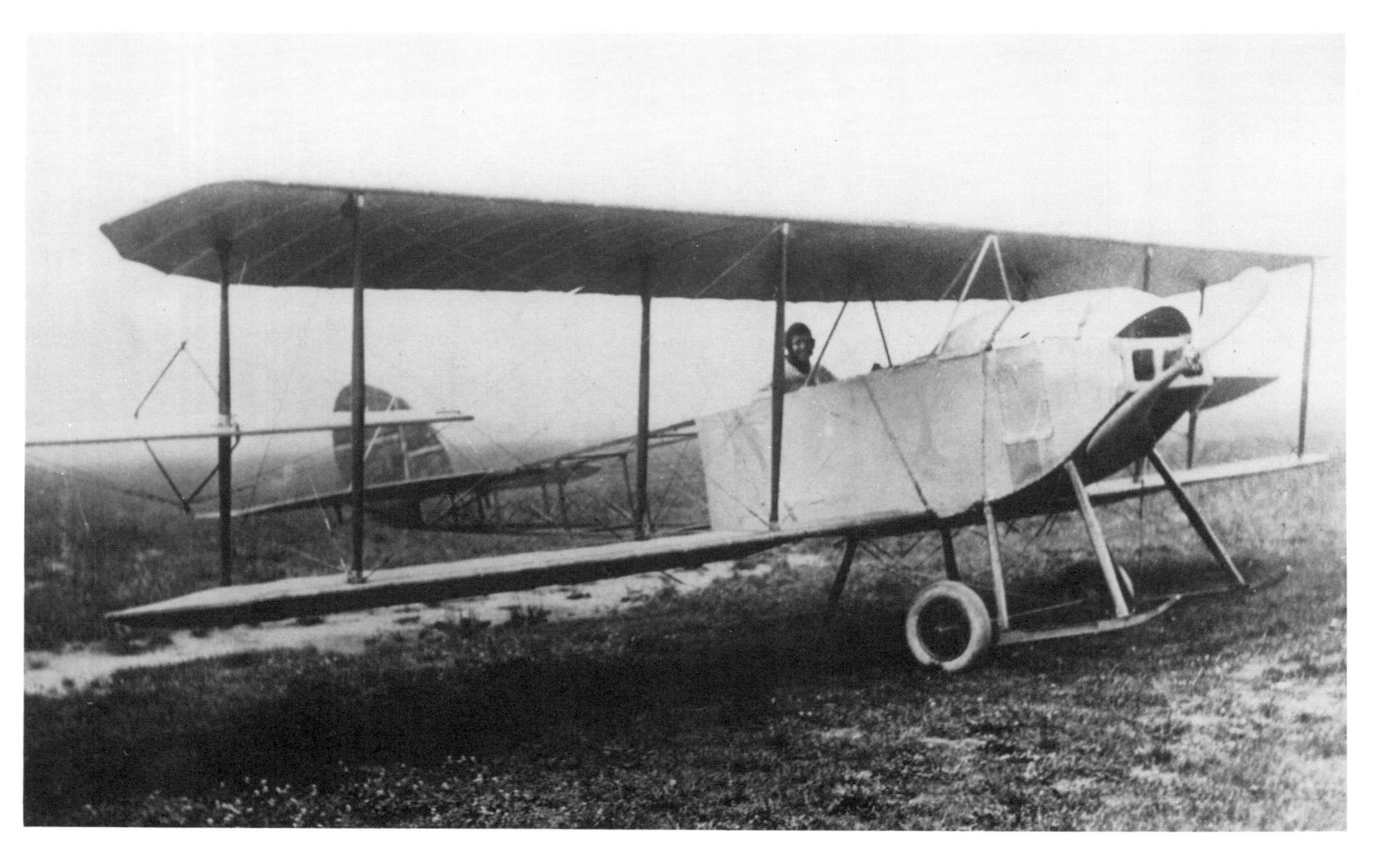

**The Lillie biplane in which W.C. Robinson made his Montreal-Ottawa flight in October 1913. The photo was taken prior to the flight, at which time, the fuselage was completely covered with fabric. The aircraft was the first design of C.M. Vought who later formed the Chance Vought Corp.**
**(C.M. Vought Coll.)**

**16 SEPTEMBER, 1913.** H.W. Blakeley made an exhibition flight on his Curtiss-type pusher biplane at Weyburn, Saskatchewan.

Ref: The Daily Province, Regina, Sask., 17 September, 1913.

**18 SEPTEMBER, 1913.** H.W. Blakeley was forced to land his Curtiss-type pusher biplane due to motor trouble between Pasqua and Moose Jaw, Saskatchewan, ending an attempted flight from Weyburn. He had completed a distance of about 90 miles.

Ref: The Morning Leader, Regina, Sask., 19 September, 1913.

**3 OCTOBER, 1913.** In a crash during an exhibition flight at Grand Junction, Colorado, Canadian-born H.W. Blakeley damaged his Curtiss-type pusher biplane beyond repair. He escaped with minor injuries.

Ref: Saskatchewan Herald, Battleford, Sask., 10 October, 1913.

**8 OCTOBER, 1913.** *The first commercial inter-city and first inter-provincial flight in Canada* was made by William Curtis Robinson in a Vought/Lillie tractor biplane (50 hp Gnome motor). He carried copies of the first edition of the newspaper, Montreal Daily Mail, from Snowdon Junction, Montreal, Quebec, to Slattery's Field, Ottawa, Ontario, with five intermediate stops. He crashed on take-off at Ottawa the following day.

Ref: Molson, K.M. Montreal to Ottawa by Air, 1913.
The CAHS Journal, Vol. 11, No. 4, Winter, 1973.

**14 OCTOBER, 1913.** James Edward Fraser, of Saint John, New Brunswick, was granted U.S. Patent No. 1,075,969 for a "Flying Machine".

Ref: Aeronautics, New York City, Vol. 13, No. 5, November, 1913.

**6 DECEMBER, 1913.** Cecil Peoli, dressed as Santa Claus, flew a Baldwin "Red Devil" biplane from the Bois Franc polo grounds, Cartierville, to Fletcher's Field, Montreal, Quebec. The flight was sponsored by Goodwin's department store.

Ref: The Montreal Gazette, Montreal, Que., 8 December, 1913.

W.A. Dean's Curtiss E flying boat "Sunfish" at Toronto Island. Pilot T.C. Macaulay is standing at the left. The upper wing extensions fitted to the Sunfish were not usually installed on the Curtiss E and F flying boats and they provide an easily distinguished mark between the Sunfish and the F flying boats of the Curtiss Aviation School. (Macaulay/NASM)

Lincoln Beachey flying at Montreal in June 1914 when he "looped-the-loop" for the first time in Canada. (A.H. Sandwell photo)

# 1914

**15 MAY, 1914.** Theodore C. Macaulay made a return flight between Toronto and Hamilton, Ontario, in W.A. Dean's Curtiss flying boat "Sunfish". A newspaper reporter accompanied him on each leg of the flight. Other passengers were given flights during stops at Hamilton and Oakville.

Ref: The Globe, Toronto, Ont., 16 May, 1914.
Hamilton, Spectator, Hamilton, Ont., 16 May, 1914.

**17 MAY, 1914.** Aerial photographs of the city of Toronto, Ontario, were taken by D.K. Billings and N.C. Pearce of "The Toronto World" from W.A. Dean's Curtiss flying boat "Sunfish" on two successive flights. It was piloted by T.C. Macaulay.

Ref: The Toronto World, Toronto, Ont., 18 and 24 May, 1914.

**25 MAY, 1914.** T.C. Macaulay crashed attempting to take off on a Curtiss biplane for an exhibition flight at Mitchell, Ontario.

Ref: The Globe, Toronto, Ont., 26 May, 1914.

**30 MAY, 1914.** Jean-Marie Landry of Quebec City, Quebec, qualified on an Anzani-powered Bleriot XI at Buc, France, for French Aviator's Brevet No. 1659, issued on 20 June, 1914.

Ref: Flight, London, England, Vol. 6, No. 26, 26 June, 1914.

**13 JUNE, 1914.** W.M. Stark flew his float-equipped Curtiss pusher biplane from Burrard Inlet to English Bay, Vancouver, British Columbia.

Ref: The Daily News-Advertiser, Vancouver, B.C., 16 June, 1914.

**25 JUNE, 1914.** Gustave Pollien made two flights from Coteau Rough Park, south Montreal, Quebec, on his Gnome-powered, Caudron-type biplane.

Ref: The Montreal Herald, Montreal, Que., 26 June, 1914.

**25 JUNE, 1914.** Tom Blakely of Calgary, Alberta, flew a Curtiss-type biplane (45 hp Maximotor engine) near that city.

Ref: Ellis, Frank H., Canada's Flying Heritage, Univ. of Toronto Press, 1954.

**27 JUNE, 1914.** *An aeroplane "looped-the-loop" for the first time in Canada* during a flying exhibition at Maisonneuve Park, Montreal, Quebec. Lincoln Beachey used his Gnome-powered special Curtiss-type pusher biplane. The exhibition was repeated on the following day.

Ref: La Presse, Montreal, Que., 29 June, 1914.
The Montreal Herald, Montreal, Que., 27, 29 June, 1914.

**1 JULY, 1914.** H.W. Blakely of New York City was seriously injured in the crash of his Baldwin biplane during a flying exhibition at Port Hope, Ontario.

Ref: The Toronto World, Toronto, Ont., 3 July, 1914.

**1 JULY, 1914.** Clair Horton carried single passengers at a rate of a-dollar-per-minute on a Curtiss pusher hydro-aeroplane for brief flights at Winnipeg Beach, Manitoba.

Ref: Manitoba Free Press, Winnipeg, Man., 2 July 1914.

The Ellis-Blakely Curtiss type pusher. (F.H. Ellis photo)

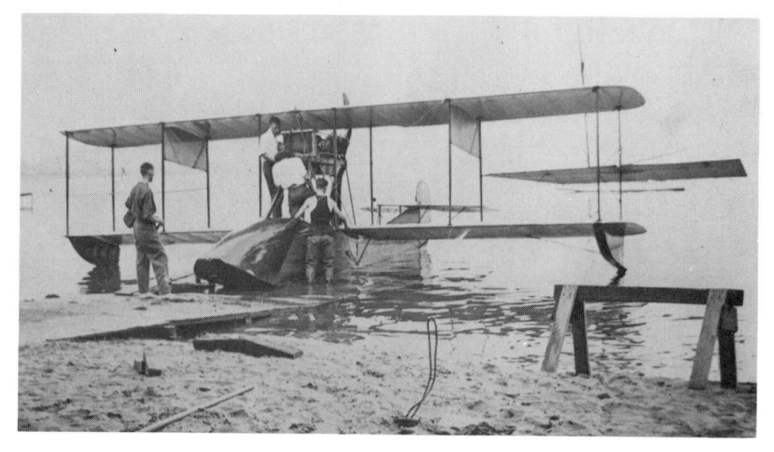

Victor Vernon's Curtiss F "Betty V" at Toronto Island 1915.
(James Coll. Toronto City Archives)

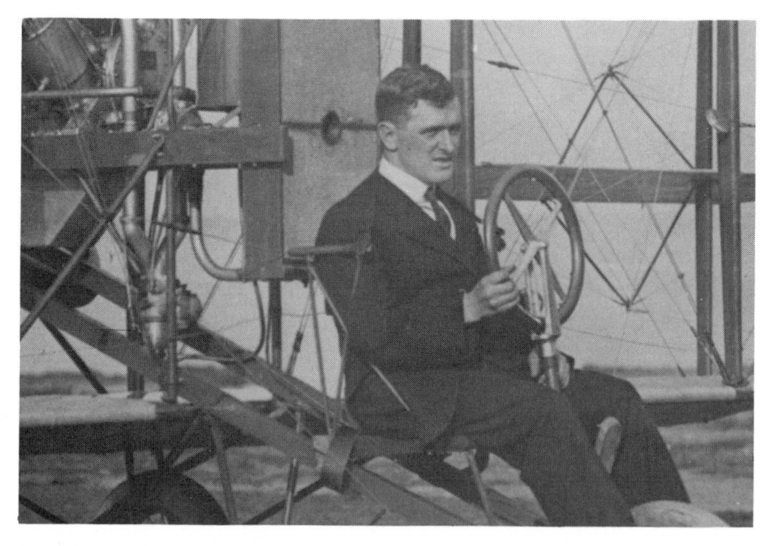

Lincoln Beachey, a pioneer pilot of both lighter-than-air and heavier-than-air machines, is seated here in a Curtiss O – powered Curtiss pusher. He appeared in a number of places in Canada and from 1913 to his death in 1915 was considered the foremost aerobatic pilot in North America. (USAF Museum)

**1 JULY, 1914.** W.M. Stark of Vancouver, British Columbia, made the first aeroplane flight at Chilliwack, B.C., on his Curtiss pusher biplane.

Ref: The Daily News-Advertiser, Vancouver, B.C., 2 July, 1914.

**2 JULY, 1914.** Frank H. Ellis made his first flight on the Blakely-Ellis Curtiss-type pusher biplane "The West Wind" near Calgary, Alberta.

Ref. Ellis, Frank H., Canada's Flying Heritage, Univ. of Toronto Press, 1954.

**2 JULY, 1914.** Canadian-born aeronaut J. Stanley Purcell drowned in the Avon River after parachuting from a hot air balloon at Windsor, Nova Scotia.

Ref: The Montreal Daily Star, Montreal, Que., 3 July, 1914.

**11 JULY, 1914.** Victor Vernon made 10 flights in his Curtiss F flying boat "Betty V" at Crystal Beach, Ontario.

Ref: Buffalo Courier, Buffalo, N.Y., 12 July, 1914.

**11 JULY, 1914.** Lincoln Beachey made two flights and "looped-the loop" on his Gnome-powered Curtiss-pusher biplane at the Canadian Industrial Exhibition, Winnipeg, Manitoba. He made two flights each day on 13, 14, 15, 16 and 17 July.

Ref: Manitoba Free Press, Winnipeg, Man., 11-18 July, 1914.

**13 JULY, 1914.** Passenger Doctor Atkinson of Selkirk, Manitoba, was injured when the Curtiss hydro-aeroplane operated by Clair G. Horton crashed into Lake Winnipeg off Winnipeg Beach, Manitoba.

Ref: Manitoba Free Press, Winnipeg, Man., 14 July, 1914.

**14 JULY, 1914.** Weldon B. Cook of Oakland, California, made two flights on a Curtiss-type hydro-aeroplane from Kootenay Lake at Nelson, British Columbia. Further flights were made on 15 and 18 July.

Ref: Ellis, Frank H., Canada's Flying Heritage, Univ. of Toronto Press, 1954.

**28 JULY, 1914.** R.B. Russell of Toronto, Ontario, made a forced landing on Lake Ontario en route from Toronto to St. Catharines in a Curtiss flying boat.

Ref: The Standard, St. Catharines, Ont., 29 July, 1914.

Jean-Marie Landry of Quebec City was licensed in France in May 1914 and was the only Canadian pioneer pilot to be licensed there. He imported a Bleriot XI monoplane to Canada in August.
(J.M. Landry photo)

The Burgess Dunne seaplane of the Canadian Aviation Corps alongside the S.S. Athenia prior to being shipped overseas.
(J.O. Leach photo)

**4 AUGUST, 1914.** Great Britain declared war on Germany. This declaration also committed Canada which was considered a "self-governing colony" at that time.

**13 AUGUST, 1914.** A Bleriot XI monoplane, bought in France, was unloaded from S.S. Reapwell at Quebec City, Quebec, for Jean-Marie Landry of that city.

Ref: The Montreal Daily Star, Montreal, Que., 14 August, 1914.

**13 AUGUST, 1914.** Weldon B. Cook flew his Curtiss-type hydro-aeroplane from Lake Okanagan at the Kelowna, British Columbia, Regatta.

Ref: Ellis, Frank H., Canada's Flying Heritage, Univ. of Toronto Press, 1954.

**31 AUGUST, 1914.** Frank H. Burnside and Charles Fay, Jr., of the Thomas exhibition flying team from Bath, New York, made aero-plane flights at the Quebec City, Quebec, Provincial Exhibition. Using the pseudonyms "Eli" and "Blanonac", they made several flights in their Thomas biplanes during the run of the fair.

Ref: L'Evénement, Quebec, Que., 1-3 September, 1914.
The Quebec Chronicle, Quebec, Que., 1-5 September, 1914.

**7 SEPTEMBER, 1914.** H.W. Blakely made the first of several flights on a Baldwin biplane during an engagement at the Great Eastern Exhibition at Sherbrooke, Quebec.

Ref: Sherbrooke DAily Record, Sherbrooke, Que., 8-10 September, 1914

**16 SEPTEMBER, 1914.** *The first Canadian military air service,* the Canadian Aviation Corps, was authorized to be formed by Colonel Sam Hughes, Minister of Militia and Defence.

Ref: Hitchins, W/C F.H. Canadian Aviation Corps.
The Roundel, Vol. 11, No. 8, October, 1959.

**16 SEPTEMBER, 1914.** William Yates Fray, of Saskatoon, Saskatchewan, received Aero Club of America Certificate No. 306 after passing his tests on 12 July, 1912, at Martin School of Aviation, Los Angeles, California, on a Martin tractor biplane with a 75 hp Curtiss engine.

**21 SEPTEMBER, 1914.** The Burgess-Dunne aircraft bought for the Canadian Aviation Corps left Lake Champlain for Quebec City, Quebec, piloted by Clifford Lawrence Webster and with Capt Ernest Lloyd Janney of the CAC as passenger. It arrived at Quebec, Que., on 29 September after delays and was shipped overseas on the 30th on board the S.S. Athenia.

Ref: Hitchins, W/C F.H. Canadian Aviation Corps.
The Roundel, Vol. 11, No. 8, October, 1959.
Farr, Lieut. (Harry A.) Canada's Air Force and the World War. Canadian Air Review, July, 1928.

Curtiss JN-3 aircraft being assembled in Toronto during the summer of 1915. (Curitss A. & M.)

Members of the first class of the Curtiss Aviation School, Toronto, shown here, were the first pilots to be licensed in Canada; Ince and Smith were the first to try their tests. (L-R) standing, D. Hay, E. Maclachlan, H. Smith, J. Day (mechanic), C. MacLaurin, I. Van Nostrand, D.G. Joy; seated, G. Gooderham, A.S. Ince, V. Carlstrom (instructor), C. Geale, W. Peberdy. (C. Geale photo)

# 1915

**4 FEBRUARY, 1915.** *First Canadian air casualty in World War I.* Lt William F.N. Sharpe was killed in a training accident in England.

**7 FEBRUARY, 1915.** British War Office asked Canadian Government to enlist candidates in Canada for the RFC.

**9 MARCH, 1915.** Flight Sub-Lt Redford Henry Mulock passed his test for Royal Aero Club Certificate No. 1103 at Eastchurch, England, on a Short biplane. Mulock was the first Canadian in the British air services to qualify for a pilot's license during World War I.

**APRIL, 1915.** British Admiralty arranged with Department of Naval Service, Ottawa, to enroll applicants for RNAS who were required to have a pilot's certificate, secured at their own expense.

**10 MAY, 1915.** Curtiss Aviation School commenced operation from Toronto Island using Curtiss F flying boats. It closed down for the winter on 7 December.

**11 JULY, 1915.** *First pilots were licensed in Canada.* A. Strachan Ince and F. Homer Smith passed their tests at Curtiss Aviation School, Toronto, Ontario, and were granted certificates No. 1519 and 1520 by Royal Aero Club of the United Kingdom.

**11 JULY, 1915.** *The first Canadian to be decorated for service in the air was Flight Sub-Lt H.J. Arnold.* He ranged the guns of two British monitors which sank the German raider S.M.S. Konigsberg while acting as an observer on a Henry Farman which was shot down. He was awarded the D.S.O.

**SUMMER, 1915.** *First series production of aircraft in Canada.* The Curtiss JN-3 is placed in production at Curtiss Aeroplanes & Motors Ltd., Toronto, Ontario. A total of 18 was produced.

**14 JULY, 1915.** *The prototype of the first aircraft type to go into series production in Canada,* the Curtiss JN-3, was test flown at Long Branch, near Toronto, Ontario, by Antony H. Jannus.

Ref: Toronto Telegram, 15 July, 1915.

**28 JULY, 1915.** The inaugural banquet of the Aero Club of Canada was held at the Walker House, Toronto, Ontario. Officers were - Honourary President, Sir John Eaton; President, B.S. Wemp; Vice-President, A.T.N. Cowley; Secretary, Snyder; Overseas Secretary, G. Williams. Among others present were - J.G. Gilpatric, V. Vernon, V. Carlstrom, T.C. Macaulay, A.H. Jannus, J.A.D. McCurdy, E.R. Grange, R.A. Logan, R.G. Delamere.

The Curtiss K, "Klava' in which T.C. Macauley competed for the Curtiss Marine Trophy at Toronto. Macauley is standing at the left. (Flying)

The Curtiss Canada prototype being readied for testing on 3 September 1915. The man in the straw hat is Chief Engineer F.G. Ericson. Note the balanced rudder fitted during the early tests. (Curtiss Museum)

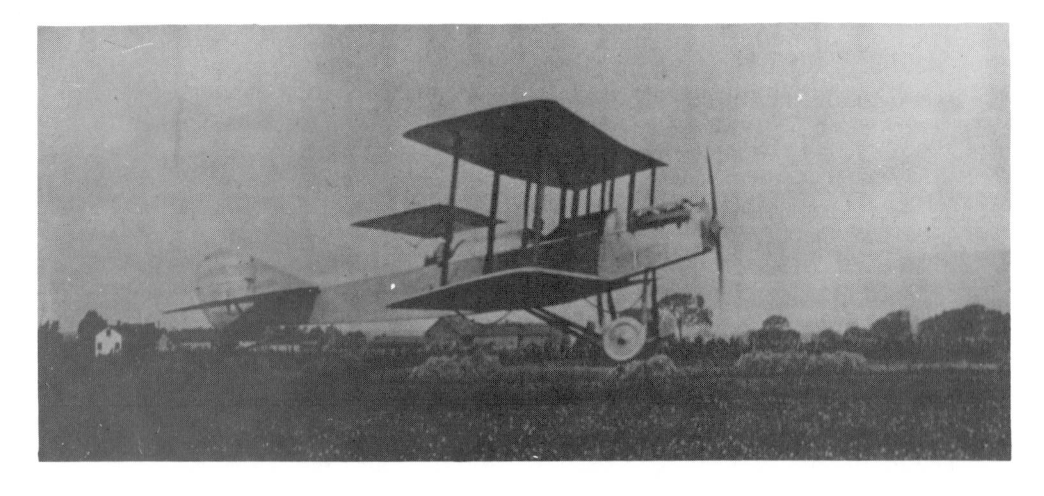

Victor Carlstrom taking off in his Curtiss R-2 during his Toronto-New York flight. (Jones/NASM)

**AUGUST, 1915.** Seal spotting from the air proposed for Newfoundland.

Ref: Aerial Age, 30 August, 1915.

**3 SEPTEMBER, 1915.** *The first twin-engined aircraft in Canada.* The Curtiss Canada prototype was tested at Long Branch, near Toronto, Ontario, by Antony H. Jannus. It was the first twin-engined aircraft to be designed and/or built and/or flown in Canada.

Ref: New York Times, 6 September, 1915.

**23 SEPTEMBER, 1915.** T.C. Macauley started competing for the Curtiss Marine Trophy by flying round trips between Toronto and Hamilton, Ontario, in the Curtiss K flying boat "Klava". He flew again for the Trophy on 17 October and altogether covered approximately 703 miles. The first five round trips were with passengers.

Ref: Flying, New York, Vol. IV, No. 11, December, 1915, p. 770.

**15 NOVEMBER, 1915.** Victor Carlstrom left Toronto, Ontario, in a Curtiss R-2 biplane and flew around the west end of Lake Ontario before heading directly for New York City, New York. He spent the night at Binghamton, N.Y., and went on the next day and that evening landed at Ridgefield, New Jersey, six miles from Manhattan. Total flying time was 6 hr. 40 min.

Ref: Aeronautics, 22 December, 1915, p. 411.

**14 DECEMBER, 1915.** *The first Canadian to be credited with bringing down an enemy aircraft* was Flight Sub-Lt Arthur Strachan Ince, RNAS. While flying as an observer for Flight Sub-Lt C.W. Graham in a Nieuport 10 off the Belgian coast, he shot down a German seaplane and was awarded the D.S.C. for his action.

Ref: Creagen, H.E., The First Canadian Aerial Victory, The Early Bird Enthusiast (later CAHS Journal), Vol. I, No. 1, January, 1963.

**Flt. Sub-Lieut. A.S. Ince at Chingford, September 1915 who became the first Canadian credited with the shooting down of an enemy aircraft.**

**(C. Geale photo)**

The M.F.P. (Polson) B-2 on the ice of Toronto Bay 29 March 1916.
(Polson Iron Works)

Miss Katherine Stinson and her Partridge-Keller "Looper" at Brandon, Manitoba, 22 July, 1916. Miss Stinson is standing directly in front of the propeller hub. (via J.W. Underwood)

Flt. Sub-Lieut. E.R. Grange, the first Canadian "ace".
(E.R. Grange photo)

# 1916

**29 MARCH, 1916.** M.F.P. (Polson) B-2 all-metal biplane prototype was test flown from the ice on Toronto Bay, Toronto, Ontario, by John Guy Gilpatric.

**15 MAY, 1916.** Curtiss Aviation School resumed its training program at Long Branch Aerodrome, Toronto, Ontario.

**30 JUNE - 3 JULY, 1916.** Miss Katherine Stinson flew at Calgary, Alberta.

Ref: Ellis, F.H. Canada's Flying Heritage, Univ. of Toronto Press, 1954.

**22 JULY, 1916.** Miss Katherine Stinson flew at Brandon, Manitoba.

**4-5 AUGUST, 1916.** Miss Katherine Stinson flew at Winnipeg, Manitoba, making a night flight.

Ref: Ellis, F.H. Canada's Flying Heritage, Univ. of Toronto Press, 1954.

**28 OCTOBER, 1916.** While trying to attack two Canadians, Lt A.G. Knight and 2/Lt A.E. McKay of 24 Squad. flying de Havilland D.H.2 single-seaters, Hauptmann O. Boelcke, the leading German fighter pilot of the time, was killed when he collided with another German aircraft.

**12 DECEMBER, 1916.** A plan to increase the strength of the RFC was approved, which included creating 20 training squadrons in Canada.

**15 DECEMBER, 1916.** Canadian Aeroplanes Ltd. was incorporated to provide training aircraft for the RFC Canada.

# 1917

**1 JANUARY, 1917.** Prototype Curtiss JN-4(Can.) was completed by Canadian Aeroplanes Ltd., Toronto, Ontario. It was tested shortly afterwards at Long Branch Aerodrome, near Toronto, Ontario, by Bertrand B. Acosta.

**4 JANUARY, 1917.** *The first Canadian 'ace',* F/S/L E.R. Grange, No. 8 (Naval) Squadron, was credited with his fifth enemy aircraft while flying a Sopwith Pup.

Ref: Creagen, Harry E. Canadian Naval Aces of WW1. CAHS Journal, Vol. 2, No. 3.

**22 FEBRUARY, 1917.** The prototype Curtiss JN-4 (Can.) was accepted by the RFC Canada at Long Branch Aerodrome, near Toronto, Ontario.

Flying started at Camp Borden on 2 April 1917, and it continued to be Canada's largest military aerodrome until the opening of Trenton Air Station in 1931. This photo was taken in 1918. (RAF Canada)

2nd Lt. L.P. (Don) Watkins who brought down the Zeppelin L.48.

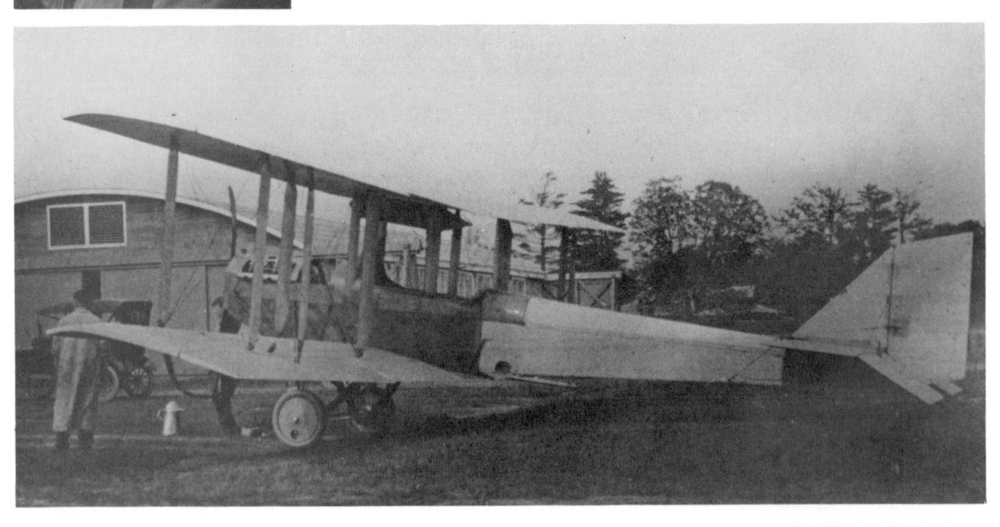

The D.H. 6 (Can.) prototype at Leaside Aerodrome. (Canadian Aeroplanes)

**27 FEBRUARY, 1917.** *The first military flying in* Canada took place when the RFC Canada began training with three Curtiss JN-4(Can.) aircraft at Long Branch Aerodrome near Toronto, Ontario.

**2 APRIL, 1917.** Flying started at Camp Borden, Ontario, with 19 aircraft on hand.

**8 APRIL, 1917.** *First military flying fatality in Canada* occurred at Camp Borden, Ontario, when Cadet J.C. Talbot died following a flying accident.

**2 MAY, 1917.** Camp Borden Aerodrome was formally taken over by RFC Canada - first of the new training fields.

**14 MAY,1917.** Flight Sub-Lt Robert Leckie and crew of Curtiss H. 12 flying boat shot down Zeppelin L. 22.

Ref: Gamble, C.F. Snowden. The Story of a North Sea Naval Air Station. Oxford University Press, 1928.

**29 MAY. 1917.** Flight Commander J. Lindsay Gordon and F/L G. Hodgson in a Curtiss H. 12 flying boat found the crew of a damaged Short seaplane who had been adrift for five days in the North Sea. They landed, rescued the two men and then taxied until picked up by a ship and towed to Great Yarmouth Air Station.

**2 JUNE, 1917.** Captain William Avery Bishop, 60 Squadron, flying a Nieuport 17, made a single-handed attack on a German aerodrome and shot down three enemy aircraft. He was awarded the Victoria Cross for this action.

**14 JUNE, 1917.** Flight Sub-Lt Basil D. Hobbs and crew of Curtiss H. 12 flying boat shot down Zeppelin L. 43.

**17 JUNE, 1917.** 2nd Lt. L.P. Watkins attacked Zeppelin L. 48 while flying a B.E.12, 6610, together with another British aircraft and L. 48 was brought down in flames near Harwich, England. He was awarded the Military Cross for his action.

Ref: Robinson, Douglas. The Zeppelin in Combat. G.T. Foulis & Co., London.

**1 JULY, 1917.** School of Aeronautics, University of Toronto, was formed.

**JULY, 1917.** Canadian prototype of de Havilland, D.H. 6 completed by Canadian Aeroplanes Ltd. and tested by Brig-Gen C.G. Hoare. First British aircraft to be license-built in Canada.

**SUMMER, 1917.** *First performance in Canada by an aerial stuntman.* Lt E.E. Ballough, R.F.C. (Canada), performed 'stunts' on his Curtiss JN-4 (Can.) after leaving the cockpit over the Deseronto, Ontario, area.

**29 AUGUST, 1917.** An agreement was signed between the RFC Canada and the U.S. Signal Corps whereby ten U.S. squadrons were to be trained in Canada that summer and two RFC wings were to be accommodated for training in Texas during the winter.

**29 AUGUST, 1917.** The Canadian Division of the Aerial League of the British Empire was incorporated with headquarters in Montreal, Quebec. It intended to stimulate aviation in all ways and many prominent Canadians were involved.

**22 SEPTEMBER, 1917.** Flight Sub-Lt N.A. Magor and crew of Curtiss H. 12 flying boat bombed and sank German submarine UB 32.

Ref: Layman, R.D. Allied Aircraft vs German Submarines, Cross & Cockade Jour., Vol. 11, No. 4, Winter, 1970.
Price, Alfred, Aircraft versus Submarines, Wm. Kimber & Co., London, 1973.

**28 SEPTEMBER, 1917.** Flight Sub-Lt Basil D. Hobbs and crew of Curtiss H. 12 made two attacks on surfaced submarine which was believed to have sunk. May have been UC-6.

Ref: Layman, R.D. Allied Aircraft vs German Submarines, 1916 - 1918. Cross & Cockade Jour., Vol. 11, No.4, Winter, 1970.

**17 NOVEMBER, 1917.** Nos. 42 and 43 Wings, RFC Canada, arrived in Texas for winter training.

**30 NOVEMBER, 1917.** Capt Andrew Edward McKeever and observer, 2/Lt L.A. Powell, 111 Squadron, shot down four enemy aircraft in their Bristol F.2B Fighter, two each.

**WINTER 1917-18.** *First ski flying in Canada.* Successful ski flying experiments were carried out by 44 Wing, RFC Canada. Skis were designed by Canadian Aeroplanes Ltd.

**Early ski experiments at Leaside.**
**(K.M. Molson Coll.)**

# 1918

**27 MARCH, 1918.** 2/Lt Alan A. McLeod, pilot, and Lt A.W. Hammond, observer, 2 Squadron flying an Armstrong-Whitworth FK. 8 were attacked by several German aircraft and their machine set on fire. McLeod climbed out on a wing and guided the aircraft to a crash landing in 'no man's land'. Both men had been wounded several times and Hammond had continued to shoot at the attackers during the descent. McLeod then dragged Hammond to the British trenches. McLeod was awarded a Victoria Cross for this action.

**30 MARCH, 1918.** First flying begun at the School of Aerial Fighting, Beamsville, Ontario.

Ref: Halliday, Hugh. The Beamsville Story. CAHS Journal, Vol. 7, No. 3, Fall, 1969.

**MARCH, 1918.** *First Canadian aviation serial publication appeared.* Aviation News was published in Toronto, Ontario, by A.F. Penton & Co. It became Aviation & Wireless News at Vol. IV, No. 3 and became Radio at Vol. 5, No. 3.

**1 APRIL, 1918.** RFC Canada became RAF Canada.

**21 APRIL, 1918.** Captain Arthur Roy Brown, 209 Squadron, was credited with shooting down Rittmeister M. Frhr. von Richthofen, the leading German fighter pilot.

**29 MAY, 1918.** Secretary of State for RAF agreed to the formation of a nucleus of Canadian squadrons within the RAF.

**5 JUNE, 1918.** Canadian Government agreed to establish air stations at Sydney and Halifax, Nova Scotia for anti-submarine operations at the suggestion of the British Admiralty.

**19 JUNE, 1918.** Major W.A. Bishop, O/C 85 Squadron, was credited with five enemy aircraft destroyed on that date.

**24 JUNE, 1918.** *First Canadian air mail.* Capt Brian Peck and Corporal E.W. Mathers flew from Montreal, Quebec, to Toronto, Ontario, in Curtiss JN-4 (Can.), C-203, carrying a small bag of mail.

**6 JULY, 1918.** Ruth Law, flying her Curtiss Pusher, gave exhibition flights at Lansdowne Park, Ottawa, Ontario, and raced Gaston Chevrolet in a car.

Ref: Ottawa Free Press, Ottawa, Ont., 8 July, 1918, p.8.

**9 JULY, 1918.** Miss Katherine Stinson flew mail from Calgary to Edmonton, Alberta, in her Curtiss Stinson Special biplane, flying time 2 hrs 5 min, elapsed time 7 hours.

Ref: Edmonton News Bulletin, Edmonton, Alta., 10 July, 1918.

The crew of the U.S. Naval Aircraft Factory prototype Felixstowe F-5L prior to its test flight 15 July 1918. (L-R) Major Wadsworth, U.S. Army; Lt. Col. J.C. Porte, RAF; Capt. F.S. McGill RAF.
(U.S. N.A.F./NASM)

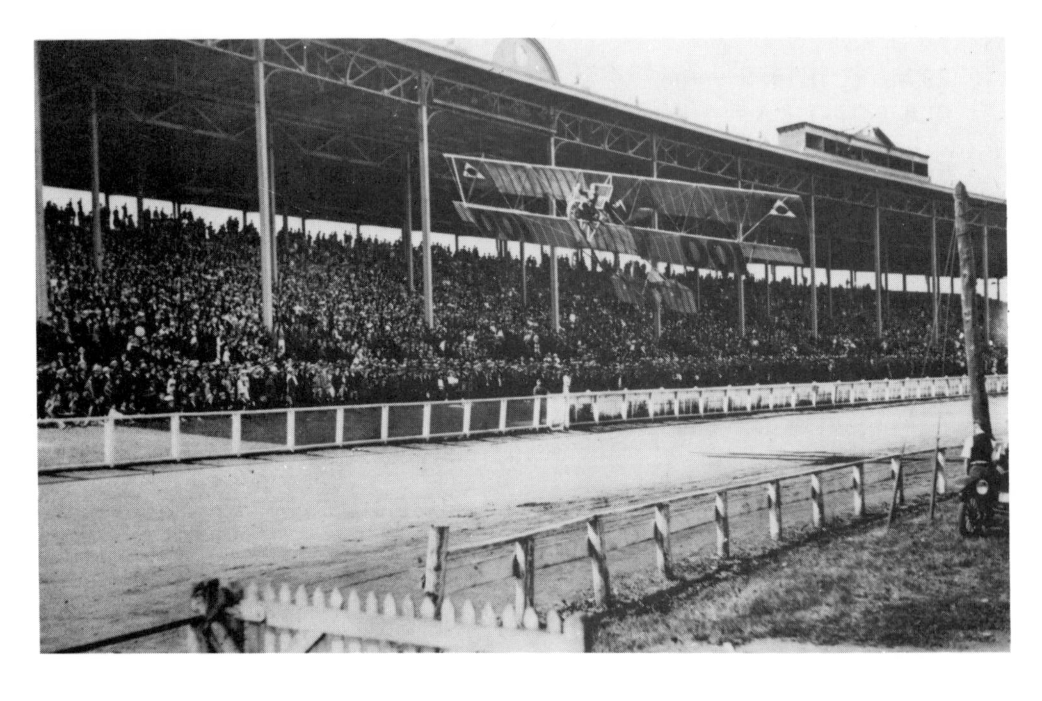

Ruth Law flying her Curtiss biplane at the Exhibition grounds. Toronto in 1918. (Mus. Sc. & Tech.)

**9-13 JULY, 1918.** Miss Katherine Stinson flew at Edmonton, Alberta.

Ref: Ellis, F.H. Canada's Flying Heritage, Univer. of Toronto Press, 1954.

**15 JULY, 1918.** Flight-Com. Frank S. McGill tested American prototype of Felixstowe F. 5L flying boat at Naval Aircraft Factory, Philadelphia, Penna.

**29 JULY, 1918.** Ruth Law gave exhibition flights at Toronto. Raced and was beaten by Gaston Chevrolet in a car.

Ref: Ottawa Free Press, Ottawa, Ont., 1 July, 1918, p.9.

**AUGUST, 1918.** The Canadian prototype of the Felixstowe F. 5L flying boat built by Canadian Aeroplanes Ltd., Toronto, Ontario, was delivered to the U.S. Naval Aircraft Factory, Philadelphia, Penna.

**5 AUGUST, 1918.** Capt Robert Leckie flying as observer with Major Egbert Cadbury in a de Havilland D.H. 4 shot down Zeppelin L. 70.

**15 AUGUST, 1918.** An airmail service by the RAF Canada completed four round trips from Toronto to Ottawa, Ontario, between 15 August and 4 September using Curtiss JN-4 (Can.) aircraft. Pilots were Lts T. Longman, E.C. Burton and A. Dunstan.

**19 AUGUST, 1918.** U.S. Naval Air Station Halifax, Nova Scotia, commissioned with Lt Richard E. Byrd commanding.

**22 AUGUST, 1918.** A Canadian Air Force detachment was formed at Halton, England, to train Canadian mechanics for two proposed Canadian squadrons.

**29 AUGUST, 1918.** Colonel Redford H. Mulock was appointed to command No. 27 Group of the Independent Force which was being equipped with Handley Page V/1500 aircraft to bomb Berlin, Germany. Col. Mulock was highest ranking Canadian in the RAF.

**31 AUGUST, 1918.** U.S. Naval Air Station North Sydney, Cape Breton Island, Nova Scotia, was commissioned with Lieut Robert Donahue commanding.

**5 SEPTEMBER, 1918.** Establishment of the Royal Canadian Naval Air Service was authorized to operate two air stations in Nova Scotia. The United States Navy was to operate the stations until the RCNAS was able to take over.

**13 SEPTEMBER, 1918.** Miss Katherine Stinson flew at Peterborough, Ontario, during the Peterborough Industrial Exhibition.

Ref: Ellis, John R. Katherine Stinson in Ontario 1918.
CAHS Journal, Vol. 9, No. 1, Spring, 1971.

The Avro 504 (Can.) prototype at Beamsville, Ontario, in October 1918. (RAF Canada)

The first Canadian-built Sunbeam Arab engine surrounded by unidentified personnel of Willys-Overland of Canada. (Willys-Overland of Canada)

**21 SEPTEMBER, 1918.** 20 flight cadets of the Royal Canadian Naval Air Service arrived at the Massachusetts Institute of Technology for training.

**OCTOBER, 1918.** The prototype of the Avro 504 (Can.), built by Canadian Aeroplanes Ltd., Toronto, Ontario, was test flown. It was intended to replace the Curtiss JN-4 (Can.) in the RAF Canada's training program.

Ref: Riddell, M.R., The Development and Future of Aviation in Canada. Journal of the Engineering Institute of Canada, March, 1919.

**27 OCTOBER, 1918.** Major William George Barker, 201 Squadron, in a Sopwith Snipe fought single-handed about 60 German aircraft. He destroyed three aircraft and was severely wounded during the engagement. He was awarded the Victoria Cross for this action which is believed to have been the greatest single combat of the war.

**11 NOVEMBER, 1918.** The Armistice was signed, ending World War I.

**20 NOVEMBER, 1918.** *First Canadian squadrons formed.* No. 1 and 2 Squadrons, Canadian Air Force were formed at Upper Heyford, England, from RAF Squadrons 81 and 123 with all-Canadian personnel.

**5 DECEMBER, 1918.** Royal Canadian Naval Air Service was demobilized.

**31 DECEMBER, 1918.** The five top scoring Canadian fighter pilots of World War I were:

| | |
|---|---|
| Lt-Col W.A. Bishop, V.C., D.S.O. & Bar, M.C., D.F.C., L. de H., C. de G. | 72 |
| Lt-Col R. Collishaw, D.S.O. & Bar, D.S.C., D.F.C., C. de G. | 60 |
| Maj D.R. MacLaren, D.S.O., M.C. & Bar, D.F.C., L. de H., C. de G. | 54 |
| Maj W.G. Barker, V.C., D.S.O., M.C. & 2 Bars, C.C., L. de H., V.M. | 53 |
| Capt W.G. Claxton, D.S.O., D.F.C. & Bar | 39 |

**1918.** *The first aviation engine was put in production in Canada.* The Sunbeam Arab was produced for the RAF by Willys-Overland of Canada Ltd. at Toronto, Ontario.

**The proposed RCNAS Officers Cap Badge 1918 as shown in "The History of Canadian Naval Aviation" by J.D.F. Kealy and E.C. Russell, 1965.**

The Sopwith Atlantic which made the first flight in Newfoundland and the first attempt at a direct trans Atlantic flight by heavier-than-air machine.
(E.W. Stedman photo)

# 1919

**28 FEBRUARY, 1919.** *First international air passenger by heavier-than-air machine arrived in Canada.* W.E. Boeing was flown to Vancouver, British Columbia, from Seattle, Washington, in a Boeing C-700 seaplane by Edward Hubbard.

**MARCH, 1919.** The installation of a wind tunnel was completed at the University of Toronto.

**3 MARCH, 1919.** *First international air mail from Canada* was flown from Vancouver, British Columbia, to Seattle, Washington, in a Boeing C-700 seaplane by E. Hubbard.

Ref: Ellis, F.H. Canada's Flying Heritage, Univer. of Toronto Press, 1954.

**25 MARCH, 1919.** No. 1 Canadian Wing, CAF, was formed in England to administer No. 1 & 2 Squadrons, CAF. Lt-Col R. Leckie was appointed its Commanding Officer.

**10 APRIL, 1919.** *The first flight in Newfoundland* was made by Harry George Hawker accompanied by Kenneth Mackenzie-Grieve in the Sopwith Atlantic biplane on the occasion of its first Newfoundland test flight. The take-off was made at Mount Pearl and a flight was made over St. John's to Quidi Vidi before returning to the aerodrome about half an hour later.

Ref: The Evening Telegram, St. John's, Nfld., 11 April, 1919.
The Daily News, St. John's, Nfld., 11 April, 1919.

**5-6 MAY, 1919.** *First commercial flight Canada-U.S.A.* Ervin E. Ballough bought a Curtiss JN-4 (Can.) in Toronto, Ontario for L. Bamberger & Co. and flew 150 lbs of raw furs to Elizabeth, New Jersey, via Thousand Islands and Watertown, New York.

Ref: Newark (N.J.) Evening News, 6 May, 1919.
Newark (N.J.) Evening News, 15 May, 1919.
Newark (N.J.) Evening News, 29 May, 1919.

**8 MAY, 1919.** USN flying boats NC-1 and NC-3, commanded by Lt-Com P.N.L. Bellinger and Com H.C. Richardson arrived at Halifax. They left for Trepassey Bay, Newfoundland, on 10th May.

**13 MAY, 1919.** Captains A. Eckly and E. Hall flew from Vancouver, British Columbia, to Victoria and returned in a Curtiss JN-4 (Can.).

**14 MAY, 1919.** USN flying boat NC-4, commanded by Lt-Com A.C. Read, arrived at Halifax, Nova Scotia, after being forced down and having to taxi to Chatham, Massachusetts. It left on 15th for Trepassey Bay, Newfoundland.

**The USN dirigible C-5 at Pleasantville, on the outskirts of St. John's, Newfoundland, 15 May 1919.**
**(via K.M. Molson)**

**A Curtiss JN-4 (Can.) of International Aerial Transport, one of the earliest Canadian air transport companies, at Armour Heights Aerodrome in 1919. (R.S. Baker photo)**

**15 MAY, 1919.** USN non-rigid airship C-5, Lt-Com Emory W. Coil commanding, arrived at St. John's, Newfoundland, after a 1,050 nautical mile flight from Montauk Point, Long Island, New York, lasting 25 hours 50 minutes. An intended trans-Atlantic flight was prevented when a storm blew the C-5 out to sea soon after its arrival.

Ref: New York Times, New York, N.Y., 9 June, 1919, p. 15.

**16 MAY, 1919.** *First trans-Atlantic flight* began when NC-1, NC-2 and NC-4 left Trepassey Bay, Newfoundland, for the Azores. NC-4 reached Horta, Azores, on 17 May and continued on to reach Plymouth, England, on 31 May to complete the flight. Both NC-1 and NC-3 were forced down on 17 May. NC-3 taxied to the Azores under her own power and the crew of NC-1 was saved.

Ref: Smith, Richard, K., First Across,Naval Institute Press, Annapolis, Md.

**16 MAY, 1919.** May Airplanes Ltd. was incorporated at Edmonton, Alberta. Court May, Managing Director; F.G. McDermid, Vice-President; Chas. Hepburn, Director.

Ref: Edmonton Daily Bulletin, Edmonton, Alta., 17 May, 1919.
Myles, Eugenie Louise. Airborne from Edmonton. The Ryerson Press, Toronto, 1959.

**18 MAY, 1919.** H.G. Hawker and K. Mackenzie-Grieve left St. John's, Newfoundland, in the Sopwith Atlantic on first direct Atlantic flight attempt. They were forced down in the ocean and were rescued.

Ref: Hawker, H.G. & Grieve, K. Mackenzie, Our Atlantic Attempt, Methuen & Co., London.

**18 MAY, 1919.** Major F.P. Raynham and Major C.W.F. Morgan crashed on take-off at Pleasantville, Newfoundland, in the Martinsyde "Raymor" on a intended direct trans-Atlantic flight.

Ref: Dalwick, R.E.R. & Harmer, C.H.C., Newfoundland Air Mails, Harmer Ltd., London, 1953.

**20 MAY, 1919.** War trophies were shipped to Canada as arranged by Lt-Col Arthur Doughty, C.M.G. (later Sir Arthur), Dominion Archivist. These included German aircraft which arrived at Toronto, Ontario, in June and were taken to Leaside Aerodrome.

Ref: Mail & Empire, Toronto, Ont., 21 May, 1919.
Mail & Empire, Toronto, Ont., 21 June, 1919.

**24 MAY, 1919.** International Aerial Transport Ltd. commenced flying operations at Leaside Aerodrome, Toronto, Ontario. They had purchased six Curtiss JN-4 (Can.) aircraft.

Ref: Toronto Star, Toronto, Ont., May 24, 1919.

The operations of the St. Maurice Forestry Protective Association began with the launching of this Curtiss HS-2L from U.S.N. Air Station at Halifax, seen here, and flying it to their Lac à La Tortue base.

(W. Kahre photo)

A crowd of Newfoundlanders gather round Alcock and Brown's Vickers Vimy at St. John's prior to the trans Atlantic flight, June 1919.

(via Museum of Sc. & Tech.)

**28 MAY, 1919.** Capt. Mansell Richard James, D.F.C., (ex 45 Squad., 9 e,a.) of Watford, Ontario, won the first Pulitzer prize by flying a Sopwith Camel from Atlantic City, New Jersey, to Boston, Massachusetts, in the best time for a long distance flight. He was lost the next day flying from Tyringham, Massachusetts, to Atlantic City and no trace of him or his aircraft has been found.

Ref: Foxworth, Thomas G. The Speed Seekers. Macdonald & Jane's Ltd., London, 1975.
AAHS Jour., Vol. 13, No. 4.
Jenkins, Harry J. Capt. Mansell James' Disappearance.
AAHS Jour., Vol. 19, No. 1

**31 MAY, 1919.** *First civil demonstration in Canada by an aerial stuntman.* J. Fieldhouse performed on a Curtiss JN-4 (Can.) flown by E.C. Hoy at Vancouver, British Columbia.

Ref: Aircraft, Vol. 1, No. 2, June, 1919.

**4 JUNE, 1919.** Britain offered Canada a gift of military aircraft. Aircraft received by Canada were: 62 Avro 504K; 12 de Havilland D.H.4; 12 de Havilland D.H. 9A; 12 S.E. 5A; 11 Felixstowe F. 3; 2 Curtiss H-16; 1 Bristol F. 2B; 1 Sopwith 7F.1 Snipe and 1 Fairey IIIC (mod.) Transatlantic.

**5-8 JUNE, 1919.** A Curtiss HS-2L was ferried from Halifax, Nova Scotia, to Lac à la Tortue near Grand Mère, Quebec, by Stuart Graham and crew for St. Maurice Forest Protective Association. Longest Canadian cross-country flight.

Ref: Molson, K.M. A History of Laurentide Air Service - Canada's First Scheduled Air Service. Can. Aero. & Space Jour., Vol. 16, No. 7, September, 1970.

**6 JUNE, 1919.** The Canadian Government passed the Air Board Act to control all flying in Canada.

Ref: Ellis, J.R., Background to the Canadian Aircraft Register. CAHS Jour., Vol. 10, No. 1, Spring, 1972.

**14-15 JUNE, 1919.** *First direct transAtlantic flight* was made by John Alcock and Arthur Whitten Brown who left St. John's, Newfoundland, in twin-engined Vickers Vimy and landed in a bog at Clifden, Ireland.

Ref: Alcock, Sir John and Brown, Sir Arthur Whitten, Our Transatlantic Flight. Wm. Kimber Co., London, 1966.

**25 JUNE, 1919.** First meeting of the Canadian Air Board was held.

Ref: Ellis, J.R. Background to the Canadian Aircraft Register. CAHS Jour., Vol. 10, No. 1, Spring, 1972.

**JULY, 1919.** The Canadian Pacific Railway amended its charter to permit it to carry passengers, mail and express by air within and beyond the Canadian borders.

The prototype Hoffar float installation on a Curtiss JN-4 (Can.)
(Mus. Sc. & Tech.)

The Handley Page V/1500 Atlantic after its forced landing at Parrsboro, N.S., 4 July 1919.
(E.W. Stedman photo)

The 'Raymor' after its take-off attempt at Quidi Vidi.
(Mus. Sc. & Tech.)

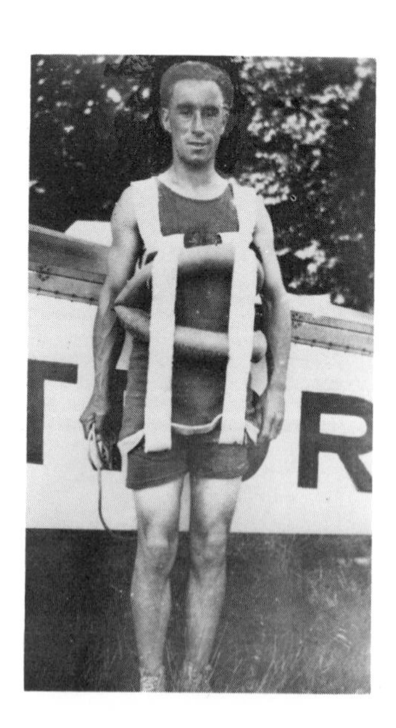

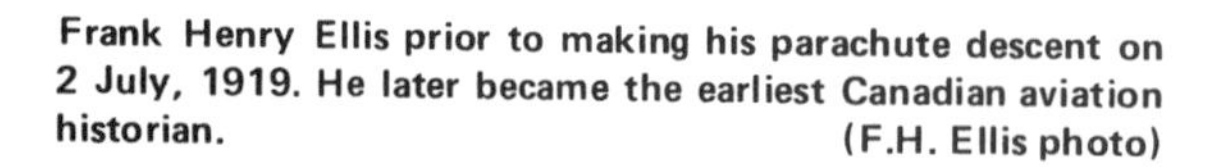

Frank Henry Ellis prior to making his parachute descent on 2 July, 1919. He later became the earliest Canadian aviation historian.
(F.H. Ellis photo)

**JULY, 1919.** Prototype float installation for Curtiss JN-4 (Can.) was built by Hoffar Bros., Vancouver, British Columbia, and tested by a "Capt. Rodgers of the Aerial League of Canada" - possibly Capt B. D. Rodgers.

Ref: --- A "New Experiment". Aircraft, Vol. 1, No. 4, August, 1919.

**4 JULY, 1919.** A Mr. Chilson tested a new parachute developed by Leslie Irvine by jumping from a Curtiss JN-4 (Can.) of Allied Aeroplanes Ltd. flown by D. Russell at Crystal Beach, Ontario.

Ref: Ellis, F.H., Canada's Flying Heritage. University of Toronto Press, 1954.

**4 JULY, 1919.** Handley Page V/1500 Atlantic, with Admiral Sir Mark Kerr and crew, left Harbour Grace, Newfoundland, for Mitchell Field, Long Island, New York. It was forced to land at Parrsboro, Nova Scotia.

Ref: Dalwick, R.E.R. & Harmer, C.H.C., Newfound Air Mails, Harmer Ltd., London, 1953.

**5 JULY, 1919.** *First parachute jump from an aeroplane by a Canadian in Canada* was made by F.H. Ellis from a Curtiss JN-4 (Can.) at Crystal Beach, Ontario.

Ref: Ellis, F.H., Canada's Flying Heritage. University of Toronto Press, 1954.

**7 JULY, 1919.** *First forest fire was spotted from the air in Canada* by S. Graham and W. Kahre.

Ref: Molson, K.M. A History of Laurentide Air Service - Canada's First Scheduled Air Service. Can. Aero. & Space Jour. Vol. 16, No. 7, September, 1970.

**12 JULY, 1919.** First permit for flight across the Canadian border was granted to Lt. O.S. Parmer and Ensign G.B. Garman, Americans. Aircraft landed at Blue Bonnets Race Track, Montreal, Quebec.

Ref: Ottawa Citizen, Ottawa, Ontario, 14 July, 1919.

**17 JULY, 1919.** Major F.P. Raynham and Lt C.H. Biddlescombe crashed on take-off at Quidi Vidi, Newfoundland, in the Martinsyde 'Raymor" on its second transAtlantic flight attempt.

Ref: Dalwick, R.E.R. & Harmer, C.H.C., Newfoundland Air Mails, Harmer Ltd., London, 1953.

**AUGUST, 1919.** *First aerial survey in what is now Canada* was a timber survey carried out in Labrador by the Owens Expedition. It was carried out by radio-equipped Curtiss JN-4 (Can.), which constituted the first use of radio in civil aircraft in what is now Canada. These flights were the first in Labrador.

Ref: Molson, K.M., Canada's First Air Survey, Aircraft, Vol. 21, No. 11, November, 1959.

The Junkers J-1 on display at the Canadian National Exhibition in August 1919. This aircraft is now in the National Aeronautical Collection at Ottawa.
(James Coll. Toronto City Archives)

The two leading Canadian entrants in the N.Y.-Toronto race were these Curtiss JN-4 (Can.)s. The near aircraft No. 62, was flown by C.A. (Duke) Schiller and the far one, No. 64, by S.S. (Dinty) Moore.
(C.A. Schiller photo)

The D.H. 4,King Alburt,which was flown from Toronto to New York non-stop by Major J.W. Simmons on 29 August 1919.
(W.C. Landrigan photo)

**5 AUGUST, 1919.** Clarence Alvin (Duke) Schiller, pilot, with Miss Lydia Collins and Frithiof Gustave Ericson as passengers set what was stated to be a new Canadian altitude record of 8,000 feet for three people. The flight was made in a modified Curtiss JN-4 (Can.) from Leaside Aerodrome, Toronto, Ontario.

Ref: Aviation News, Vol. 2, No. 8, October, 1919.

**7 AUGUST, 1919.** *The first flight over the Canadian Rocky Mountains* was made by Ernest C. Hoy who flew from Vancouver, British Columbia, to Calgary, Alberta, in a Curtiss JN-4 (Can.) via Vernon, Grand Forks, Cranbrook and Lethbridge. He crashed on an attempted return flight via another route at Golden, B.C., on 11 August.

Ref: - - - -, First Successful Trans Rocky Flight Aircraft, Vol. 1, No. 4,

**9 AUGUST, 1919.** *First exhibit of historic aircraft in Canada* was held at the Canadian National Exhibition, Toronto, Ontario. Aircraft on display included Major W.G. Barker's V.C. - winning Sopwith Snipe, 2/Lt. F. Sowery's Zeppelin-destroying B.E. 2C, a Fokker D-VII fighter and a Junkers J 1 ground attack machine.

Ref: Mail & Empire, Toronto, Ont., 9 August, 1919.
Toronto Star, Toronto, Ont., August, 1919

**15 AUGUST, 1919.** A trans-Canada flight was proposed starting from Halifax, Nova Scotia. It was to begin about 20 September in a de Havilland D.H.4 aircraft piloted by Lt D.K. Trim with Lt W.H. Welsh as navigator.

Ref: Ottawa Citizen, Ottawa, Ont., 15 August, 1919, p. 12.

**16 AUGUST, 1919.** Handley Page was to set up a Canadian company at Morrisburg, Ontario. Officers were to include Wm. H. Workman and Mark Kerr of London, England, and R. Chalmers and W.H. McGannon, coal merchants, of Morrisburg. (Not carried out).

Ref: Toronto Star, Toronto, Ont., 16 August, 1919.

**25-29 AUGUST, 1919.** The New York-Toronto Air Race took place.

Ref: Molson, K.M. The New York-Toronto Air Race CAHS Jour. Vol. 9, No. 3, Fall, 1971.

**23 AUGUST - 6 SEPTEMBER, 1919.** A daily exhibition of formation and stunt flying was given at the Canadian National Exhibition, Toronto, Ontario, by a team led by Col. W.G. Barker and composed of Capts James, L.B. Hyde-Pearson and Dallin, flying Fokker D VII fighters. This is believed to be the first public exhibition of formation flying in Canada.

Ref: The Evening Telegram, Toronto, Ontario, 25 August, 1919, p. 17.

**29 AUGUST, 1919.** First non-stop flight Toronto-New York. Major J.W. Simmons, USAS, and passenger flew direct to New York City, New York, from Toronto, Ontario, in 3 hours 44 minutes in D.H.4.

Ref: Mail & Empire, Toronto, Ont., 30 August, 1919, p. 1.

**The Supermarine Sea Lion which Basil Hobbs flew in the 1919 Schneider Trophy Race. (Flight photo)**

**The Curtiss JN-4 (Can.) in which Capt. Stevens and Lt. Barnhill flew mail from Truro, N.S., to Charlottetown, P.E.I. (N.A. Pelletier photo)**

**30 AUGUST, 1919.** W.R. "Wop" May flew Detective J. Campbell from Edmonton to Coalbranch, Alberta, in a Curtiss JN-4 (Can.). Campbell was in pursuit of a murderer. This is the first use of aircraft by a Canadian police department.

Ref: Myles, E.L. Airborne from Edmonton. Ryerson Press, Toronto. 1959

**10 SEPTEMBER, 1919.** Basil D. Hobbs flew a specially modified Supermarine Sea Lion flying boat in the Schneider Trophy contest at Bournemouth, England. He was forced to land by fog.

Ref: Barker, Ralph. The Schneider Trophy Races. Chatto & Windus Ltd., London, 1971.

**29 SEPTEMBER, 1919.** Capt Lawrence Stevens and Lt Logan Barnhill carried mail from Truro, Nova Scotia to Charletown, Prince Edward Island, in a Curtiss JN-4 (Can.).

Ref: Ellis, J.R. A Maritime First. CAHS Journal, Vol. 7, No. 2, Summer, 1969.

**9 OCTOBER, 1919.** The Handley Page V/1500 Atlantic, with Mark Kerr and crew, left Parrsboro, Nova Scotia, for Mitchel Field, Long Island. They landed at Greenport, Long Island, New York.

Ref: Kerr, Mark. Land, Sea, and Air. Longmans, Green & Co., London, 1927.

**OCTOBER, 1919.** First photographic survey operations in Canada carried out by S. Graham and W. Kahre. (Note survey in August in Labrador which was not in Canada in 1919.)

Ref: Molson, K.M. A History of Laurentide Air Service - Canada's First Scheduled Air Service. Can. Aero. & Space Jour., Vol. 16, No. 7, September, 1970.

**31 DECEMBER, 1919.** Legislation covering the operation of aircraft in Canada was passed by Parliament.

Ref: Ellis, J.R. Background to the Canadian Aircraft Register. CAHS Jour., Vol. 10, No. 1, Spring, 1972.

**The Handley Page V/1500 Atlantic over Long Island, N.Y. (E.W. Stedman Coll.)**

The Laurentide Co.'s base at Lac à la Tortue, Quebec, in September 1920. The aircraft are, left to right, a Curtiss Seagull and a Curtiss HS-2L. (S. Graham photo)

This Curtiss JN-4 (Can.) of the Aerial Service Co., Regina, Sask., was the first aircraft to be civilly registered in Canada. (W.L. West photo)

# 1920

**1920.** Laurentide Co. took over air operations of St. Maurice Forest Protective Association.

Ref: Molson, K.M. A History of Laurentide Air Service - Canada's First Scheduled Air Service. Can. Aero. & Space Jour., Vol. 16, No. 7, September, 1970.

**17 JANUARY, 1920.** Air regulations were published in Canada Gazette and became law.

Ref: Ellis, J.R. Background to the Canadian Aircraft Register. CAHS Jour., Vol. 10, No. 1, Soring, 1972.

**24 JANUARY, 1920.** *First Canadian private pilot's license was issued* to James Stanley Scott, Ottawa, Ontario.

**28 JANUARY, 1920.** No. 1 Squadron, CAF, was disbanded in England.

**5 FEBRUARY, 1920.** No. 2 Squadron, CAF, and No. 1 Canadian Wing Headquarters were disbanded in England.

**18 FEBRUARY, 1920.** Formation of a Canadian Air Force was authorized by Order-in-Council as a non-professional, non-permanent force under the Air Board.

**15-16 APRIL, 1920.** First Washington, D.C. - Ottawa, Ontario, flight. Lt-Col H.E. Hartney and Capt H.T. Douglas made the trip in a de Havilland D.H.4 and stopped at Ithaca, New York. They landed at Bowesville aerodrome, Ontario. (later Uplands).

Ref: Ottawa Journal, Ottawa, Ont., 17 April, 1920, p. 1-5.

**19 APRIL, 1920.** Lt-Col H.E. Hartney and Capt H.T. Douglas left Ottawa, Ontario, in a de Havilland D.H.4 on return trip to Washington, D.C. They proceeded via Toronto, Ont., and dropped mail bags at various towns en route.

**19 APRIL, 1920.** New Air Board was constituted by Order-in-Council under Hon Hugh Guthrie, Chairman.

**20 APRIL, 1920.** *The first civil aircraft was registered in Canada.* A Curtiss JN-4 (Can.) was registered G-CAAA in the name of Aerial Service Co., of Regina, Saskatchewan.

Ref: Ellis, John R. The Canadian Civil Register G-CAAA to G-CACH. CAHS Journal, Vol. 10, No. 1, Spring, 1972.

**20 APRIL, 1920.** *First Canadian air engineer's license was issued* to Robert McCombie, Regina, Saskatchewan.

Bishop-Barker Aeroplanes' Sopwith Dove photographed in New York prior to coming to Canada. This was the prototype Dove and the aircraft in which Major W.G. Barker had carried the Prince of Wales as a passenger in England.
(Arens/NASM)

Ormer L. Locklear, the celebrated American aerial stuntman of the early post-WWI period and the first man to change planes in the air. (W.R. May Coll.)

The Martinsyde Type A Mk. I with which Price Bros. & Co. Ltd. started their aerial operations.
(A. Murray photo)

**17 MAY, 1920.** Lt-Col A.K. Tylee, OBE, was appointed Air Officer Commanding, CAF, with rank of Air Commodore, for a period of nine months.

**28 MAY 1920.** Mail was carried on a return flight from Toronto to Hamilton, Ontario, by A.K. Colley in a Curtiss JN-4 (Can.).

**4 JUNE, 1920.** W.G. Barker left New York, New York, for Toronto, Ontario, in a Sopwith Dove (became G-CAAY), the same aircraft in which he flew the Prince of Wales over London, England.

Ref: Mail & Empire, Toronto, Ont., 4 June, 1920, p. 5.

**18 JUNE, 1920.** A de Havilland D.H.4 piloted by Capt H.T. Douglas, USAS, accompanied by Capt J.A. Royer, CAF, landed at Whitehorse, Yukon Territory, to make arrangements for a proposed American round-the-world flight. This was the first aircraft to land at Whitehorse.

**18 JUNE, 1920.** The first aircraft were taken on strength by the Canadian Air Force. They were four Avro 504Ks, registered G-CYAA to G-CYAD.

Ref: Griffin, J.A., Canadian Military Aircraft, Serials & Photographs, 1920-1968. Canadian War Museum, Ottawa, Ont.

**28 JUNE - 1 JULY, 1920.** *The first change of aircraft in flight in Canada* was performed by Ormer L. Locklear, at Calgary, Alberta.

Ref: Calgary Herald, Calgary, Alta., 29 June, 1920, p. 1.
Calgary Herald, Calgary, Alta., 2 July, 1920, p. 1.

**30 JUNE, 1920.** A provisional establishment of 1,340 officers and 3,905 airmen for the CAF was authorized by Order-in-Council.

**JULY, 1920.** Price Bros. & Co. Ltd. started an aviation department and commenced flying operations in the Lake St. John district of Quebec.

**5 JULY, 1920.** Camp Borden, Ontario, was taken over by the CAF from Department of Militia & Defence to serve as a training centre.

**5-8 JULY, 1920.** Ormer L. Locklear changed aircraft in flight along with other aerial stunts at Edmonton, Alberta.

Ref: Ronnie, Art. Locklear: The Man Who Walked on Wings. A.S. Barnes & Co., New York, 1973.
Edmonton Morning Bulletin, Edmonton, Alta., 3 July, 1920.

**6-8 JULY, 1920.** Fokker D VII, 8493/18, was exhibited at University of Alberta, Edmonton, Alberta, a donation of the Canadian Government.

Ref: Edmonton Morning Bulletin, Edmonton, Alta., 2 July, 1920.

Four early licensed pilots taking a refresher course at Camp Borden during the winter of 1920-21, including the holders of licenses Nos. 1 and 2. L-R, E.G. MacPherson, Comm. Lic. 12; R.G. Groome, Comm. Lic. 1; C.R. McNeill, Comm. Lic. 41; H.S. McCelland, Comm. Lic. 2. (E.G. MacPherson photo)

W.R. (Wop) May's Curtiss JN-4 (Can.) at Grande Prairie after his flight of 19 August, 1920. (W.R. May photo)

**11 JULY, 1920.** Capt G.H. Simpson and mechanic Beal walked out to Webbwood, Ontario, near Sudbury, after their aircraft belonging to the Spanish River Pulp & Paper Co. was forced to land on a small lake. They had been missing a week. Aircraft was probably the Aeromarine 40L, G-CABM. First incident of this type in Canada.

Ref: Mail & Empire, Toronto, Ont., 12 July, 1920.

**22 JULY, 1920.** *First Canadian mining claim staked with the use of aircraft* by S. Graham and crew in Curtiss HS-2L.

Ref: Molson, K.M. A History of Laurentide Air Service - Canada's First Scheduled Air Service. Can. Aero. & Space Jour. Vol. 16, No. 7, September, 1970.

**25 JULY, 1920.** The First Alaska Air Expedition of the USAS reached Saskatoon, Saskatchewan, under command of Capt St. Clair Street. It proceeded on to Edmonton, Alberta, on the 27th and to Wrangell, Alaska, which it reached on 13 August, going via Jasper, Alberta, Prince George, and Hazelton, British Columbia.

Ref: Ellis, Frank H. Canada's Flying Heritage, Univer. of Toronto Press, 1954.

**27 JULY, 1920.** First freight by air in Manitoba. Capt M.G. Dover and Lt C.P. Thornton flew 50 lbs. of tobacco from Winnipeg to Dauphin, Man. Afterwards they planned on proceeding to Kamsack and Pelly, Saskatchewan.

Ref: Manitoba Free Press, Winnipeg, Man., 27 July, 1920, p. 1.
Mail & Empire, Toronto, Ont., 28 July, 1920.

**31 JULY, 1920.** *First Canadian commercial pilot's* license was issued to Roland J. Groome, Regina, Saskatchewan.

**SUMMER, 1920.** The Canadian Air Force photographed the City of Ottawa, Ontario, and completed a mosaic map. First aerial photography by the CAF.

**9 AUGUST, 1920.** *First ambulance flight in Canada.* Lt Townley, who had "started some old war wounds" was flown from Camp Borden to Toronto, Ontario, in 45 minutes (pilot D.G. Joy.).

Ref: Mail & Empire, Toronto, Ont., 10 August, 1920.

**17 AUGUST, 1920.** First flight to James Bay. W.R. Maxwell, pilot, and G.A. Doan flew from Remi Lake to Moose Factory, Ontario, in a Curtiss HS-2L.

Ref: Maxwell, W.R., Flying Boat Operations in Northern Ontario: 1920. CAHS Journal, Vol. 11, No. 3, Fall, 1973.

**19 AUGUST, 1920.** W.R. (Wop) May left Edmonton, Alberta, on a trip to Grand Prairie in the Peace River district, via Whitecourt, in a Curtiss JN-4 (Can.).

Ref: Edmonton Morning Bulletin, Edmonton, Alta., 20 August, 1920, p. 1.

Two stages of the first Trans Canada Flight from Halifax, N.S. to Vancouver, B.C. are captured by Canada's leading aviation artist R.W. Bradford. The October 1920 event was sponsored by the Canadian Air Board, flown by Canadian Air Force crews.
Above: The arrival of Col. Robert Leckie and Major Basil Hobbs at Rivière du Loup, P.Q. in darkness and a driving rain, using a Curtiss HS-2L.
Below: The final stage of the flight through the Rockies, flown by Captain G.A. "Tommy" Thompson in a D.H. 9A with Col. Arthur Tylee as passenger. (Nat. Mus. Sc. & Tech.)

**26-28 AUGUST, 1920.** Capt. H. Allan Wilson flew from Halifax, Nova Scotia, to Ottawa, Ontario, via Fredericton, Quebec and Montreal, in a Curtiss HS-2L flying boat.

**28 AUGUST, 1920.** *First ambulance flight in northern Canada.* W.R. Maxwell in Curtiss HS-2L flew J.W. Thompson from Moose Factory to Remi Lake (near Cochrane), Ontario, for hospitalization for mastoids.

Ref: Maxwell, W.R. Report on Flying Boat Operations in Northern Ontario. CAHS Jour., Vol., No. 11, No. 3, Fall, 1973.

**SEPTEMBER, 1920.** W.R. May and G.W. Gorman made a non-stop flight from Edmonton to Peace River Crossing, Alberta, in a Curtiss JN-4(Can.).

Ref: ---- The Flying Man in Industry. Imperial Oil Review, February, 1921.

**2 SEPTEMBER, 1920.** First volume carriage of air mail in Canada. W.R. Maxwell carried 100 pounds of mail from Remi Lake, to Moose Factory, Ontario, in a Curtiss HS-2L.

**3 SEPTEMBER, 1920.** Four de Havilland D.H.4 aircraft of the U.S. Army Air Service reached Dawson, Yukon Territory, on their return flight to the U.S. Flight proceeded via Whitehorse, Telegraph Creek, Hazelton and Edmonton.

**1 OCTOBER, 1920.** Refresher training began at Camp Borden, Ontario.

**7-17 OCTOBER, 1920.** First trans-Canada flight from Halifax, Nova Scotia, to Vancouver, British Columbia, completed in 49 hrs. 7 min. flying time by CAF.

Ref: Manning, W/C R.V. The First Trans-Canada Flight. Can. Geographical Journal, Vol. LXIX, No. 3, September, 1964.

**15 OCTOBER, 1920.** First Canadian international mail service started between Seattle, Washington, and Victoria, British Columbia. Operated by Edward Hubbard using a Boeing C-700 seaplane initially and later a Boeing B-1 flying boat. Last trip was flown by Percy Barnes, 29 June, 1937.

Ref: Davies, R.E.G. Eddie Hubbard's Airline. Air Pictorial, November, 1966.

**15-17 OCTOBER, 1920.** Hector Dugal, pilot, F.H. Ellis and F.J. Stanley, passengers, flew from Winnipeg to The Pas, Manitoba, in an Avro 504K.

Ref: Ellis, Frank H. Canada's Flying Heritage, Univ. of Toronto Press, 1954.

**The two Junkers JL-6 aircraft of Imperial Oil Ltd. photographed at Fort Simpson.** **(via F.H. Ellis)**

**The D.H. 9 in which F.S. Cotton carried the first air mail in Newfoundland.** **(via A.J. Jackson)**

**14 NOVEMBER, 1920.** Frederick Sidney Cotton arrived in Newfoundland and started flying operations shortly afterwards as the Aerial Survey Company (Newfoundland) Ltd.

Ref: Barker, Ralph, Aviator Extraordinary - The Sidney Cotton Story, Chatto & Windus, London, 1969.

**14 DECEMBER, 1920.** USN balloon, A-5598, landed 20 miles northeast of Moose Factory, Ontario, after leaving Rockaway Air Station, Long Island, New York, on 12 December. It became the object of an extensive search. The crew, Lieuts L.A. Kloor, Walter Hinton and Stephen A. Farrel were guided to Moose Factory by natives and were stated to be in poor condition on their arrival on 28 December.

Ref: New York Times, New York, N.Y., 3 January, 1921, p. 1.
8 January, 1921, p. 1.
14 July, 1921, p. 6.

**1920.** J.W. Norcross, of Canada Steamship Lines, proposed the purchase of Vickers Vimy seaplanes for an aerial service between Montreal, Toronto and New York to be inaugurated in the summer of 1921.

Ref: Edmonton Morning Bulletin, Edmonton, Alta., 25 November, 1920, p. 14

# 1921

**JANUARY, 1921.** The Aerial Survey Co. (Newfoundland) started operation. It was formed by F.S. Cotton, Alan S. Butler and V. Sidney Bennett.

**JANUARY, 1921.** Capt E.L. Janney, of Northern Canada Traders Ltd., planned an air service from Peace River, Alberta, to Fort Norman, Northwest Territories, using dirigibles.

Ref: Edmonton Bulletin, 21 January, 1921.
Edmonton Bulletin, 28 January, 1921.

**24 MARCH, 1921.** Exploration flight commenced down the Mackenzie River from Peace River Crossing Alberta, by two Junkers JL-6 aircraft piloted by George W. Gorman and Elmer G. Fullerton. Both propellers were broken at Fort Simpson, Northwest Territories, and new ones were made there by William R. Hill and Walter Johnson.

Ref: Molson K.M. Early Flying Along the Mackenzie. CAHS Journal Vol. 20 No. 2.

**28 MARCH, 1921.** The first air mail in Newfoundland was flown from Botwood to Fogo by F.S. Cotton in a de Havilland D.H.9.

Ref: Dalwick, R.E.R. & Harmer, C.H.C., Newfoundland Air Mails, Harmer Ltd., London, 1953.

The Aeromarine 75 Santa Maria in Toronto Harbour on 14 May, 1921. (Toronto Harbour Commission)

C.O. Prest and his aircraft the "Polar Bear" at Prince Rupert, B.C. The aircraft is believed to be a much modified Curtiss JN-4D. (Public Archives Canada)

**5 APRIL, 1921.** The first of the two 'homemade' propellers was successfully tested on a Junkers JL-6 by E.G. Fullerton at Fort Simpson, Northwest Territories. The second was tested on 20 April. The propellers were made by William R. Hill and Walter Johnson.

Ref: Molson K.M. Early Flying Along the Mackenzie. CAHS Journal Vol. 20 No. 2.

**11 APRIL, 1921.** The first Canadian Air Force flying fatality occurred at Camp Borden, Ontario when S/L K. Tailyour crashed in an Avro 504K while performing aerobatics.

**21 MAY, 1921.** J.M. Larsen of New York City, New York, bought Edmonton Aircraft Ltd. and property on 124th Street, Edmonton, Alberta, and planned to initially assemble and then build Junkers aircraft there.

Ref: Edmonton Bulletin, Edmonton, Alta., 12 May, 1921, p. l.
Edmonton Bulletin, Edmonton, Alta., 12 July, 1921, Supplement.
Edmonton Bulletin, Edmonton, Alta., 6 October, 1921, p.12.

**9 MAY, 1921.** J.M. Larsen of New York City, New York, planned to fly to the Arctic from Edmonton, Alberta, for both sightseeing and photography using two Junkers JL-6 aircraft. He intended to visit Coronation Gulf and Victoria Land as well as other places. The trip was planned for the summer of 1921, but was cancelled completely in the fall.

Ref: Edmonton Bulletin, Edmonton, Alta., 9 May, 1921, p. 9.
Edmonton Bulletin, Edmonton, Alta., 12 May, 1921, p. 1.
Edmonton Bulletin, Edmonton, Alta., 20 June, 1921, p. 6.

**10 MAY, 1921.** The Aeromarine 75 (modified Felixstowe F.5L) 'Santa Maria" arrived at Montreal, Quebec, piloted by Capt Theodore L. Tibbs. It left for Toronto, Ontario, on 14 May and proceeded on to Buffalo, New York, the same day. The aircraft was on a delivery flight to Detroit, Michigan, combined with a route survey for a possible air service from New York City.

Ref: Binns, Jack, Cross-Country in a Flying Boat, U.S. Air Service, July, 1921, p. 23.

**28 JUNE, 1921.** Harvey N. Hyslop flew Dr A.L. Lynch of Saskatoon, Saskatchewan, to Humboldt, 70 miles away, in 57 minutes to save the life of a man with a heart attack. (Aircraft probably was the Curtiss JN-4 (Can.), G-CAAJ.)

Ref: The Edmonton Bulletin, Edmonton, Alta., 29 June, 1921, p. 7.

**JULY, 1921.** Clarence Oliver Prest and Morton Bach attempted to fly from Mexico to Siberia via the United States, Canada and Alaska in a modified Curtiss JN-4D "Polar Bear I". They landed at Lethbridge and Edmonton, Alberta (16 August), and Hazelton, British Columbia. The flight terminated at Prince Rupert, British Columbia, when the aircraft was demolished by a windstorm.

Ref: Edmonton Bulletin, Edmonton, Alta., 17 August, 1921, p. 1 & 2.
Wiley, Frank W., Montana and the Sky.

F.S. Cotton made the first flight to Labrador from Newfoundland in this Martinsyde Type A Mk. I. (E. Parsons photo)

This Dayton-Wright F.P. 2 was the first twin-engined civil aircraft to be registered in Canada. (Mus. Sc. & Tech.)

The Vickers Viking IV of Laurentide Air Service was the first amphibian in Canada. It is seen here at Remi Lake, Ontario. (F.T. Jenkins photo)

**8 OCTOBER, 1921.** L. Reese, an American, was killed at Regina, Saskatchewan, while changing from one Curtiss JN-4 (Can.) to another. As a result, regulations were introduced forbidding performances by aerial stuntmen.

# 1922

**1922.** Laurentide Air Service Ltd. was formed to take over the air operations of the Laurentide Co. T. Hall, President; H.D. Wilshire, Vice-President & Managing Director.

Ref: Molson, K.M. A History of Laurentide Air Service - Canada's First Scheduled Air Service. Can. Aero. & Space Jour., Vol. 16, No. 7, September, 1970.

**5 FEBRUARY, 1922.** The first winter flight to James Bay was made by J. Hervé St. Martin, accompanied by W.R. Maxwell, in an Avro 504K, G-CAAE.

Ref: Molson, K.M., A History of Laurentide Air Service - Canada's First Scheduled Air Service, Can. Aero. & Space Jour., Vol. 16, No. 7, September, 1970.

**3 MARCH, 1922.** The first flight to Labrador was made by F.S. Cotton in a Martinsyde Type A Mark I aircraft. He flew from Botwood, Newfoundland, to Battle Harbour, Labrador, via St. Anthony, Nfld. He continued on to Cartwright on 6 March.

Ref: Dalwich, R.E.R. & Harmer, C.H.C., Newfoundland Air Mails, Harmer Ltd., London, 1954.

**1 JUNE, 1922.** The first twin-engined aircraft to be registered civilly in Canada was the Dayton-Wright F.P.2, N-CAED, which was registered to the Dayton-Wright Airplane Co., Dayton, Ohio.

Ref: Ellis, J.R., The Canadian Civil Aircraft Register. The CAHS Jour., Vol. 10, No. 3, Fall, 1972.

**5 JUNE, 1922.** *The first amphibious aircraft in Canada* was the Napier Lion-powered Vickers Viking IV, G-CAEB, registered to Laurentide Air Service Ltd. of Montreal, Quebec.

Ref: Ellis, J.R., The Canadian Civil Aircraft Register. The CAHS Jour., Vol. 10, No. 3, Fall, 1972.

**28 JUNE, 1922.** The National Defence Act was passed by Parliament to combine the Department of Militia and Defence, Department of Naval Service, and the Air Board in one new Department.

**JULY, 1922.** Fairchild Aerial Surveys (of Canada) Ltd. was established.

**15 JULY, 1922.** John W. Miller in a Curtiss Seagull flying boat started a timber survey for the Chicago Tribune newspaper at Shelter Bay, Quebec. He also performed an ambulance flight during the survey.

Ref: A Timber Survey for the Chicago Tribune, Aviation, 11 September, 1922, p. 319.

This Canadian prototype of the Vickers Viking IV was the first aircraft built by Canadian Vickers Ltd. and the first to be made in Canada since World War I. (RCAF)

Fairchild Aerial Surveys (of Canada) Ltd., started their flying operations with this Curtiss Experimental Flying Boat. It was built with the hull and tail surfaces of a Curtiss Seagull and new wings.
(Mus. Sc. & Tech.)

**MID JULY, 1922.** C.O. Prest again attempted a flight via a circuitous route from Mexico to Siberia, but was forced down 40 miles from Eagle, Yukon Territory. He shot a caribou to survive and the aircraft was, apparently, damaged beyond repair (see July, 1921).

Ref: New York Times, New York, N.Y., 12 May, 1922, p. 14.
New York Times, New York, N.Y., 23 July, 1922, Sect. 2, p. 12.

**18 JULY, 1922.** S/L Robert Archibald Logan sailed from Quebec City, Quebec, to survey the suitability of the Canadian Arctic for flying operations.

Ref: Report of the Air Board 1922. King's Printer, Ottawa.
Ellis, F.H. Canada's Flying Heritage, University of Toronto Press, 1954.

**SEPTEMBER, 1922.** Dominion Aerial Exploration Ltd. was formed by Harry Stephen Quigley and it took over the flying operations of Price Bros. & Co.

# 1923

**15 FEBRUARY, 1923.** His Majesty the King approved the designation Royal Canadian Air Force for the Canadian Air Force.

**12 MARCH, 1923.** Weekly Order No. 21/23 was issued to promulgate the new title Royal Canadian Air Force for the Canadian Air Force. New title was first used in orders and correspondence the following day.

**15 MAY, 1923.** The first course of Provisional Pilot Officers began training at Camp Bordon, Ontario.

**29 JUNE, 1923.** RCAF was re-organized and the Civil Operations Branch of the Air Board was combined with the RCAF under W/C J.L. Gordon as Acting Director.

**SUMMER 1923.** *First use of radio by Canadian civil aviation company.* Laurentide Air Service established a radio station at Sudbury, Ontario.

Ref: Molson, K.M. A History of Laurentide Air Service - Canada's First Scheduled Air Service. Can. Aero. & Space Jour. Vol. 16, No. 7, September, 1970.

**26 JULY, 1923.** First aircraft constructed in Canada since World War I, a Vickers Viking IV, was delivered to the RCAF.

**AUGUST, 1923.** Fairchild Aerial Surveys (of Canada) Ltd. started their own flying operation with a flying boat. Previously they had rented an aircraft to fly their camera man.

**27 AUGUST, 1923.** The first flight from Prince Edward Island to the Magdalen Islands, Quebec, in the Gulf of St. Lawrence was made by Squadron Leader A.B. Shearer in a Curtiss HS-2L flying boat.

The Standard J-1 which Fairchild Aerial Surveys (of Canada) Ltd., operated during the winter of 1923-24 to provide year-round service in the Canadian bush for the first time. (Fairchild)

The first scheduled air passenger in Canada, W.J. Hacker, stands on the dock at Angliers with some Laurentide Air Service personnel. L-R, R.S. Grandy, J.S. Williams, W.J. Hacker and C.S. (Jack) Caldwell.

(Laurentide)

**NOVEMBER, 1923.** Fairchild Aerial Surveys (of Canada) Ltd. rented a Standard J-1 and became the first Canadian company to provide year-round service in bush flying field.

**27 SEPTEMBER, 1923.** J.V. Elliot Ltd. was incorporated at Hamilton, Ontario. Name was changed to Elliot Air Service Ltd. on 15 February, 1928, by Order-in-Council.

# 1924

**1 JANUARY, 1924.** Department of National Defence was created to combine the Department of Militia and Defence, Department of Naval Service and the Air Board.

**22-24 JANUARY, 1924.** Air Vice Marshal Sir Sefton Brancker, Director of Civil Aviation, British Air Ministry, visited Montreal, Quebec, and Ottawa, Ontario, at the invitation of the Department of National Defence. He met with Canadian aviation officials and was given information on Canadian aviation conditions.

**30 MARCH, 1924.** First seal spotting flight was carried out by Roy Stanley (Bill) Grandy in an Avro 554 "Baby" aircraft off the Newfoundland coast, near Harbour Deep.

Ref: Grandy, R.S. Seal Spotting Operations off Newfoundland in 1924. CAHS Journal, Vol. 15, No. 2, 1977.

**1 APRIL, 1924.** RCAF was placed on a permanent basis and The King's Regulations and Orders for the Royal Canadian Air Force and Pay and Allowance Regulations came into effect.

**22 APRIL, 1924.** First of 13 Curtiss HS-2L's was delivered to Ontario Provincial Air Service at Toronto, Ontario, by H.D. Wilshire for Laurentide Air Service Ltd. This was the beginning of the OPAS.

Ref: Molson, K.M. A History of Laurentide Air Service - Canada's First Scheduled Air Service. Can. Aero. & Space Jour. Vol. 16.

**6 APRIL, 1924.** Four Douglas DWC seaplanes on a round-the-world flight landed at Prince Rupert, British Columbia. The "Seattle" was damaged on landing, but was repaired and the flight continued to Sitka, Alaska, on the 10th.

Ref: Thomas, Lowell. The First World Flight. Houghton Mifflin Co. Boston, 1925.

**MAY, 1924.** W/C J.S. Scott returned to Canada after completing the course at the RAF Staff College - the first RCAF officer to do so.

**23 MAY, 1924.** *The first Canadian scheduled air service began.* It was operated by Laurentide Air Service Ltd. between Angliers, Lake Fortune and Rouyn, Quebec. The first scheduled air passenger in Canada was mining engineer, W.J. Hacker.

Ref: Molson, K.M., A History of Laurentide Air Service - Canada's First Scheduled Air Service. Can. Aero. & Space Jour., Vol. 16, No. 7, September, 1970.

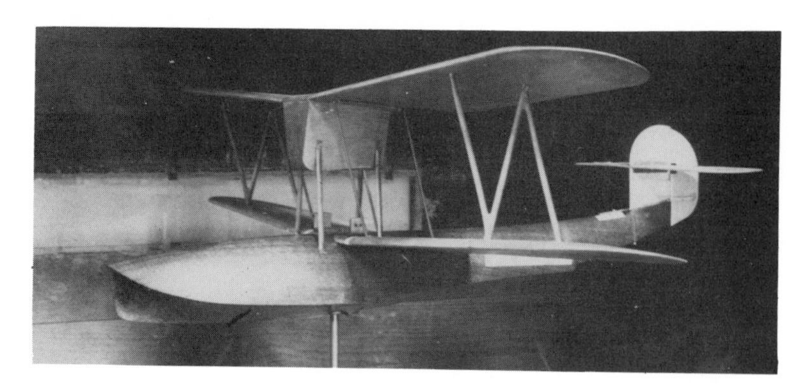

The model of the Canadian Vickers Vedette prototype in the University of Toronto wind tunnel. The N-struts were incorporated for convenience in model making only and were not a design feature.
(N.R.C. Coll.)

C.S. (Jack) Caldwell's Thomas Morse S-4C at Dayton in September 1924. It was fitted with a long range tank above the wing center section for the trip.
(Mus. Sc. & Tech.)

Pilot E.A. Alton receiving the bag of mail at Estevan prior to starting his flight of October 1, 1924.
(via N.A. Pelletier)

**JULY, 1924.** The first wind tunnel tests in Canada of a complete model aircraft, the Canadian Vickers Vedette, were carried out at the University of Toronto.

**3 AUGUST, 1924.** HMCS Thiepval picked up Major Stuart MacLaren and crew from wrecked Vickers Vulture amphibian at Bering Island, Alaska, the end of their attempted round-the-world flight and brought them to Prince Rupert, British Columbia.

Ref: ---- Canada Played Stirring Role in MacLaren's Famous Flight. Montreal Daily Star, Montreal, Que., 6 November, 1924, p. 26 & 38.

**31 AUGUST, 1924.** Two Douglas DWC seaplanes on a round-the-world flight landed at Icy Tickle, Labrador, from Ivigtut, Greenland. They left on 2 September for Hawkes Bay, Newfoundland, and went on to Pictou, Nova Scotia, on 3rd. They left for Casco Bay, Maine, on the 5th.

Ref: Thomas, Lowell, The First World Flight, Houghton Mifflin Co., Boston, 1925.

**3 SEPTEMBER, 1924.** *The first Canadian regular air mail service began.* It was operated by Laurentide Air Service between Haileybury, Ontario, and Angliers and Rouyn, Quebec.

Ref: Molson, K.M., A History of Laurentide Air Service - Canada's First Scheduled Air Service, Can. Aero. & Space Jour., Vol. 16, No. 7, September, 1970.

**11 SEPTEMBER, 1924.** Miss Norma Garden, of New York, made a hot air balloon ascension at the Central Canada Exhibition, Ottawa, Ontario, but could not release her parachute and was forced to ride her cooling balloon down. Close to earth, the parachute broke loose and Miss Garden had a narrow escape from serious injury or death.

Ref: The Ottawa Journal, Ottawa, Ont., 12 September, 1924, p. 2. The Citizen, Ottawa, Ont., 12 September, 1924, p. 4.

**SEPTEMBER, 1924.** C.S. (Jack) Caldwell piloted a Thomas Morse S-4C in 'On-to-Dayton' Race and flew from Three Rivers, Quebec, to Dayton, Ohio, via Ottawa and Camp Borden, Ontario, and Detroit, Michigan.

**1 OCTOBER, 1924.** E.A. Alton attempted an air mail flight from Estevan, Saskatchewan, to Winnipeg, Manitoba, in a Standard J-1 aircraft. Flight was terminated at Bienfait, Saskatchewan, by an accident.

**3 NOVEMBER, 1924.** *First aerial stowaway in Canada.* An unidentified man stowed away on a Curtiss HS-2L piloted by C.S. (Jack) Caldwell from Rouyn to Angliers, Quebec.

Ref: Molson, K.M., A History of Laurentide Air Service - Canada's First Scheduled Air Service. Can. Aero. & Space Jour., Vol. 16, No. 7, September, 1970.

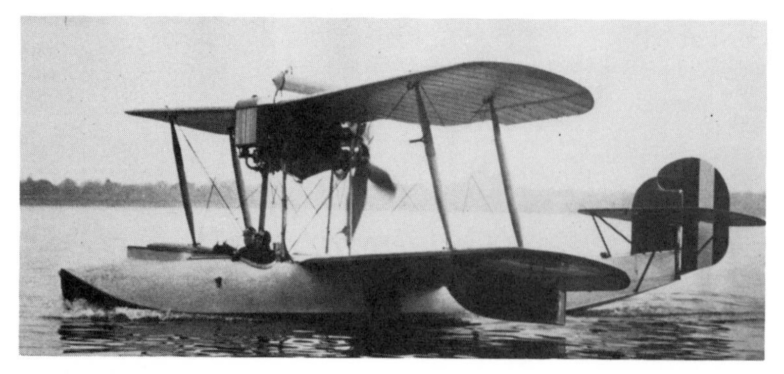

The Wolseley Viper-powered Canadian Vickers Vedette prototype being tested on 4 November 1924. (Canadian Vickers)

The modified D.H. 9 of Laurentian Air Service which operated briefly, in the winter air service, 1925. (RCAF)

Northern Air Service's Curtiss HS-2L which took over the air transport operations into the Quebec goldfields. Pilot B.W.Broach has his leg outside the cockpit.

(via K.M. Molson)

**4 NOVEMBER, 1924.** The prototype Canadian Vickers Vedette was test flown at Montreal, Quebec, by F/O W.N. Plenderleith, RAF.

Ref: Molson, K.M. Canadian Vickers Vedette. Canadian Aeronautics & Space Jour., Vol. 10, No. 8, October, 1964.

**20 DECEMBER, 1924.** The first RCAF Wings Parade took place at Camp Borden, Ontario, when W/C L.S. Breadner presented wings to F/L F.C. Higgins, P/O B.G. Carr-Harris and P/P/Os C.M. Anderson, W.J. Durnin, C.R. Slemon and W.C. Weaver.

# 1925

**21 JANUARY, 1925.** A winter air service was started between Larder Lake, Ontario, and Rouyn, Quebec. It was operated by Laurentide Air Service Ltd.

Ref: Molson, K.M. A History of Laurentide Air Service - Canada's First Scheduled Air Service. Can. Aeronautics & Space Jour., Vol. 16, No. 7, September, 1970.

**29 JANUARY, 1925.** A library of aerial photographs was authorized by Order in Council P.C. 108. This library became known as the National Air Photographic Library in 1937.

Ref: Thomson, Don W. Skyview Canada. Department of Energy, Mines & Resources, Ottawa, 1975.

**10 FEBRUARY, 1925.** Pacific Airways, Ltd. was formed by D.R. MacLaren and took over the fishery patrol from RCAF.

**APRIL, 1925.** The wearing of parachutes in flight in RCAF aircraft was made obligatory.

**APRIL, 1925.** Northern Air Service, Ltd. was formed to provide air transport to the Rouyn goldfields of Quebec. It commenced operations on 18 May with a flight from Haileybury, Ontario, to Rouyn.

**9 JUNE, 1925.** Canadian Airways Ltd. (old) was formed by H.S. Quigley and took over operations of Dominion Aerial Explorations Ltd.

**12 AUGUST, 1925.** *First landing in the Canadian Arctic* was made by a Loening amphibian piloted by Lt-Com. R.E. Byrd and Floyd Bennett on the east coast of Ellesmere Island.

**25 AUGUST, 1925.** The MacMillan Arctic Expedition completed 15 days flying and explored Ellesmere Island.

A Curtiss HS-2L of the Ontario Provincial Air Service at Red Lake on the last trip of the October air lift. A typical early snowfall lightly covers the trees.

(G.A. Thompson Coll.)

The Curtiss Lark of Patricia Airways & Explortion in the early spring of 1926.

(via K.M. Molson)

J.D. McKee's Douglas MO-2BS photographed at the USN Air Station at Anacostia, Washington, D.C. in July 1926.

(U.S. Nat. Archives)

**OCTOBER, 1925.** Ontario Provincial Air Service flew men and supplies to develop Howey gold find at Red Lake, Ontario, during the first week of October. J.R. Ross was senior pilot in charge and he was assisted by R.C. Guest, H.A. Oaks, T.G.M. Stephens and J.R. Vachon.

# 1926

**5 JANUARY, 1926.** The first Armstrong-Whitworth Siskin fighter was taken on strength by the RCAF. This was the first post-WWI operational type aircraft of the RCAF.

**MARCH, 1926.** Patricia Airways & Exploration Co. was formed to provide an air service in the Red Lake district of Ontario.

**3 MARCH, 1926.** Air service to Red Lake, Ontario began. J.V. Elliot and A.H. Farrington of Elliot Air Service flew two Curtiss JN-4 (Can.)'s with a passenger in each from Hudson to Red Lake, Ontario.

Ref: Parrott, D.F., The Red Lake Gold Rush. D.F. Parrott. Red Lake, Ont., 1967.

**12 APRIL, 1926.** The Curtiss Lark of Patricia Airways and Exploration Co. arrived at Red Lake, Ontario, after a delivery flight from New York City, New York, piloted by C.S. (Casey) Jones to Buffalo, N.Y., and by W.R. Maxwell from there to Red Lake.

Ref: Parrott, D.F. The Red Lake Gold Rush. D.F. Parrott. Red Lake, Ont., 1967.

**14 APRIL, 1926.** H.A. (Doc) Oaks commenced flying operations in the Red Lake district for Patricia Airways & Exploration Ltd.

Ref: Parrott, D.F. The Red Lake Gold Rush. D.F. Parrott. Red Lake, Ont., 1967.

**10 MAY, 1926.** The first commercial aircraft, a Canadian Vickers Vedette, G-CAFF, to be built in Canada for a civil company, Fairchild Aerial Surveys Ltd., was launched at Montreal, Quebec.

Ref: Montreal Gazette, Montreal, Que., 10 May, 1926.

**JUNE, 1926.** Fairchild Air Transport Ltd. was formed.

**JULY, 1926.** Compagnie Aérienne Franco-Canadienne was incorporated. It operated in Quebec only and was primarily concerned with photography and forestry work for the Quebec Government.

**11-19 SEPTEMBER, 1926.** *The first transcontinental seaplane flight* was made by J. Dalzell McKee and S/L Albert Earl Godfrey who flew a Douglas M0-2BS seaplane from Montreal, Quebec to Vancouver, British Columbia.

Ref: Molson, K.M., The McKee Flight. The CAHS Jour., Vol. 2, No. 4, Winter, 1964.

H.A. Oaks the sole pilot upon the formation of Western Canada Airways Ltd. and the Fokker Universal Aircraft, photographed at Hudson, Ontario in January 1926. (H.A. Oaks photo)

The men who carried out the Churchill airlift, left to right, S.A. Cheesman, J.R. Ross, Bernt Balchen and Fred J. Stevenson, photographed after their return on 17 April 1927. (Balchen photo)

The Curtiss HS-2L in which F.V. Robinson and crew carried out the Canadian search for Nungesser & Coli. (Mus. Sc. & Tech.)

**10 DECEMBER, 1926.** Western Canada Airways Ltd. was incorporated with James A. Richardson of Winnipeg, Manitoba, as President and only shareholder.

Ref: Molson, K.M. Pioneering in Canadian Air Transport. James Richardson & Sons. Winnipeg, 1974.

**27 DECEMBER, 1926.** Western Canada Airways started flying operations from Hudson, Ontario, into the Red Lake district with one Fokker Universal aircraft. H.A. (Doc) Oaks was pilot and manager.

Ref: Molson, K.M. Pioneering in Canadian Air Transport. James Richardson & Sons. Winnipeg, 1974.

# 1927

**24 JANUARY, 1927.** A flight of 12 U.S. Army Curtiss Hawks commanded by Major T.G. Lamphier visited Ottawa, Ontario, from Selfridge Field, Michigan.

Ref: New York Times, New York, N.Y., 25 January, 1927, p. 25.

**FEBRUARY, 1927.** Fairchild Aviation Ltd. was formed and absorbed Fairchild Aerial Surveys (of Canada) and Fairchild Air Transport Ltd.

**FEBRUARY, 1927.** J.M. Clarke, L.T. Palmer and F/O Gilbert Jenkins (of Melbourne, Australia) planned a trans Pacific flight in a Sikorsky seaplane. Vancouver to Honolulu and then to Sidney, N.S.W., via Fanning Island and Fiji.

Ref: New York Times, New York, N.Y., 23 February, 1927, p. 5.

**22 MARCH, 1927.** *Largest airlift of freight in Canada began.* 17,894 pounds of freight was flown from Cache Lake to Churchill, Manitoba, between 22 March and 17 April. J.R. Ross was in charge for Western Canada Airways; pilots F.J. Stevenson and Bernt Balchen flew Fokker Universals.

Ref: MacKay, Alice First Freight Flies North. The Beaver, September, 1947.

**18 MAY, 1927.** Marchese Francesco de Pinedo reached Shippegan, New Brunswick, after a flight across the South Atlantic and up the coast.

Ref: Dalwick, R.E.R. & Harmer, C.H.C. Newfoundland Air Mails. Harmer & Co., London, 1953.

**20 MAY, 1927.** Marchese Francesco de Pinedo arrived at Trepassey, Newfoundland, from Shippegan, New Brunswick, in a Savoia-Marchetti S.55 flying boat. Left for Azores on 23 May. Landed 200 miles short and was towed in.

Ref: Dalwick, R.E.R. & Harmer, C.H.C. Newfoundland Air Mails. Harmer & Co., London, 1953.

**28 MAY-7 JUNE, 1927.** F.V. Robinson and crew in a Curtiss HS-2L of Canadian Airways Ltd. (old) conducted a search for Nungesser and Coli along the North Shore of the St. Lawrence going as far east as the Straits of Belle Isle.

Ref: Molson, K.M. The Canadian Search for Nungesser and Coli. Can. Aviation Historical Soc. Journal Vol. 15, No. 2, Summer 1977.

The Fokker Universal, Jeanne d'Arc, which carried out the search in Newfoundland for Nungesser and Coli. This was, also, the first aircraft to visit St. Pierre & Miquelon.
(via K.M. Molson)

P/O C.L. Bath taxiing out at Whycomah, N.S., in his Keystone Puffer to carry out a dusting flight. Note the dust streaks on the lower aft fuselage.
(S.A. Cheesman photo)

W.R. Turnbull and his variable pitch propeller installed on the Avro 504K at Camp Borden, Ontario. (Turnbull/N.R.C.)

**MAY-JUNE, 1927.** A search for Nungesser and Coli was carried out in Newfoundland by F.S. Cotton and C.C. Caldwell in a Fokker Universal.

Ref: Barker, Ralph. Aviator Extraordinary - The Sidney Cotton Story. Chatto & Windus. London, 1969.

**1 JUNE, 1927.** Western Canada Airways inaugurated weekly air service from Winnipeg to Long Lake, Manitoba, via Lac du Bonnet.

Ref: Molson, K.M. Pioneering in Canadian Air Transport. James A. Richardson & Sons. Winnipeg, 1974.

**8 JUNE, 1927.** J.E. Jellison of Elliot Air Service flew newly-weds, Dr. & Mrs. James Nesbitt, from Toronto to Hamilton, Ontario, in a Curtiss JN-4 (Can.), G-CAFX. Another aerial honeymoon was taken on 27 July, 1927, by Mr. & Mrs. Alex. Beemer who flew from London to Niagara Falls, Ont., piloted by a Captain Brodie.

Ref: Hamilton Spectator, Hamilton, Ont., 28 July, 1927.

**13 JUNE, 1927.** First flight to St. Pierre and Miquelon was made by F.S. Cotton and C.C. Caldwell from Newfoundland in a Fokker Universal. This was also the first aircraft flight in the island.

Ref: Hamilton Spectator, Hamilton, Ont., 14 June, 1927, p. 1.

**18 JUNE - 27 JULY, 1927.** *First forest dusting in Canada* was carried out by F/O C.L. Bath in a Keystone Puffer seaplane at Cape Breton Island, Nova Scotia.

Ref: Hitchins, F.H. Air Board, Canadian Air Force and Royal Canadian Air Force. Canadian War Museum, 1972.

**24 JUNE, 1927.** Authority was given to acquire and develop an aerodrome site at St. Hubert, Quebec, near Montreal, which was to include a mooring mast for dirigibles for contemplated trans-Atlantic airship service.

**29 JUNE, 1927.** Miss Rose Tracey jumped with a parachute from a Curtiss JN-4 (Can.), G-CAFX, piloted by Joseph Earle Jellison and became the second Canadian woman to jump from an aeroplane in flight. The first Canadian woman to parachute from an aeroplane was Miss Jean Sykes of Toronto, but the date is not known.

Ref: Hamilton Spectator, Hamilton, Ont., 29 June, 1927, p. 5.

**29 JUNE, 1927.** First flight test of the Turnbull variable pitch propeller was carried out at Camp Borden, Ontario, by F/L G.E. Brookes on Avro 504K, G-CYFL. Note preliminary whirling tests were carried out on 6 June by F/L G.E. Wait.

Ref: The Turnbull Variable Pitch Propeller. Aviation, 20 February, 1928, p. 446.
J.H. Parkin. Wallace Rupert Turnbull, 1870-1954. Canadian Aeronautical Journal, Vol. 2, Nos. 1 & 2, Jan. & Feb., 1956.

Charles Lindbergh arriving at Uplands Airport in the Spirit of St. Louis on 1 July 1927, in a cloud of dust.
(A.O. Adams photo)

The Spirit of the Valley of the Moon, a D.H. 60 Moth, and the first of the type in Canada, photographed at Wakeham Bay, Quebec in 1928. (RCAF)

A crowd of interested spectators await the takeoff of the Brock & Schlee Stinson from Harbour Grace 27 August 1927. (Mus. Sc. & Tech.)

**29 JUNE, 1927.** E.L. Janney planned an Ottawa-London, England, flight to start 11 July.

Ref: New York Times, New York, N.Y., 30 June, 1927, p. 6.

**1 JULY, 1927.** Air Services re-organized under the Department of National Defence. The RCAF continued as the military branch. New branches, the Civil Government Air Operations, Controller of Civil Aviation and an Aeronautical Engineering Division, were responsible to the Deputy Minister.

**2 JULY, 1927.** At the invitation of the Canadian Government to help celebrate the 50th Anniversary of Confederation, Charles Augustus Lindbergh flew to Ottawa, Ontario, in his Ryan NYP "Spirit of St. Louis". He was escorted by 12 Curtiss Hawks from Selfridge Field, Michigan, two of which collided at Ottawa, killing one pilot. He departed on 4 July after circling Ottawa for 35 minutes. Uplands airport was named Lindbergh Field in his honour. The "Spirit", preserved in Washington, D.C., bears the flags of all countries visited by this famous aircraft except Canada which is omitted, probably by oversight.

Ref: Lindbergh, Charles A., The Spirit of St. Louis. Charles Scribner, New York, 1953.

**4 JULY, 1927.** The technical training of boys, 15 to 18 years of age was inaugurated at Camp Borden to supply mechanics for the RCAF.

**17 JULY, 1927.** Hudson Strait Expedition sailed for Arctic from Halifax, Nova Scotia. Expedition is organized by Department of Marine and Fisheries to gather information on ice conditions in Hudson Strait to aid in establishing new port of Churchill, Manitoba. Aviation personnel supplied by RCAF.

Ref: Manning D.F.C., W/C R.V. The Hudson Strait Expedition 1927-8. Can. Geo. Jour. Vol. LXII, No. 2, Feb., 1961.

**27 JULY, 1927.** *First flight by a Canadian aircraft in the high Arctic.* A de Havilland D.H. 60, Moth seaplane, G-CAHK, piloted by S/L T.A. Lawrence and F/L A.A. Leitch at Port Burwell, Labrador.

Ref: Manning, W/C R.V. The Hudson Strait Expedition 1927-28. Canadian Geographical Journal, Vol. LXII, No. 2.

**26 AUGUST, 1927.** William Brock, pilot, and Edward Schlee arrived at Harbour Grace, Newfoundland, from Old Orchard Beach, Maine, in the Stinson SM-1, Detroiter, "The Pride of Detroit". They left the next day for London, England, and then continued to Tokyo, Japan.

Ref: Aviation Year Book 1928. Aeronautical Chamber of Commerce, New York, 1928.

**28 AUGUST, 1927.** Terrance B. Tully and James V. Medcalf left London, Ontario, on a projected flight to London, England, in the Stinson Detroiter "Sir John Carling". They were forced to return by fog.

Ref: Ellis, Frank H. Canada's Flying Heritage. Univ. of Toronto Press, 1954.

The Stinson SM-1, "Sir John Carling" and its crew before setting off from London, Ontario in September 1927. (J.F. McNulty Coll.)

Stinson SM-1, "Royal Windsor" and its colourful pilot C.A. "Duke" Schiller. (S.A. Cheesman Coll.)

A Curtiss HS-2L brings the first overseas mail to Montreal, from Rmouski. (CAL Archives)

**AUGUST - SEPTEMBER, 1927.** During 5 weeks of this period, F.J. Stevenson of Western Canada Airways carried 45,708 lbs of freight into Cold Lake from The Pas, Manitoba, in a Fokker Universal.

Ref: Molson, K.M. Pioneering in Canadian Air Transport. James A. Richardson & Sons, Winnipeg, 1974.

**AUGUST, 1927.** Land for St. Hubert Airport was purchased by the Canadian Government. It was first used by aircraft for experimental mail flights in November 1927. Hangars, lighting and mooring tower were completed later. Covering 729 arpents (about 620 acres), it was the largest Canadian airport for many years.

Ref: Report on Civil Aviation 1927. King's Printer, Ottawa, 1928.

**6 SEPTEMBER, 1927.** T.B. Tully and J.V. Medcalf arrived at Harbour Grace, Newfoundland, from Old Orchard Beach, Maine, in the Stinson SM-1, Detroiter, "Sir John Carling". They had left London, Ontario, on 1 September. They departed for London, England, on 7 September and were lost at sea.

Ref: Ellis, Frank H., Canada's Flying Heritage. Univ. of Toronto Press, 1953.

**7 SEPTEMBER, 1927.** C.A. (Duke) Schiller and Phillip S. Wood arrived at Harbour Grace, Newfoundland, in the Stinson SM-1, Detroiter, "Royal Windsor" for projected flight to London, England. Flight was called off on 10 September.

Ref: Ellis, Frank H. Canada's Flying Heritage. Univ. of Toronto Press, 1954.

**8 SEPTEMBER, 1927.** R.H. Storer proposed a flight from Vancouver, British Columbia, to Australia to take place in the spring of 1928.

Ref: Hamilton Spectator, Hamilton, Ont., 8 September, 1927.

**16 SEPTEMBER, 1927.** First of ten experimental air mail flights during the fall between Montreal and Father Point, Quebec, to connect with incoming and outgoing liners, was carried out by Canadian Airways (old) in a Curtiss HS-2L piloted by H.S. Quigley and S. Graham. Up to three days were saved on transAtlantic mail.

Ref: Report on Civil Aviation 1927. King's Printer, Ottawa, 1928.

**21 SEPTEMBER, 1927.** C.A. (Duke) Schiller and P.S. Wood entered the New York-to-Spokane Derby in their Stinson SM-1 Detroiter "Royal Windsor". They were forced down at Billings, Montana.

Ref: New York Times, New York, N.Y., 23 September, 1927, p. 1.

**23 SEPTEMBER, 1927.** The Honourable R.J. Ralston announced the terms for assistance to flying clubs by the Canadian Government.

Ref Hamilton Spectator, Hamilton, Ont., 24 September, 1927.

**6 OCTOBER, 1927.** Western Canada Airways commenced its first contract air mail service between Lac du Bonnet, Wadhope and Bisset in Manitoba.

Ref: Molson, K.M. Pioneering in Canadian Air Transport. James A. Richardson & Sons. Winnipeg, 1974.

The inauguration of the mail service to Pelee Island on 30 November 1927. Pilot Banghart is seated on the Waco 9 on the right but the others are unidentified. (K.M. Molson Coll.)

Canadian Transcontinental Airways started operations with two Fairchild FC-2W sisterships, one of which is shown here at Lac Ste. Agnes, Quebec. (Fairchild)

**18 OCTOBER, 1927.** Count Jacques de Lesseps and his mechanic were lost in a Schreck flying boat, in the Gulf of St. Lawrence near Ste. Félicité, Quebec.

Ref: Montreal Daily Star, Montreal, Que., 19, 21 & 22 October, 1927.

**27 OCTOBER, 1927.** First overseas mail is brought to Ottawa, Ontario, by air from Father Point, Quebec, by a Fairchild FC-2 seaplane of Fairchild Aviation Ltd. piloted by H.M. Pasmore.

Ref: Ellis, F.H. Canada's Flying Heritage. University of Toronto Press, 1954.

**30 NOVEMBER, 1927.** Winter mail service between Leamington and Pelee Island, Ontario, began. The initial flight was made by F.I. Banghart in a Waco 9 aircraft.

**DECEMBER, 1927.** Canadian Transcontinental Airways Ltd. formed at Quebec City, Quebec.

**25 DECEMBER, 1927.** Canadian Transcontinental Airways commenced the first winter air mail service from Quebec City, Quebec, along the North Shore of the St. Lawrence River.

**1927.** The Trans-Canada (McKee) Trophy was awarded to H.A. (Doc) Oaks for his work in organizing and operating air transport in Northern Ontario, Manitoba and Saskatchewan.

**1927.** Harmon Trophy for Canada was awarded to F.J. Stevenson, pilot, Western Canada Airways.

**Fred J. Stevenson, winner of the Harmon Trophy for Canada in 1927.**
**(C.A. Schiller Coll.)**

**The Magdalen Island mail service which began on 11 January 1927, was operated by a Fairchild FC-2W on a unique float-ski gear which proved unsatisfactory.**
**(E.J. Cooper photo)**

**Jack Caldwell's snow-bound Avro Avian being dug out at Grindstone, Magdalen Islands, during the seal spotting operation of March 1928. (C.S. Caldwell photo)**

**General Airways started operations from this base at Amos, Quebec, using these two aircraft, a D.H. 60 Moth and a Fairchild FC-2. This photo taken 12 October 1928 after an early snowstorm. (R.S. Baker photo)**

# 1928

**11 JANUARY, 1928.** First air mail service to Magdalen Islands, Quebec, commenced. It was operated by Canadian Transcontinental Airways from Moncton, New Brunswick, using a Fairchild FC-2W aircraft; E.J. Cooper was the pilot.

Ref: Ellis, F.H. Canada's Flying Heritage. University of Toronto Press, 1954.

**FEBRUARY, 1928.** Reid Aircraft Co. Ltd. was formed at Montreal, Quebec, by W.T. Reid.

**13 FEBRUARY, 1928.** Prospectors Airways Ltd. was formed for aerial prospecting.

**15 FEBRUARY, 1928.** Elliot Air Service Ltd. was formed and took over operations of J.V. Elliot Ltd.

**17 FEBRUARY, 1928.** F/O A. Lewis, F/Sgt N.C. Terry and Eskimo "Bobby" were lost in Fokker Universal, G-CAHG, which landed on an ice floe off Labrador. "Bobby" guided the crew to shore.

Ref: Manning, D.E.C., W/C R.V. The Hudson Strait Expedition 1927-28. Canadian Geographical Journal, Vol. LXII, No. 2, February, 1961.

**19 FEBRUARY. 1928.** A weekly winter service was inaugurated between Moncton, New Brunswick, and Charletown, Prince Edward Island, by Canadian Transcontinental Airways Ltd.

**MARCH, 1928.** Successful seal spotting flights were carried out by C.S. (Jack) Caldwell in an Avro 594 Avian in early March, the first of the season. The aircraft was based at Grindstone, Magdalen Islands, Quebec.

Ref: The Financial Post, August 31, 1928, p. 15.

**MARCH, 1928.** De Havilland Aircraft of Canada Ltd. was formed at Toronto, Ontario. It served as a sales and service outlet for aircraft made in England by its parent company until it entered the manufacturing business in 1938.

**MARCH, 1928.** Canadian Air Review commenced publication.

**MARCH, 1928.** Northern Aerial Minerals Exploration Ltd. was formed by John E. Hammell to take advantage of aircraft in the search for minerals.

**8 MARCH, 1928.** General Airways Ltd. was formed at Toronto, Ontario. It commenced operations in June from a base at Amos, Quebec.

Eileen M. Vollick, Canada's first licensed woman pilot.
(D. Miles photo)

Charles Lindbergh after landing at Quebec City 25 April, with serum for the ailing Floyd Bennett.
(J.M. Landry)

The Bremen crew at Murray Bay, Quebec 26 April 1928. Left to right, Baron Guenther von Huenefeld, Capt. Hermann Koehl, Clarence Chamberlin, Major James Fitzmaurice, Bernt Balchen and C.A. "Duke" Schiller (back to camera). (Wide World)

**13 MARCH, 1928.** *First Canadian woman to become a licensed pilot.* Miss Eileen M. Vollick passed her test for a Private Pilot's License (No. 77) at Hamilton, Ontario, on a Curtiss JN-4(Can.). Her instructors were J. Earle Jellison, Leonard J. Tripp and Richard Turner of Elliot Air Service. Miss Vollick had also made several parachute jumps, her first being on 30 July, 1927.

Ref: Vollick, Eileen M. How I Became Canada's First Licensed Woman Pilot. Canadian Air Review, June, 1928, p. 14, 42, & 43.

**31 MARCH, 1928.** De Havilland Aircraft of Canada Ltd. commenced operations.

**13 APRIL, 1928.** Capt Hermann Koehl, Major James C. Fitzmaurice and Baron Guenther von Huenefeld landed on Greenly Island, Labrador, in the Junkers W-33 "Bremen", after completing the first westward Atlantic flight.

Ref: Koehl, Capt Herman, Fitzmaurice, Major James C., & von Huenefeld, Baron Guenther. The Three Musketeers of the Air. G.P. Putnam. New York, 1928.

**15 APRIL, 1928.** C.A. (Duke) Schiller, flying a Fairchild FC-2W, reached the stranded crew of the "Bremen" on Greenly Island, Labrador.

Ref: Ellis F.H. Canada's Flying Heritage. University of Toronto Press, Toronto, 1954.

**25 APRIL, 1928.** C.A. Lindbergh landed on the Plains of Abraham, Quebec City, Quebec, in a Curtiss Falcon carrying pneumonia serum for Floyd Bennett.

Ref: New York Times, 25 April, 1928, p. 11.

**26 APRIL, 1928.** The Breman's crew was flown from Greenly Island, Labrador, to Murray Bay, Quebec, in a Ford 4-AT piloted by Bernt Balchen, and then on to New York City, New York, the following day.

**28 APRIL, 1928.** Regular summer air service from Rimouski to Montreal, Quebec, was started to connect with ocean liners.

**1 MAY, 1928.** Pacific Airways was bought by Western Canada Airways Ltd.

**1 MAY, 1928.** The Toronto Flying Club started flying operations at Leaside Aerodrome, the first Canadian club to do so.

Ref: The Financial Post, May 3, 1929.

**4 MAY, 1928.** The Saskatoon Aero Club started flying operations at the Club field, Saskatoon, Saskatchewan, the second club to do so.

Ref: The Financial Post, May 3, 1929. p.20

The Montreal Light Aeroplane Club's first aircraft, instructor and air engineer, the DH.60 Moth, G-CAKD, Capt. Hugh "Tony" Spooner and A.G.W. Adams. The Cirrus powered D.H.60 was the original aircraft type issued to all the flying clubs in Canada in 1928. (A.G.K. Edward photo)

The Stinson SB-1 Detroiter with which Great Western Airways started operations. (G.R. Spradbrow photo)

**12 MAY, 1928.** The Montreal Light Aeroplane Club started flying operations at St. Hubert Aerodrome.

Ref: The Financial Post, May 3, 1929, p.20.

**24 MAY, 1928.** Stevenson Aerodrome was opened at Winnipeg, Manitoba.

Ref: Our Bases - Stevenson Aerodrome, Winnipeg. The Bulletin, Vol. 1, No. 12, p. 1.

**24 MAY, 1928.** The Hamilton Aero Club started flying operations at the Club field, Hamilton, Ontario.

Ref: The Financial Post, May 3, 1929, p.20.

**28 MAY, 1928.** The Winnipeg Flying Club started flying operations at Stevenson Field, Winnipeg, Manitoba.

Ref: The Financial Post, May 3, 1929, p.20.

**29 MAY, 1928.** The Regina Flying Club started flying operations at the Regina Municipal Airport.

Ref: The Financial Post, May 3, 1929, p.20.

**JUNE, 1928.** International Airways Ltd. was formed and took over operations of Elliot Air Service Ltd.

**JUNE, 1928.** Canadian Aviation commenced publication.

**5 JUNE, 1928.** Amelia Earhart, William S. Stulz and Louis Gordon landed at Halifax, Nova Scotia, after flying from Boston, Massachusetts, in a Fokker F. VII/3m seaplane "Friendship". They flew to Trepassey, Newfoundland, on the 6th and left for Wales on the 17th. Amelia Earhart became the first woman to cross the Atlantic by air.

Ref: Earhart, Amelia. 20 Hrs. 40 Mins. - Our Flight in the Friendhsip. G.P. Putnam, New York, 1928.

**13 JUNE, 1928.** The Edmonton & Northern Alberta Aero Club started flying operations at the Club field at Edmonton, Alberta.

Ref: The Financial Post May 3, 1929. p.20

**20 JUNE, 1928.** Great Western Airways Ltd. started operations at Calgary, Alberta, with one Stinson SB-1, Detroiter.

Ref: Financial Post, August 31, 1928, p.19

**23 JUNE, 1928.** Joaquin Pachero and Fritz Bieler took off from Walker Airport, Windsor, Ontario, on a non-stop flight to Mexico City, Mexico, in Stinson SM-1, NX5829. They were forced down at Tampico, Mexico, due to fuel shortage.

Ref: New York Times, New York, N.Y., 24 June, 1928, p. 20.
New York Times, New York, N.Y., 25 June, 1928, p. 8.

**The Bellanca J. "North Star," photographed at Cartierville airport just before its trans Atlantic flight attempt. It later became the famous "Pathfinder" of Roger Q. Williams and Lewis Yancey. (A.G.K. Edward photo)**

**Passengers from the Clarke Steamship SS North Shore and local residents attend the dedication of a cairn to the Bremen crew on Greenly Island, July 1928. (Clarke Transportation)**

**The Dornier Wal of Frank Courtney which was the first Canadian registered aircraft to make a trans Atlantic flight attempt. (F.T. Courtney photo)**

**28 JUNE, 1928.** Bellanca J "North Star" was damaged on take-off for a transatlantic flight at Cap de la Madeleine, Quebec, Ulrich Koenemann, pilot, Thea Rasche, and M. Zebora, mechanic. Mrs. James Stillman financed the flight.

Ref: New York Times, New York, N.Y., 26 June, 1928, p.27.
New York Times, New York, N.Y., 29 June, 1928, p. 10.
Ellis, F.H. & E.M. Atlantic Air Conquest Wm. Kimber, London, 1963.

**JULY, 1928.** Fast Air Service Transport Ltd. was incorporated.

Ref: Air Transportation, 28 July, 1928, p. 10.

**7-15 JULY, 1928.** *First Canadian aircraft show* was opened by Maj-Gen J.H. MacBrien at Craig Street Drill Hall, Montreal, Quebec.

Ref: Air Transportation, 7 July, 1928, p. 1.
Air Transportation, 21 July, 1928, p. 11.

**8 JULY, 1928.** The Victoria Aero Club started flying operations at the Club field, Victoria, British Columbia.

Ref: The Financial Post, May 3, 1929, p.20.

**25 JULY, 1928.** A cairn and plaque was dedicated on Greenly Island to commemorate the landing of the German Junkers Bremen, the first airplane to fly non-stop across the Atlantic east to west.

Ref: Ellis, Frank H. Canada's Flying Heritage.
University of Toronto Press, 1954.

**25 JULY, 1928.** National Air Transport Ltd. began operations at Toronto, Ontario.

**28 JULY, 1928.** The London Aero Club started flying operations at the Club field, London, Ontario.

Ref: The Financial Post, May 3, 1929, p.20

**AUGUST, 1928.** Commercial Airways Ltd. started operations. (Note that this is Commercial Airways of Edmonton, Alberta, and is not be be confused with other Commercial Airways companies.)

**2 AUGUST, 1928.** Frank T. Courtney and crew were forced down in the Atlantic 500 miles from the Azores in a Dornier Wal, G-CAJI. The crew was rescued and the aircraft later brought to Montreal, Quebec. The flight was financed by a Canadian, Elwood B. Hosmer.

Ref: Frank T. Courtney. The Eighth Sea. Doubleday & Co., New York, 1972.

**7 AUGUST, 1928.** *The first tri-motored aircraft registered in Canada was* a Ford 4-AT, G-CATX, of British Columbia Airways Ltd., Victoria, British Columbia.

The Stinson SM-1 "Greater Rockford" at Cochrane, Ontario on its projected flight to Sweden. Left to right, B.R.J. "Fish" Hassell and P.D. "Shorty" Cramer. (via R.S. Baker)

The American registered Fairchild FC-2W-2, in which S/L A.E. Godfrey made his trans-Canada seaplane flight of September 1928. (RCAF)

Pilot Brintnell signs for express packages before leaving on the experimental air mail flight 13 September 1928. Left to right, J. Hunter, J. Bracken, Premier of Alberta; A. MacNeill, all passengers on the flight; W.L. Brintnell and express company representative. (W.C.A. Coll.)

**10 AUGUST, 1928.** Continental Aero Corp. was formed at Montreal, Quebec.

**16 AUGUST, 1928.** Bert R.J. (Fish) Hassell, pilot, and Parker (Shorty) Cramer landed at Cochrane, Ontario, in their Stinson SM-1 Detroiter "Greater Rockford" on the first leg of a projected flight from Rockford, Illinois, to Stockholm, Sweden. They left on the 18th and force landed on the Greenland icecap.

Ref: Ellis, F.H. & E.M. Atlantic Air Conquest. Wm. Kimber, London, 1963.

**23 AUGUST, 1928.** B.C. Airways Ltd. commenced a scheduled air service between Vancouver, British Columbia, Victoria, B.C., and Seattle, Washington.

**25 AUGUST, 1928.** The Ford 4-AT of B.C. Airways crashed in Puget Sound in fog and the two crew and five passengers were killed. Vancouver-Victoria-Seattle service terminated.

**28 AUGUST, 1928.** C.H. (Punch) Dickins left Winnipeg, Manitoba, in a Fokker Super Universal with Lt-Col C.D.H. MacAlpine on long inspection trip of 3,956 miles in northern Canada, including a flight across the barren lands for first time. They returned to Winnipeg on 9 September.

Ref: Molson, K.M. Pioneering in Canadian Air Transport.
James Richardson & Sons Ltd., Winnipeg, 1974.

**5-8 SEPTEMBER, 1928.** A seaplane flight from Ottawa, Ontario, to Vancouver, British Columbia, was carried out by S/L A.E. Godfrey and F/S M. Graham of the RCAF in a U.S.-registered Fairchild FC-2W2 fitted with long-range tanks, on personal loan to S/L Godfrey by Sherman M. Fairchild.

**8 SEPTEMBER, 1928.** The Border Cities Aero Club started flying operations at Walker Airport, Walkerville, Ontario.

Ref: The Financial Post, May 3, 1929.

**12 SEPTEMBER, 1928.** W.H.E. Drury with M.E. Oliphant as passenger won the Windsor, Ontario, to Los Angeles, California race in a Waco Ten.

Ref: Drury Wins International Air Derby. Canadian Aviation, Vol. I, No. 5, October, 1928, p. 12.

**13-20 SEPTEMBER, 1928.** First survey flight over the Prairie Air Mail Route was made by W.L. Brintnell in a de Havilland D.H.61, Giant Moth, for Western Canada Airways.

Ref: Molson, K.M. Pioneering in Canadian Air Transport.
James Richardson & Sons, Winnipeg, 1974.

**15 SEPTEMBER, 1928.** The Calgary Aero Club started flying operations at the Calgary Municipal Airport.

Ref: The Financial Post, May 3, 1929, p.20

Above: The prototype Reid Rambler at Cartierville Airport. J.R. Douglas, engine installation engineer is in the cockpit.
(Reid Aircraft)

Right: Lt-Commander H.C. MacDonald just before boarding his Moth at Harbour Grace Newfoundland, 1928.
(Mus. Sc. & Tech.)

Below: T.M. "Pat" Reid and H.A. "Doc" Oaks' two aircraft, a Fokker Super Universal and Fairchild FC-2W-2 respectively, at Richmond Gulf at the end of their long flight down the eastern shore of Hudson Bay for N.A.M.E. on 11 Jan. 1929.
(Mus. Sc. & Tech.)

**29 SEPTEMBER, 1928.** The prototype Reid Rambler was test flown by Martin Berlyn at Cartierville, Quebec.

**1 OCTOBER, 1928.** Daily scheduled passenger and mail service was inaugurated between Montreal, Quebec, and Albany and New York, New York, by Canadian Colonial Airways Ltd.

**1 OCTOBER, 1928.** Daily mail service commenced between Montreal, Quebec, and Toronto, Ontario, by Canadian Airways Ltd. (old) replacing previous tri-weekly service.

**17 OCTOBER, 1928.** Com.H.C. MacDonald left Harbour Grace, Newfoundland, for London, England, in de Havilland D.H.60, Moth. He was lost at sea.

Ref: Ellis, Frank H. Canada's Flying Heritage, Univ. of Toronto Press, 1953.

**14 NOVEMBER, 1928.** Hudson Strait Expedition returned to Quebec City, Quebec.

Ref: Manning, D.F.C., W/C R.V. The Hudson Strait Expedition 1927-8. Can. Geo. Jour. Vol. LXII, No. 2, February, 1961.

**16 NOVEMBER, 1928.** A daily experimental air mail service was started by Western Canada Airways over the Prairie Air Mail Route which was continued for twenty days.

Ref: Molson, K.M. Pioneering in Canadian Air Transport. James Richardson & Sons, Winnipeg, 1974.

**26 NOVEMBER, 1928.** Leonard S. Flo left Walker Airport, Windsor, Ontario, in a Spartan C3-2 biplane on non-stop flight to Havana, Cuba. He was forced to land at Key West, Florida, due to illness from anti-sleep pills.

Ref: New York Times, New York, N.Y., 27 November, 1928, p. 14.
New York Times, New York, N.Y., 28 November, 1928, p. 29.

**10-29 DECEMBER, 1928.** Daily experimental mail service was carried out by Western Canada Airways between Winnipeg, Manitoba, and Regina, Saskatchewan, Regina and Calgary, Alberta, and Regina and Edmonton, Alberta.

**DECEMBER, 1928.** Compagnie Aérienne Franco-Canadienne bought property at Pointe aux Trembles (Montreal), Quebec, previously rented, to build an air base.

Ref: Air Transportation. 8 December, 1928, p. 15.

**1928.** The Trans-Canada (McKee) Trophy was awarded to C.H. (Punch) Dickins for his flight across the Barren Lands.

# 1929

**JANUARY, 1929.** T.M. (Pat) Reid and H.A. (Doc) Oaks flew into Hudson Bay area. First winter flights in this area.

Dr. M.R. Bow hands W.R. "Wop" May the diptheria antitoxin at Edmonton which is to be flown to Fort Vermilion. (W.R. May Coll.)

This D.H.60 Moth, CF-CAK, was the first aircraft registered in the new CF- registration series. (R. Reid photo)

The Bellanca CH-200 in which G.W. Halderman and J. Hayden flew from Windsor, Ontario, to Havana. (Bellanca photo)

**2 JANUARY, 1929.** Interprovincial Airways Ltd. was formed and took over flying operations and aerial survey work of Fairchild Aviation Ltd.

**2-3 JANUARY, 1929.** W.R. (Wop) May and J.V. Horner flew diphtheria antitoxin from Edmonton to Fort Vermilion, Alberta, in a wheel-equipped Avro 594 Avian.

Ref: Ellis, Frank H. The Saviours of Little Red River. Western Wings, October, 1959.

**3 JANUARY, 1929.** A Fairchild FC-2W-2 and a Fokker Super Universal of N.A.M.E. Ltd. piloted by H.A. (Doc) Oaks and T.M. (Pat) Reid reached Richmond Gulf on the east coast of Hudson Bay having left Cochrane , Ontario, on December 29.

Ref: Edmonton Journal. January 3, 1929.

**16 JANUARY, 1929.** The Vickers Syndicate was formed and shortly bought control of International Airways, Canadian Airways (old), Canadian Transcontinental Airways and Interprovincial Airways. The last company comprised the aircraft operating portion of Fairchild Aviation Ltd.

Ref: Molson, K.M. Pioneering in Canadian Air Transport. James Richardson & Sons, Winnipeg, 1974.

**23 JANUARY, 1929.** An air service was started down the Mackenzie River, C.H. (Punch) Dickins left Fort McMurray, Alberta, in a Fokker Super Universal of Western Canada Airways and continued north to Fort Simpson, Northwest Territories.

Ref: Molson, K.M. Pioneering in Canadian Air Transport. James Richardson & Sons, Winnipeg, 1974.

**28 JANAURY, 1929.** The first aircraft in the new CF- series was registered CF-CAK in the name of the Hamilton Aero Club, a de Havilland D.H.60 Moth. The CF- series was introduced on 1 January, 1929, and continued until 31 December, 1973.

**28 JANUARY, 1929.** The Pratt & Whitney Aircraft Co. of Hartford, Connecticut, announced the formation of a Canadian company which would start operation in leased quarters at Longueuil, Quebec.

Ref: New York Times, January 28, 1929.

**23 FEBRUARY, 1929.** George W. Haldeman, pilot, and James Hayden flew from Windsor, Ontario, to Havana, Cuba - 1,404 miles in 12 hrs 56 min in a Bellanca CH-200.

**MARCH, 1929.** National Air Transport Ltd. operated Windsor-Toronto, Ontario, service.

Ref: Air Transportation. 9 March, 1929, p. 38.

**MARCH, 1929.** Curtiss-Reid Aircraft Ltd. let a contract for construction of new factory at Cartierville Airport, Quebec.

The new de Havilland factory completed in 1929 on Sheppard Avenue beside the CN tracks. The wooden hangar with MOTH on the roof had been moved from Mt. Dennis. (DHC photo)

The Sikorsky used in the Toronto-Buffalo service is christened by Mrs. Howard Ferguson, 15 July, when the mail contract began. (Toronto City Archives)

**APRIL, 1929.** De Havilland Aircraft of Canada bought 70-acre site on Sheppard Avenue, Toronto, Ontario.

Ref: Air Transportation. 6 April, 1929, p. 131.

**4 MAY, 1929.** USN balloon No. 1 landed at Savage Harbour, Prince Edward Island, winner of National Elimination Balloon Race; 952 miles in 42 hrs 20 mins.

**4-11 MAY, 1929.** The *Montreal Aircraft Exhibition* was held at the Stadium Building, *Montreal, Quebec.*

**17 MAY, 1929.** *The first Canadian to save his life by parachute* was Canadian Vickers test pilot Colin Spenser (Jack) Caldwell, who parachuted from a spinning Vedette flying boat at Montreal, Quebec.

**25 MAY, 1929.** An air meet was held at Winnipeg, Manitoba. First air meet in western Canada.

**JUNE, 1929.** Boeing Aircraft of Canada Ltd. was formed at Vancouver, British Columbia, by the Boeing Airplane Co. and Hoffar-Beeching Shipyards.

**3 JUNE, 1929.** An Ottawa, Ontario, air meet was sponsored by Ottawa Flying Club.

**6 JUNE, 1929.** Hamilton City Airport was opened.

Ref: Air Transportation. 16 May, 1929, p. 16.

**8 JUNE, 1929.** Flight was planned from Saskatoon, Saskatchewan, to London, England, via Fort Churchill, Nottingham Island, Port Burwell, Greenland and Iceland by Ben Brotman and Bruce (Reg) Ronald in a Lockheed Vega.

Ref: New York Times, New York, N.Y., 9 June, 1929, p. 2.

**20 JUNE, 1929.** C.S. (Jack) Caldwell and two passengers were killed when they hit high tension wires over the St. Lawrence River at Montreal, Quebec, in a Fokker Super Universal.

Ref: Montreal Daily Star, Montreal, Que., 21 June, 1929, p. 1.

**29 JUNE, 1929.** Scheduled passenger service was begun between Toronto, Ontario, and Buffalo, New York, by Colonial Western Airways Inc. using Sikorsky S-38 amphibians.

Ref: Long, C.D. Buffalo - Toronto by Air. CAHS Journal, Vol. 8, No. 3, Fall, 1970.

The crew of the "'Untin' Bowler" in front of their Sikorsky before leaving Chicago. L-R, Robert Wood, reporter, Parker D. Cramer, co-pilot and Robert H. Gast, pilot. (Chicago Tribune)

The Fokker G-CASC used by W. Leigh Brintnell in his flight from Vancouver, B.C. to Winnipeg, Man. in July 1929. (WCA Archives)

**1 JULY, 1929.** *Canada's western Arctic coast was reached by air for first time.* C.H. (Punch) Dickins landed at Aklavik, Northwest Territories, in a Fokker Super Universal of Western Canada Airways Ltd.

Ref: Molson, K.M. Pioneering in Canadian Transport. James Richardson & Sons Ltd., Winnipeg, 1974.

**1 & 2 JULY, 1929.** The First Maritime Provinces Air Pageant was held at Moncton, New Brunswick, to mark the opening of Moncton Municipal Airport.

**7 JULY, 1929.** Sikorsky S-38, "'Untin' Bowler" with pilot Robert Gast & crew, landed in Hudson Strait on a flight from Chicago to Berlin. It flew to Port Burwell on 9th and aircraft was destroyed by sea there on 14th.

Ref. Ellis, F.H. & E.M. Atlantic Air Conquest. Wm. Kimber, London, 1963.

**7 JULY, 1929.** D.S. Zimmerly flew non-stop from Brownsville, Texas, to Winnipeg, Manitoba, in 16 hours in a Barling NB-3.

Ref: Air Transportation. 20 July, 1929, p. 8.

**19 JULY, 1929.** The Aviation Corporation of Canada was formed and took over control of four eastern Canada air transport companies from the Vickers Syndicate (see January 26).

Ref: Molson, K.M. Pioneering in Canadian Air Transport. James A. Richardson & Sons, Winnipeg, 1974.

**19 JULY, 1929.** Capt Ross G. Hoyt arrived at Edmonton, Alberta, in a Curtiss Hawk on a flight from New York to Nome, Alaska. He left for Whitehorse, Yukon Territory.

**21 JULY, 1929.** Capt Ross G. Hoyt force landed his Curtiss Hawk at Valemoubt, British Columbia, on return flight to New York from Nome, Alaska, via Whitehorse, Yukon Territory.

Ref: New York Times, New York, N.Y., 22 July, 1929, p. 3.

**27 JULY, 1929.** W.L. Brintnell in the Fokker F.VII/3m of Western Canada Airways flew from Vancouver, British Columbia, to Winnipeg, Manitoba, in 10 hours, 30 minutes flying time with a stop at High River, Alberta. First time route had been flown with only one stop.

Ref: Molson, K.M. Pioneering in Canadian Air Transport. James Richardson & Sons. Winnipeg, 1974.

**JULY, 1929.** An Aeronautics Section was established by the National Research Council, Ottawa, Ontario, under the direction of J.H. Parkin.

**AUGUST, 1929.** The Bellanca Aircraft of Canada Ltd. was formed at Montreal, Quebec, to sell and service Bellanca aircraft, with the ultimate intention of manufacturing them as the market developed.

Members of the 1929-30 Wilkins Antarctic Expedition. L-R, Parker D. Cramer, first pilot; Sir Hubert Wilkins, leader, S.A. (Al) Cheesman, second pilot; Orval Porter, mechanic.
(photo S.A. Cheesman)

**12 AUGUST, 1929.** John G. (Tex) Rankin flew from Vancouver, British Columbia, to Agua Caliente, Mexico - 1,350 miles in 13 hrs, 7 mins in a Great Lakes 2T-1.

Ref: Air Transportation. 29 August, 1929, p. 35.

**26 AUGUST, 1929.** *First emergency parachute jump made by a member of the RCAF.* Sgt J.M. Ready jumped from de Havilland D.H.60 Moth, G-CYXH, over Windigo Island, Lac du Bonnet, Manitoba, after controls failed in a dive.

**9 SEPTEMBER, 1929.** The two aircraft of the MacAlpine party landed at Dease Point on the Arctic coast of the Northwest Territories out of fuel.

Ref: Molson, K.M. Pioneering in Canadian Air Transport. James Richardson & Sons. Winnipeg, 1974.

**20 SEPTEMBER, 1929.** Plans for a search for the missing MacAlpine party were begun.

Ref: Molson, K.M. Pioneering in Canadian Air Transport. James Richardson & Sons. Winnipeg, 1974.

**28 SEPTEMBER, 1929.** Silas Alward Cheesman sailed from New York as a pilot with Sir Hubert Wilkins's 1929-30 Antarctic expedition. He was the first Canadian to participate in the aerial exploration of the Antarctic.

Ref: Thomas, Lowell. Sir Hubert Wilkins, Arthur Barker Ltd., London, 1962.

**5 OCTOBER, 1929.** The Fifth National (Ford) Air Tour left Windsor for Toronto, Ontario. It went on to Montreal, Quebec, on the 6th via Ottawa, Ont., and left for Portland, Maine, on the 7th.

**5-6 OCTOBER, 1929.** Montreal Air Pageant was held at St. Hubert, Quebec.

**9 OCTOBER, 1929.** W.H. Cannon and Leonce Lizotte in a Travel Air 6000 of Curtiss-Reid Airways Ltd. were lost on a flight from St. Félicien to Chibougamau, Quebec. Crash site was found by Indians near Riviére au Fortin in December 1930.

Ref: New York Times, New York, N.Y., 26 December, 1930, p. 3.

**9 OCTOBER, 1929.** Urban F. Diteman arrived at St. John's, Newfoundland, from Fredericton, New Brunswick, in the Barling NB-3 "Golden Hind". He left from Harbour Grace on 22 October for London, England and was lost at sea.

Ref: Ellis, F.H. & E.M. Atlantic Air Conquest. Wm. Kimber, London, 1963.

**NOVEMBER, 1929.** The Canadian Flying Clubs Association was formed to co-ordinate the clubs activities and represent them in dealing with the Government.

**The two search aircraft at Cambridge Bay, picking up the members of the stranded MacAlpine party, November 6, 1929. (W.C.A. Archives)**

**The three Bellanca CH-300s of Commercial Airways being readied at Fort McMurray for their first air mail flight down the Mackenzie River on December 10, 1929. (W.R. May photo)**

**NOVEMBER, 1929.** T.M. (Pat) Reid was appointed to lead the C.B. Eielson search in Alaska.

Ref. Reid, T.M.(Pat). The Search for Carl Ben Eielson. CAHS Journal, Vol. 6, Nos. 2 & 3, Summer & Fall, 1968.

**3 NOVEMBER, 1929.** The missing MacAlpine party, guided by Eskimos, reached the Hudson's Bay Post at Cambridge Bay, on Victoria Island, Northwest Territories.

Ref: Molson, K.M. Pioneering in Canadian Air Transport. James Richardson & Sons. Winnipeg, 1974.

**4 DECEMBER, 1929.** All members of the missing MacAlpine party reached civilization, having been brought out by aircraft under difficult circumstances.

Ref: Molson, K.M. Pioneering in Canadian Air Transport. James Richardson & Sons. Winnipeg, 1974.

**9 DECEMBER, 1929.** A daily air mail service was inaugurated between Moncton, New Brunswick, and Montreal, Quebec, by Canadian Airways Ltd. (old).

**10 DECEMBER, 1929.** Commercial Airways Ltd. of Edmonton, Alberta, commenced operating an airmail route down the Mackenzie River under contract to the Post Office Department.

**1929.** *First Canadian woman obtained a Master's Degree in Aeronautical Engineering.* Miss E.G. MacGill obtained her M.S.E. at University of Michigan.

**1929.** The Trans-Canada (McKee) Trophy was awarded to W.R. (Wop) May for his flight carrying diphtheria antitoxin from Edmonton to Fort Vermilion, Alberta (see 2-3 January).

**T.M. (Pat) Reid, photographed beside his Fairchild during the search for Carl Ben Eilson.**

**(G. Swartman photo)**

The Fairchild KR-21, CF-AKR, in which W.G. Barker was killed at Rockcliffe. It is seen here at Farmingdale, N.Y. before leaving for Canada and has a pair of skis lashed to its center section struts. (Fairchild)

The Southern Cross rests at Harbour Grace after circling all night, waiting for the fog to clear. (Mus. Sc. & Tech.)

# 1930

**1 JANAURY, 1930.** The Aircraft Engine Laboratory started operations at National Research Council, Ottawa, Ontario. Initial work was confined to fuels and lubricants.

**23 JANUARY, 1930.** First complete airport lighting system in Canada commenced operation at Calgary, Alberta.

Ref: Brett, R.de R. Canada's First Completely Lighted Airport Described. Canadian Air Review. May, 1930, p. 21.

**5 FEBRUARY, 1930.** Mrs J.M. Miller, New York City, N.Y., was issued Canadian commercial pilot's license, No. 631, the first to be issued to a woman.

**3 MARCH, 1930.** The inaugural flight over the Prairie Air Mail Route was carried out by Western Canada Airways Ltd.

Ref: Molson, K.M. Pioneering in Canadian Air Transport. James Richardson & Sons. Winnipeg, 1974.

**12 MARCH, 1930.** W.G. Barker was killed in a flying accident at Rockcliffe Aerodrome, Ottawa, Ontario, while demonstrating a Fairchild KR-21.

**APRIL, 1930.** A special demonstration (aerobatic) flight of Armstrong-Whitworth Siskin fighters was formed at Camp Borden, Ontario, by the RCAF.

**25 JUNE, 1930.** Sir Charles Kingsford Smith and crew arrived at Harbour Grace, Newfoundland, from Ireland in the Fokker F.VII/3m, "Southern Cross". They left the following day for New York City, N.Y.

Ref: Ellis, F.H. & E.M. Atlantic Air Conquest. Wm. Kimber, London, 1963.

**27 JUNE, 1930.** Canadian Airways, Ltd. was incorporated. (Also see 25 November, 1930.)

**29 JUNE, 1930.** Roger Q. Williams and J. Erroll Boyd landed back at New York City, N.Y., after a return non-stop flight to Bermuda in the Bellanca WB-2, "Columbia".

Ref: New York Times, New York, N.Y., 30 June, 1930.

**6 JULY, 1930.** S/L C.S. Wynne-Eaton, RAF, crashed on take-off from Lester's Field, St. John's, Newfoundland, in his D.H.80A, Puss Moth, G-AAXI, when his special tail skid dolly failed to release on a trans Atlantic flight attempt.

Ref: Ellis, E.H. & E.M. Atlantic Air Conquest. Wm. Kimber. London, 1963.

**The R-100 at St. Hubert Airport during its visit in August 1930. This was the only occasion that a large rigid dirigible visited Canada. (RCAF)**

**Henry Mears and the Lockheed Vega "City of New York" which crashed on takeoff in Newfoundland. (Lockheed)**

**The famous Bellanca "Columbia" on the beach at Tresco, Scilly Isles after its second Atlantic flight of 9-10 October, 1930. It was the first aircraft to make two Atlantic crossings. (via G.C. Kohn)**

**31 JULY, 1930.** *First aircraft towed glider flight in Canada.* A.H. Wilson, in a Boeing Canada primary glider, was towed into the air by J.H. Holley in a Fleet Model 2 at Vancouver, British Columbia.

Ref: Judge, T.R. The Fleeting Thirties; The B.C. Era (Sect. 1). CAHS Journal, Vol. 13, No. 4, Winter, 1975.

**1 AUGUST, 1930.** The British dirigible R-100 arrived at St. Hubert Airport, Montreal, Quebec, after a flight from Cardington, England. On 9-10 August, it made a flight over the Province of Ontario and returned to St. Hubert. It left on 13 August for the return flight to England.

Ref: Ellis, F.H. & E.M. Atlantic Air Conquest. Wm. Kimber, London, 1963.

**2 AUGUST, 1930.** John Brown, pilot, and Henry Mears landed at Harbour Grace, Newfoundland, in their Lockheed Vega "City of New York" after a flight from New York. Continuing a projected world flight, a tire blew on take-off and the aircraft was wrecked.

Ref: Ellis, F.H. & E.M. Atlantic Air Conquest. Wm. Kimber, London, 1963.

**23 AUGUST, 1930.** Wolfgang von Gronau, navigator, Eduard Zimmer, pilot, and crew reached Cartwright, Labrador, in a Dornier Wal flying boat on a flight from Greenland. They left on the 24th and landed at Queensport, Nova Scotia. They flew to Halifax, Nova Scotia, on the 25th and left for New York on the 26th.

Ref: Ellis, F.H. & E.M. Atlantic Air Conquest. Wm. Kimber. London, 1963.

**5 SEPTEMBER, 1930.** W.E. Gilbert flew over the North Magnetic Pole in a Fokker Super Universal.

**14 SEPTEMBER, 1930.** Sixth National Air Tour arrived at Stevenson Field, Winnipeg, Manitoba. It left for Brandon, Manitoba, and Saskatoon, Saskatchewan on the 15th. It went on to North Battleford, Saskatchewan, and Edmonton, Alberta, on the 16th. It arrived at Calgary, Alberta, the following day and went on to Lethbridge, Alberta, and Great Falls, Montana, on the 18th.

**17 SEPTEMBER, 1930.** An air meet was held at Edmonton, Alberta, by Edmonton & Northern Alberta Aero Club and the Edmonton Chamber of Commerce.

Ref: Canadian Aviation, Vol. 3, No. 11, November, 1930, p. 15.

**8 OCTOBER, 1930.** J. Erroll Boyd, pilot, and Harry P. Connor, navigator, arrived at Harbour Grace, Newfoundland, from Charlottetown, Prince Edward Island in the Bellanca WB-2 "Columbia".

**9-10 OCTOBER, 1930.** *J. Erroll Boyd became first Canadian to fly the Atlantic* when he and Harry P. Connor landed at Tresco, Scilly Isles, in Bellanca WB-2 "Columbia" after flying from Harbour Grace, Newfoundland.

Ref: Ellis, F.H. & E.M. Atlantic Air Conquest. Wm. Kimber. London, 1963.

The D.H. 60 Moth, CF-AGL, in which A.D. Sullivan and D. Fraser brought the first air mail to Newfoundland from Canada. (via A.G.K. Edward)

Joe Walsh beside the lost Junkers when he and Wasson reached it on November 28, 1930. (Mus. Sc. & Tech.)

**22 OCTOBER, 1930.** Sherwin Cottingham bought the Bellanca WB-2 "Columbia" and presented it to J. Erroll Boyd.

Ref: New York Times, New York, N.Y., 23 October, 1930.

**19 NOVEMBER, 1930.** First airmail from Canada arrived at St. John's, Newfoundland. A D.H. 60 Moth of Newfoundland Airways arrived at Mount Pearl, near St. John's, piloted by D.C. Fraser, with A.D. Sullivan as passenger. Flight originated at Toronto, Ontario, on 4 November.

Ref: Dalwick, R.E.R. & Harmer, C.H.C. Newfoundland Air Mails 1919-1939. H.R. Harmer Ltd. London, 1953.

**24 NOVEMBER, 1930.** E.J.A. Burke's Junkers F-13 missing since 11 October, was sighted on the Liard River, British Columbia, by Everett Wasson. The passengers had survived but Burke died of exposure.

Ref: Ellis, F.H., Canada's Flying Heritage. Univ. of Toronto Press, 1954.

**25 NOVEMBER, 1930.** Canadian Airways, Ltd. came into operating reality with acquisition of companies controlled by the Aviation Corporation of Canada and Western Canada Airways Ltd.

Ref: Molson, K.M. Pioneering in Canadian Air Transport. James A. Richardson & Sons. Winnipeg, 1974.

**1930.** The Trans-Canada (McKee) Trophy was awarded to J.H. Tudhope for his development of air mail routes.

**Soon after Canadian Airways started operating in November 1930 its insignia became a familiar emblem in Canadian skies from coast to coast. (Canadian Airways Archives)**

J.G. Hall's Lockheed Altair in which he flew from Vancouver to Aqua Caliente on 19 June, 1931. (Lockheed)

Ruth Nichols and the Lockheed Vega that crashed on landing at Saint John, N.B., on 22 June, 1931. (Pratt & Whitney)

The Hoiris/Hillig Bellanca "Liberty" at Harbour Grace before its successful Atlantic crossing 24 June. (Mus. Sc. & Tech.)

# 1931

**3 FEBRUARY, 1931.** Winnipeg, Manitoba-Pembina, North Dakota, air service was inaugurated by Canadian Airways. First international service operated by Canadian Airways Ltd.

**APRIL, 1931.** Airmail contracts were curtailed.

Ref: Molson, K.M. Pioneering in Canadian Air Transport. James A. Richardson & Sons. Winnipeg, 1974.

**15 MAY, 1931.** Commercial Airways Ltd. of Edmonton was purchased by Canadian Airways Ltd.

Ref: Molson, K.M. Pioneering in Canadian Air Transport. James A. Richardson & Sons. Winnipeg, 1974.

**26 MAY, 1931.** J.D. Parkinson took off from Cartierville Airport, Montreal, Quebec, in the prototype Curtiss-Reid Rambler III in an attempt to establish a new Canadian altitude record. The barograph froze and only recorded 18,000 ft. although it was believed that 22,000 ft. was reached.

Ref: Montreal Daily Star, Que., 30 May, 1931, p.42.

**6 JUNE, 1931.** Barker Field was opened at Toronto, Ontario, by Mrs. W. G. Barker and Lt. Col. W. A. Bishop.

**15 JUNE, 1931.** The radio beam was flown by a commercial flight for the first time in Canada. Pilot E.W. Stull in a Fokker F.14A of Canadian Airways flew from Winnipeg, Manitoba, to Moose Jaw, Saskatchewan.

**19 JUNE, 1931.** James Goodwin Hall flew from Vancouver, British Columbia, to Agua Caliente, Mexico, in 7 hrs, 48 mins in a Lockheed Altair.

Ref: New York Times, New York, N.Y., 20 June, 1931, p. 3.

**JUNE 1931.** The first tests of the new wind tunnel at the National Research Council, Ottawa, Ontario, were carried out during the second week of June.

Ref: Montreal Daily Star, Montreal, Que., 13 June, 1931.

**22 JUNE, 1931.** Ruth Nichols crashed on landing at Saint John, New Brunswick, in a Lockheed Vega on a projected Atlantic flight from New York.

Ref: Ellis, F.H. & E.M. Atlantic Air Conquest. Wm. Kimber. London, 1963.

**22 JUNE, 1931.** Holger Hoiris, pilot, and Otto Hillig landed at Harbour Grace, Newfoundland, from New York, in the Bellanca CH-300 Pacemaker "Liberty". They left on 24th for Denmark, but landed at Krefeld, Germany.

Ref: Ellis, F.H. & E.M. Atlantic Air Conquest. Wm. Kimber. London, 1963.

Frank Hawks' record setting Travel Air R. Texaco No. 13, photographed at Rockcliffe, Ontario, 3 July, 1931. (RCAF)

An interested crowd from Harour Grace watch the "Justice for Hungary" prepare for its Atlantic flight. (Mus. Sc. & Tech.)

John Webster and the Curtiss-Reid Rambler III which he flew in the 1931 King's Cup Air Race, photographed at Cartierville, Quebec. (Curtiss-Reid)

**23 JUNE 1931.** Wiley Post, pilot, and Harold Gatty, navigator, landed at Harbour Grace, Newfoundland, in their Lockheed Vega, "Winnie Mae" from New York. They left four hours later for England on a round the world flight.

Ref: Ellis, F.H. & E.M. Atlantic Air Conquest. Wm. Kimber. London, 1963.

**30 JUNE, 1931.** Wiley Post and Harold Gatty arrived at Edmonton, Alberta, from Fairbanks, Alaska, in their Lockheed Vega "Winnie Mae", on a round-the world flight. They left 1st July for Cleveland, Ohio.

Ref: Ellis, F.H. & E.M. Atlantic Air Conquest. Wm. Kimber. London, 1963.

**1 JULY, 1931.** The Trans-Canada Air Pageant started at Hamilton, Ontario, and toured Canadian cities until 12 September.

Ref: Canadian Aviation, March April, 1932, Vol. V, No. 3, p.8.

**2 JULY, 1931.** Frank Monroe Hawks landed at Quebec City, Quebec, on the RMS "Empress of Britain" after a European tour. He took off from the pier at Wolfe's Cove and flew to the Quebec Airport in his Travel Air Mystery S.

Ref: New York Times, New York N.Y., 3 July, 1931, p. 8.

**3 JULY, 1931.** F.M. Hawks completed the following record breaking flights in his Travel Air Mystery S: Quebec-Montreal 48 min, Montreal-Toronto 108 min, Toronto-Ottawa 70 min, Ottawa-Montreal 32 min.

Ref: New York Times, New York, N.Y., 3 July, 1931, p. 5.

**4 JULY, 1931.** Seventh National (Ford) Air Tour left Walker Airport, Windsor, Ontario, for start of tour.

**7 JULY, 1931.** F.M. Hawks flew from Montreal, Quebec, to New York in 1 hr, 45 min in his Travel Air Mystery S.

Ref: New York Times, New York, N.Y., 8 July, 1931, p. 1.

**13 JULY, 1931.** Capts Alexander Magar (christened Sandor Wilczek) and George Endres arrived at Harbour Grace, Newfoundland, from New York in their Lockheed Sirius "Justice for Hungary". They left on the 15th for Budapest, Hungary, but landed at Bieske, Hungary. (Magar was a resident of Windsor, Ontario.)

Ref: Allen, Richard Sanders. Revolution in the Sky.
Stephen Greene Press. Brattleboro, Vt. 1964.

**15 JULY, 1931.** M and C Aviation Ltd. was incorporated at Prince Albert, Saskatchewan.

**25 JULY, 1931.** John C. Webster placed thirteenth in King's Cup Air Race in England flying a Curtiss-Reid Rambler III.

Oliver Pacquette, left, and Parker Cramer beside their Packard diesel-powered Bellanca CH-300. (Unknown)

The Lindberghs taxi out in their Lockheed Sirius at Aklavik, N.W.T., on 8 August, 1931. This was the last stop in Canada on their flight to the Orient. (W.R. May photo)

Von Gronau's Dornier Wal at Long Lac, Ontario. The unidentified men on board are believed to be local residents. (S.A. Cheesman photo)

**28 JULY, 1931.** Parker (Shorty) Cramer and Oliver Louis Pacquette landed on the Abitibi River near Cochrane, Ontario, from Detroit, Michigan, in a Packard diesel-powered Bellanca CH-300, Pacemaker seaplane. They left for Rupert House, Quebec, on the 29th, flew to Great Whale River, Quebec, on 30th, and on 31th flew to Wakeham Bay on Hudson Strait. They left 1 August for Greenland. They were lost at sea on their last leg from Lerwick, Shetland Isles, to Denmark.

Ref: Ellis, F.H. & E.M. Atlantic Air Conquest. Wm. Kimber. London, 1963.

**30 JULY, 1931.** Col. & Mrs. C.A. Lindbergh landed on the Ottawa River at Rockcliffe Air Station, Ottawa, Ontario, in their Lockheed Sirius seaplane after a flight from North Haven, Maine. They left the next day for Moose Factory, Ontario. They flew to Churchill, Manitoba, on 2 August; to Baker Lake, Northwest Territories on 3 August; and to Aklavik, Northwest Territories, 4 August. They left Aklavik 8 August for Point Barrow, Alaska on their flight to the Orient.

Ref: Lindbergh, Anne Morrow. North to the Orient. Harcourt, Brace and Co., New York. 1935.

**10 AUGUST, 1931.** John C. Webster was killed in the crash of a Curtiss-Reid Rambler at St. Hubert Airport, Montreal, Quebec.

**15-16 AUGUST, 1931.** The 3rd Canadian Air Pageant was held at St. Hubert Airport, Montreal, Quebec.

Ref: Montreal Daily Star, Montreal, Que., 18 August, 1931.

**18 AUGUST, 1931.** Edwin L. Preston, pilot, and Robert H. Collingnon, radio operator, landed at Goderich, Ontario, from Detroit, Michigan, on the first leg of a projected survey flight for Transamerican Airlines Corp. of the northern air route to Copenhagen, Denmark. They were flying a Packard diesel-powered Stinson SM-2A seaplane and were repeating the original survey (see 28 July, 1931). They proceeded to Rupert House, Quebec, via Sudbury and Cockrane, Ontario, on 20 August. By 27 August they reached Port Harrison, Quebec, and were waiting for fuel. Due to the delay and lateness of the season the flight was terminated and they returned to Detroit on 6 September.

Ref: New York Times, New York, 19,21, 24, 28, & 30 August and 7 September, 1931.

**28 AUGUST, 1931.** W. von Gronau, E. Zimmer and crew landed at Port Harrison, Quebec, in their Dornier Wal flying boat after flying from Greenland. They flew to Long Lac, Ontario, on the 31st and went on to Chicago, Illinois, on 1 September.

Ref: Ellis, F.H. & E.M. Atlantic Air Conquest. Wm. Kimber. London, 1963.

**29 AUGUST - 7 SEPTEMBER, 1931.** RCAF aerobatic team performed at the National Air Races, Cleveland, Ohio.

Above:
G.W. Dean and Fairchild's Pitcairn PCA-2 autogiro. Dean made the first loop in an autogiro with this machine. (via J.A. Smith)

Right:
S/L H.J.L. (Bert) Hinkler who flew from Toronto to London, England, via the South Atlantic route October-December 1931. (DHC photo)

Below:
The Laird Solution which Major J.H. Doolittle flew from Ottawa to Mexico City via Washington, Birmingham and Corpus Christi on 20 October, 1931. (Arens/NASM)

**31 AUGUST, 1931.** Dr. J. Clarence Webster announced the donation of the John C. Webster Memorial Trophy in memory of his son. It was to be competed for annually by amateur pilots.

Ref: Montreal Daily Star, Montreal, Que., 1 September, 1931.

**SEPTEMBER, 1931.** Trenton Air Station was opened by the RCAF.

**SEPTEMBER 1931.** The first loop in an autogiro was performed by Godfrey W. Dean in a Pitcairn PCA-2 autogiro CF-ARO, owned by Fairchild Aircraft Ltd., at Willow Grove, Pennsylvania, during the week beginning 12 September.

Ref: Montreal Daily Star, Montreal, Que., 17 September, 1931, p. 31.

**8 SEPTEMBER, 1931.** The Tip Top Aerial Derby handicap race was flown in southern Ontario with start and finish at Toronto.

Ref: Hotson, Fred. W. The Tip Top Aerial Derby. CAHS Journal, Vol. 5, No. 4, Winter 1967.

**20 OCTOBER, 1931.** S/L H.J.L. (Bert) Hinkler, RAAF, left Toronto Ontario in a Canadian-registered D.H.80A Puss Moth on a long flight through the United States, South America, across the South Atlantic and terminating at London, England. This D.H.80A, CF-APK, was the first Canadian-registered aircraft to cross the Atlantic.

Ref: Ellis, F.H. & E.M. Atlantic Air Conquest. Wm. Kimber. London, 1963.

**20 OCTOBER, 1931.** Major James Harold Doolittle flew from Ottawa, Ontario, to Washington, D.C., and then on to Mexico City, Mexico via Birmingham, Alabama, and Corpus Christi, Texas, in 11 hrs 56 min in a Laird Solution.

**27 NOVEMBER, 1931.** The Junkers Ju52/1m, CF-ARM, was test flown at Longueuil, Quebec, after shipment from Germany. It remained the largest civil aircraft in Canada until 1938 when the twin-engined Lockheed 14 was introduced by Trans-Canada Airlines.

**1 DECEMBER, 1931.** James Wedell flew from Agua Caliente, Mexico, to Vancouver, British Columbia, via Reno, Nevada, in 6 hrs, 40 min in his Wedell-Williams Special.

Ref: New York Times, New York, N.Y., 2 December 1931, p. 19.

**1 DECEMBER, 1931.** F.M. Hawks flew from Vancouver, British Columbia, to Grenada, California, in his Travel Air Mystery S.

Ref: New York Times, New York N.Y., 1 December, 1931, p. 19.

**1931.** The National Research Council's first wind tunnel commenced operation at John Street, Ottawa, Ontario.

**1931.** The Trans-Canada (McKee) Trophy was awarded to G.H.R. Phillips for forest fire protection work with the Ontario Provincial Air Service.

Lou Reichers' Lockheed Altair Golden Eagle in which he flew from Montreal to Havana on 28 April, 1932. Reichers is second from the left. The upper surfaces of the aircraft were finished in gold leaf. It was later renamed Miss Liberty – see 13 May, 1932. (via R.S. Allen)

The Dornier DO-X rests on Dildo Harbour, Newfoundland, on its way to the Azores. (Mus. Sc. & Tech.)

# 1932

**23 JANUARY, 1932.** F.M. Hawks flew from Agua Caliente, Mexico, to Vancouver, British Columbia, and return in 13 hrs, 44 min in a Travel Air Mystery S.

**30 JANUARY, 1932.** Mackenzie Air Service Ltd. was formed at Edmonton, Alberta.

**15 FEBRUARY, 1932.** Almost all air mail routes were cancelled by the Canadian Government. Individual routes were shut down at various times beginning in April.

Ref: Molson, K.M. Pioneering in Canadian Air Transport. James Richardson & Sons. Winnipeg, 1974.

**31 MARCH, 1932.** RCAF appropriations were reduced by 67 per cent which necessitated a reduction in strength of 78 officers, 100 airmen and 110 civilians - almost 20 per cent of the total.

**28 APRIL, 1932.** Louis T. Reichers flew from Montreal, Quebec, to Havana, Cuba; 1,786 miles in 9 hrs in Lockheed Altair "Golden Eagle".

Ref. New York Times, New York, N.Y., 29 April, 1932, p. 19.

**13 MAY 1932.** Louis T. Reichers landed at Harbour Grace, Newfoundland, in a Lockheed Altair, "Miss Liberty". He left immediately for Dublin, Ireland, but landed by a ship, out of fuel, near the Irish coast.

Ref: Allen, Richard Sanders. Revolution in the Sky. Stephen Greene Press. Brattleboro, Vt. 1964.

**19 MAY, 1932.** Dornier DO-X with Capt F. Christensen and crew arrived at Dildo Harbour, Newfoundland, from New York and continued to Holyrood. It left 21 May for the Azores.

Ref: Ellis, F.H. & E.M. Atlantic Air Conquest. Wm. Kimber. London, 1963.

**20 MAY, 1932.** Amelia Earhart arrived at Harbour Grace, Newfoundland, and departed for Ireland in a Lockheed Vega. First woman pilot to fly Atlantic and first to fly in Newfoundland.

Ref: Ellis, F.H. & E.M. Atlantic Air Conquest. Wm. Kimber. London, 1963.

**30 MAY, 1932.** USN balloon landed at Hatton, Saskatchewan, winning the National balloon race.

**JUNE, 1932.** A gas turbine engine was made in Fort William, Ontario, by L.E. Lasley.

Ref: Canadian Aviation, Vol. V, No. 6, June, 1932, p. 20.

**7 JUNE, 1932.** Arrow Airways Ltd. was incorporated with its main operating base at The Pas, Manitoba.

R.H. Storer, left, and B.R. Ronald, with the Waco ATO in which they made the proposed non-stop Montreal-Vancouver flight attempt in 1932. (via Mrs. R.H. Storer)

Jim Mollison watches his D.H. 80A, "The Hearts Content", warming up at Pennfield Ridge, N.B. before leaving for New York. (L.M. Harrison photo)

The "Green Mountain Boy" at Harbour Grace on its intended flight to Oslo Norway was later lost at sea 26 August, 1932. (Mus. Sc. & Tech.)

**4 JULY, 1932.** Waco ATO "Vancouver Sun" with pilot R.H. Storer, and passenger Bruce Ronald, left Montreal, Quebec, on a proposed non-stop flight to Vancouver, British Columbia. Intended in-flight refueling arrangements broke down and it only reached Regina, Saskatchewan, that night after a forced landing at Sudbury, Ontario.

Ref: New York Times, New York, N.Y., 5 July, 1932, p. 18.

**5 JULY, 1932.** J. Mattern and B. Griffin arrived at Harbour Grace, Newfoundland, from New York and left for Berlin, Germany in a Lockheed Vega.

**25 JULY, 1932.** W. von Gronau, G. Roth and crew landed at Cartwright, Labrador, from Greenland in the Dornier Wal flying boat "Gronland Wal". They flew direct to Montreal, Quebec, on the 26th and then went on to Chicago, Illinois, on 2 August.

Ref: Ellis, F.H. & E.M. Atlantic Air Conquest. Wm. Kimber. London, 1963.

**9 AUGUST, 1932.** W. von Gronau, G. Roth and crew again entered Canada on their westward flight and landed their Dornier Wal "Gronland Wal" at Lac du Bonnet, Manitoba. They went on to Cormorant Lake, Manitoba, on the 13th; to Lac la Biche, Alberta, on the 16th; to Prince Rupert, British Columbia, on the 18th. They left for Alaska on the 21th.

Ref: Ellis, F.H. & E.M. Atlantic Air Conquest. Wm. Kimber, London, 1963.

**19 AUGUST, 1932.** J.A. Mollison landed at Pennfield Ridge, New Brunswick, from Portmarnock Strand, Ireland, in a D.H.80A Puss Moth. He left for New York on 21 August. First westward Atlantic solo flight.

Ref: Ellis, F.H. & E.M. Atlantic Air Conquest. Wm. Kimber. London, 1963.

**20-21 AUGUST, 1932.** The Fourth Annual Air Pageant was held at St. Hubert Airport, Montreal, Quebec.

Ref: Canadian Aviation, August, 1932, Vol. V, No. 8, p. 16.
Canadian Aviation, September, 1932, Vol. V, No. 9, p. 3.

**23 AUGUST, 1932.** Thor Solberg and Carl Peterson ditched their Bellanca K "Enna Jettick" after engine failure off south coast of Newfoundland. The crew reached shore and the aircraft later towed to Placentia Bay.

Ref: Ellis, F.H. & E.M. Atlantic Air Conquest. Wm. Kimber. London, 1963.

**23 AUGUST, 1932.** Clyde Allen Lee and John Bochken were forced down at Burgeo, Newfoundland, on a flight from Barre, Vermont, to Harbour Grace in the Stinson SM-1, Detroiter, "Green Mountain Boy". They continued on the 24th to Harbour Grace and left for Oslo, Norway, on the 26th. They were lost at sea.

Ref: Ellis, F.H. & E.M. Atlantic Air Conquest. Wm. Kimber. London, 1963.

The Hutchinson Flying Family and crew at St. John's, N.B. L-R, P. Redpath, navigator; G. Altifissh, radio operator; N.W. Alley, photographer; G.R. Hutchinson, pilot; Miss Janet Lee Hutchinson; Miss Katherine Hutchinson; J. Ruff, mechanic; Mrs. G.R. Hutchinson. (L.M. Harrison photo)

The Wedell Williams Special, used by Wedell in his Ottawa-Mexico flight of 23 October. (Mus. Sc. & Tech.)

**23 AUGUST, 1932.** George R. Hutchinson and his 'flying family' landed at Saint John, New Brunswick, in the Sikorsky S-38B "City of Richmond" after a flight from New York. They went on to Port Menier, Anticosti Island, Quebec, on the 24th; to Hopedale, Labrador, on the 30th. They left for Greenland on 2 September. Flight terminated off the Greenland coast on 11 September, but all were saved.

Ref: Ellis, F.H. & E.M. Atlantic Air Conquest. Wm. Kimber, London, 1963.

**10 SEPTEMBER, 1932.** The Rolls Royce-powered Supermarine S-6B, Schneider Cup winner (406.997 mph) was shown at the Canadian National Exhibition, Toronto, Ontario.

Ref: Aero Digest Sept. 1932, P. 74.

**5 OCTOBER, 1932.** The first action was taken to form Non-Permanent Active Air Force units when approval was given to form No. 1 (Army Co-operation) Wing with Nos. 10, 11 and 12 Squadrons located at Toronto, Ontario, Vancouver, British Columbia and Winnipeg, Manitoba.

**12 OCTOBER - 10 DECEMBER, 1932.** J.R. Hebert, of Montreal, Quebec, flew from London, England, to Cloncurry, Australia, in a D.H.60 Moth, CF-ADC.

Ref Ellis, Joyce. A Gipsy Moth's Migration. CAHS Journal, Vol. 3, No. 1, Spring, 1965.

**23 OCTOBER 1932.** James Robert Wedell flew from Ottawa, Ontario, to Mexico City, Mexico, in 11 hrs, 53 mins in his Wedell-Williams Special "Miss Patterson".

**FALL, 1932.** An unemployment relief scheme was announced by Maj-Gen A.G.L. McNaughton to construct a series of intermediate airports across Canada for a future trans-Canada airway.

**1 NOVEMBER, 1932.** Government air services were re-organized to conform with reduced appropriations. RCAF, Civil Government Air Operations and Aeronautical Engineering Division were placed under a single Senior Officer. The Controller of Civil Aviation remained separate under the Deputy Minister.

**1932.** An aircraft engine test cell was set up by the Engine Laboratory of the National Research Council, Ottawa, Ontario, on their John Street property.

**1932.** The Trans-Canada (McKee) Trophy was awarded to Maurice Burbidge for his record in flying instruction.

**1932.** The John C. Webster Memorial Trophy for amateur pilots was won by E.C. Cox of the Montreal Light Aeroplane Club.

General Balbo's Savoia Machetti S-55 flying boats being refuelled at Longueuil on 15 July 1933. (via J.F. McNulty)

Frank Hawks' famous Northrop Gamma "Sky Chief". (via J.W. Underwood)

# 1933

**MAY, 1933.** Manitoba Government Air Service commenced operations with five ex-RCAF Canadian Vickers Vedette flying boats from a main base at Lac du Bonnet, Manitoba.

**11 JUNE 1933.** First non-stop flight between New York and St. Marc, Haiti, was made by J. Erroll Boyd, pilot, Robert G. Lyon, co-pilot and Harold P. Davis, passenger, in the Bellanca WB-2, "Columbia" in 24 hours 8 minutes.

**7 JULY 1933.** J. Erroll Boyd, pilot, and Robt. G. Lyon, co-Pilot, flew from Port au Prince, Haiti, to Washington, D.C., in the Bellanca WB-2, "Columbia".

**11 JULY, 1933.** Col & Mrs C.A. Lindbergh arrived at Halifax, Nova Scotia, in their Lockheed Sirius, "Tingmissartoq", from College Point, Long Island, New York, via South Pond, Maine. They flew to Cartwright, Labrador, on the 14th via St. John's, Newfoundland. They left for Greenland on the 21st.

Ref: Ellis, F.H. & E.M. Atlantic Air Conquest. Wm. Kimber. London, 1963.

**12 JULY 1933.** General Italo Balbo, leading a flight of 24 Savoia Marchetti S-55 flying boats, landed at Cartwright, Labrador, on a flight to Chicago, Illinois, from Orbetello, Italy. He flew to Shediac, New Brunswick, on the 13th; to Montreal, Quebec, on the 14th. He left for Chicago on the 16th.

Ref: Ellis, F.H. & E.M. Atlantic Air Conquest. Wm. Kimber. London, 1963.

**28 JULY, 1933.** General Italo Balbo leading a flight of 24 Savoia Marchetti S-55 flying boats, landed at Shoal Harbour, Newfoundland, on a return flight to Italy from Chicago via New York. He left for the Azores on 8 August.

Ref: Ellis, F.H. & E.M. Atlantic Air Conquest. Wm. Kimber. London, 1963.

**22 JULY, 1933.** Wiley Post landed at Edmonton, Alberta, in his Lockheed Vega, "Winnie May" on his solo round the world flight. He refuelled and took off for a direct flight to New York.

Ref: Ellis, F.H. & E.M. Atlantic Air Conquest. Wm. Kimber. London, 1963.

**25 JULY, 1933.** F.M. Hawks arrived at Regina, Saskatchewan, after 10 hr 42 min non-stop flight from New York in his Northrop Gamma, "Sky Chief".

Ref: New York Times, 26 July, 1933, p. 3.

**AUGUST, 1933.** First Maritime Air Tour.

Ref: Canadian Aviation, Vol. VI, No. 9, September, 1933, p. 6.

The White Eagle (former Liberty) after its landing at Harbour Grace. It was repaired and back a year later as the City of Warsaw. (Mus. Sc. & Tech.)

Jim Mollison makes a final walk-around check prior to his attempted takeoff from Wasage Beach in 1933. (via D. Williams)

**4 AUGUST, 1933.** F.M. Hawks flew from Regina, Saskatchewan, to Bridgeport, Conn., 1,700 miles, in 7 hrs 50 min in his Northrop Gamma 'Sky Chief'.

Ref. New York Times, 5 August, 1933, p. 8.

**8 AUGUST, 1933.** The Bellanca CH-300, Pacemaker, "White Eagle", piloted by Emil Bergin and with Joseph and Benjamin Adamowicz passengers, landed at Harbour Grace, Newfoundland, on a projected flight to Warsaw, Poland. It was damaged on landing and flight terminated.

Ref: Ellis, F.H. & E.M. Atlantic Air Conquest. Wm. Kimber. London, 1963.

**19-20 AUGUST, 1933.** Fifth Annual Canadian Air Pagent at St. Hubert Airport, Montreal, Quebec. A goodwill flight from New York headed by Amy Mollison and F.M. Hawks attended.

Ref: Canadian Aviation, Vol. VI, No. 9, September, 1933.
New York Times, New York, N.Y., 20 August, 1933, p. 18.

**22 AUGUST, 1933.** J. Erroll Boyd announced that he would attempt to beat the solo endurance record at Toronto, Ontario, but damaged his Bellanca WB-2, "Columbia". on the 24th.

Ref: New York Times, New York, N.Y., 23 August, 1933, p. 19.
New York Times, New York, N.Y., 24 August, 1933, p. 3.

**25-26 AUGUST, 1933.** F.M. Hawks flew from Vancouver, British Columbia, to Quebec City via Kingston, Ontario, and Montreal, Quebec, in 17 hrs 10 min in his Northrop Gamma, 'Sky Chief'.

Ref: Canadian Aviation, Vol. VI, No. 9, September, 1933, p. 12.
New York Times, New York, N.Y., 27 August, 1933, p. 3.

**3 OCTOBER, 1933.** James & Amy Mollison made three unsuccessful attempts to take off from Wasaga Beach, Ontario, on a projected flight to Bagdad in a D.H.84, Seafarer II.

**1933.** The Trans-Canada (McKee) Trophy was awarded to W.E. Gilbert for his bush flying and his flight to the North Magnetic Pole.

**1933.** The John C. Webster Memorial Trophy for amateur pilots was won by E.C. Cox of the Montreal Light Aeroplane Club.

**Edward C. Cox (later S/L RCAF) of the Montreal Light Aeroplane Club who won the Webster Trophy three years in a row, 1932-33-34. (photo 1929)**
**(Pub. Arch. Can. PA 126217)**

The Bellanca, City of Warsaw (formerly Liberty and later White Eagle) at Harbour Grace in 1934. It crossed safely June 29-30. (Mus. Sc. & Tech.)

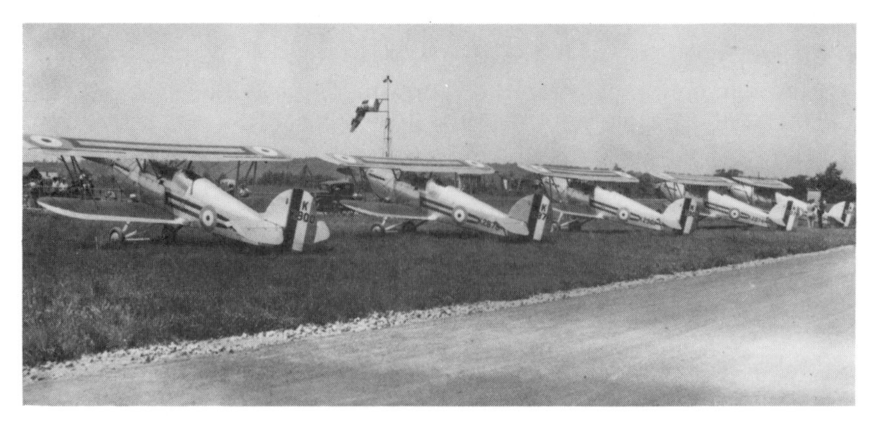

The Hawker Furies of No. 1 Squadron, RAF, at Hamilton, Ontario, in July 1934. (via G. Clow)

Reid & Ayling's "Trail of the Caribou" (formerly "Seafarer II") at Wasaga Beach prior to its successful flight in 1934. (DHC photo)

# 1934

**15 MARCH, 1934.** Prairie Airways Ltd. was incorporated at Moose Jaw, Saskatchewan.

**MAY, 1934.** Capreol & Austin Air Services Ltd. commenced operations at Toronto.

**11 JULY, 1934.** Wings Ltd. was formed.

**28 JUNE, 1934.** The Bellanca CH-300 Pacemaker"City of Warsaw", piloted by Holger Hoiris; Joseph and Benjamin Adamowicz passengers, landed at Harbour Grace, Newfoundland. It left on the 29th for Warsaw.

Ref: Ellis, F.H. & E.M. Atlantic Air Conquest. Wm. Kimber. London, 1963.

**18 JUNE - 27 JULY, 1934.** A visiting flight of five Hawker Fury aircraft from No. 1 Squadron, RAF, gave demonstrations at Ontario and Quebec cities.

**8-9 AUGUST, 1934.** *First direct flight from Canadian mainland to Europe.* James R. Ayling and Leonard G. Reid left Wasaga Beach, Ontario, in their D.H.84 Dragon "The Trail of the Caribou", and landed at Heston Airport, London, England.

Ref: Ellis, F.H. & E.M. Atlantic Air Conquest. Wm. Kimber. London, 1963.

**21 AUGUST, 1934.** Dr. Richard U Light, pilot, and Robert F. Wilson, engineer/radio-operator, landed at Sydney, Nova Scotia, in the Bellanca CH-400 Skyrocket "Asulinak", seaplane on a round-the-world flight. They left for Deer Lake, Newfoundland, on the 22nd went to Cartwright, Labrador, on the 23rd. They left 27 August for Greenland.

Ref: Ellis, F.H. & E.M. Atlantic Air Conquest. Wm. Kimber. London, 1963.

**27 AUGUST, 1934.** John Grierson landed at Lake Harbour, Baffin Island, after a flight from Greenland in his D.H.83 Fox Moth "Robert Bruce" and went on to Povungnetuk, Quebec, the same day. He flew to Eastmain, Que., via Fort George on the 29th and went to Ottawa, Ontario, on the 30th. He left for New York on 10 September.

Ref: Grierson, John. Challenge to the Poles. G.T. Foulis & Co. London, 1964.

**30 AUGUST, 1934.** United Air Transport Ltd. was formed at Edmonton, Alberta.

**1 SEPTEMBER, 1934.** Formation of Nos. 15 (Fighter) and 18 (Bomber) Squadrons of Non-Permanent Active Air Force at Montreal, Quebec, was authorized.

The Fairchild Super 71 under test at Longueuil, with Dale Atkinson in the cockpit. (Fairchild photo)

Charles Ulm's Airspeed Envoy, "Stellis Australis", at St. Hubert Aerodrome in November 1934. (J.H. Lymbumer photo)

**31 OCTOBER, 1934.** The prototype Fairchild Super 71 was test flown at Longueuil, Quebec, by D.S.E. Atkinson. It was the first aircraft designed in Canada specifically for bush flying, but it used a wing from the U.S.-designed Model 71, very slightly modified.

**19 NOVEMBER, 1934.** C.T.P. Ulm, J.S. Skilling and G. Littlejohn together with their Airspeed Envoy, Stella Australis, arrived at Quebec City, Quebec on R.M.S. Ascania. They flew to St. Hubert Airport, Montreal, Quebec on the 20th where they carried out fuel consumption tests for a trans Pacific flight. They left Montreal on the 23rd and departed from Oakland, California on 3 December for Honolulu, Hawaii. They were lost at sea.

Ref: The Montreal Daily Star, 19 November - 8 December, 1934.

**28 DECEMBER, 1934.** Quebec Airways Ltd. was incorporated.

**1934.** The Trans-Canada (McKee) Trophy was awarded to F/L E.G. Fullerton for his work in the RCAF.

**1934.** The John C. Webster Memorial Trophy for amateur pilots was won by E.C. Cox of the Montreal Light Aeroplane Club.

**Quebec Airways Limited was a subsidiary of Canadian Airways Limited, localized in the province of Quebec. The insignia was similar to CAL and seen primarily along the mail runs of the St. Lawrence River.**

C.H. (Punch) Dickins, O.B.E., Trans Canada, (McKee) Trophy winner 1928. (WCA Archives)

W.R. (Wop) May, O.B.E., Trans. Canada, (McKee) Trophy winner 1929. (Can. Airways Archives)

Dominion Skyways Limited main base of operations Rouyn, P.Q. during 1935. (S.L. Walker photo)

# 1935

**1 JANUARY, 1935.** C.H. (Punch) Dickins and W.R. May were awarded the Order of the British Empire.

**1 JANUARY, 1935.** The first awards were made to RCAF personnel. S/L R.S. Grandy received the Order of the British Empire and F/S H.J. Winny the British Empire Medal.

**6 JANUARY, 1935.** Dr Richard U. Light, pilot, and Robert F. Wilson, engineer/radio-operator, left Vancouver, British Columbia, in their Bellanca CH-400 Skyrocket "Asulinak" seaplane to continue their flight around the world. They had arrived on the R.M.S. "Empress of Canada" from Manila.

Ref: Ellis, F.H. & E.M. Atlantic Air Conquest. Wm. Kimber. London, 1963.

**JANUARY, 1935.** Quebec Airways Limited started operations.

Ref: Molson, K.M. Pioneering in Canadian Air Transport. James Richardson & Sons. Winnipeg, 1974.

**23 JANUARY, 1935.** Dominion Skyways Ltd. was formed at Montreal, Quebec, and absorbed Northern Skyways.

**4 FEBRUARY, 1935.** Starratt Airways & Transportation Ltd. was formed and took over the operations of Northern Transportation Co.

**2 APRIL, 1935.** Pan-American Airways started Fairbanks-Juneau, Alaska service via Whitehorse, Yukon Territory, using Lockheed 10 aircraft.

**15 MAY, 1935.** Formation of No. 19 (Bomber) Squadron of the NPAAF at Hamilton, Ontario, was authorized.

**3 JUNE, 1935.** Squadron Leader George Eric Brookes was awarded the Order of the British Empire.

**1 JUNE, 1935.** Formation of No. 20 (Bomber) Squadron of the NPAAF at Regina, Saskatchewan, was authorized.

**18 JULY, 1935.** Pilot Thor Solberg and navigator Paul Oscanyan arrived at St. Hubert Airport, Montreal, Quebec, in a Loening C-2 amphibian "Leif Ericsson" on a flight from New York to Norway. They left on the 19th for St. Pierre, Quebec, and went on to Cartwright, Labrador, on the 24th. They left Cartwright on the 28th for Greenland.

Ref: Ellis, F.H. & E.M. Atlantic Air Conquest. Wm. Kimber. London, 1963.

The prototype Noorduyn Norseman returning after its first flight November 14, 1935. (Noorduyn photo)

The Northrop Gamma Polar Star warming up prior to the start of its historic trans-Antarctic flight. This aircraft is now in the National Air & Space Museum, Washington. (J.H. Lymburner photo)

W.M. Archibald (L) with chief pilot Page McPhee in front of their D.H. Dragonfly at Toronto 1936. (F.W. Hotson photo)

**20 JULY, 1935.** Warrant Officer 1 Anthony Augustine Rabnett was made a Member of the British Empire.

**20 JULY, 1935.** Ist Western Canada Annual Air Show was held at Vancouver, British Columbia.

Ref: Judge, T.R. The Fleeting Thirties, Pt. 2. CAHS Journal, Vol. 13, No. 4, Winter 1975.

**20 JULY, 1935.** About 40 aircraft arrived at Cartierville Airport, Montreal, Quebec, on a Goodwill Flight from New York.

Ref: New York Times, New York, N.Y., 21 July, 1935, Sect. 2, p. 2.

**26 AUGUST, 1935.** Harold L. Farquhar and Fritz Beiler landed at Toronto, Ontario, from New York in their Beech 17R, G-ADLE, on their westward trip to England. They left Canada at Aklavik, Northwest Territories, for Nome, Alaska, after landing at Sault Ste. Marie, Ontario, Lac du Bonnet and Cormorant Lake, Manitoba, Fort McMurray, Alberta, and Fort Norman, N.W.T.

Ref: Berry, Peter, Westwards to England. AAHS Journ., Vol. 13, No. 4

**17 OCTOBER, 1935.** The Bellanca WB-2 "Columbia" was destroyed by fire in a service hangar at the Bellanca factory, New Castle, Delaware, as it was being readied for a motion picture on its career.

**14 NOVEMBER, 1935.** The prototype Noorduyn Norseman was tested at Pointe aux Trembles, Quebec, by W.J. McDonough. First all-Canadian-designed bush aircraft.

**23 NOVEMBER - 5 DECEMBER, 1935.** Lincoln Ellsworth and Herber Hollick-Kenyon, pilot, flew 2,100 miles across the Antarctic and made four landings enroute in a Northrop Gamma.

Ref: Grierson, John. Challenge to the Poles. G.T. Foulis. London, 1964.

**1935.** The Trans-Canada (McKee) Trophy was awarded to W.M. Archibald for his work in utilizing aircraft in mining development.

**1935.** The John C. Webster Memorial Trophy for amateur pilots was won by G.R. McGregor of the Kingston Flying Club.

**Gordon R. McGregor won the Webster Memorial Trophy 1935 & 36. He became a distinguished fighter pilot in WW II, and later, President of Trans Canada Airlines (Air Canada).**

**(photo Karsh Ottawa/Air Canada)**

The Vultee V-1A of Canadian Colonial Airways, used on the New York-Montreal-Ottawa route and which opened the Montreal-Ottawa leg.
(J.S. Beilby photo)

Matt Berry and the two missing RCAF flyers he found on Sept. 16, 1936. (L-R) F/L S.W. Coleman,LAC J.A. Fortey and A.M. Berry.
(via D.D. MacLaren)

Mrs. Berl Markham's Percival Vega Gull after its landing at Bauline Cove, Nova Scotia. (via W.R. Richardson)

# 1936

**1 APRIL, 1936.** The first Canadian Public Transport Pilot's License was issued to D.G. Joy, an Inspector of the Civil Aviation Branch, Department of National Defence.

**16 MAY, 1936.** Capreol & Austin Air Service Ltd. changed its name to Austin Airways Ltd.

**24 MAY, 1936.** Wilson H. Clarke, Chief Pilot of General Airways Ltd., and six passengers were killed in crash of a Bellanca CH-300 Pacemaker at Lake Puskatamika, Quebec.

**20 JULY, 1936.** First proving flight of the extension of the Newark-Montreal air service to Ottawa, Ontario, was carried out by a Vultee V-1A.

Ref: The Gazette, Montreal, Que., July 21, 1936.

**JUNE, 1936.** Newfoundland Skyways Ltd. started operations.

**1 AUGUST, 1936.** 2nd Western Canada Annual Air Show was held at Vancouver, British Columbia.

Ref: Judge, T.R. The Fleeting Thirties, Pt. 2. CAHS Journal, Vol. 13, No. 4, Winter, 1975.

**4 AUGUST, 1936.** The first of the modern air transports to be registered in Canada arrived at Vancouver, British Columbia, from California. It was a Lockheed 10A Electra, CF-AZY, of Canadian Airways which went into service immediately on the Vancouver-Seattle route.

Ref: Molson, K.M. Pioneering in Canadian Air Transport. James Richardson & Sons. Winnipeg, 1974.

**17 AUGUST - 16 SEPTEMBER, 1936.** A search in the Northwest Territories was carried out for a missing RCAF Fairchild 71 piloted by F/L S.W. Colman. A.M. (Matt) Berry of Canadian Airways found the missing aircraft.

**5 SEPTEMBER, 1936.** Mrs Beryl Markham landed at Bauline Cove, Cape Breton Island, Nova Scotia, in her Percival Vega Gull 'Messenger" after a flight from Abingdon, England.

Ref: Ellis, F.H. & E.M. Atlantic Air Conquest. Wm. Kimber. London, 1936.

**14 SEPTEMBER, 1936.** Harry T. (Dick) Merrill, pilot, and Harry Richman landed at Musgrave Harbour, Newfoundland, owing to fuel shortage on a flight from England to New York in the Vultee V-1A, "Lady Peace". They continued the same day to Harbour Grace and went on to New York on the 21st. This completed the first round-trip crossing of the Atlantic by air.

Ref: Dalwick, R.E.R. & Harmer, C.H.C. Newfoundland Air Mails. Harmer Ltd. London, 1953.

The Lieutenant-Governor of Manitoba, W.J. Tupper (L) presents the HARMON TROPHY FOR CANADA to Joseph Stevenson, father of Fred Stevenson.

The medallion awarded posthumously to Captain F.J. Stevenson for his pioneer commercial flying in the north. (via F.H. Ellis)

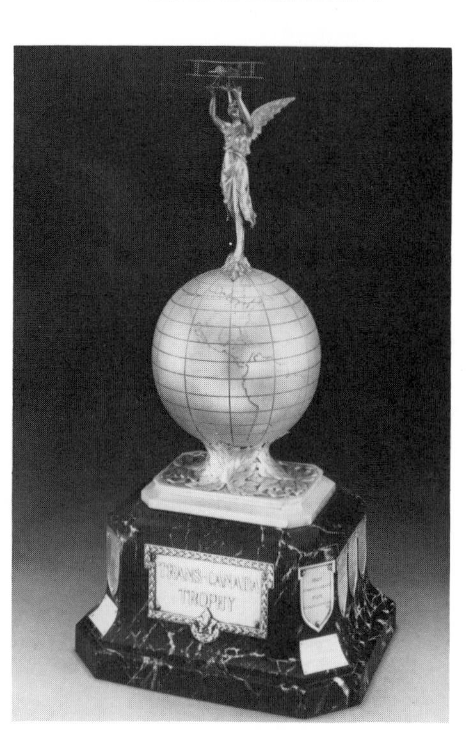


The stirling silver "Trans-Canada Trophy" also known as the "McKee Trophy" stands three feet and rests on a solid base of marble. It was awarded to A.M. "Mat" Berry in 1936 for his rescues in the north.

(via K.M. Molson)

**20 OCTOBER, 1936.** The Harmon Trophy for Canada, awarded to F.J. Stevenson for 1927, was presented posthumously to his father, Joseph Stevenson, by the Lieutenant-Governor of Manitoba, W.J. Tupper at Winnipeg, Manitoba.

Ref: Winnipeg Free Press, 22 October, 1936.

**28 OCTOBER, 1936.** J.A. Mollison landed at Harbour Grace, Newfoundland, from New York in the Bellanca 28-70 Flash "Miss Dorothy". He left on the 29th for London, England, which he reached in 9-1/4 hrs, a new record.

Ref: Ellis, F.H. & E.M. Atlantic Air Conquest. Wm. Kimber. London, 1963.

**2 NOVEMBER, 1936.** The Department of Transport was established and took over control of civil aviation from the Department of National Defence.

**1936.** The Trans-Canada (McKee) Trophy was awarded to A.M. Berry for his bush flying and two rescues made in the north.

**1936.** The John C. Webster Memorial Trophy for amateur pilots was won by G.R. McGregor of the Kingston Flying Club.

**The WEBSTER TROPHY, in memory of John C. Webster, awarded annually to the best amateur pilot in Canada.**
**(Muc. Sc. & Tech.)**

The four D.H. 90 Dragonfly aircraft of the first RCMP Air Division, 1937.

The original staff of the RCMP Air Division: (L-R): R.H. Barker, T.R. Michelson, G.F. Hart, W.R. Munroe, Superintendant R.E. Mercer, M.P. Fraser, L. Dubuc, P.M. Grant and W.E. Barnes.
(C.D. Long photos)

The Lockheed 12A Electra Jr. on its arrival at Vancouver after its flight from Montreal, 31 July 1937. Hon. C.D. Howe is in front of the doorway in the light suit. This aircraft is now in the National Aviation Museum.
(G.C. Bulger photo)

# 1937

**1 JANUARY, 1937.** Formation of No. 13 (Fighter) and No. 21 (Fighter) Squadrons of NPAAF at Calgary, Alberta, and Quebec City, Quebec, was authorized.

**16 JANUARY, 1937.** Yukon Southern Air Transport Ltd. was incorporated (formerly McConachie Air Transport Ltd.).

**6 APRIL, 1937.** A Bill was passed by Parliament authorizing the formation of Trans-Canada Air Lines Ltd.

**5 MAY, 1937.** The newly-formed Air Division of the Royal Canadian Mounted Police accepted its first aircraft, a D.H.90 Dragonfly.

Ref: Gardiner, E.P. Winged Mounties. CAHS Journal, Vol. 6, No. 4, Winter, 1968.

**12 MAY, 1937.** An RCAF detachment of eight officers and 22 airmen under the command of W/C H. Edwards participated in Coronation ceremonies of H.M. the King at London, England.

**23 MAY, 1937.** A scheduled air service was started between Montreal and Rouyn, Quebec. Inaugural flight was made by F.I. Young in a Waco ZQC-6 of Dominion Skyways Ltd.

Ref: The Montreal Gazette, Montreal, Que., 24 May, 1937.
Northern News, Kirkland Lake, Ontario, 25 May, 1937.

**3-6 JULY, 1937.** *First Atlantic crossing by commercial aircraft.* Pan-American Sikorsky S-42 "Clipper III" Capt Harold Gray flew from Port Washington, New York, to Southampton, England, via Shediac, New Brunswick and Botwood, Newfoundland.

**5 JULY, 1937.** A Ford 6-AT of United Air Transport Ltd., piloted by G.W.C. McConachie, inaugurated a regular air service from Edmonton, Alberta, to Whitehorse, Yukon Territory.

Ref: Edmonton Journal, Edmonton, Alta., 5 July, 1937.

**5-8 JULY, 1937.** Imperial Airways Short S.23 "Cavalier" Capt A.S. Wilcockson, flew from Foynes, Ireland, to Montreal, Quebec, via Botwood, Newfoundland and on to New York on 9 July.

**31 JULY, 1937.** A Lockheed 12A Electra Jr., piloted by J.H. Tudhope and J.D. Hunter, flew from Montreal, Quebec, to Vancouver, British Columbia, with intermediate stops.

Ref: Ellis, F.H. Canada's Flying Heritage. University of Toronto Press, 1954.

The Lockheed 10E used by Sir Hubert Wilkins during the winter of 1937-38 in the search for the lost Russian aviators. A Consolidated PBY flying boat had been used during August and September. (G.C. Gill photo)

The Fairchild 45-80 Sekani prototype at Longueuil, which was first flown on 24 August 1937. (Fairchild)

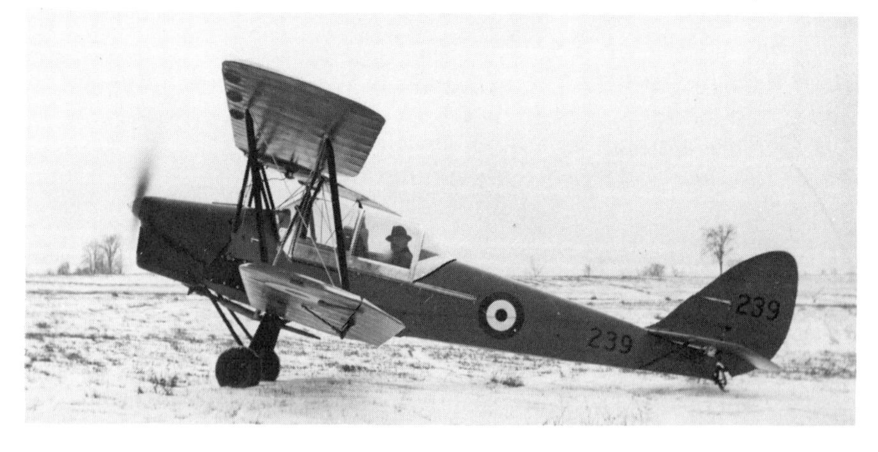


The first Canadian made Tiger Moth, D.H. 82A (Can) taxis for its first flight with P.C. Garratt at the controls. (F.W. Hotson photo)

**19 AUGUST, 1937.** Extensive search flights commenced penetrating deep in the Arctic by Sir Hubert Wilkins with pilots H. Hollick-Kenyon and S.A. Cheesman for S. Levanevsky and crew, missing on a trans-Arctic flight from Moscow. Search flights continued until March, 1938.

Ref: Grierson, John. Challenge to the Poles. G.T. Foulis & Co. London, 1964.

**24 AUGUST, 1937.** The Fairchild 45-80, Sekani, prototype was test flown at Longueuil, Quebec, by A.S. Schneider.

Ref: The Montreal Daily Star, Montreal, Que., 28 August, 1937.

**28-29 AUGUST, 1937.** An Air Pageant was held at St. Hubert Airport, Montreal, Quebec.

**1 SEPTEMBER, 1937.** Trans-Canada Air Lines flew its first regular service on the Vancouver-Seattle route in a Lockheed 10A Electra, CF-AZY, piloted by Captain E.P.H. (Billy) Wells and First Officer F.M. McGregor.

**SEPTEMBER, 1937.** A course in Aeronatical Engineering under Professor T.R. Loudon was established at the University of Toronto, Toronto, Ontario.

**SEPTEMBER, 1937.** Canadian Car & Foundry Ltd. opened its aircraft plant at Fort William, Ontario.

**15 NOVEMBER, 1937.** Squadrons of the NPAAF were renumbered by adding 100 to their number, e.g., No. 10 Squadron became No. 110 Squadron.

**21 DECEMBER, 1937.** First aircraft manufactured by De Havilland Aircraft of Canada Ltd. was test flown at Downsview, Ontario, by P.C. Garratt, a D.H.82A Tiger Moth, RCAF 239.

Ref: Long, C.D. The Tiger Moth in Canada. CAHS Journal, Vol. 7, No. 4, Winter, 1969.

**1937.** The Trans-Canada (McKee) Trophy was awarded to J.P. Romeo Vachon for his work in developing flying along the North Shore of the St. Lawrence River.

**1937.** The John C. Webster Memorial Trophy for amateur pilots was won by B.J. Bouchier of the Toronto Flying Club.

**1937.** The Aeronautical Museum was organized during the year under the sponsorship of the Associate Committee on Aeronautical Research. Exhibits were housed in the National Research Council, Ottawa, Ontario, and artifacts formed nucleus of the National Aviation Museum in 1960.

The Fleet 50 prototype at Fort Erie, Ont. 1937. (Fleet)

F.W. Fuller in his Seversky SEV-S2 which he flew from Vancouver to Oakland in 3 hrs. 8 min. on 28 May 1938.

The Short Mercury being refuelled at Longueuil after its trans Atlantic flight. (Shell Oil)

# 1938

**22 FEBRUARY, 1938.** The Fleet 50 Freighter prototype was test flown at Fort Erie, Ontario, by W.J. Sanderson.

Ref: McIntyre, M.L. The Fleet 50, Freighter. CAHS Journal, Vol. 7, No. 1, Spring, 1969.

**1 MARCH, 1938.** Western Air Command with Headquarters at Vancouver, British Columbia, was formed to control all RCAF units in British Columbia, Alberta, Saskatchewan and Manitoba.

**1 APRIL, 1938.** Formation of No. 114 (Bomber), No. 116 (Com. & Army Co-op.) and No. 117 (Fighter) Squadrons of NPAAF at London, Ontario, Halifax, Nova Scotia and Saint John, New Brunswick, was authorized.

**13 APRIL, 1938.** Ground was broken at Malton Airport, Toronto, Ontario, for the new plant of the Aircraft Division of the National Steel Car Corp. Plant later became Victory Aircraft Ltd. and Avro Aircraft Ltd.

**10 MAY, 1938.** Trans-Canada Air Lines received its first Lockheed 14.

**28 MAY, 1938.** Frank W. Fuller Jr. flew from Vancouver, British Columbia, to Oakland, California, in his Seversky SEV-S2 in 3 hrs 8 min, 43 sec.

**21 JULY, 1938.** The Short "Mercury" landed at Montreal, Quebec, piloted by Captain D.C.T. Bennett after being air-launched at Foynes, Ireland.

**25 JULY, 1938.** Short "Mercury" landed at Botwood, Newfoundland, piloted by Capt D.C.T. Bennett on its return flight to England.

**15 SEPTEMBER, 1938.** Air Training Command of the RCAF with Headquarters at Toronto, Ontario, was formed.

**1 OCTOBER, 1938.** A regular air mail service was started between Winnipeg, Manitoba, and Vancouver, British Columbia, by Trans-Canada Air Lines.

**27 OCTOBER, 1938.** Ginger Coote Airways Ltd. was incorporated at Vancouver, British Columbia.

**19 NOVEMBER, 1938.** RCAF became directly responsible to the Minister of National Defence instead of the Chief of the General Staff and achieved equal status with the RCN and Canadian Army.

Inset: (L-R): H.O. West, P.G. Johnson, D.B. Colyer, H.T. Lewis.

Missing from photo: W.P.A. Straith, M.B. Barclay.

Trans Canada Operations personnel in 1942: (L-R back row) D.R. MacLaren, W.S. Thompson, W.W. Fowler, J.T. Bain, F.M. McGregor, W.F. English, Dr. E. Dwyer, T.M. Shields DOT, E.W. Stull, J.H. Sandgathe, J.T. Dyment, (L-R front row): P.W. Baldwin, E.P. Wells, S.S. Stevens, R.F. George, J.A. Wilson Controller of Civil Aviation, O.T. Larson, R.A. Rawson, A.M. Sutherland. (Air Canada)

**1 DECEMBER, 1938.** The Non-Permanent Active Air Force was renamed the Auxiliary Active Air Force.

**1 DECEMBER, 1938.** Regular air mail service was extended east to Montreal, Quebec, from Vancouver, British Columbia, by Trans-Canada Air Lines.

**17 DECEMBER, 1938.** The Canadian Car & Foundry FBD-1 prototype, the first Canadian designed fighter, was test flown at Fort William, Ontario, by George Adye.

**1938.** The Trans-Canada (McKee) Trophy was awarded to Trans Canada Airlines' operating personnel for their work in setting up the airline.

**1938.** The John C. Webster Memorial Trophy for amateur pilots was won by G.R. McGregor of the Kingston Flying Club.

**The first Canadian fighter, the Canadian Car & Foundry FBD-1 at Fort William, Ont.**
**(Can. Car & Fdry.)**

Passengers on the first Trans Canada Airlines revenue flight preparing to leave Sea Island, Vancouver in Lockheed 14 H-2, CF-TCK. Mrs. E. Malleck holds baby Carol Anne, beside Mrs. E. Flaherty. Second from right is Grant McConachie and far right, F.W. Crickard. (Air Canada)

James A. Richardson, called the "Father of Canadian Civil Aviation" for his support of the industry during the 1920s and 1930s. (Can. Airways Arch.)

# 1939

**14 FEBRUARY, 1939.** First Canadian tests of the Worth oil dilution system were carried out by Canadian Airways Ltd. in a Junkers W-34, CF-AQW, at Sioux Lookout, Ontario.

Ref: Molson, K.M. Pioneering in Canadian Air Transport. James Richardson & Sons. Winnipeg, 1974.

**17 FEBRUARY, 1939.** First Hawker Hurricane fighters were received by the RCAF at Sea Island Airport, Vancouver, British Columbia.

**1 APRIL, 1939.** Passenger service was inaugurated between Montreal-Vancouver and to Lethbridge and Edmonton by Trans-Canada Air Lines.

**14 MARCH, 1939.** Yukon Southern Air Transport Ltd. was formed and took over the operations of United Air Transport Ltd.

**28 APRIL, 1939.** Brig. General Vladimir Kokkinaki and Major Mikhail Gordienko landed on Miscou Island, New Brunswick, after a flight from Moscow, Russia, in the prototype of the DB-3 bomber, the Ilyushin TsKB-30 "Moskva".

Ref: Ellis, F.H. & E.M. Atlantic Air Conquest. Wm. Kimber. London, 1963.

**15 MAY, 1939.** Carl Backman arrived at Botwood, Newfoundland, from Bangor, Maine, in his Monocoupe 90A. He left on 16 May for Leksand, Sweden, and was lost at sea.

Ref: Ellis, F.H. & E.M. Atlantic Air Conquest. Wm. Kimber. London, 1963.

**28 MAY, 1939.** Thomas H. Smith crashed in the bush north of St. John's, Newfoundland, in the Aeronca 65C "Baby Clipper" after leaving Old Orchard Beach, Maine, on a projected flight to London, England. Wreckage of the aircraft was found during the war and a note from the uninjured pilot stated he was walking north.

Ref: Ellis, F.H. & E.M. Atlantic Air Conquest. Wm. Kimber. London, 1963.

**26 JUNE, 1939.** The first regular Atlantic air mail service over the northern route began. Pan-American Airways Boeing 314 flying boat "Yankee Clipper" arrived at Botwood, Newfoundland, from Port Washington, New York, via Shediac, New Brunswick. Capt Harold E. Gray was in command and 20 official passengers were on board together with 2,543 pounds of mail. It left on the 27th for Foynes, Ireland.

**26 JUNE, 1939.** James A. Richardson, President of Canadian Airways Ltd., died at Winnipeg, Manitoba.

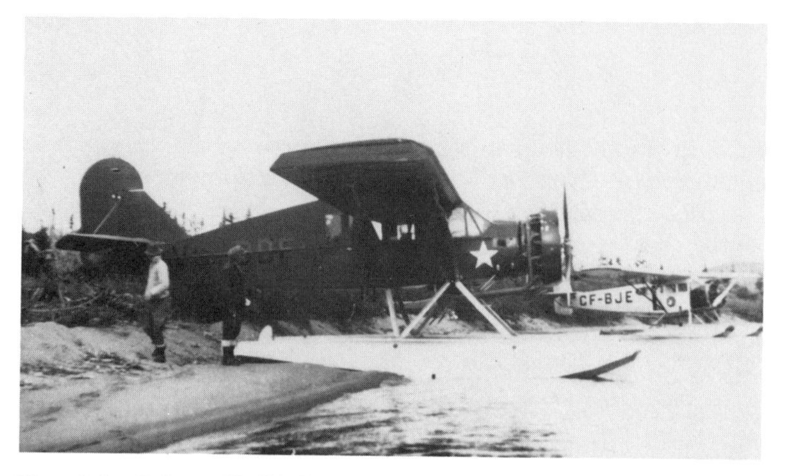


The missing Bellanca Ch-400 Skyrocket as found beached on an unnamed lake which was later named Bellanca Lake. The Fairchild 71C of Norman Forester who found the missing machine is at the right. (via R.M. Shortill)

The Canadian Westland Lysander prototype taxis in at Malton after its initial flight on 16 Aug. 1939. (C. Wright)

The trappers cabin in Labrador in which pilot J. Fecteau and his passengers took shelter and died. (Can. Airways Arch.)

**3 JULY, 1939.** Pilot Clifford Frechette and air engineer Edward Gaynor were missing on flight from North West River to Seven Islands, Quebec, in a Newfoundland Skyways' Bellanca Skyrocket. Missing aircraft was found 25 September and bodies of missing men on 3 October.

**8-9 JULY, 1939.** First passenger service was inaugurated over North Atlantic. Pan-American Boeing 314 "Yankee Clipper", Capt Arthur E. Laporte, flew from Port Washington, New York, to Southhampton, England via Shediac, New Brunswick, and Botwood, Newfoundland. 17 passengers, who were invited guests, were on board.

**18 JULY, 1939.** Airmail and passenger service was inaugurated between Montreal-Ottawa-Toronto, via Muskoka, by Trans-Canada Air Lines.

**6 AUGUST, 1939.** Imperial Airways first regular Atlantic flight made by the Short S.23 flying boat, "Caribou", commanded by Capt J.C. Kelly Rogers, arrived at Botwood, Newfoundland. It left for Montreal, Quebec, the same day. The return flight left Montreal on the 11th.

**11 AUGUST, 1939.** Alexander Loeb and Richard Decker took off from Point Michaud Beach, Cape Breton Island, Nova Scotia, for Dublin, Ireland, in their Wright J-6 powered Ryan C-1 "Shalom". They were lost at sea.

Ref: Ellis, F.H. & E.M. Atlantic Air Conquest. Wm. Kimber. London, 1963.

**16 AUGUST, 1939.** Canadian prototype of the Westland Lysander II was test flown at Malton, Ontario, by E.L. Capreol.

**26 AUGUST, 1939.** RCAF squadrons began moving to war stations.

**1 SEPTEMBER, 1939.** RCAF was placed on active service.

**3 SEPTEMBER, 1939.** Great Britain and France declared war on Germany.

**10 SEPTEMBER, 1939.** Canada declared war on Germany.

**12 SEPTEMBER, 1939.** Pilot J. Fecteau and two passengers were missing in a Canadian Airways' D.H.89A Dragon Rapide on a flight from Moisie, Quebec, to North West River, Labrador. They were subjects of an extensive search, but bodies were only found in March 1940 by a trapper in his cabin.

Ref: Globe & Mail, Toronto, Ont., 27 September, 1939, p. 1 & 2.
Globe & Mail, Toronto, Ont., 8 March, 1940, p. 10.

**The Junkers W-34, CF-ASN which was used on the longest ambulance flight in the history of Canadian Airways. (Can. Airways Archives)**

**Fleet 16B Finch IIs lined up at a typical EFTS. Finches and DH Tiger Moths did virtually all elementary training in the BCATP until superseded by the Fairchild Cornell in 1943. (L. Johnson photo)**

**14 SEPTEMBER, 1939.** *First RCAF war casualties.* Northrop Delta was missing in New Brunswick with pilot WO2 J.E. Doan and Cpl D.A. Rennie. Aircraft was found north of Fredericton, New Brunswick, in July 1958.

**18 SEPTEMBER, 1939.** RCAF Manning Pool (later No. 1 Manning Depot) was formed at Toronto, Ontario.

**29-30 SEPTEMBER, 1939.** *First member of RCAF flew over enemy territory.* S/L W.I. Clements, attached to No. 53 Squadron, RAF, made a night reconnaissance over Hamm-Hanover area from Metz, France.

**27 NOVEMBER - 20 DECEMBER, 1939.** The longest ambulance flight in Canadian history was carried out by a Junkers W-34 of Canadian Airways piloted by W.E. Catton from Winnipeg, Manitoba, to Repulse Bay, Northwest Territories and return.

Ref: Mackay, Armour. Mercy Flight. The Beaver, March, 1948.

**17 DECEMBER, 1939.** The government of the United Kingdom, Canada, Australia and New Zealand signed an agreement at Ottawa, Ontario, to set up the British Commonwealth Air Training Plan in Canada for the training of aircrew. The Plan was to be administered and organized by the RCAF.

**1939.** The Trans-Canada (McKee) Trophy was awarded to M.A. Seymour for his work in the formation and operation of the Canadian Flying Clubs Association.

**1939.** The John C. Webster Memorial Trophy for amateur flying was won by Dr. R.J. Simard of the Montreal Light Aeroplane Club. No further competitions were held until 1947.

**Murton A. Seymour receives the Trans Canada (McKee) Trophy from C.G. "Chubby" Power, on 5 June 1940 in Ottawa. (RCAF)**

The first TCA passenger flight, Moncton, N.B. to Montreal, P.Q., 15 Feb. 1940. L-R: R.J.S. Weatherston, F.M. Smith, Capt. J. Storie, G. Mongeau, stewardess, D. Rushton, L.T. LeBlanc, First Officer R.L. Smith, Mrs. J.W. St. Pierre, F.M. Brown, R.E. McBeath and J.E. Butler. (Air Canada)

Pilot staff Dominion Skyways (Training) Ltd. # 1 AOS Toronto 1940. Back Row L-R: W. Hughes, F. Baillie, R. Leslie, B. McKinney, R. Smuch, A. Mitten, D. Duggan, A. Leach, R. LeRoy, W. Walker, Front Row L-R: E. Hamel, W. Resseguier, H. Seiger, W. Woollett, C.R. Troup, R. Mulhern, C.A. Schiller, W. Hilchie. (via J. Lucas)

# 1940

**1 JANUARY, 1940.** RCAF Overseas Headquarters at London, England, was formed.

**1 JANUARY, 1940.** Trans-Canada Air Lines extended its trans-continental airmail service east to Moncton, New Brunswick, and passenger service was started on 15 February.

**JANUARY, 1940.** Dr. W.R. Franks and F/L W.G. Riddell, using Fleet Finch 1021 tested the first anti-G suit ever worn in an aircraft. Conceived and developed by Dr. Franks, the tests were carried out at Camp Borden, Ontario.

**16 FEBRUARY, 1940.** *First RCAF squadron sailed for overseas.* No. 110 Army Co-operation Squadron sailed from Halifax, Nova Scotia, for Liverpool, England.

**1 APRIL, 1940.** Trans-Canada Air Lines inaugurated a second daily transcontinental service.

**5 APRIL, 1940.** Dominion Skyways (Training) Ltd. was incorporated which was the first of several private companies formed to operate training schools for the RCAF.

**15 APRIL, 1940.** No. 1 Initial Training School was officially opened at the Eglington Hunt Club, Toronto, Ontario. It absorbed the Ground Training School at Trenton, Ontario.

**20 MAY, 1940.** The second RCAF squadron commenced its move overseas when the advance party of No. 112 (AC) "City of Winnipeg" Squadron sailed from Montreal, Quebec, for Liverpool, England. The second party of the squadron sailed from Halifax, Nova Scotia, on 8 June.

**23 MAY, 1940.** Ministry of National Defence for Air was created and Hon C.G. Power was appointed Minister.

**23 MAY, 1940.** *First RCAF officer entered combat.* S/L F.M. Gobeil, an RCAF exchange officer and C.O. of No. 242 Squadron, RAF, engaged a Messerschmitt Bf 109 near Berck, France.

**25 MAY, 1940.** *First RCAF officer destroyed an enemy aircraft.* S/L F.M. Gobeil, an RCAF exchange officer and C.O. of No. 242 Squadron, RAF, shot down a Messerschmitt Bf 110 near Menin, Belgium.

**27 MAY, 1940.** No. 1 Air Observers School, operated by Dominion Skyways (Training) Ltd., was officially opened at Malton, Ontario, and was the first such school activated.

**The Manuan dam which was constructed with the aid of a large air lift of equipment and material during 1940 and 1941. (via J. Kirk)**

**A Hawker Hurricane of No. 1 Squadron, the first RCAF squadron to go into action. (Ken Smith photo)**

**JUNE, 1940.** The RCAF ensign was approved by H.M. the King. The design was based on the RAF ensign with a red maple leaf replacing the inner red circle of the RAF roundel.

**8 JUNE, 1940.** No. 1 (F) Squadron, augmented by personnel of No. 112 (F) "City of Montreal" Squadron, sailed from Halifax, Nova Scotia, for Liverpool, England.

**17 JUNE, 1940.** A detachment of five Douglas B-18 Digbys from No. 10 (BR) Squadron at Dartmouth, Nova Scotia, commenced operation from Gander Airport, Newfoundland. This was the first RCAF operation in Newfoundland.

**24 JUNE, 1940.** The first four Elementry Flying Training Schools - No. 1 at Malton, Ontario, No. 2 at Fort William, Ontario, No. 3 at London, Ontario, and No. 4 at Windsor Mills, Quebec , were officially opened. They were operated by local flying clubs.

**22 JULY, 1940.** First BCATP pupils reported to No. 1 SFTS at Camp Borden, Ontario, for service flying training.

**1 AUGUST, 1940.** First flights of the Manuan air lift were made. Over 3,000 tons of freight were transported from Beauchêne to Manuan, Quebec, for the construction of power dams.

Ref: Molson, K.M.,Pioneering in Canadian Air Transport.
James A. Richardson & Sons. Winnipeg, 1974.

**5 AUGUST, 1940.** No. 2 SFTS was officially opened at Uplands Airport, Ottawa, Ontario, by the Governor-General.

**15 AUGUST, 1940.** The first RCAF victory in the Battle of Britain was scored by S/L E.A. McNab who destroyed a Dornier Do 215 while with No. 111 Squadron (RAF).

**16 AUGUST, 1940.** An agreement between the Canadian Pacific Railway and the British Ministry of Aircraft Production was initialled regarding the manning and dispatching of aircraft from North America to the British Isles and elsewhere. Pilots of BOAC had arrived in Montreal on 30 July and 1 August to assist in setting up the operation.

**17 AUGUST, 1940.** No. I (Fighter) Squadron became operational and commenced patrols from its base at Northolt, England.

**26 AUGUST, 1940.** *The first RCAF squadron went into action.* No. 1 (Fighter) Squadron engaged the enemy in the Battle of Britain and destroyed three and damaged four enemy aircraft while losing one pilot, F/O R.L. Edwards, who was the RCAF's first battle casualty.

Ref: ---- The R.C.A.F. Overseas - The First Four Years.
Oxford University Press, Toronto, 1944.

The Ferry Command monument at Gander Airport, Newfoundland, to commemorate the first flight of Lockheed Hudsons to Aldergrove, near Belfast, Ireland. The Hudson on the stone pedestal bears the same markings as that flown by D.C.T. Bennett when he led the first seven delivery aircraft across the Atlantic on 10 Nov. 1940. (Gander Photo Shop)

**1 OCTOBER, 1940.** S/L J.A. Kent, No. 303 Squadron (RAF), of Winnipeg, Manitoba, flying a Hawker Hurricane, fought 40 enemy fighters over the south coast of England. He destroyed one and was awarded the D.F.C. about 10 days later.

Ref: Kent, Gp. Capt. J.A. One of the Few. Wm. Kimber. London, 1971.

**22 OCTOBER, 1940.** S/L E.A. McNab, No. 1 Squadron, was awarded the D.F.C. for services in the Battle of Britain. Three days later F/L G.R. McGregor and F/O B.D. Russel, No. 1 Squadron, were also awarded the D.F.C.

**11 NOVEMBER, 1940.** Seven Lockheed Hudson aircraft, led by Capt D.T.C. Bennett, left Gander Airport, Newfoundland, on the first Atlantic ferry flight to Britain.

**19 NOVEMBER, 1940.** The formation of the Air Cadet League of Canada was authorized by Order-in-Council.

**24 NOVEMBER, 1940.** First BCATP graduates arrived overseas at Liverpool, England. They had graduated from No. 1 Air Navigation School at Trenton, Ontario, on 24 October.

**1 DECEMBER, 1940.** Trans-Canada Air Lines routed trans-continental service directly through Montreal-Ottawa-Toronto and eliminated Muskoka.

**9 DECEMBER, 1940.** No. 2 Squadron was formed at Digby, Lincolnshire, England, on the renumbering of No. 112 (AC) Squadron.

**1940.** The Trans-Canada (McKee) Trophy was awarded to T.W. Siers for his work in developing the Worth oil dilution system.

Pilots of 402 Squadron RCAF with their Commanding Officer, W/C Gordon R. McGregor (under prop. spinner) Jan. 1941. (W.F.H. Cann)

Passengers on the first official TCA flight from Toronto to New York discuss their trip with stewardess Georgie Ingram. (L-R) Herbert J. Symington, Miss Ingram, John Charles Thomas, C.D. Howe and C.L. Burton. (Air Canada)

# 1941

**7 JANUARY, 1941.** RCAF squadrons overseas were renumbered in the 400 series to avoid confusion with RAF squadrons. No. 110 became No. 400, No. 1 became No. 401 and No. 2 became No. 402.

**7 JANUARY, 1941.** Trans-Canada Air Lines received the first of its Lockheed 18 Lodestar aircraft.

**20 FEBRUARY, 1941.** Sir Frederick Banting was killed in a crash in Newfoundland of a Lockheed Hudson piloted by Capt. J. Mackey.

**1 MARCH, 1941.** No. 402 Squadron became operational at Digby, Lincolnshire, England.

**1 MARCH, 1941.** No. 403 (Fighter) Squadron was formed at Bagington, England.

**15 APRIL, 1941.** No. 404 (Coastal Fighter) Squadron was formed in England.

**15 APRIL, 1941.** *First RCAF offensive patrol over enemy territory.* Patrol was carried out by 12 pilots of 402 (Fighter) Squadron flying Hawker Hurricanes over the Boulogne area in France and was led by W/C G.R. McGregor.

**15 APRIL, 1941.** Trans-Canada Air Lines extended its service east to Halifax, Nova Scotia, and increased the frequency over Toronto-Halifax route to five daily trips.

**23 APRIL, 1941.** No. 405 (Bomber) Squadron was formed in England.

**8 MAY, 1941.** No. 407 (Coastal) Squadron was formed in England.

**10 MAY, 1941.** No. 406 (Night Fighter) Squadron was formed in England.

**10 MAY, 1941.** Trans-Canada Air Lines inaugurated a Toronto-New York service with two trips daily which was increased to three trips daily on 16 June.

**MAY, 1941.** Nickel Belt Airways commenced operations at Sudbury, Ontario, having taken over Wicks Air Service.

**27 MAY, 1941.** The agreement between the Canadian Pacific Railway and the British Ministry of Aircraft Production in regard to the ferrying aircraft overseas was terminated and the operation was taken over by Atfero until 31 July; the RAF Ferry Command took over on 1 August.

**12/13 JUNE, 1941.** *First RCAF bomber attack* was carried out by No. 405 (Bomber) Squadron against Schwerte (SE of Dortmund).

**16 JUNE, 1941.** No. 441 (Fighter) Squadron was formed in England.

**17 JUNE, 1941.** No. 409 (Night Fighter) Squadron was formed in England.

**24 JUNE, 1941.** No. 408 (Bomber) Squadron was formed in England.

**30 JUNE, 1941.** No. 410 (Night Fighter) Squadron was formed in England.

**30 JUNE, 1941.** No. 412 (Fighter) Squadron was formed in England.

**1 JULY, 1941.** No. 413 (Coastal) Squadron was formed in England.

**2 JULY, 1941.** The formation of the Canadian Women's Auxiliary Air Force was authorized by Order-in-Council.

**12 AUGUST, 1941.** No. 414 (Army Co-operation) was formed in England.

**20 AUGUST, 1941.** No. 415 (Coastal) Squadron was formed in England.

**1/2 SEPTEMBER, 1941.** The first RCAF night fighter victory was scored by F/O R.C. Fumerton and Sgt L.P.S. Bing in a Bristol Beaufighter of 406 Squadron over Bedlington, England.

**23 SEPTEMBER, 1941.** The formation of University Training Squadrons was approved.

**25 OCTOBER, 1941.** Eastern Air Command made its first attack on an enemy submarine off coast of Newfoundland. The attack made by No. 10 Squadron and the bomb did not explode.

**10 NOVEMBER, 1941.** *First George Cross was awarded to RCAF.* Awarded to LAC K.M. Gravel posthumously for his attempted rescue of his pilot from burning wreckage of a D.H.82C Tiger Moth at Calgary, Alberta.

**15 NOVEMBER, 1941.** No. 418 (Intruder) Squadron was formed in England.

**18 NOVEMBER, 1941.** No. 416 (Fighter) Squadron was formed in England.

**27 NOVEMBER, 1941.** No. 417 (Fighter) Squadron was formed in England.

**7 DECEMBER, 1941.** No. 419 (Bomber) Squadron was formed in England.

**7 DECEMBER, 1941.** Canada declared war on Japan and immediate steps were taken to strengthen the Pacific Coast defences.

**19 DECEMBER, 1941.** No. 420 (Bomber) Squadron was formed in England.

**22 DECEMBER, 1941.** A daily air service between Montreal, Quebec, and Quebec City was inaugurated by Quebec Airways Ltd. using Beachcraft 18A aircraft. A preliminary flight had been carried out on December 19 by pilot H. S. Jones Jr.

Ref: Montreal Gazette, December 20, 1941.

**27 DECEMBER, 1941.** No. 404 (Coastal Fighter) Squadron provided air support for a Commando raid on Vaagso, Norway.

**1941.** The Trans-Canada (McKee) Trophy was awarded to A.D. McLean for his work in establishing early airmail routes and especially in preparing airports for the British Commonwealth Air Training Plan.

**The Trans Canada (McKee) Trophy presentation Jan. 1943 L-R: J.A. Wilson, A.D. "Dan" McLean (recipient) A/V/M A.T.N. Cowley, A/M L.S. Breadner. (RCAF)**

Air Vice Marshall E.W. Stedman who became the first Director General of Air Research in the RCAF.
(Dir. of History)

Quebec Airways Beech 18A of the Montreal Quebec City run that was taken over by Canadian Pacific Airlines in 1942. (Pub. Arch. Can. PA 126213)

A Short Sunderland of 422 (Coastal) Squadron in England. (DND PL 40991)

# 1942

**JANUARY, 1942.** No. 121 (Composite) Squadron was formed at Dartmouth, Nova Scotia.

**1 JANUARY, 1942.** No. 124 (Ferry) Squadron was formed at Rockcliffe, Ontario.

**2 JANUARY, 1942.** No. 14 (Fighter) Squadron was formed at Sea Island, Vancouver, British Columbia.

**10 JANUARY, 1942.** No. 122 (Composite) Squadron formed at Patricia Bay, British Columbia.

**15 JANUARY, 1942.** No. 123 (Army Co-operation Training) Squadron formed at Debert, New Brunswick.

**3 FEBRUARY, 1942.** The Canadian Women's Auxiliary Air Force was renamed the Royal Canadian Air Force (Women's Division).

**12 FEBRUARY, 1942.** Nine Canadian squadrons participated in attacks on the German warships, "Scharnhorst", "Gneisenau" and "Prinz Eugen", which had escaped from Brest, France.

**15 FEBRUARY, 1942.** No. 113 (BR) Squadron formed at Yarmouth, Nova Scotia.

**1 MARCH, 1942.** An Accidents Investigation Branch of the RCAF was formed.

**18 MARCH - 6 APRIL, 1942.** No. 413 (Coastal) Squadron flew from the Shetland Isles to a new base on Ceylon.

**23 MARCH, 1942.** A new position of Director General of Air Research in the RCAF was created and A/V/M E.W. Stedman was selected to fill it.

**24 MARCH, 1942.** Canadian Pacific Air Lines Ltd. was formed by changing the name of United Air Services Ltd. The airway companies acquired by the Canadian Pacific Railway during 1941 commenced operating under the new name in May. These companies were: Arrow Airways Ltd., British Yukon Naviagation Co., Canadian Airways Ltd., Dominion Skyways Ltd., Mackenzie Air Service Ltd., Prairie Airways Ltd., Quebec Airways Ltd., Starratt Airways & Transportation Ltd., Wings Ltd., and Yukon & Southern Air Transport Ltd. (including their subsidiary Ginger Coote Airways Ltd.)

**2 APRIL, 1942.** No. 422 (Coastal) Squadron was formed in England.

Squadron Leader (later Brig. Gen.) L.J. Birchall who earned the title of "The Savior of Ceylon" in the action of 4 April 1942. (Dir. of History)

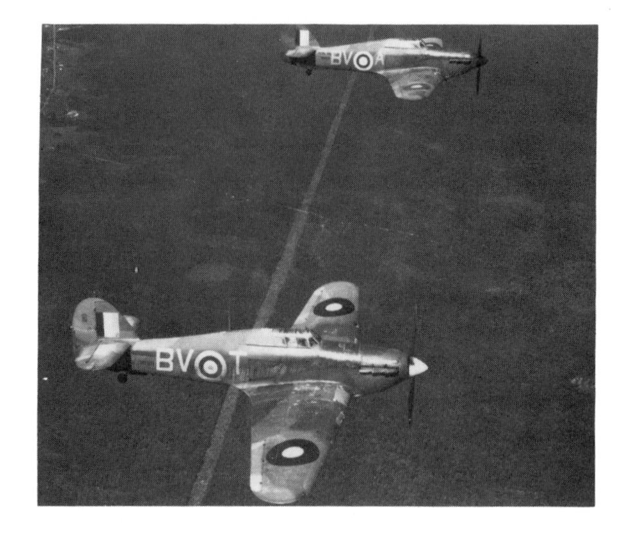


Hawker Hurricanes of the 126 (Fighter) Squadron in an early training flight. (DND REA 253-48)

Capt. N. Trerice and Supt. W. Fowler discuss TCA's inaugural passenger flight (Moncton, N.B. to Newfoundland) with G/C Ross of the RCAF. (Air Canada)

**4 APRIL, 1942.** S/L L.J. Birchall and crew of Consolidated Catalina of No. 413 Squadron sighted Japanese naval force steaming to attack Ceylon and gave warning before being shot down and taken prisoner. S/L Birchall was awarded the D.F.C. for this action.

**9 APRIL, 1942.** No. 421 (Fighter) Squadron was formed in England.

**10 APRIL, 1942.** No. 132 (Fighter) Squadron was formed at Tofino, British Columbia.

**20 APRIL, 1942.** No. 126 (Fighter) Squadron was formed at Dartmouth, Nova Scotia.

**1 MAY, 1942.** Trans-Canada Air Lines inaugurated service to St. John's, Newfoundland, from Moncton, New Brunswick, via Sydney, Nova Scotia.

**1 MAY, 1942.** No. 130 (Fighter) Squadron was formed at Bagotville, Quebec.

**13 MAY, 1942.** University Air Training Corps was established by Order-in-Council. 23 UAT Squadrons were formed during the war.

**17 MAY, 1942.** No. 404 (Coastal Fighter) Squadron participated in an attack on the German cruiser "Prinz Eugen" in the Skagerrak.

**18 MAY, 1942.** No. 145 (BR) Squadron was formed at Torbay, Newfoundland.

**18 MAY, 1942.** No. 423 (Coastal) Squadron was formed in England.

**19 MAY, 1942.** No. 162 (BR) Squadron was formed at Yarmouth, Nova Scotia.

**30-31 MAY, 1942.** Nos. 405, 408, 419 & 420 (Bomber) Squadrons participated in the first 1,000 aircraft attack on Germany directed at Cologne.

**2-8 JUNE, 1942.** Nos. 8, 111 & 118 Squadrons moved to Alaska to join No. 115 Squadron already there to work with U.S. forces against the Japanese threat.

**4 JUNE, 1942.** No. 417 (Fighter) Squadron arrived in Egypt to serve with the Desert Air Force.

**7 JUNE, 1942.** No. 128 (F) squadron was formed at Sydney, Nova Scotia.

**7 JUNE, 1942.** No. 119 (BR) Squadron formed at Sydney, Nova Scotia.

The Canadian D.H. 98 Mosquito prototype which was first flown on 23 September 1942. (DHC)

The Canadian Vickers prototype of the Consolidated PBY-5A Canso being towed out for its first official test 5 Dec. 1942. (Can. Vickers)

**15 JUNE, 1942.** No. 135 (Fighter) Squadron was formed at Patricia Bay, British Columbia.

**15 JUNE, 1942.** No. 147 (BR) Squadron was formed at Sea Island, Vancouver, British Columbia.

**25 JUNE, 1942.** No. 425 (Bomber) Squadron was formed in England.

**27 JULY, 1942.** Sgt G.F. Beurling flying a Supermarine Spitfire of No. 249 (RAF) Squadron destroyed four enemy aircraft over Malta.

**1 JULY, 1942.** No. 133 (Fighter) Squadron was formed at Boundary Bay, British Columbia.

**4 JULY, 1942.** No. 127 (Fighter) Squadron was formed at Gander, Newfoundland.

**7 JULY, 1942.** F/S P.M.G. Thomas and crew in a Bristol Bolingbroke of No. 115 Squadron attacked Japanese submarine Ro 32 while on patrol from Annette Island, Alaska. Submarine was damaged and later was sunk by U.S. Navy ships.

**19 AUGUST, 1942.** Six fighter and two army co-operation squadrons of the RCAF supported the Canadian attack on Dieppe, France.

**28 AUGUST, 1942.** No. 129 (Fighter) Squadron was formed at Dartmouth, Nova Scotia.

**23 SEPTEMBER, 1942.** The Canadian D.H.98 Mosquito prototype was test flown at Downsview, Ontario, by G.R. Spradbrow and F.H. Burrell.

Ref: Sharp, C.M. & Bowyer, M.J.F. Mosquito Faber & Faber Ltd. London, 1967.

**25 SEPTEMBER, 1942.** S/L K.A. Boomer, CO of No. 111 Squadron, destroyed a Japanese Nakajima A6M2-N (Ruff) fighter over Kiska, Alaska. This was the only RCAF air combat in the North American theatre of war.

**5 NOVEMBER, 1942.** The Canadian Government expropriated the facilities of the Aircraft Division of National Steel Car Corp. at Malton, Ontario, and began their operation as a crown corporation, Victory Aircraft Ltd.

**5 DECEMBER, 1942.** The Canadian Vickers prototype of the Consolidated Canso was test flown at St. Hubert Airport, Quebec, by E.C.W. Dobbin and crew.

P/O G.F. Beurling who was Canada's top scoring fighter pilot of World War II.
(via G.N. Irwin)

T.M. (Pat) Reid, popular pioneering Canadian pilot who received the Trans Canada (McKee) Trophy for the combined years of 1942-43.
(via K.M. Molson)

**31 JULY, 1942.** S/L N.E. Small and crew in a Lockheed Hudson of No. 113 Squadron sunk the German submarine U 754 southeast of Cape Sable, Nova Scotia. This was the first sinking by Eastern Air Command.

**1 OCTOBER, 1942.** No. 149 (TB) Squadron was formed at Dartmouth, Nova Scotia.

**14 OCTOBER, 1942.** P/O G.F. Beurling flying a Supermarine Spitfire of No. 249 (RAF) Squadron destroyed three enemy aircraft over Malta, but was shot down and wounded himself.

**15 OCTOBER, 1942.** No. 424 (Bomber) Squadron was formed in England.

**15 OCTOBER, 1942.** No. 426 (Bomber) Squadron was formed in England.

**30 OCTOBER, 1942.** F/O D.F. Raymes and crew in a Douglas B-18 Digby of No. 10 (BR) Squadron destroyed the German submarine U 520 far out in the Atlantic Ocean.

**30 OCTOBER, 1942.** F/O E.L. Robinson and crew in a Lockheed Hudson of No. 145 (BR) Squadron destroyed the German submarine U 658 320 miles east of St. John's, Newfoundland.

**7 NOVEMBER,** Nos. 427 & 428 (Bomber) Squadrons were formed in England.

**7 NOVEMBER, 1942.** No. 429 (Bomber) Squadron was formed in England.

**8 NOVEMBER, 1942.** Pilots equipped with anti-G suits carried out combat operations for the first time in history. They were members of 807 Squadron Fleet Air Arm wearing the Canadian designed Franks suit and flew Supermarine Seafires over Oran, Algeria.

**9 NOVEMBER, 1942.** No. 431 (Bomber) Squadron was formed in England.

**1942.** A new engine test facility was opened by the Engine Laboratory, National Research Council, Ottawa, Ontario, on their Montreal Road property.

**1942-43.** The Trans-Canada (McKee) Trophy was awarded to T.M. Reid for his efforts to advance Canadian aviation.

The outstanding building in Allerton Park, York, England used as headquarters for No. 6 RCAF Bomber Group from 1 Jan. 1943 to the end of the war.
(DND via J. Griffin)

An Avro Anson Mk I as used by No. 4 Air Observer School in the training of navigators at London, Ont.
(via K.M. Molson)

# 1943

**1 JANUARY, 1943.** No. 6 (RCAF) Group was formed under command of A/V/M G.E. Brookes to serve in RAF Bomber Command. It originally comprised Nos. 408, 419, 420, 424, 425, 426, 427 & 428 (Bomber) Squadrons. Later it was expanded to 14 squadrons.

**1 JANUARY, 1943.** No. 430 Army Co-operation Squadron was formed in England.

**JANUARY, 1943.** The RCAF badge was approved by H.M. the King.

**4 JANUARY, 1943.** The Avro 652A Anson V prototype was test flown at Montreal, Quebec.

**22 APRIL, 1943.** The Air Cadet Corps was made a component of the RCAF by Order-in-Council.

**26/27 APRIL, 1943.** No. 405 (Bomber) Squadron, now transferred to No. 8 Pathfinder Group (RAF), carried out its first Pathfinder operation.

**1 MAY, 1943.** No. 432 (Bomber) Squadron was formed in England.

**4 MAY, 1943.** First paratroop training jumps were carried out at Camp Shilo, Alberta, by the Canadian Army and No. 2 Detachment of No. 165 (HT) Squadron.

**4 MAY, 1943.** S/L B.H. Moffit and crew of a Consolidated Canso of No. 5 (BR) Squadron, Eastern Air Command, sunk the German submarine U 630 in the West Atlantic Ocean.

**13 MAY, 1943.** F/L J. Musgrave and crew of a Short Sunderland of No. 423 Squadron attacked the German submarine U 630 in the Atlantic. U 630 had been crippled on the 12th by and RAF Consolidated Liberator and was finished after Musgrave's attack by two ships of the Royal and Royal Canadian Navies.

Ref: Prince, Alfred. Aircraft Versus Submarine. Wm. Kimber. London, 1973.

**14 MAY, 1943.** LAC K.G. Spooner was awarded the George Cross posthumously. Spooner, a student navigator with no pilot training, took over the controls of an Avro Anson of No. 4 Air Observers School, London, Ontario, after the pilot had fainted. After three occupants had safely bailed out, the aircraft crashed in Lake Erie and Spooner was killed.

The transfer of mail during the first Vancouver/Victoria flight by T.C.A. (L-R) Ron George, Ops. Mgr. T.C.A., R.W. Mayhew, MP for Victoria and G.H. Clarke, Postal Services. (Air Canada)

Crew and passengers of the first T.C.A. Transatlantic flight. (L-R) Harold Thomae, Capt. M.B. Barclay, A.J. Blackwood, Capt. A. Rankin, C.S. Hewett, W. Houston, J.R.K. Main, C.S. Ritchie, G. Nettleton, Capt. R.M. Smith, Capt. R.F. George and S/L J.R. Gilmore. (Air Canada)

**16/17 MAY, 1943.** No. 617 (RAF), Squadron, led by W/C G.P. Gibson (RAF), breached the Mohne and Eder Dams in the German Ruhr. Twenty-nine of 133 men in the attack were members of the RCAF and seven of them were decorated.

**JUNE, 1943.** The first four-engined civil aircraft was registered in Canada, a British-built Avro 683 Lancaster III, CF-CMS, to Department of Munitions & Supply, Ottawa, Ontario. It was operated on transatlantic service by Trans-Canada Air Lines.

**6 JUNE, 1943.** Trans-Canada Air Lines extended its service from Vancouver to Victoria, British Columbia. Prior to this the Vancouver-Victoria route had been serviced by Canadian Airways and its successor, Canadian Pacific Airlines, using D.H.89A seaplanes.

**15 JUNE, 1943.** No. 434 (Bomber) Squadron was formed in England.

**23 JUNE - 1 JULY, 1943.** *First transatlantic glider flight.* A Waco CG4A, co-pilot S/L F.M. Gobeil, was towed from Montreal, Quebec to Preswick, Scotland, in stages by a Douglas C-47 Dakota piloted by F/L W.S. Longhurst, a Canadian in the RAF.

Ref. Gobril, F.M. By Glider Across The Atlantic.
CAHS Journal, Vol. 14 No. 1, Spring 1976

**26 JUNE, 1943.** 331 Wing, comprised of Nos. 420, 424, and 425 (Bomber) Squadrons and commanded by G/C C.R. Dunlap, commenced operations in Tunisia.

**11-12 JULY, 1943.** F/O J.H. Turnbull, No. 600 Squadron (RAF), flying a Bristol Beaufighter, destroyed three Junkers Ju 88 bombers in a night interception over Sicily.

**22 JULY, 1943.** *The first regular Canadian transatlantic air service was inaugurated.* It was operated by Trans-Canada Air Lines for the Canadian Government using converted Avro 683 Lancaster aircraft.

**28/29 JULY, 1943.** No. 6 (RCAF) Group despatched over 200 bombers for the first time on an attack on Hamburg, Germany; 22 bombers did not return.

**29 JULY, 1943.** The Canadian prototype of the Curtiss Helldiver, designated SBW-1, was test flown at Fort William, Ontario, having been built by Canadian Car & Foundry Co.

**1 AUGUST, 1943.** RCAF Staff College formed at Armour Heights, Toronto, Ontario. It was officially opened on 4 October.

**The prototype Avro Lancaster X at Malton just prior to its christening ceremony. During the ceremony, the RCAF ensign was dropped revealing its name "Rhur Express". (Victory Aircraft)**

**1 AUGUST, 1943.** The prototype Avro 683 Lancaster X was test flown at Malton, Ontario, by E.H. Taylor and crew. It was christened "Ruhr Express" on 6 August.

**4 AUGUST, 1943.** F/L A.A. Bishop and crew of a Short Sunderland of No. 423 Squadron sank the German submarine U 489. The Sunderland was shot down; five crew members were lost and six saved.

**17/18 AUGUST, 1943.** The RCAF contributed 74 aircraft to the RAF attack on the German rocket experimental facility at Peenemunde.

**24 AUGUST, 1943.** P/O D.F. McRae and crew, flying a Vickers Wellington of No. 179 (RAF) Squadron, sank the German submarine U 134.

**6 SEPTEMBER, 1943.** P/O D.F. McRae and crew, flying a Vickers Wellington of No. 179 (RAF) Squadron, attacked and badly crippled the German submarine U 760 which was forced to Vega Harbour, Spain, where it was interned.

**7 SEPTEMBER, 1943.** P/O E.M. O'Donnell and crew of a Vickers Wellington of No. 407 Squadron sank the German submarine U 669 to the west of the Bay of Biscay.

**15 SEPTEMBER, 1943.** First Avro 683 Lancaster X arrived in England after a transatlantic delivery flight.

**19 SEPTEMBER, 1943.** F/L R.F. Fisher and crew of a Consolidated Liberator of No. 10 Squadron sank the German submarine U 341 in the North Atlantic.

**23 SEPTEMBER, 1943.** The Avro 652A Anson VI prototype was test flown at Cartierville, Quebec.

**8 OCTOBER, 1943.** F/L A.H. Russell and crew of a Short Sunderland of No. 423 Squadron sank the German submarine U 610 in the North Atlantic.

**18 OCTOBER, 1943.** No. 168 (Heavy Transport) Squadron was formed at Rockcliffe, Ottawa, Ontario.

**26 OCTOBER, 1943.** F/L R.M. Aldwinckle and crew of a Consolidated Liberator of No. 10 Squadron sank the German submarine U 420 in the North Atlantic.

F/O R.D. (Joe) Schultz of Bashaw, Alberta (L) and F/O Vernon Williams of Hamilton, Ontario after their triple victory in Dec. 1943. (via DHC)

Boeing Fortress II, of No. 168 (H.T. ) "Mailcan" Squadron RCAF, taken at Rockcliffe. (Pub. Arc. Can. PA-65072)

**6 NOVEMBER, 1943.** Spilsbury and Hepburn Ltd., Vancouver, British Columbia, purchased a Waco YKC-S, CF-AWK, and started flying operations. The company later became Queen Charlotte Airlines Ltd.

**18 NOVEMBER, 1943.** F/O D.F. McRae and crew, flying a Vickers Wellington of No. 179 (RAF) Squadron, sank the German submarine U 211.

**22 NOVEMBER, 1943.** G/C C.R. Dunlap assumed command of No. 139 Wing (RAF), comprised of three squadrons of North American Mitchell aircraft. This was the only time an RCAF officer commanded a RAF operational wing.

**10-11 DECEMBER, 1943.** F/O R.D. Schultz, 401 Squadron, flying a D.H.98 Mosquito, destroyed three Dornier Do 217 bombers in a night interception sortie.

**15 DECEMBER, 1943.** A Boeing Fortress, of No. 168 (HT) Squadron, piloted by W/C R.B. Middleton left Rockcliffe, Ontario, with mail for Canadian servicemen overseas. This began RCAF air transport operations on a global scale.

**Before the start of the first "Mailcan" flight to Prestwick, (L-R) A/M R. Leckie, W/C Findlay, W/C Bruce Middleton, Air Minister C.G. Power and W/C Lewis Leigh. (RCAF via Z.L. Leigh)**

The HMS Puncher manned by RCN crews, at Esquimalt, B.C. 3 June 1944.
(Pub. Arc. Can. PA-112871)

A Canso from No. 164 Squadron operating from Reykjavik, Iceland. (DND RF 64-1928)

# 1944

**1 JANUARY, 1944.** A/M R. Leckie succeeded A/M L.S. Breadner as Chief of the Air Staff. A/M Breadner became Air Officer, Commanding-in-Chief, RCAF Overseas.

**4-5 JANUARY, 1944.** Six Handley Page Halifax aircraft of No. 428 Squadron carried out the first high-level mine laying in the harbour at Brest, France, from 14-15,000 ft.

**12 JANUARY, 1944.** The Cabinet approved the manning of the aircraft carriers H.M.S. "Nabob" and "Puncher" by crews from the RCN.

**24 JANUARY, 1944.** No. 162 Squadron began operations from Reykjavik, Iceland.

**11 FEBRUARY, 1944.** F/O P.W. Heron and crew of a Vickers Wellington, No. 407 Squadron, sank the German submarine U 283 in the North Atlantic.

**16 FEBRUARY, 1944.** A gradual reduction of the British Commonwealth Air Training Plan started.

**1 MARCH, 1944.** No. 170 (Ferry) Squadron was formed at Winnipeg, Manitoba.

**10 MARCH, 1944.** F/L S.W. Butler and crew flying a Short Sunderland attacked and damaged the German submarine U 625 which had to be abandoned by its crew.

**15 MARCH, 1944.** The following squadrons were disbanded. Nos. 119 (BR), 128 (F), 130 (F), 147 (BR), 149 (BR) and 163 (F).

**SPRING, 1944.** The Canadian Flying Clubs Association became the Royal Canadian Flying Clubs Association.

**17 APRIL, 1944.** F/O T.C. Cooke and crew of a Consolidated Canso of No. 162 Squadron sank the German submarine U 342 southwest of Iceland.

**24 APRIL, 1944.** F/L F.G. Fellows and crew of a Short Sunderland of No. 423 Squadron sank the German submarine U 311 southwest of Ireland.

**4 MAY, 1944.** F/L L.J. Bateman and crew of a Vickers Wellington of No. 407 Squadron sank the German submarine U 846 west of the Bay of Biscay.

Members of RCAF No. 418 Squadron in front of Mosquito "Moonbeam McSwine". (L-R) S/L H.D. Cleveland, F/S F. Day, Lt. Lou Luma, F/O C.G. Finlason. (DND PL 28482)

One of the Spitfires of No. 126 Wing RCAF that helped destroy 12 enemy aircraft over Normany 7 June 1944. (DND 34970)

**2 MAY, 1944.** Two D.H. Mosquitoes of No. 418 Squadron (crews S/L C.C. Scherf (RAAF), F/O W.A.R. Stewart and F/O J.T. Caine, P/O E.W. Boal) on a daylight intrusion mission to the Baltic coast destroyed ten aircraft on the ground, one in the air and damaged four more on the ground.

**16 MAY, 1944.** Two D.H.98 Mosquitoes of No. 418 Squadron, crewed by S/L C.C. Scherf with F/O C.G. Finlayson, navigator, and S/L H.D. Cleveland with FS F. Day (RAF), navigator, destroyed six enemy aircraft in the air and two on the ground during a daylight intrusion to the Baltic coast.

**MAY-JUNE, 1944.** Recruiting for RCAF was suspended and recruiting centres disbanded.

**1 JUNE, 1944.** North West Air Command was formed at Edmonton, Alberta, under command of A/V/M T.A. Lawrence.

**3 JUNE, 1944.** F/L R.E. McBride and crew in a Consolidated Canso of No. 162 Squadron sank the German submarine U 477 north of the Shetland Isles.

**6 JUNE, 1944.** Thirty-seven RCAF bomber, fighter and coastal squadrons took part in operations for the invasion of Normandy, France.

**7 JUNE, 1944.** No. 126 (RCAF) Wing (Nos. 401, 411 and 412 (Fighter) Squadrons) destroyed 12 enemy aircraft and probably destroyed or damaged five more over the Normandy beaches.

**8 JUNE, 1944.** F/O K.O. Moore and crew of a Consolidated Liberator, of No. 224 Squadron (RAF) sank two German submarines, the U 629 and the U 373, in 22 minutes off the French island of Ushant (Ouessant).

Ref: Price, Alfred. Aircraft versus Submarines. Wm. Kimber. London, 1973.

**10-27 JUNE, 1944.** Three RCAF fighter wings moved to France, Nos. 144, 127 and 143.

**11 JUNE, 1944.** F/O L. Sherman and crew in a Consolidated Canso of No. 162 Squadron sank the German submarine U 980 north of the Shetland Isles.

**12 JUNE, 1944.** While attacking Cambrai, France, an Avro Lancaster X of No. 419 squadron was shot down in flames. P/O A.C. Mynarski, the mid upper gunner, made repeated attempts to free the tail gunner trapped in his turret. With clothing and parachute on fire, he finally gave up and jumped, but succumbed to his burns. Miraculously, the tail gunner survived the crash and Mynarski was posthumously awarded the Victoria Cross.

Ref. Roberts, Leslie. There Shall Be Wings. Clarke, Irwin & Co. Toronto, 1959.

S/L Russ Bannock and F/O Bob Bruce in front of their mosquito named after the comic character "Hairless Joe". (DHC)

Flight Lieutenant David Ernest Hornell, V.C. (via Directorate of History)

**13 JUNE, 1944.** W/C C.G.W. Chapman and crew in a Consolidated Canso of No. 162 Squadron sank the German submarine U 715 north of the Shetland Isles.

**13 JUNE - 31 AUGUST, 1944.** No. 418 Squadron was the most successful RCAF squadron countering the German V-1 bomb attacks on England with 82 destroyed. S/L R. Bannock, with navigator, F/O R.R. Bruce, were the most successful team with 18-1/2 destroyed.

**24 JUNE, 1944.** F/L D.E. Hornell and crew in a Consolidated Canso of No. 162 Squadron sank the German submarine U 1225 north of the Shetland Isles. Badly damaged, the Canso landed, on fire, on the ocean and sank. The crew was picked up 21 hours later, but two had died from exposure and Hornell later succumbed. Hornell was awarded the Victoria Cross for this action.

Ref: Roberts, Leslie. There Shall Be Wings. Clarke, Irwin & Co. Toronto, 1959.

**28 JUNE, 1944.** A/C A.D. Ross, Sgt J.R. St. Germain, Corp M. Marquet, LAC M.M. McKenzie and LAC R.R. Wolfe made repeated attempts to rescue the crew of a burning bomber of No. 425 Squadron in spite of bomb explosions. All the crew were saved. Ross lost his right hand and McKenzie and Wolfe were also injured. For their actions Ross, St. Germain and Marquet were awarded the George Medal and McKenzie and Wolfe the British Empire Medal.

Ref: Coughlin, Tom. The Dangerous Sky - Canadian Airmen in World War II. Ryerson Press, Toronto, 1968.

**28 JUNE, 1944.** Twenty-six enemy aircraft were destroyed by the three RCAF fighter wings over Normandy.

**30 JUNE, 1944.** F/L R.E. McBride and crew of a Consolidated Canso of No. 162 Squadron attacked the German submarine U 478 which was later sunk by a Consolidated Liberator of No. 86 Squadron (RAF).

**1 JULY, 1944.** The transatlantic air service operated by Trans-Canada Air Lines was increased to three round trips per week.

**28-29 JULY, 1944.** No. 6 Group sent 234 bombers to attack Hamburg, Germany, and 22 did not return. This was the first time it had launched over 200 bombers.

**AUGUST, 1944.** Turbo Research Ltd. was started at Toronto, Ontario.

**17-20 AUGUST, 1944.** Three RCAF fighter wings destroyed or damaged over 2,000 enemy vehicles in the Falaise area.

**26/27 AUGUST, 1944.** While attacking a German submarine, a Vickers Wellington of No. 172 (RAF) squadron was shot down in the Atlantic. Four crew members escaped to a dinghy. F/O R.B. Ray, the navigator, refused to get into it so his injured companions might be accommodated. Although wounded himself, he held on to the dinghy for several hours before he died. He was awarded the George Cross for his action.

Ref. Roberts, Leslie. There Shall Be Wings. Clarke, Irwin & Co. Toronto, 1959.

**4 SEPTEMBER, 1944.** No. 437 (Transport) Squadron was formed in England.

**11 SEPTEMBER, 1944.** F/O J.N. Farren and crew of a Short Sunderland of No. 423 Squadron participated in the sinking of the German submarine U 484 with two ships of the RCN north of Ireland.

**17-23 SEPTEMBER, 1944.** No. 437 Squadron took part in the airborne landings at Eindhoven, Grave and Arnhem in the Netherlands.

**OCTOBER, 1944.** Canadair Ltd., a Crown company, was formed and took over the aircraft operations of Canadian Vickers Ltd., at Cartierville, Quebec on 17 November.

**OCTOBER, 1944.** The closing of British Commonwealth Air Training Plan schools was accelerated.

**OCTOBER, 1944.** No. 435 (Transport) Squadron was formed in England.

**OCTOBER, 1944.** No. 436 (Transport) Squadron was formed.

**5 OCTOBER, 1944.** Five pilots of No. 401 Squadron destroyed a Messerschmitt Me 262, the first jet aircraft brought down by either the RAF or RCAF.

**6-7 OCTOBER, 1944.** No. 6 (RCAF) Group sent 293 bombers to attack Dortmund, the largest force sent out by the Group.

**1 DECEMBER, 1944.** No. 2 Air Command, established at Winnipeg, Manitoba, took over duties of Nos. 2 and 4 Training Commands disbanded on 30 November.

**9 DECEMBER, 1944.** No. 664 (Air Observation Post) Squadron was formed at Andover, England. The flying personnel came from the Royal Canadian Artillery and other personnel from the RCAF.

**29 DECEMBER, 1944.** F/L R.J. Audet, flying a Supermarine Spitfire of No. 411 (Fighter) Squadron near Rheine, Germany, destroyed five enemy fighters in his first combat.

Ref: Coughlin, Tom. The Dangerous Sky. Ryerson Press. Toronto, 1968.

**30 DECEMBER, 1944.** S/L C.G.W. Taylor and crew flying a Vickers Wellington of No. 407 Squadron sank the German submarine U 772 in the English Channel.

**31 DECEMBER, 1944.** The University Air Training Squadrons were disbanded.

**1944.** The Trans-Canada (McKee) Trophy was awarded to J.A. Wilson for exceptional service in the advancement of Canadian aviation while Controller of Civil Aviation.

# 1945

**16 JANUARY, 1945.** No. 1 Air Command was established at Trenton, Ontario, to take over duties of the disbanded Nos. 1 and 3 Training Commands.

**FEBRUARY, 1945.** No. 665 (Air Observation Post) Squadron was formed at Andover, England. The flying personnel came from the Royal Canadian Artillery and other personnel from the RCAF.

**5 FEBRUARY, 1945.** No. 9 (Transport) Group was formed at Rockcliffe, Ottawa, Ontario. It comprised Nos. 12 (Comm), 168 (HT), 124 (Ferry), 164 (T), 165 (T) and 170 (Ferry) Squadrons.

**MARCH, 1945.** No. 666 (Air Observation Post) Squadron was formed at Andover, England. The flying personnel came from the Royal Canadian Artillery and the other personnel from the RCAF.

**31 MARCH, 1945.** The British Commonwealth Air Training Plan was terminated as scheduled, a total of 131,553 aircrew had been trained.

| Trade | RCAF | RAF | RAAF | RNZAF | Total |
|---|---|---|---|---|---|
| Pilot | 25,747 | 17,796 | 4,045 | 2,220 | 49,808 |
| Nav B | 5,154 | 3,113 | 699 | 829 | 9,795 |
| Nav W | 421 | 3,847 | – | 30 | 4,298 |
| Nav | 7,280 | 6,922 | 944 | 724 | 15,870 |
| A/Bomber | 6,659 | 7,581 | 799 | 634 | 15,673 |
| WO/AG | 12,744 | 755 | 2,875 | 2,122 | 18,496 |
| Naval AG | – | 704 | – | – | 704 |
| AG | 12,917 | 1,392 | 244 | 443 | 14,996 |
| FE | 1,913 | – | – | – | 1,913 |
| Total | 72,835 | 42,110 | 9,606 | 7,002 | 131,553 |

The Fleet 80 Canuck prototype. (Fleet Aircraft)

H.M.S. "Formidible" leaving Sidney, Australia, June 1945. (Imp. War Mus.)

**25 APRIL, 1945.** The last bombing attack was carried out by No. 6 (RCAF) Group with 192 aircraft dropping over 902 of bombs on Wangerooge Island.

**2 MAY, 1945.** D.H.98 Mosquito aircraft of No. 404 Squadron shared in the sinking of the German submarine U 2359 in the Kattegat - the last RCAF submarine sinking.

**7 MAY, 1945.** All German forces surrendered unconditionally. The instrument of surrender was signed at Berlin, Germany, on 8 May, V E Day.

**25 MAY, 1945.** No. 8 Squadron was disbanded.

**31 MAY, 1945.** Nos. 126, 160, and 161 Squadrons were disbanded.

**MAY - JUNE, 1945.** No. 6 (RCAF) Group (Squadron Nos. 405, 419, 419, 425, 425, 431, and 434) flew to Canada in their Canadian Avro Lancaster X's. The intention to equip them with Avro Lincolns for the war against Japan was abandoned with the Japanese surrender.

**JUNE, 1945.** Associated Airways Ltd., Edmonton, Alberta, started operations with two aircraft, a D.H.82C Tiger Moth and a D.H.90 Dragonfly.

**JUNE, 1945.** No. 5, 116 & 145 Squadrons were disbanded.

**4 JUNE, 1945.** The Fleet 80 Canuck prototype, designed and built by J.O. Noury, was test flown by Thomas Fredric Williams.

**9 JULY, 1945.** An RCAF Supermarine Spitfire from Rivers, Manitoba, photographed the eclipse of the sun, for the first time in history, from 34,000 feet.

**25 JULY, 1945.** No. 7 Squadron was disbanded.

**7 AUGUST, 1945.** Nos. 4 and 6 Squadrons were disbanded.

**SUMMER, 1945.** Four 'Canadianized' squadrons were formed by the Royal Naval Fleet Air Arm.

**9 AUGUST, 1945.** Lt. R.H. Gray, RCN, flying a Vought Corsair from the deck of H.M.S. Formidable , attacked a Japanese destroyer. Hit and on fire, Gray continued the attack and sank the destroyer before plunging into the waters of Onagawa Bay, Japan. Gray was awarded a posthumous Victoria Cross for this action.

The RCAF's first jet aircraft, the Gloster Meteor III, EE311, at Malton, Ont., in October 1945.
(K.M. Molson photo)

The Avro 694 Lincoln XV at Malton, Ontario. (A. Tee photo)

**14 AUGUST, 1945.** Japan agreed to make an unconditional surrender which was signed on 2 September.

**15 AUGUST, 1945.** No. 10 Squadron was disbanded.

**31 AUGUST, 1945.** No. 11 Squadron was disbanded.

**10 SEPTEMBER, 1945.** Nos. 133 and 135 Squadrons were disbanded.

**22 SEPTEMBER, 1945.** Trans-Canada Air Lines received its first Douglas DC-3. The type was introduced on its routes the following year.

**28 SEPTEMBER, 1945.** The RCAF accepted its first jet aircraft, a Gloster Meteor Mk. III, EE311, which is believed to be the first jet aircraft to fly in Canadian skies.

**30 SEPTEMBER, 1945.** No. 170 (Ferry) Squadron was disbanded.

**30 SEPTEMBER, 1945.** Nos. 121 and 167 Squadrons were disbanded.

**30 SEPTEMBER, 1945.** No. 122 Squadron was disbanded.

**1 OCTOBER, 1945.** RCAF Maintenance Command was formed at Uplands, Ottawa, Ontario.

**15 OCTOBER, 1945.** Nos. 423 and 433 (Bomber) Squadrons were disbanded.

**19 OCTOBER - 16 NOVEMBER, 1945.** No. 168 (HT) Squadron flew medical supplies contributed by the Canadian Red Cross from Rockcliffe Airport to Poland. One Boeing Fortress crashed at Munster, Germany, during the operation killing the five crew members.

**25 OCTOBER, 1945.** The Victory Aircraft-built Avro 694 Lincoln XV prototype was test flown at Malton, Ontario, by E.H. Taylor.

**30 OCTOBER, 1945.** No. 166 Squadron was disbanded.

**31 OCTOBER, 1945.** No. 165 (Transport) Squadron was disbanded.

**1 DECEMBER, 1945.** Avro Canada Ltd. was formed and took over the facilities of Victory Aircraft Ltd. at Malton, Ontario, with about 400 key personnel who had been kept on from the wartime production programme.

**1 DECEMBER, 1945.** A Royal Canadian Naval Air Station was established at Dartmouth, Nova Scotia.

**19 DECEMBER, 1945.** The Cabinet approved the formation of an Air Component of the Royal Canadian Navy.

**31 DECEMBER, 1945.** No. 426 (Transport) Squadron was disbanded.

**31 DECEMBER, 1945.** The strength of the RCAF had now been reduced to 58,047 from 181,235 a year previous.

**31 DECEMBER, 1945.** The five top-scoring Canadian fighter pilots of World War II were:

| | |
|---|---|
| F/L G.F. Beurling, D.S.O., D.F.C., D.F.M. | 31 |
| S/L H.W. McLeod, D.S.O., D.F.C. and Bar | 21 |
| S/L V.C. Woodward, D.F.C. and Bar | 21 |
| F/O W.E. McKnight, D.F.C. and Bar | 16 |
| G/C R.W. McNair, D.S.O., D.F.C. and 2 Bars | 16 |

**1945.** The Trans-Canada (McKee) Trophy was awarded to G.W.G. McConnachie for his work in establishing northern air routes, especially in the Yukon.

**1945.** The Soaring Association of Canada was formed under a Federal charter. A gliding instructor's school was established at Carp, Ontario.

**The first Canadian aircraft carrier H.M.C.S. "Warrior" shown in March 1947.**
**(DND PA 114008)**

# 1946

**17 JANUARY, 1946.** An RCAF roundel with a red maple leaf in centre in place of the red circle of the RAF was approved for use on RCAF aircraft.

**24 JANUARY, 1946.** The first Canadian aircraft carrier, H.M.C.S. "Warrior", was commissioned.

**1 FEBRUARY, 1946.** Recruiting for the RCAF resumed to fill vacancies in some ground trades.

**15 FEBRUARY - 6 MAY, 1946.** The RCAF provided an air drop supply to a Canadian Army expedition, "Exercise Musk-Ox", across the Barren Lands from Churchill, Manitoba, to Edmonton, Alberta, via Victoria Island and Fort Churchill.

**22 FEBRUARY, 1946.** The Post-War Plan for the RCAF was announced. It provided for a Regular Force of 16,100, an Auxiliary Force of 4,500 and a Reserve of 10,000. There were to be eight Regular and 15 Auxiliary Squadrons.

**15 MARCH, 1946.** The RCAF Fighter Wing, Nos. 411, 412, 416 and 443 Squadrons, was disbanded. It was serving with the British Air Forces of Occupation.

**31 MARCH, 1946.** No. 435 Squadron was disbanded.

**15 APRIL, 1946.** Colonial Airlines inaugurated Ottawa, Ontario-New York air service, via Montreal, Quebec.

**15 APRIL, 1946.** The formation of the first post-war Auxiliary Squadrons was authorized: Nos. 400(Toronto), 401(Montreal), 402(Winnipeg), 418(Edmonton), 424(Hamilton), 438(Montreal) and 442(Vancouver).

**21 APRIL, 1946.** No. 168 (Heavy Transport) Squadron was disbanded at Rockcliffe, Ottawa, Ontario. It had completed 636 trans-Atlantic flights between 15 December 1943 and 2 March 1946.

**22 APRIL, 1946.** The first flight of a tailless glider developed at National Research Council, Ottawa, from a design by Prof. G.T.R. Hill. Flight was made at Namao, Alberta, and the glider was piloted by S/L R. Kronfeld (RAF) in towed flight by an RCAF Douglas Dakota piloted by F/O Robertson.

**MAY, 1946.** Facilities and personnel of Turbo Research Ltd. were taken over by Avro Canada Ltd. They became the Engine Division of Avro Canada Ltd.

The DHC-1 Chipmunk prototype later went to England as G-AKEY. (DHC)

The Fairchild F-11 Husky prototype on its trail flight at Longueuil, Que. Note the added fins on the tailplane for this occasion. (Fairchild)

The Douglas/Canadair DC-4M North Star prototype. (Canadair)

**22 MAY, 1946.** The DHC-1 Chipmunk prototype was test flown at Downsview, Ontario, by W.I.P. Fillingham.

**31 MAY, 1946.** Nos. 427(B), 429(B) and 664(AOP) Squadrons were disbanded.

**15 JUNE, 1946.** No. 437 Squadron was disbanded.

**14 JUNE, 1946.** Fairchild F-11 Husky prototype was test flown on floats at Longueuil, Quebec, by A.M. Mackenzie.

**22 JUNE, 1946.** No. 436 Squadron was disbanded.

**26 JUNE, 1946.** The Air Cadets were renamed the Royal Canadian Air Cadets by permission of H.M. the King.

**1 JULY, 1946.** The transatlantic service was increased to five round trips weekly by Trans-Canada Air Lines.

**20 JULY, 1946.** The prototype Douglas DC-4M North Star was test flown at Cartierville, Quebec, by R. Brush and A.J. Lilly.

**1 OCTOBER, 1946.** The RCAF returned to a peacetime footing and many Regular Force personnel were reduced in rank.

**24 DECEMBER, 1946.** J. Wade and J.G. (Pat) Twist, flying a Grumman Goose, rescued three men from an ice floe in the Gulf of St. Lawrence after a D.H. 89A of Canadian Pacific Air Lines had made a forced landing. Three more survivors were rescued by boat on 26 December.

Ref: Woollett, W., . . . And Six Survived, CAHS Journal Vol. 19, No. 1.

**31 DECEMBER, 1946.** The RCAF (Women's Division) was dissolved.

**31 DECEMBER, 1946.** During the year, the RCAF photographed 401, 033 square miles of Canadian territory which included rediscovery of the Spicer Islands in Foxe Basin in the Arctic Archipelago.

**1946.** The Trans-Canada (McKee) Trophy for 1946 was awarded to G/C Z.L. Leigh in recognition of 20 years' service to Canadian civil and military aviation. Presentation was made on 30 April, 1947.

The first RCAF helicopter, a Sikorsky S-51, at Rockcliffe, Ontario. (K.M. Molson photo)

Pilot Gil McLaren in the North Star M 1 on the inauguration of transatlantic North Star service. (Air Canada)

The first Canadian designed helicopter, the Intercity Airlines SG-VI-C, under test. (via L. Milberry)

# 1947

**16 JANUARY, 1947.** The Minister of National Defence announced that the Services would be built up to 75 per cent of the permanent strengths proposed in February 1946.

**23 JANUARY, 1947.** It was announced that control of Canadair Ltd. had been acquired by the Electric Boat Co. of New York.

**FEBRUARY, 1947.** A course was inaugurated at Edmonton, Alberta, for 'para-rescue jumpers'.

**1 MARCH, 1947.** Air Commands were reorganized. Nos. 1 & 2, together with Eastern and Western Air Commands, were disbanded. Central (Trenton, Ont.) and North-West (Edmonton, Alta.) Air Commands were formed. No. 10 Group (Halifax, N.S.), No. 11 Group (Winnipeg, Man.), No. 12 Group (Vancouver, B.C.) were formed. Also formed were Maintenance Command at Ottawa, Ont. and No. 9 (T) Group at Rockcliffe, Ottawa, Ontario.

**5 APRIL, 1947.** The RCAF acquired its first heliocopter, a Sikorsky H-5. This aircraft, RCAF 9601, is now in the National Aeronautical Collection, Ottawa, Ontario.

Ref: Griffin, J.A. Canadian Military Aircraft, Serials & photographs, 1920-1968. Canadian War Museum, Ottawa, 1969.

**15 APRIL, 1947.** The first Canadian-built transport aircraft entered scheduled service when a TCA Canadair-built Douglas DC-4M-1 North Star flew from Goose Bay, Labrador, to Prestwick, Scotland, in 8 hrs, 39 mins.

**6-28 MAY, 1947.** First General Assembly of the International Civil Aviation Organization was held at Montreal, Quebec.

**JULY-AUGUST, 1947.** A party of 46 Royal Canadian Air Cadets visited Britain and a group from British Air Training Corps visited Canada.

**9 JULY, 1947.** The first Canadian designed helicopter, the Intercity Airlines SG Mk. VI-C, was successfully flown at Dorval, Quebec, by H.J. Eagle Jr.

Ref: Milberry, L. Aviation in Canada. McGraw-Hill Ryerson, Toronto, 1979.

**19 JULY, 1947.** F/L J.F. Drake and crew left Rockcliffe Air Station in an RCAF Consolidated Canso to re-establish the location of the North Magnetic Pole.

The prototype DHC-2 Beaver taxiing in after its initial test. It is now in the National Aeronautical Collection at Ottawa.
(DHC photo)

Airmen gather for the 1948 presentation of the McKee Trophy: (L-R) left row: "Barney" Rawson, Jim Mollison, "Punch" Dickins, J.A. Wilson, Romeo Vachon, "Pat" Reid, "Moss" Burbidge, and "Murt" Seymour. Right row: John Fauquier, Lewis Leigh, Dan McLean, "Doc" Oaks, George Phillips, Tom Siers, and "Wop" May.
(Roberts: Winnipeg Tribune)

**16 AUGUST, 1947.** The DHC-2 Beaver prototype was test flown at Downsview, Ontario, by Russell Bannock.

**SEPTEMBER, 1947.** First RCAF cadets began training at RCN-RCAF College at Royal Roads, British Columbia.

**1 SEPTEMBER, 1947.** A/M W.A. Curtis succeeded A/M R. Leckie as Chief of the Air Staff.

**2 SEPTEMBER - 14 OCTOBER, 1947.** S/L C.N. Burridge and crew completed a 7,000 mile voyage from Patricia Bay, British Columbia, to Dartmouth, Nova Scotia, via the Panama Canal in RCAF high speed rescue launch "Takuli".

**15 SEPTEMBER, 1947** Edgar H. Atkin, Chief Designer, Avro Canada Ltd., delivered the fifth British Commonwealth Lecture to the Royal Aeronautical Society in London, England, which was entitled "Inter-City Transport Development in Commonwealth Routes".

**NOVEMBER, 1947.** The first post-war RCAF aircrew trainees, 21 cadets, began indoctrination training at No. 1 Manning Depot, Toronto, Ontario.

**DECEMBER, 1947.** The first engine was tested in new Cold Weather Test Station for jet engines set up at Fort Churchill, Manitoba, by the National Research Council.

**1947.** The Trans-Canada (McKee) Trophy was awarded to B.A. Rawson for his work with Trans-Canada Air Lines.

**1947.** The John C. Webster Memorial Trophy for amateur pilots was won by C.W. Wilson of the Aero Club of B.C.

An RCAF D.H. 100 Vampire at DH Canada. (DHC photo)

The Avro Canada Chinook, the first Canadian jet engine. (Avro Canada)

Canada's aircraft carrier, HCMS "Magnificent". (DND)

# 1948

**23 JANUARY, 1948.** The RCAF commenced taking delivery of the D.H. 100 Vampire MK1, *the first jet fighter to enter RCAF squadron service.*

**6 FEBRUARY, 1948.** The Intercity Airlines SG-VI-D Grey Gull helicopter, the production version of the machine, was test flown at Dorval, Quebec, by H.J. Eagle Jr.

Ref: Milberry, L. Aviation in Canada. McGraw-Hill Ryerson, Toronto, 1979.

**8 FEBRUARY, 1948.** The RCAF Flyers ice hockey team won the Olympic and World's Amateur Ice Hockey championships in Switzerland.

**17 MARCH, 1948.** *The first Canadian jet engine was run successfully.* The Chinook, designed and built by the Engine Division of Avro Canada Ltd., was tested at Malton, Ontario. (Details of the Lasley engine and its test, if any, are not known - see June 1932.)

**23 MARCH, 1948.** H.M.C.S. "Warrior" was paid off and returned to the Royal Navy.

**1 APRIL, 1948.** Air Transport Command was formed and No. 9 (T) Group was disbanded.

**7 APRIL, 1948.** H.M.C.S. "Magnificent" was commissioned.

**1 MAY, 1948.** A Montreal-Toronto-Bermuda service was inaugurated by Trans-Canada Air Lines.

**10 JUNE, 1948.** The RCAF Association (of Air Force veterans) was formed.

**20 MAY, 1948.** G.F. Beurling, top-scoring Canadian fighter pilot of World War II, was killed in an aircraft accident at Rome, Italy.

**14 JULY, 1948.** *First jet aircraft fly the Atlantic Ocean.* Six D.H.100 Vampire fighters of No. 54 Squadron (RAF) landed at Goose Bay, Labrador, after a flight from England via Scotland, Iceland and Greenland.

Ref: Robertson, Peter. Ocean Hop. CAHS Journal, Vol. 6, No. 2, Spring, 1968.

**7 AUGUST, 1948.** F.W. (Casey) Baldwin, the first Canadian to pilot an heavier-than-air flying machine, died at Neareagh, Nova Scotia.

The National Research Council tailless glider which was towed from Namao, Alberta to Arnprior, Ontario. (DND PL 39148)

Trans Canada Air Lines North Star at Oakes Airport in Nassau opening the Caribbean service. (Air Canada)

**1 SEPTEMBER, 1948.** Formation of a Fighter Operational Training Unit at St. Hubert, Quebec, was authorized. No. 410, the first RCAF jet fighter squadron, began training on 1 December.

**10-13 SEPTEMBER, 1948.** The NRC tailless glider made a 2,300 mile towed flight from Namao, Alberta to Arnprior, Ontario, via Winnipeg, Chicago and Toronto. The glider was piloted by F/Ls C.F. Phripp and G.A. Lee and was towed by an RCAF Douglas Dakota.

**12-24 SEPTEMBER, 1948.** The RCAF and the USAF carried out a search for a missing RN aircraft with RN and USN naval attachés on board which was lost on a flight from Churchill, to The Pas, Manitoba. The RCAF found and rescued the missing men.

**19 NOVEMBER, 1948.** Fairey Aviation Co. of Canada was established and took over the facilities of the Clark-Ruse Aircraft Co. at Dartmouth, Nova Scotia.

**NOVEMBER, 1948.** The Roundel, the RCAF service publication, made its first appearance.

**1 DECEMBER, 1948.** Montreal-Toronto-Nassau-Kingston-Port of Spain service was inaugurated by Trans-Canada Air Lines.

**11 DECEMBER, 1948.** Canada and Newfoundland, a British Colony, agreed on Terms of Union and Newfoundland became the 10th province on 31 March 1949.

**15 DECEMBER, 1948.** No. 2401 Radar Squadron (Auxiliary) - later designated Aircraft Control and Warning Squadron - was formed at Montreal, Quebec.

**28 DECEMBER, 1948.** The Minister of Nation Defence, Brooke Claxton, outlined an expanded defence program which included an increase in personnel, reconditioning of air stations and development and production of jet fighters.

**1948.** The Trans-Canada (McKee) Trophy was awarded to F/O R.B. West for his and the RCAF's work in search-and-rescue operations.

**1948.** The John C. Webster Memorial Trophy for amateur pilots was won by J.H. Blackburn of the Edmonton Flying Club.

The Avro Canada Orenda engine, the first Canadian jet engine to go into production. (Avro Canada)

The Avro C-102 Jetliner taking off at Malton, Ont. (Avro Canada)

# 1949

**14-15 JANUARY, 1949.** *The first non-stop trans-Canada flight* was made by F/O J.A.F. Jolicoeur and crew who flew a RCAF Douglas DC-4M North Star from Vancouver, British Columbia, to Halifax, Nova Scotia, in 8 hours, 32 minutes for an average speed of 329 mph for the 2,785-mile flight.

**10 FEBRUARY, 1949.** The prototype Orenda jet engine, designed and built by the Engine Division of Avro Canada Ltd., made its first test run at Malton, Ontario.

**28 MARCH, 1949.** The first Canadair-built Douglas DC-4M Argonaut left Dorval Airport, Montreal, Quebec, for delivery to BOAC in charge of Capt A.J. Lilly.

**1 APRIL, 1949.** The RCAF Maintenance Command was renamed Air Material Command; Central Air Command became Training Command; No. 10 Group became Maritime Group; and No. 11 Group became Tactical Group.

**27 JUNE, 1949.** Found FBA-1A prototype was test flown at Malton, Ontario, by S.R. Found.

**13 JULY, 1949.** Canadian Pacific Airlines' first scheduled trans-Pacific flight left Vancouver, British Columbia, bound for Sydney, Australia, via San Francisco, Honolulu, Fiji and Auckland. The aircraft was a Douglas DC-4M North Star.

**30 JULY - 7 AUGUST, 1949.** The Soaring Association of Canada held their second annual soaring meet at Kingston, Ontario. Al. Pow qualified for a Silver C, the second Canadian to do so, and set a new Canadian glider endurance record of 6 hrs, 16 mins.

**10 AUGUST, 1949.** *The first Canadian jet aircraft and the world's second jet transport,* the Avro Canada C-102 Jetliner was test flown at Malton, Ontario, by J.H. Orrell and crew.

Ref: Rogers, D.H. Testing the Jetliner. CAHS Journal, Vol. 10, No. 1, Spring, 1972.

**4-6 SEPTEMBER, 1949.** First Canadian aircraft appeared in the National Air Races, Cleveland, Ohio. F/L J.H.G. McArthur, RCAF, flying a Rolls-Royce Griffin-powered Supermarine Spitfire XIV, CF-GMZ, placed third in the Tinnerman Race. He qualified as an alternate starter in the Thompson Race, but did not fly the race.

McKee Trophy winners present at the RFCA meeting in 1950. (L-R) seated: Grant McConachie, Dennis Yorath, J.A. Wilson. standing: Dan. McLean, "Barney" Rawson, "Murt" Seymour, "Wop" May and Romeo Vachon. (Capital Press)

The Avro Canada CF-100 prototype, the first Canadian-designed jet fighter. (RCAF)

**15 SEPTEMBER, 1949.** John Dure established a new Canadian soaring endurance record of 8 hours. He took off from Carp, Ontario, in a Grunau sailplane and landed at Breckenridge, Quebec.

**15 SEPTEMBER, 1949.** No. 421 Squadron was reformed at Chatham, New Brunswick. Equipped with D.H.100 Vampire, fighters, it was second RCAF jet squadron.

**1 NOVEMBER, 1949.** Air Defence Group was moved to St. Hubert, Quebec. It had been formed 1 December 1948, located at Ottawa, Ontario.

**1949.** *First Silver "C" badge was earned by a Canadian glider pilot,* Ovila Boudreault, of the Gatineau Gliding Club, Ottawa, Ontario.

**1949.** The Trans-Canada (McKee) Trophy was awarded to D.K. Yorath for his work in developing private flying and especially with the Royal Canadian Flying Clubs Association.

**1949.** The John C. Webster Memorial Trophy for amateur pilots was won by D.R. Jacques of the Aero Club of B.C.

# 1950

**2 JANUARY - 8 FEBRUARY, 1950.** A RCAF Douglas DC-4M North Star carrying the Hon. L.B. Pearson, made a round-the-world flight over the following route; Rockcliffe-Gander-Azores-Gibraltar-Malta-Fayid-Karachi-Negombo-Karachi-Delhi-Rangoon-Singapore-Hong Kong-Tokyo-Wake Island-Hawaii-Fairfield-Rockcliffe. Flying time. 125.20 hrs.

**19 JANUARY, 1950.** The prototype Avro Canada CF-100 was test flown at Malton, Ontario, by S/L W.A. (Bill) Waterton, RAF.

**31 MARCH, 1950.** No. 405 Squadron was reformed at Greenwood, Nova Scotia, equipped with Avro 683 Lancaster 10MR aircraft.

**4 JUNE, 1950.** Frank H. Brame set a new Canadian glider record by flying a Loudon glider from Oshawa, Ontario, to Kingston, Ontario, a distance of 118 miles in 5 hrs 42 mins and also earned his Silver 'C' badge for the flight.

**5 JUNE, 1950.** RCAF Colours were presented to the Force by the Governor-General, Field Marshal Earl Alexander of Tunis, at Ottawa, Ontario.

The modified Avro Lancaster 10-0 fitted with two Avro Canada Orenda engines. (J.F. McNulty photo)

The Canadair-built, North American Sabre 1. (Canadair)

**13 JULY, 1950.** The first Canadian jet engine was air tested. A modified Avro 683 Lancaster X was flown at Malton, Ontario, which incorporated two Orenda engines.

**27 JULY, 1950.** RCAF moved in support of United Nations action in Korea. No. 426 (Transport) Squadron began airlift of supplies to Tokyo, Japan.

**29 JULY - 6 AUGUST, 1950.** The Soaring Association of Canada held its third annual soaring meet at St. Eugene, Ontario, and logged over 100 hours of gliding.

**9 AUGUST, 1950.** The Canadian prototype of the North American F-86 Sabre 1, which was assembled from U.S.-made parts, was test flown at Dorval, Quebec, by A.J. Lilly.

**26 SEPTEMBER, 1950.** The Institute of Aerophysics was officially opened at the University of Toronto. The Institute had been in full operation since January.

Ref The Institute of Aerophysics. Aircraft and Airport, Vol. 12, No. 11, November, 1950.

**1 OCTOBER, 1950.** No. 411 Squadron (Auxiliary) was formed at Toronto, Ontario.

**15 OCTOBER, 1950.** First Technical Training Unit was formed in the RCAF Auxiliary at Vancouver, British Columbia. Eight others were formed in next three years.

**DECEMBER, 1950.** No. 2 Flying Training School was opened at Gimli, Manitoba, by the RCAF and the first students arrived in January.

**1950.** The Trans-Canada (McKee) Trophy was awarded to C.C. Agar for outstanding work in developing heliocopter operations in Canada.

**1950.** The John C. Webster Memorial Trophy for amateur pilots was won by E.O. Mann of the Aero Club of B.C.

**RCAF 426 Squadron North Star at Haneda on United Nations support. (DND PL 51259)**

A No. 404 Squadron Lancaster at Greenwood. (RCAF)

A formation of No. 410 Squadron Sabres. (DND PL 52447)

# 1951

**JANUARY, 1951.** No. 421 Squadron was transferred to England for training with the RAF. It was the first RCAF squadron to go overseas in peacetime.

**8 JANUARY, 1951.** No. 416 Squadron was reformed at Uplands Air Station, Ottawa, Ontario. It was initially equipped with North American Mustang IV aircraft.

**1 MARCH, 1951.** No. 441 Squadron was reformed at St. Hubert, Quebec, and equipped with D.H.100 Vampire fighters.

**30 MARCH, 1951.** F/L J.A.O. Levesque, attached to the USAF in Korea, destroyed a MIG-15 in combat. First RCAF victory in Korea.

**18 APRIL, 1951.** James C. Floyd, Project Engineer of the Avro Canada C-102, was presented with the Wright Brothers Award by the Society of Automobile Engineers at the Hotel Statler, New York City, for his paper "The Avro C-102 Jetliner", presented on 9 January, 1950. The award was for the best aeronautical paper of the year and J.C. Floyd was the first non-American to receive it. (The first Canadian to receive it was John A. McKillop in 1968.)

**30 APRIL, 1951.** No. 404 Squadron was reformed at Greenwood, Nova Scotia, and equipped with Avro 683 Lancaster 10MR aircraft.

**4 MAY, 1951.** First Canadian-trained students from NATO countries graduated as navigators at Summerside, Prince Edward Island.

**MAY, 1951.** Recruiting of women for the RCAF was resumed but they now entered directly into the RCAF and not into a separate Women's Division.

**19 MAY, 1951.** No. 410 Squadron began re-equipping with North American Sabre fighters. It was the first RCAF squadron to receive this new fighter.

**1 JUNE, 1951.** Air Defence Group at St. Hubert, Quebec, was redesignated Air Defence Command.

**20 JUNE, 1951.** First Orenda-powered Avro Canada CF-100 was tested at Malton, Ontario.

No. 439 Squadron Sabres at the start of "Operation Leapfrog". (DND PL 54283)

P.C. "Phil" Garratt, General Manager of DH Canada (L), receives the Trans Canada (McKee) Trophy from A/M W.A. Curtis. (DHC)

**28 JULY - 5 AUGUST, 1951.** The Soaring Association of Canada's fourth annual gliding meet was held at the Waterloo-Wellington Airport, near Kitchener, Ontario.

**31 JULY, 1951.** A Canadian Pacific Airlines' Douglas DC-4 crashed on a flight from Vancouver, British Columbia, to Anchorage, Alaska and 36 were killed.

**1 AUGUST, 1951.** No. 413 Squadron was reformed at Bagotville, Quebec, and equipped initially with D.H.100 Vampire fighters.

**18-19 AUGUST, 1951.** A RCAF aerobatic team flying D.H.100 Vampire fighters performed at the National Air Races at Detroit, Michigan.

**19 AUGUST, 1951.** Miss Margaret M. Carson and Miss Betty McCanse won the Women's International Air Race between Orlando, Florida, and Windsor, Ontario, flying a Stinson 105.

**1 SEPTEMBER, 1951.** No. 439 Squadron was reformed at Uplands, Ottawa, Ontario, and equipped with North American Sabre fighters.

**1 SEPTEMBER, 1951.** No. 443 Squadron was reformed at Westminister, British Columbia.

**15 OCTOBER, 1951.** RCAF Ground Observer Corps was formed.

**1 NOVEMBER, 1951.** No. 1 Fighter Wing was formed in England and on 15 November was established at North Luffenham where No. 410 Squadron was relocated.

**13 NOVEMBER, 1951.** First DHC-2 Beaver, an L-20A, was turned over to the U.S. Army at Downsview, Ontario.

**15 DECEMBER, 1951.** No. 421 Squadron returned after training in England and was relocated at St. Hubert, Quebec and re-equipped with North American Sabre fighters.

**1951.** The Trans-Canada (McKee) Trophy was awarded to P.C. Garratt for his long aviation career and especially for developing de Havilland Aircraft of Canada Ltd.

**1951.** The John C. Webster Memorial Trophy for amateur pilots was won by D. Fisher of the Kingston Flying Club.

Sabre fighters while enroute from Ottawa, Canada to Luffenham, England. (DND PL 54944)

RCAF Sabres lined up at their new base at Grostenquin Germany. (DND PL 55446)

# 1952

**2 JANUARY, 1952.** RCAF Air Division Europe Planning was formed at Paris, France, to prepare for the establishment of RCAF units in Europe.

**12 FEBRUARY, 1952.** No. 441 Squadron left St. Hubert, Quebec, to join No. 1 Fighter Wing in England.

**30 MAY - 15 JUNE, 1952.** Twenty-one North American Sabre fighters of No. 439 Squadron flew from Uplands, Ottawa, Ontario, to their new base at North Luffenham, England, in stages.

**1 JULY, 1952.** No. 434 Squadron was reformed at Uplands, Ottawa, Ontario, and was equipped with North American Sabre fighters.

**1 JULY, 1952.** No. 407 Squadron was reformed at Comox, British Columbia, and was equipped with Avro 683 Lancaster 10 MR aircraft.

**SUMMER, 1952.** Enheat Aircraft was formed at Amherst, Nova Scotia, by Enamel & Heating Co., Ltd. of Sackville, New Brunswick, to utilize the former aircraft facility of Canadian Car & Foundry Ltd.

**1 AUGUST, 1952.** No. 427 Squadron was reformed at St. Hubert, Quebec, and was equipped with North American Sabre fighters.

**AUGUST, 1952.** No. 1 Air Division Headquarters was formed at Paris, France.

**28 SEPTEMBER - 11 OCTOBER, 1952.** Nos. 416, 421 and 430 Squadrons flew from Canada to their new base at Grostenquin, Germany, in stages where they formed No. 2 Fighter Wing.

**1 OCTOBER, 1952.** No. 1 Air Division was formed as an operational command of the 4th Allied Tactical Air Force. Headquarters were temporarily in Paris, France.

**1 NOVEMBER, 1952.** No. 414 Squadron was reformed at Bagotville, Quebec.

**18 DECEMBER, 1952.** An Avro Canada CF-100 exceeded Mach 1 in a dive while piloted by J. Zurakowski. It was the first straight-winged aircraft to do so without rocket power.

The ill-fated D.H. 106 Comet of Canadian Pacific Airlines, the first jet aircraft of any Canadian airline. (DH)

The DHC-2 Beaver Mk II prototype on its initial flight over Toronto, 10 March 1953. (DHC)

**22 DECEMBER, 1952.** The Canadian prototype Lockheed T-33 Silver Star was test flown at Cartierville, Quebec, by W.S. Longhurst.

**30 DECEMBER, 1952.** A R-1340 Wasp engine, the first built in Canada, went on test at Canadian Pratt & Whitney Aircraft Ltd., Longueuil, Quebec.

**1952.** The Trans-Canada (McKee) Trophy was awarded to S/L K.R. Greenaway for his work in northern navigation and developing the twilight computer. Presentation was made on 22 May, 1953.

**1952.** The John C. Webster Memorial Trophy for amateur pilots was won by T.A. Wells of the Chilliwack Flying Club.

# 1953

**1 JANUARY, 1953.** No. 422 Squadron was reformed at Uplands, Ottawa, Ontario, and was equipped with North American Sabre fighters.

**23 JANUARY, 1953.** F/L E.A. Glover was awarded the D.F.C. Attached to the USAF in Korea, F/L Glover destroyed three MIG-15's and damaged two others.

**31 JANUARY, 1953.** Air Marshal C.R. Slemon succeeded Air Marshal W.A. Curtis as Chief of the Air Staff.

**FEBRUARY, 1953.** Rimouski Airlines Ltd. had its name changed to Quebecair Inc.

**1 MARCH, 1953.** No. 444 Squadron was formed at St. Hubert, Quebec, and equipped with North American Sabre fighters.

**3 MARCH, 1953.** Canadian Pacific Airlines' first D.H.106 Comet crashed on take-off at Karachi, Pakistan, on its delivery flight, killing all 11 on board.

**7 MARCH, 1953.** Nos. 413, 427 and 434 Squadrons began flying their North American Sabres from Canada to Zweibrucken, Germany, forming No. 3 Fighter Wing.

**MARCH, 1953.** The DHC-2 Mk.2 prototype, an Alvis Leonides-powered Beaver, was test flown by G.A. Neal.

The Orenda powered North American Sabre 3 in which Jaqueline Cochran exceeded Mach 1. (Canadair)

The first of the RCAF's two D.H. 106 Comets. (K.M. Molson photo)

RCAF Sabres of No. 2 Fighter Wing at Baden Soellingen, Germany. (DND PL 80494)

**1 APRIL, 1953.** No. 436 Squadron was reformed at Dorval, Quebec, and equipped with Fairchild C-119 aircraft.

**1 APRIL, 1953.** No. 445 Squadron was formed at North Bay, Ontario, and equipped with Avro Canada CF-100 aircraft.

**9 APRIL, 1953.** A North American Harvard of the RCAF collided with a TCA Douglas DC-4M at Moose Jaw, Saskatchewan. Thirty-seven were killed including T.M. (Pat) Reid.

**10 APRIL, 1953.** No. 1 Air Division Headquarters completed its move from Paris, to Metz, France.

**18 MAY, 1953.** Miss Jacqueline Cochran exceeded Mach 1 in an Orenda-powered, Canadair-built, North American Sabre, and became the first woman to do so.

Ref: Cochran, Jacqueline. The Stars at Noon. Atlantic Monthly Press. 1954.

**20 MAY, 1953.** The first of two RCAF D.H. 106 Comet aircraft was flown to Canada from England. It was the RCAF's first jet transport.

**30 MAY, 1953.** Central B.C. Airways Ltd. changed its name to Pacific Western Airlines Ltd. and at the same time absorbed Associated Air Taxi Ltd., Associated Aero Services Ltd., Associated Air Taxi (Powell Lake) and Port Alberni Airways Ltd.

**1 JUNE, 1953.** No. 423 Squadron was reformed at St. Hubert, Quebec, and equipped with Avro Canada CF-100 fighters.

**30 JULY, 1953.** North American Sabre 5, Avro Orenda-powered, was test flown at Cartierville, Quebec, by W.S. Longhurst.

**27 AUGUST - 4 SEPTEMBER, 1953.** Nos. 414, 422 and 444 Squadrons, comprising No. 4 Fighter Wing, flew from Canada to their new base at Baden Soellingen, Germany.

**1 OCTOBER, 1953.** No. 440 Squadron was reformed at Bagotville, Quebec, and equipped with Avro Canada CF-100 fighters.

**1953.** The Trans-Canada (McKee) trophy was awarded to F.I. Young for his work in developing the National Air Show at Toronto, Ontario.

**1953.** The John C. Webster Memorial Trophy for amateur pilots was won by E.G. McLarty of the Calgary Flying Club.

R.D. Hiscocks receives the first McCurdy Award from John A.D. McCurdy in Ottawa 1954.
(Newton Ottawa via DHC)

Guests at the formal opening of the new de Havilland plant in Downsview include (L-R) Sir Geoffrey de Havilland, Frank T. Hearle, F.B. Halford, Hon C.D. Howe, Air Marshal C.R. Slemon and Major General F.R. Dent.
(DHC photo)

# 1954

**JANUARY, 1954.** The Canadian Aeronautical Institute was formed and incorporated the Toronto Branch of the Institute of Aeronautical Sciences, the Ottawa Branch of the Royal Aeronautical Society and the Montreal-based Institute of Aircraft Technicians.

**2 JANUARY, 1954.** Avro Canada Ltd. was reorganized. Avro Canada Ltd. became parent, or holding company, controlling Avro Aircraft Ltd., the former Aircraft Division of Avro Canada, and Orenda Engines Ltd., the former Engine Division.

**16 JANUARY, 1954.** Toronto-Tampa route was extended to Mexico by Trans-Canada Air Lines.

**4 FEBRUARY - 17 MARCH, 1954.** The Canadair C-5 aircraft of No. 412 Squadron flew Prime Minister Louis St. Laurent around the world.

**26 FEBRUARY, 1954.** Trans-Canada Air Lines received its first Lockheed 1049 Constellation aircraft.

**15 MARCH, 1954.** No. 419 Squadron was reformed at North Bay, Ontario, and was equipped with Avro Canada CF-100 fighters.

**11 APRIL, 1954.** S/L R.G. Christie flew from Vancouver, British Columbia, to Ottawa, Ontario, in 3 hrs, 46 mins flying time with stops at Calgary, Alberta, and Winnipeg, Manitoba. He was flying a Canadair-built North American Sabre V.

**25 MAY, 1954.** The first presentation of the McCurdy Award was made to R.D. Hiscocks at the first annual dinner of the Canadian Aeronautical Institute held at the Chateau Laurier, Ottawa, Ontario.

**21 JUNE, 1954.** No. 428 Squadron was reformed at Uplands, Ottawa, Ontario, and equipped with Avro Canada CF-100 fighters.

**8 JULY, 1954.** The Canadian Aeronautical Institute was granted a charter. Its first publication, the C.A.I. Log, appeared in September and was replaced by the C.A.I. Journal in April 1956.

**29 SEPTEMBER, 1954.** De Havilland Aircraft of Canada Ltd.'s new plant at Downsview, Ontario, was opened by the Right Honourable C.D. Howe.

**1 OCTOBER, 1954.** Nos. 425 and 432 Squadrons were formed at St. Hubert and Bagotville, Quebec, and equipped with Avro Canada CF-100 fighters.

The first Vickers Viscount arrives in Canada. (Air Canada)

The Orenda Iroquois jet engine designed to power the Avro Canada CF-105. (Orenda)

**14-15 OCTOBER, 1954.** First joint meeting of the Institute of the Aeronautical Sciences and the Canadian Aeronautical Institute was held at the Mount Royal Hotel, Montreal, Quebec.

**1 NOVEMBER, 1954.** No. 409 Squadron was reformed at Comox, British Columbia, and equipped with Avro Canada CF-100 fighters.

**15 NOVEMBER, 1954.** No. 433 Squadron was reformed at Cold Lake, Alberta, and equipped with Avro Canada CF-100 fighters.

**26 NOVEMBER, 1954.** Wallace Rupert Turnbull, Canada's first aeronautical scientist, died at Saint John, New Brunswick.

Ref: The Engineering Journal, January, 1955.

**13 DECEMBER, 1954.** The first Vickers Viscount was accepted by Trans-Canada Air Lines at Dorval, Quebec.

**15 DECEMBER, 1954.** The Orenda Iroquois jet engine, designed for the Avro CF-105 Arrow, made its first test run.

**1954.** The Trans-Canada (McKee) Trophy was awarded to W/C J.G. Wright for his development of the R-Theta Computor. Presentation was made on 11 May, 1955.

**1954.** The John C. Webster Memorial Trophy for amateur pilots was won by R.F. Parvis of the Winnipeg Flying Club. Trophy was retired and late placed in the National Aviation Museum, Ottawa, which was absorbed by the Museum of Science and Technology.

**The J.C. Webster Memorial Trophy on display at the National Aviation Museum in Ottawa. It has since been re-activiated.**
**(Mus. Sc. & Tech.)**

The Canadian prototype Helio H-391B Courier. (K.M. Molson photo)

Canadian Pacific Airlines over-the-pole service to Europe. (CP Air)

The Canadian prototype Doman LZ-5 helicopter. (K.M. Molson photo)

# 1955

**1 FEBRUARY, 1955.** The Canadian prototype Helio Courier built by Fleet Manufacturing Ltd., Fort Erie, Ontario, was test flown at Fort Erie.

**24 MARCH, 1955.** Three Avro Canada CF-100 fighters flew to England. First Canadian-designed aircraft to cross the Atlantic.

**1 APRIL, 1955.** Trans-Canada Air Lines introduced the Vickers Viscount into regular service and was first North American airline to use turbine-powered aircraft.

**2 MAY, 1955.** Trans-Canada Air Lines inaugurated transcontinental scheduled cargo service using Douglas DC-4M North Star aircraft, converted to freighters.

**5 MAY, 1955.** An agreement was concluded between the United States and Canada for the construction and operation of distant early warning (DEW) radar defence line.

**4 JUNE, 1955.** Canadian Pacific Airlines introduced an over-the-pole European service using Douglas DC-6B aircraft.

**4 JUNE, 1955.** The Canadian prototype Doman LZ-5 helicopter built by Fleet Manufacturing Ltd., Fort Erie, Ontario, was test flown at Fort Erie.

**20-28 JUNE, 1955.** All 12 squadrons of No. 1 Air Division in Europe took part in "Carte Blanche" exercise featuring 3,000 aircraft.

**4 JULY, 1955.** An Anti-Submarine Helicopter Squadron was formed at H.M.C.S. "Shearwater", Dartmouth, Nova Scotia.

**1 SEPTEMBER, 1955.** No. 12 Air Defence Group at Vancouver, British Columbia, was redesignated No. 5 Air Division.

**6 OCTOBER, 1955.** Dr. J.J. Green, National Research Council, Ottawa, Ontario, delivered the eleventh British Commonwealth Lecture to the Royal Aeronautical Society in London, England, which was entitled "The Growth of Aeronautical Research in Canada During the Post-War Decade".

**30 SEPTEMBER - 15 NOVEMBER, 1955.** The Canadair C-5 of No. 412 Squadron, captained by W/C W.G.S. Miller, flew External Affairs Minister L.B. Pearson around the world.

**OCTOBER, 1955.** Avro Canada Ltd. purchased a controlling interest in Canadian Car & Foundry Ltd.

The Canadair C-5 transport served Canadian government officials and visiting dignitaries. (K.M. Molson photo)

The prototype Alvis Leonides powered Fairchild Husky. (R. Halford photo)

The Alexander Graham Bell Museum at Baddeck, N.S. (N.S. Film Bureau)

**11 OCTOBER, 1955.** No. 433 Squadron moved from Cold Lake, Alberta, to North Bay, Ontario.

**1955.** The Trans-Canada (McKee) Trophy was awarded to G.L. McGinnis for work in establishing DEW Line sites.

# 1956

**16 JANUARY, 1956.** S/L L. Hill and F/L A. Bowman flew a Lockheed T-33 Silver Star from Vancouver, British Columbia, to Dartmouth, Nova Scotia, in 6 hrs, 17 mins, including a 25-minute stop at Fort William, Ontario.

**9 FEBRUARY, 1956.** Arrangements were concluded for the purchase of Associated Airways Ltd. of Edmonton, Alberta, by Pacific Western Airways Ltd.

**20 MARCH - 5 APRIL, 1956.** The Canadair C-5 of No. 412 Squadron, captained by W/C W.G.S. Miller, flew Governor-General Massey on a tour of the Canadian Arctic and overflew the North Pole on 24 March.

**29 JUNE - 13 JULY, 1956.** A Canadian soaring team captained by Frank Woodward of Toronto competed in the World Soaring Meet at St. Yon, France.

**6 JULY, 1956.** The prototype of the Alvis Leonides-powered Fairchild Husky, known as the Super Husky, was test flown at Vancouver, British Columbia, by A.M. McKenzie.

**10 JULY, 1956.** Sgt D.E. Stevenson twice entered an aviation fuel fire at Montmedy, France, and brought it under control. He was awarded the George Medal.

**28 JULY - 5 AUGUST, 1956.** The National Soaring Meet was held at Cap de la Madeleine, Quebec.

**18 AUGUST, 1956.** The Alexander Graham Bell Museum was opened at Baddeck, Nova Scotia, by Mrs Gilbert Grosvenor and Mrs Daniel Fairchild.

**30 AUGUST, 1956.** Four North American Sabres, of No. 1 Overseas Ferry Unit, flew from Vancouver, British Columbia, to Dartmouth, Nova Scotia. First section: pilots F/L R.H. Annis and F/O R.J. Childerhose took 5 hrs. 30 min. including a ten minute stop at Gimli, Manitoba. Second section: pilots F/Os B.J. McComiskey and B. Merklinger took 5 hrs. 12 min. including two stops of seven minutes at Gimli, Manitoba, and St. Hubert, Quebec.

**11 SEPTEMBER, 1956.** Canada's leading fighter pilot of WWI, A/M W.A. Bishop, died at West Palm Beach, Florida.

**22 OCTOBER, 1956.** An officer exchange program was inaugurated between the RAAF and RCAF.

**22 OCTOBER, 1956.** No. 401 Squadron (Auxiliary) was first of six Auxiliary squadrons to be equipped with North American Sabre fighters.

**1-4 NOVEMBER, 1956,** No. 445 Squadron flew from Uplands, Ottawa, Ontario, to Marville, France. It was the first Avro Canada CF-100-equipped squadron to join No. 1 Air Division.

**20 NOVEMBER, 1956.** It was announced that No. 435 (Transport) Squadron would move from Namao, Alberta, to Capodichino, Naples, Italy, to assist UNEF in the Egyptian-Israeli crisis.

**9 DECEMBER, 1956.** A Douglas DC-4M of Trans-Canada Air Lines crashed into Mt. Slesse, British Columbia, 62 people were killed.

**1956.** The Trans-Canada (McKee) Trophy was awarded to S/L R.T. Heaslip for his contribution to helicopter operations during the Mid-Canada radar line construction.

**Squadron Leader R.T. (Bob) Heaslip who won the McKee trophy for his pioneering of helicopter operations.**
**(via R.T. Heaslip)**

# 1957

**9 JANUARY, 1957.** F/L Sabourin landed his damaged Lockheed T-33 after a rocket had exploded at Rivers, Manitoba. He was awarded the George Medal.

**17 JANUARY, 1957.** The aircraft carrier H.M.C.S. "Bonaventure" was commissioned.

**11-12 MAY, 1957.** No. 440 Squadron flew its Avro Canada CF-100 aircraft from Bagotville, Quebec, to Zweibruecken, Germany, in 28 hrs, 50 mins to join No. 1 Air Division.

**12-16 FEBRUARY, 1957.** No. 423 Squadron flew its Avro Canada CF-100 aircraft from St. Hubert, Quebec, to Grostenquin, France, to join No. 1 Air Division.

**28 MARCH, 1957.** The prototype Canadair CL-28 Argus, a development of the Bristol Britannia, made its first flight at Cartierville, Quebec, piloted by W.S. Longhurst and crew.

**15 MAY, 1957.** The RCAF Central Experimental and Proving Establishment at Ottawa was moved from Rockcliffe Air Station to Uplands Air Station.

**14 JUNE, 1957.** H.M.C.S. "Magnificent" was paid off and returned to the Royal Navy.

**30 JUNE, 1957.** The aerial surveying of Canada was completed. The photographing of Canada from the air, which was begun in the 1920's, was completed by 408 Squadron in the Arctic Archipelago.

Ref: RCAF Wraps Up its Shoran Project Canadian Aviation, August, 1957, p. 57.

**4 JULY, 1957.** The last NATO students arrived for training by the RCAF.

**20-27 JULY & 3-10 AUGUST, 1957.** The Canadian National Soaring Meet was held at Brantford, Ontario.

**6 AUGUST, 1957.** F/L W.J. Marsh rescued the pilot of a crashed North American Sabre at Chatham, New Brunswick. He was awarded the George Medal. Four assisting airmen, Cpl T.G. Onarheim, LACs R.W. Henderson, J.J. Gommer and D.C. Meier, were awarded the Queen's Commendation for Brave Conduct.

**11 AUGUST, 1957.** A Douglas DC-4 of Maritime Central Airways crashed near Issoundun, Quebec, killing all 79 people aboard.

**The Avro Canada CF-105 Arrow prototype on its initial flight. (Avro Canada)**

**The DHC-4 Caribou test crew: (L-R) George Neal, H. Brinkman and Dave Fairbanks. (DHC photo)**

**1 SEPTEMBER, 1957.** A/M C.R. Slemon retired as Chief of the Air Staff and was succeeded by A/M H.L. Campbell.

**4 OCTOBER, 1957.** The Avro Canada CF-105 Arrow prototype was rolled out from the plant at Malton, Ontario.

**DECEMBER, 1957.** Fifty-three Avro Canada CF-100 Mk.5 all-weather fighters were delivered to the Belgian Air Force.

# 1958

**25 MARCH, 1958.** The Avro CF-105 Arrow prototype was test flown at Malton, Ontario, by J. Zurakowski.

**18 APRIL, 1958.** *The first Canadian aircraft exceeded Mach 1.0 in level flight.* The Avro CF-105 Arrow prototype exceeded M 1.5 at 50,000 feet during a test flight at Malton, Ontario, piloted by J. Zurakowski.

**12 MAY, 1958.** North American Air Defence Command (NORAD) was established by agreement signed in Washington, D.C., by the United States and Canada.

**30 JULY, 1958.** The DHC-4 Caribou prototype was test flown at Downsview, Ontario, by George Neal and David Fairbanks.

**18 AUGUST, 1958.** Gordon Oates became first Canadian to win the Diamond C, the top gliding rating, at Brantford, Ontario.

**30 AUGUST, 1958.** The Guynemer Trophy for aerial gunnery supremacy in the Allied Air Forces, Central Europe, was won by No. 1 Air Division. It was won again in 1959 and 1960 by No. 1 Air Division.

**9 OCTOBER, 1958.** J.C. Floyd, Vice President, Engineering, Avro Aircraft Ltd., delivered the fourteenth British Commonwealth Lecture to the Royal Aeronautical Society in London, England, which was entitled "The Canadian Approach to All Weather Interceptor Development".

**18 OCTOBER, 1958.** The last Canadian-built North American Sabre, the 1,815th produced, was delivered to representatives of West Germany.

**28 OCTOBER - 20 DECEMBER, 1958.** The Canadair C-5 of the RCAF piloted by W/C W.K. Carr and crew, flew Prime Minister Diefenbaker on a round-the-world tour.

**4 DECEMBER, 1958.** The last Avro CF-100 was rolled from the production line at Malton, Ontario.

The reproduction of the A.E.A. Silver Dart in flight at Baddeck, N.S., on 23 Feb. 1959. (via Maj. J. Wood)

The monument at Baddeck, N.S., commemorating the flight of the A.E.A. Silver Dart. (via K.M. Molson)

**19 DECEMBER, 1958.** The first scheduled commercial jet transport flight arrived in Canada, a D.H. 106 Comet of BOAC, which landed at Dorval Airport, Montreal, Quebec.

**1958.** The Trans-Canada (McKee) Trophy was awarded to J. Zurakowski for his test flying of the Avro Canada CF-105 Arrow.

# 1959

**20 FEBRUARY, 1959.** The contract for the design and manufacture of the Avro CF-105 Arrow was cancelled by the Canadian Government.

**23 FEBRUARY, 1959.** A reproduction of the A.E.A. Silver Dart was flown at Baddeck, Nova Scotia, by W/C P.A. Hartman on the fiftieth anniversary of powered flight in Canada. Pilot of the original Silver Dart, J.A.D. McCurdy, witnessed the flight.

Ref: Walker, F/L C. Silver Dart Re (Air) born(e). CAHS Journal. Vol. 2, No. 4, Winter, 1964.
Hartman, W/C Paul A. Flying Vintage Aircraft. CAHS Journal, Vol. 9, No. 3, Fall, 1971.

**16 MAY, 1959.** The newly-formed RCAF aerobatic team, the Golden Hawks, flying gold-finished North American Sabres, performed its first demonstration at Torbay, Newfoundland. Other demonstrations were given across Canada with the final 1959 show being given at Windsor, Ontario, on 20 September.

**15 JUNE, 1959.** A monument, erected by the Canadian Aeronautical Institute, was unveiled at Alexander Graham Bell Museum, Baddeck, Nova Scotia, commemorating the flight of the A.E.A. Silver Dart in 1909.

Ref: The Silver Dart Monument. The Canadian Aeronautical Journal, September, 1959, p. 284.

**1 JULY, 1959.** The Commonwealth Air Force Memorial, commemorating 798 men and women who lost their lives in Canada and adjacent waters and lands, and who have no known graves, was unveiled at Ottawa, Ontario, by Her Majesty the Queen.

**1 JULY, 1959.** Joint RCN-RCAF Maritime Commands were established on the East and West Coasts.

**OCTOBER, 1959.** A RCAF Canadair CL-28 Argus flew non-stop from Hawaii to North Bay, Ontario, in 20 hrs, 10 mins.

**24 NOVEMBER, 1959.** The Canadair CL-44D Yukon entered RCAF service.

**1959.** The Trans-Canada (McKee) Trophy was awarded to J.A.D. McCurdy for his early flights and later service to aviation in Canada.

The Canadair CL-41 Tutor prototype. (K.M. Molson photo)

The prototype of the swing tail version of the Canadair CL-44. (Canadair photo)

# 1960

**JANUARY, 1960.** An RCAF detachment equipped with two Avro CF-100 flighters (Operation Lookout) was established to monitor radiation from U.S. rocket nose cones re-entering the atmosphere.

**13 JANUARY, 1960.** The Canadair CL-41 Tutor prototype made its first flight at Cartierville, Quebec, piloted by Ian MacTavish.

**MARCH, 1960.** F/O C.C. Battock, flying a North American Sabre over Germany, refused to abandon his disabled aircraft and made a safe landing in poor weather conditions. He was awarded the Air Force Cross.

**5-7 MARCH, 1960.** A RCAF Douglas DC-4M flew medical supplies and personnel to Radat, Morocco, for relief of earthquake victims at Agadir.

**24 MAY, 1960.** After the pilot of his Avro CF-100 suffered a lack of oxygen, navigator F/O C.M. Alexander assisted him to make a safe landing. He was awarded the Air Force Cross.

**28 MAY, 1960.** Following earthquakes in Chile, Douglas DC-4M's of No. 426 Squadron flew 25 tons of medical supplies, shelters, food and a field hospital for the relief of victims.

**18 JULY, 1960.** RCAF Douglas DC-4M's started the airlift of 22 tons to assist in UN operations in the Republic of the Congo (now Zaire).

**11 AUGUST, 1960.** The Found FBA-2A prototype was test flown at Malton, Ontario, by Stanley Haswell.

**25 SEPTEMBER, 1960.** Trans-Canada Air Lines received its first Douglas DC-8 jet transport.

**11 OCTOBER, 1960.** The Hon G.R. Pearkes, V.C., D.S.O., retired as Minister of National Defence and was replaced by the Hon Douglas Harkness.

**25 OCTOBER, 1960.** The National Aviation Museum was opened at Uplands Airport, Ottawa, Ontario, by the Hon J. Angus MacLean, acting in place of Prime Minister John Diefenbaker.

**18 NOVEMBER, 1960.** The prototype of the swing-tail version of the Canadair CL-44 was test flown at Cartierville, Quebec, by W.S. Longhurst and G.T. McLean.

**1960.** The Trans-Canada (McKee) Trophy was awarded to W/C W.G. Leach, of the Institute of Aviation Medicine, Toronto, Ontario, for his research into high altitude flying.

The Avian 2/180 gyroplane. (via Aircraft magazine)

The Avro Canada Avrocar under test at Malton, Ont. (Avro Canada photo)

The development and use of oversize, low pressure, tires as seen here on a Piper PA-18 Super Cub, to enable landings on unprepared surfaces in the Arctic, won the McKee Trophy for W.W. Phipps. (K.M. Molson photo)

# 1961

**16 FEBRUARY, 1961.** The Avian 2/180 gyroplane was test flown at Georgetown, Ontario.

**16 MAY, 1961.** The Avro VZ-9V Avrocar prototype made its first untethered flight at Malton, Ontario, piloted by W.J. (Spud) Potocki.

**26 MAY, 1961.** Lockheed CF-104 Starfighter Canadian prototype (Canadair CL-90) was test flown at Palmdale, California.

**30 MAY 1961.** The Canadian Pratt & Whitney PT-6, the first Canadian prop-jet engine, was test flown in a modified Beech 18 at Downsview, Ontario, piloted by R.H. Fowler and J. McNeal.

**25 JUNE, 1961.** J.A.D. McCurdy, the first man to pilot an heavier-than-air aircraft in Canada, died at Montreal, Quebec, aged 74 years.

**14 JULY, 1961.** The Canadian Pratt & Whitney PT-6 (U.S. military designation T-74) successfully completed the 50-hour Preliminary Flight Rating Test of U.S. Navy.

**JUNE, 1961.** The RCAF carried out an airlift of insecticides from Toronto, Ontario, to Saskatchewan to curb a plague of grasshoppers and cut worms.

**1 MAY 1961.** No. 415 Squadron was formed at Summerside, Prince Edward Island, equipped with Canadair CL-28 Argus aircraft.

**28 MARCH, 1961.** The RCAF received its first Lockheed CF-104 Starfighters.

**1 OCTOBER, 1961.** The RCAF took over the operation of Station Beausejour, Manitoba, from the USAF, the first of eleven Pinetree radar sites to be transferred to RCAF control.

**28 DECEMBER, 1961.** The first RCAF Bomarc missile unit, No. 446 (SAM) Squadron, was formed at North Bay, Ontario.

**1961.** The Trans-Canada (McKee) Trophy was awarded to W.W. Phipps for his work in northern flying and particularly the development of low pressure big wheels for landing on unprepared surfaces in the Arctic islands.

The newly acquired Curtiss JN-4 (Can.) was first displayed unrestored and stripped of fabric at the request of the RCAF on Air Force Day, 9 June, at Rockcliffe Air Station. (K.M. Molson photo)

The Junkers W-34 is presented to the National Aviation Museum by Mrs. W.M. Benidickson, daughter of its donor, Mrs. J.A. Richardson. The Minister of Natural Resources, Walter Dinsdale (L), accepts it for the Museum. Ferry pilot John Racey is in the center. (Mus. of Sc. & Tech.)

# 1962

**1 JANUARY, 1962.** RCAF Air Transport Command began regular scheduled flights between Trenton, Ontario, and Marville, France.

**8 FEBRUARY, 1962.** The RCAF began extensive aerial photography of cloud and ice conditions in the Gulf of St. Lawrence to supplement information gathered by U.S. satellite.

**8 FEBRUARY, 1962.** The National Aviation Museum purchased a Curtiss JN-4 (Can.) in Honeoye Falls, New York, a type which performed much of the early military and civil flying in Canada. It was overhauled and placed on display in May 1964, and the display was officially opened on 24 July, 1964.

**20 FEBRUARY, 1962.** RCAF Avro CF-100s observed the launch of U.S. astronaut John Glenn and monitored infra-red rays and radion emissions in conjunction with USAF aircraft at Cape Canavenal, Florida.

**6 APRIL, 1962.** The Consolidated Canso was withdrawn from RCAF service.

**8 APRIL, 1962.** S/L F.G. McLaren and F/L I.K. McKenzie rescued an occupant of a crashed and burning DHC-1 Chipmunk trainer. Both were severely burned and were awarded the George Medal.

**JULY, 1962.** No. 425 Squadron, the first RCAF Squadron to be equipped with McDonnell CF-101 Voodoo fighters, moved to its permanent station at Bagotville, Quebec, after re-equipping at Namao, Alberta.

**21 JULY 1962.** A new Canadian endurance record was set by a Canadair CL-44D Yukon aircraft of the RCAF which was airborne 23 hrs, 51 mins and covered approximately 7,000 miles.

**SEPTEMBER, 1962.** An RCAF Canadair CL-44D Yukon flew emergency supplies to Teheran, Iran, following severe earthquakes there.

**14 SEPTEMBER, 1962.** A/M H.L. Campbell retired as Chief of the Air Staff and was succeeded by A/M C.R. Dunlap.

**17 SEPTEMBER, 1962.** A Junkers W-34, CF-ATF, was presented to the National Aviation Museum by Mrs William Benidickson on behalf of her mother, Mrs James A. Richardson.

**28 SEPTEMBER, 1962.** The Canadian-built Alouette satellite was launched at Vandenberg, California, by a Thor-Agena B rocket.

A 430 Squadron Sabre in formation with a Lockheed CF-104 of No. 1 Air Division.
(DND PL 147905)

The short-lived Found FBA-2C prototype. Note the tall vertical tail fitted.
(J.F. McNulty photo)

A typical Pinetree radar installation at Foymount. (DND PL 101370)

**23 OCTOBER - 28 NOVEMBER, 1962.** RCAF Air Defence Command units were alerted during the Cuban missile crisis.

**15 DECEMBER, 1962.** No. 427 Squadron of No. 1 Air Division was re-equipped with Lockheed CF-104 aircraft. All eight Air Division squadrons were re-equipped with CF-104 aircraft by 2 March, 1964.

**31 DECEMBER, 1962.** The four Avro Canada CF-100 squadrons with No. 1 Air Division - Nos. 419, 423, 440 and 445 Squadrons - were disbanded.

**1962.** The Trans-Canada (McKee) Trophy was not awarded.

# 1963

**JANUARY, 1963.** The Canadian Aviation Historical Society was formed and issued its first Journal. (Original name was Early Birds Association of Canada and Vol. 1, No. 1 only was issued under the name of The Early Bird Enthusiast.)

**1 FEBRUARY, 1963.** Canadian Pratt & Whitney Aircraft Co., Ltd., changed its name to United Aircraft of Canada Ltd.

**FEBRUARY, 1963.** Sixteen Nigerians arrived in Canada for aircrew training by the RCAF.

**10 APRIL, 1963.** When an RCAF pilot became ill through oxygen failure, his navigator, F/O D.F. Parker, directed and assisted him to a safe landing. F/O Parker was awarded the Air Force Cross.

**13 MAY, 1963.** NORAD Region Headquarters was moved from St. Hubert, Quebec, to North Bay, Ontario.

**12 JUNE, 1963.** The Found FBA-2C prototype was test flown at Malton, Ontario.

**JUNE, 1963.** A Canadair CL-44D Yukon of the RCAF flew emergency supplies to East Pakistan to provide relief following a severe cyclone.

**1 JULY 1963.** The last of the eleven Pinetree radar stations was transferred to RCAF jurisdiction by the USAF.

**20 JULY, 1963.** In order to observe an eclipse of the sun, an RCAF Canadair CL-44D Yukon flew a party of scientists down the track of its shadow.

**OCTOBER, 1963.** Maritime Central Airways Ltd. was purchased by Eastern Provincial Airways Ltd.

The prototype DHC-2 III Turbo Beaver on its initial test flight, 31 Dec. 1963. On this occasion it had a Mk II Beaver vertical tail installed. (DHC photo)

The same Turbo Beaver prototype on amphibious/floats after completing its certification. The noticeable changes include a new vertical tail and wing fences. (DHC photo)

**28 SEPTEMBER, 1963.** The Semi-Automatic Ground Environment (SAGE) system at North Bay, Ontario, for directing air defense, became operational.

**3 OCTOBER, 1963.** The D.H. 106 Comet aircraft were retired from RCAF service.

**11 OCTOBER, 1963.** The Vertol CH-113 Voyageur helicopter entered RCAF service.

**29 OCTOBER, 1963.** The first Canadair CL-41 Tutor jet trainer entered RCAF service.

**31 OCTOBER, 1963.** LAC H.F. Schulz rescued an RCAF officer on board a Canadair CL-44D Yukon aircraft, who was in danger of being sucked out of a cargo door. LAC Schulz was awarded the British Empire Medal for Gallantry.

**29 NOVEMBER, 1963.** A Douglas DC-8 of Trans-Canada Air Lines crashed near Ste. Thérèse, Quebec, killing all 118 people aboard.

**31 DECEMBER, 1963.** The DHC-2 Mk.3 Turbo Beaver prototype was test flown at Downsview, Ontario, by R.H. Fowler.

**1963.** The Trans-Canada (McKee) Trophy was awarded to F.A. McDougall for developing new techniques of forest fire suppression.

**Frank A. MacDougall 1963** **(MNR ONT.)**

Air Marshal C.L. Annis addresses a gathering at the retirement of the Lancaster from the RCAF.
(J.S. Beilby photo)

The first flight of the de Havilland Canada DHC-5 Buffalo, one of the four that went to the U.S. Army.
(DHC photo)

# 1964

**7 FEBRUARY, 1964.** The RCAF announced the Golden Hawks aerobatic team which had been active since 1959 would be disbanded.

**20 FEBRUARY, 1964.** In order to rescue a stranded seal hunter, a Grumman Albatross piloted by F/L R.W. Cass landed among floe ice. Cpl P.E. Blank effected a rescue in a rubber boat in spite of choppy seas. F/L Cass was awarded the Air Force Cross and Cpl Blank the British Empire Medal for Gallantry.

**12-23 MARCH, 1964.** The RCAF carried out an airlift to Cyprus to supply a Canadian peace-keeping force.

**31 MARCH, 1964.** Nos. 403, 406, 424, 442 and 443 Squadrons of the Auxiliary RCAF were disbanded.

**1 APRIL, 1964.** The Avro 683 Lancaster X aircraft was retired from the RCAF.

**9 APRIL, 1964.** The DHC-5 Buffalo prototype was test flown at Downsview, Ontario, by R.H. Fowler and A. Saunders.

**16 MAY, 1964.** The Canadian Aircraft Operator commenced publication.

**6 JUNE, 1964.** The historic aircraft collections of the Canadian War Museum, National Aviation Museum and the Royal Canadian Air Force were displayed together for the first time at the Rockcliffe RCAF Station at Ottawa, Ontario. The three collections together were designated the National Aeronautical Collection.

**31 JULY, 1964.** A/M C.R. Dunlap retired as Chief of the Air Staff and became Deputy Commander of NORAD.

**1 AUGUST, 1964.** A/M C.R. Slemon, the last original RCAF officer, retired after serving as Deputy Commander of NORAD.

**22 SEPTEMBER, 1964.** The Clairco Super Cheetah was test flown by D. Saunders at St. Jean, Quebec.

**5-13 OCTOBER, 1964.** The RCAF provided air transportation and honour guards during the visit of Her Majesty Queen Elizabeth II to Canada.

**1964.** The Trans-Canada (McKee) Trophy was not awarded.

The prototype de Havilland Canada DHC-6 Twin Otter first flown by R.H. Fowler and M. Saunders. (DHC photo)

A press photo of Grant McConachie in his office shortly before his death in 1965. (CP Air photo)

# 1965

**JANUARY, 1965.** Trans-Canada Air Lines' name was changed to Air Canada.

**3 MARCH, 1965.** F/L K.A. Harvey, RCAF, after having an engine failure in a jet fighter, elected to make an emergency landing rather than bail out and have the aircraft crash in a populated area. He was awarded the Air Force Cross.

**7 MAY, 1965.** The Canadair CL-84 prototype was test flown in hovering flight by W.S. Longhurst at Cartierville, Quebec.

**20 MAY, 1965.** The DHC-6 Twin Otter prototype was test flown at Downsview, Ontario, by R.H. Fowler.

**29 MAY - 13 JUNE, 1965.** A Canadian team competed in World Gliding Championships at South Cerney, England.

**31 MAY, 1965.** The North American Harvard was retired as an RCAF service trainer after 26 years' of service.

**29 JUNE, 1965.** G.W.G. McConachie, President of Canadian Pacific Airlines and former bush pilot, died suddenly at Long Beach, California.

**23 OCTOBER, 1965.** The Basic Helicopter Training Unit, Rivers, Alberta, became an integrated unit of the Canadian Armed Forces by providing instruction for RCN, Canadian Army and RCAF personnel.

**28 JULY, 1965.** F/L W.R. Barnes, RCAF, flying a Lockheed CF-104 at night, suffered engine failure near Munich, Germany. He refused to bail out or approach over a populated area to a suitable base, but elected to land at an alternate base with inadequate facilities. He was awarded the Queen's Commendation for Brave Conduct.

**18 JULY, 1965.** F/L D.M. Campbell, RCAF, twice descended in his helicopter into the tree tops, on one occasion at night, in order to rescue the occupants of a crashed aircraft. He was awarded the Air Force Cross.

**8 DECEMBER, 1965.** The Douglas DC-4M North Star was retired from the RCAF.

**31 DECEMBER, 1965.** P.C. Garratt retired as Chairman and Managing Director of De Havilland aircraft of Canada after being active in aviation since 1915.

**1965.** The Trans-Canada (McKee) Trophy was not awarded.

# INDEX

The chronological nature of this publication favours an index of dates rather than page numbers. Aircraft, companies, people, places etc. are all listed alphabetically and referred to by date, month and year. Months are shown: Ja, Fe, Mr, Ap, My, Je, Jl, Ag, Se, Oc, No and De. Years prior to 1900 are given in full; others show the last two digits only. (e.g. 28 Ja '37/)

**AIRCRAFT (heavier than air)**


A.E.A. – Red Wing 12, 17 Mr '08/
– White Wing 18, 23 My '08/
– June Bug 20 Je '08/
– Silver Dart 06 De '08/ 23 Fe '09/ 02 Ag '09/ 23 Fe '59/ 15 Je '59/
Aeromarine 75 (modified Felixstowe F-5L) 10 Ma '21/
Aeronca 65C 28 My :39/
Aeromarine 40L 11 Jl '20/
Airspeed Envoy 19 No '34/
Antoinette – type (monoplane) 26 Mr '10/
Armstrong-Whiteworth FK. 8 27 Mr '18/
Armstrong-Whiteworth Siskin 05 Ja '26/ Ap '30/
Avian 2/180 16 Fe '61/
Avro 504 (Can) Oc '18/
Avro 504K 04 Je '19/ 18 Je '20/ 15-17 Oc .20/ aa Ap '21/ 05 Fe '22/ 29 Je '27/
Avro 554 Baby 30 Mr '24/
Avro 594 Avian Mr '28/ 02-03 Ja '29/
Avro 652A Anson 04 Ja '43/ 14 My :43/ 23 Se '43
Avro 683 Lancaster Je '43/ 22 Jl '43/ 01 Ag '43/ 12 Je '44/ My-Je '45/ 31 Mr '50/ 13 Jl '50/ 30 Ap '51/ 01 Jl '52/ 01 Ap '64/
Avro 694 Lincoln XV My-Je '45/ 25 Oc '45/
Avro Canada C-102 Jetliner 10 Ag '49/ 18 Ap '51/
Avro Canada CF-100 Canuck 19 Ja '50/ 20 Je '51/ 18 De '52/ 01 Ap '53/ 01 Je '53/ 01 Oc '53/ 15 Mr '54/ 21 Je '54/ 01 Oc '54/ 01 No '54/ 01-04 No '54/ 15 No '54/ 24 Mr '55/ 01-04 No '54/ 11-12 My '57/ 12-16 Fe '57/ De '57/ 4 De '58/ Ja '60/ 24 My '60/ 20 Fe '62/ 31 De '62/
Avro CF-105 Arrow 15 De '54/ 04 Oc '57/ 25 Mr '58/ 18 Ap '58/ '59/ 20 Fe '59/
Avro VZ-9V Avrocar 16 My '61/

Baldwin "Red Devil" 11 Se '11/ 15 Jl '12/ 02, 25, 26 Se '12/ 30 Je .13/ 04 Jl '13/ 05, 11 Se '13/ 06 De '13/ 01 Jl '14/ 07 Se '14/
Barling NB-3 07 Jl '29/ 09 Oc '29/
Beech 17R. G-ADLE 26 Ag '35/
Beech 18 22 De '41/
Beech 18 30 My '61/
Bell Cygnet 1 06 De '07/
Bellanca WB-2 29 Je '30/ 08 Oc '30/ 09-10 Oc '30/ 22 Oc '30/ 11 Je '33/ 07 Jl '33/ 22 Ag .33/ 17 Oc '35/
Bellanca J "North Star" 28 Je '28/
Bellanca K 23 Ag '32/
Bellanca CH-200 23 Fe '29/
Bellanca CH-300 Pacemaker 22 Je '31/ 28 Jl '31/ 08 Ag '33/ 28 Je '34/ 24 My '36/
Bellanca CH-400 Skyrocket 21 Ag '34/ 06 Ja '35/ 03 Jl '39/
Bellanca 28-70 Flash 28 Oc '36/
Benoist biplane 22, 24 My '12/
Bleriot XI monoplane 16 My '10/ 25, 26, 27, 28, 29, 30 Je '10/ 01, 02, 03, 04, 05, 08, 09, 11, 12, 13, 15, 16 Jl '10/ 02 Ag '10/ 31 De '10/ 22 Mr '11/ 02 Ag '11/ 30 My '14/ 13 Ag '14/
Bleriot – type monoplane 26 Mr '10/ 03 Jl '11/ 04 Se '11/ 28 De '11/ 19 Je '12/ 24, 28 Jl '13/ 12 Ag '13/
Boeing C-700 seaplane 28 Fe '19/ 03 Mr '19/ 15 Oc '20/
Boeing B-1 flying boat 15 Oc '20/
Boeing B-17 Fortress 19 Oc-16 No '45/
Boeing B-17 Fortress 15 De '43/ 19 Oc-16 No '45/
Boeing 314 26 Je '39/ 08-09 Jl '39/
Borel monoplane 10 Jl '12/ 26 Ag '12/ 02 Se '12/
Bristol F.2B 04 Je '19/
Bristol Bolingbroke 07 Jl '42/
Bristol Beaufighter 01-02 Se '41/ 11-12 Jl '43/
Bristol Britannia 28 Mr '57/
Burgess-Dunne 21 Se '14/
Burgess – Wright 19 Je '12/ 17 Jl '12/ 14, 22 Se '12/

Canadair C-5 04 Fe-17 Mr '54/ 30 Se-15 No '55/ 20 Mr-05 Ap '56/ 28 Oc-20 De '58/
Canadair CL-28 Argus 28 Mr '57/ Oc '59/ 1 My '61/
Canadair CL-41 Tutor 13 Ja '60/ 29 Oc '63/
Canadair CL-44 18 No '60/
Canadair CL-44D Yukon 24 No '59/ 21 Jl '62/ Se '62/ Je '63/ 20 Jl '63/ 31 Oc '63/
Canadair CL-84 07 My '65/
Canadair CL-90 (Lockheed Cf-104 Starfighter) 26 My '61/
Can. Aerodrome – Baddeck No. 1 12 Ag '09/
– Baddeck No. 2 25 Se '09/ 07, 09 Mr '10/ 24, 26, 27, 28, 29 Je '10/
Can. Aerodrome Hubbard "Mike" monoplane 05 Ap '10/ 04 Jl '10/
Canadian Car & Fdry. FBD-1 17 De '38/
Canadian Vickers Vedette Jl '24/ 04 Se '24/ 10 My '26/ 17 My '29/ My '33/

Felixstowe F-5L 15 Jl '18/ Ag '18/ 10 Ma '21/
Fleet Model 2 31 Jl '30/
Fleet 50 Freighter 22 Fe '38/
Fleet 16R Finch I Ja '40/
Fleet 80 Canuck 4 Je '45/
Fokker VII 09 ag '19/ 23 Ag-06 Se '19/
06-08 Jl '20/
Fokker Universal 27 De '26/ 22 Mr '27/
My-Je '27/ 13 Je '27/ Ag-Se '27/
17 Fe '28/
Fokker F. VII/3m 05 Je '28/ 27 Jl '29/
25 Je '30/
Fokker Super Universal 28 Ag '28/
03, 23 Ja '29/ 20 Je '29/ 01 Jl '29/
05 Se '30/
Fokker F.14A 15 Je '31/
Ford 4-AT 26 Ap '28/ 07, 25 Ag '28/
Ford 6-ATS 05 Jl '37/
Found FBA-1A 27 Je '49/
Found FBA-2A 11 Ag '60/
Found FBA-2C 12 Je '63/

Gage Tractor 23, 24 My '12/ 10 Ag '12/
Gibson Multi-plane 12 Ag '11/
Gibson Twin-plane 08, 24 Se '10/
Gloster Meteor Mk III 29 Se '45/
Great Lakes 2T-1 12 Ag '29/
Grumman Albatross 20 Fe '64/
Grumman G-21 Goose 24 De '46/
Grunau Sailplane 15 Se '49/

Handley Page V/1500 29 Ag '18/ 04 Jl '19/
09 Oc '19/
Handley Page Halifax 04-05 Ja '44/
Hawker Fury 18 Je-27 Jl '34/
Hawker Hurricane 17 Fe '39/ 01 Oc '40/
15 Ap '41/
Helio H-391B Courier 01 Fe '55/

Ilyushin TsKB-30 28 Ap '39/
Intercity Airlines SG Mk VI 09 Jl '47/

Junkers J1 09 Ag '19/
Junker JL-6 24 Mr '21/ 05 Ap '21/ 09 My '21/
Junkers F-13 24 No '30/
Junkers W-33 13 Ap '28/ 25 Jl '28/
Junkers W-34 14 Fe '39/ 27 No-20 De '39/
17 Se '62/
Junkers Ju 52/1m, CF-ARM 27 No '31/
Junkers Ju 88 11-12 Jl '43/

Keystone Puffer 18 Je-27 Jl '27/ 13 Jl '27/

Laird Solution 20 Oc '31/
Lesh Montreal No. 1 glider Ag '07/ 31 Ag '07/
Lesh Montreal No. 2 glider Se '07/
Lockheed Vega 08 Je '29/ 02 Ag '30/ 22, 23,
30 Je '31/ 20 My '32/ 05 Jl '32/
22 Jl '33/
Lockheed Sirius 13, 30 Jl '31/ 11 Jl '33/
Lockheed Altair 19 Je '31/ 13 My '32/
28 Sg '32/
Lockheed 10A Electra 02 Ap '35/ 04 Ag '36/
01 Se '37/
Lockheed 12A Electra Jr. 01 Ag '37/
Lockheed 14 27 No .31/ 10 My '38/
Lockheed 18 Lodestar 07 Ja '41/
Lockheed Hudson 11 No '40/ 20 Fe '41/
31 Jl '42/ 30 Oc '42/
Lockheed L1049 Constellation 26 Fe '54/
Loening amphibian 12 Ag '25/
Loening C-2 amphibian 18 Jl '35/
Lockheed/Canadair T-33 Silver Star 22 De '52/
16 Ja '56/ 09 Ja '57/
Lockheed Canadair CF-104 Starfighter
28 Mr '61/ 26 My :61/ 15 De '62/
29 Jl '65/
Loudon Glider 04 Je '50/

Martin tractor biplane 16 Se '14/
Martinsyde "Raymor" 18 My '19/ 17 Jl '19/
Martinsyde Type A Mark 1 03 Ma '22/
McDonnell CF-101 Voodoo Fighter Jl '62/
Messerschmidt Bf 109 23 My '40/
Messerschmidt Bf 110 25 My '40/
Messerschmitt Me 262 05 Oc '44/
McCurdy-Willard biplane 27 Jl '11/ 02 Ag '11/
Mikoyan and Gurevich MiG-15 20 Mr '51/
23 Ja '53/
Moisant monoplane 03 Jl '11/ 15 Ag '11/
Monocoupe 90A 15 My '39/
Morane/Borel monoplane 29 Ag '11/ 09 Oc '11

Nakajima A6M2-N 25 Se '42/
NC-1 08, 16 My '19/
NC-2 16 My '19/
NC-3 08 My '19/
NC-4 14, 16 My '19/
Nieuport monoplane 23 Jl '12/
Nieuport 10 14 De '15/
Nieuport 17 02 Je '17/
Noorduyn Norseman 12 No '35/ 17 De '59/
North American Harvard 09 Ap '53/
31 My '65/
North American B-25 Mitchell 22 No '43/
North American P-51 Mustang 08 Ja '51/
Northrop Delta 14 Se '39/
Northrop Gamma 25 Jl '33/ 04, 25-26 Ag '33/
23 No-05 De '35/
North American/Canadair F-86 Sabre
09 Ag '50/ 19 My '51/ 01 Se '51/
15 De '51/ 30 My-15 Je '52/ 01 Jl '52/
01 Ag '52/ 01 Ja '53/ 01, 07 Mr '53/
18 My '53/ 30 Jl '53/ 11 Ap '54/
30 Ag '56/ 22 Oc '56/ 06 Ag '57/
18 Oc '58/ 16 My '59/ Mr '60/

Pepper brothers' biplane 01 Ag '11/
Percival Vega Gull 05 Se '36/
Pitcairn PCA-2 Autogiro Se '31/
Polson (M.F.P.) biplane 29 Mr '16/

R.A.F. B.E. 2C 09 Ag '19/
R.A.F. B.E. 12 17 Je '17/
R.A.F. S.E. 5A 04 Je '19/
Reid Rambler 29 Se '28/
Reiflin (Curtiss-type) pusher biplane 06 Jl '12/
Rex biplane 16 Je '13/ 13 Jl '13/
Ryan NYP "Spirit of St. Louis" 02 Jl '27/
Ryan C-1 11 Ag '39/

Savoia-Marchetti S.55 20 My '27/
12, 28 Jl '33/

Schreck flying boat 18 Oc '27/
Seversky SEV-S2 28 My '38/
Short biplane 09 Mr '15/
Short seaplane 29 My '17/
Short S.23 05-08 Jl '37/ 06 Ag '39/
Short "Mercury" 21, 25 Jl '38/
Short Sunderland 13 My '43/ 04 Ag '43/ 08 Oc '43/ 10 Mr '44/ 24 Ap '44/ 11 Se '44/
Sikorsky seaplane Fe '27/
Sikorsky S-38 amphibian 29 Je '29/ 07 Jl '29/ 23 Ag '32/
Sikorsky S-42 03-06 Jl '37/
Sikorsky H-5 05 Ap '47/
Sopwith Pup 04 Ja '17/
Sopwith Camel 28, 29 My '19/
Sopwith 7F.1 Snipe 27 Oc '18/ 04 Je '19/ 01 Ag '19/
Sopwith Atlantic 18 Mr '19/ 10 Ap '19/
Sopwith Dove 04 Je '20/
Spartan C3-2 26 No '28/
Standard J-1 No '23/ 01 Oc '24/
Stinson SB-1 Detroiter 20 Je '28/
Stinson SM-1 Detroiter 26, 28 Ag '27/ 06, 07, 21 Se '27/ 23 Je '28/ 16 Ag '28/ 23 Ag '32/
Stinson SM-2A 18 Ag '31/
Stinson 105 19 Ag '51/
Supermarine Sea Lion flying boat 10 Se '19/
Supermarine Spitfire 27 Jl '42/ 14 Oc '42/ 29 De '44/ 09 Jl '45/ 04-06 Se '49/
Supermarine Seafire 08 No '42/

Thomas Morse S-4C Se '24/
Travel Air 6000 09 Oc '29/
Travel Air Mystery S 02 Jl '31/ 03 Jl '31/ 07 Jl '31/ 01 De '31/ 23 Ja '32/

V-1 (flying bomb) 13 Je '44
Vertol CH-113 Voyageur Helicopter 11 Oc '63/
Vickers Vimy 14-15 Je '19/ '20/
Vickers Viking IV 05 Je '22/ 26 Jl '23/ 25 Jl '25/
Vickers Vulture 03 Ag '24/
Vickers Viscount 13 De '54/ 01 Ap '55/
Vickers Wellington 24 Ag '43/ 06, 07 Se '43/ 18 No '43/ 11 Fe '44/ 04 My '44/ 26-27 Ag '44/ 30 De '44/
Vought/Lillie tractor biplane 08 Oc '13/
Vought F4U Corsair 09 Ag '45/
Vultee V-1A 20 Jl '36/ 14 Se '36/

Waco ATO 04 Jl '32/
Waco 10 30 No '27/ 12 Se '28/
Waco YKC-S 06 No '43/
Waco ZQC-6 23 My '37/
Waco CG4A 23 Je-01 Jl '43/
Wedell-Williams Special 01 De '31/ 23 Oc '32/
Westland Lysander II 16 Ag '39/
Wright biplane 25, 27, 28, 29, 30 Je '10/ 01, 02, 03, 04, 08, 09, 11, 14, 15, 16 Jl '10/ 13, 22 Jl '11/ 05 No '12/ 04 Se '13/

**AIRCRAFT (lighter than air)**

USN Balloon A-5598 14 De '20/
Dirigible C-5 airship 15 My '19/
Dirigible California Arrow II 26 Se '07/
Dirigible R-100 01 Ag '30/
Dirigible Strobel 01 Jl '08/ 09 Ag '09/
Dirigible Zeppelin L.22 14 My '17/
Dirigible Zeppelin L.43 14 Je '17/
Dirigible Zeppelin L.48 17 Je '17/
Dirigible Zeppelin L.70 05 Ag '18/

**AWARDS**

Air Force Cross 24 My '60/ 10 Ap '63/ 20 Fe '64/ 03 Mr '65/ 28 Jl '65/
British Empire Medal for Gallantry 20 Fe '64/
Commonwealth Air Force Memorial 01 Jl '59/
Curtiss Marine Trophy 23 Se '15/
Diamond C 18 Ag '58/
George Medal 10 Jl '56/ 09 Ja '57/ 06 Ag .57/ 8 Ap '62/
Guynemer Trophy 30 Ag '58/
John C. Webster Memorial Trophy 31 Ag '31/ '32/ '33/ '34/ '35/ '36/ '37/ '38/ '39/ '47/ '48/ '49/ '50/ '51/ '52/ '53/ '54/
McCurdy Award 25 My '54/
Order of the British Empire 03 Je '35/
Pulitzer Prize 28 My '19/
Queen's Commendation for Brave Conduct 06 Ag '57/ 28 Jl '65/
The Trans-Canada (McKee) Trophy '27/ '28/ '29/ '30/ '31/ '32/ '33/ '34/ '35/ '36/ '37/ '38/ '39/ '40/ '41/ '42-'43/ '44/ '45/ '46/ '47/ '48/ '49/ '50/ '51/ '52/ '53/ '54/ '55/ '56/ '58/ '69/ '60/ '61/ '62/ '63/ '64/ '65/
Victoria Cross 2 Je '17/ 27 Mr '18/ 23 Oc '18/ 12, 24 Je '44/ 09 Ag '45/

**COMPANIES/ORGANIZATIONS**

Aerial Experiment Association 01 Oc '07/ 06 De '07/ 13 Ja '08/ 12, 17 Mr '08/ 18, 23 My '08/ 20 Je '08/ 13 Jl '08/ 06 De '08/ 23 Fe '09/ 31 Mr '09/
Aerial League of the British Empire 29 Ag '17/
Aerial League of Canada Jl '19/
Aerial Service Co. 20 Ap '20/
Aerial Survey Company (Newfoundland) Ltd. 14 No '20/ Ja '21/
Aero Club of B.C. '47/ '49/ '50/
Aero Club of Canada 31 Mr '09/ 28 Jl '15/
Aeronautical Engineering Division 01 Jl '27/ 01 No '32/
Aeronautical Museum '37/
Aeronautical Society of Canada 02 Se '09/
Aeronautical Society of Great Britain 28 J1 '09/

Department of Munitions and Supply Je '43/
Department of National Defence 01 Ja '24/
01 Jl '27/ 01 Ap '36/ 02 No '36/
Department of Naval Service 01 Ja '24/
Department of Transport 02 No '36/
Dominion Aerial Exploration Ltd. Se '22/
9 Je '25/
Dominion Skyways Ltd. 23 Ja '35/ 23 My '37/
24 Mr '42/
Dominion Skyways (Training) Ltd. 05 Ap '40/
27 My '40/

Eastern Provincial Airways Limited Oc '63/
T. Eaton Co. Ltd. 07 Jl '10/
Edmonton Aircraft Ltd. 21 My '21/
Edmonton & Northern Alberta Aero Club
13 Je '28/ 17 Se '30/
Edmonton Chamber of Commerce 17 Se '30/
Edmonton Flying Club '48/
Elliot Air Service Ltd. 27 Se '23/ 03 Mr '26/
08 Je '27/ 15 Fe '28/ 13 Mr '28/ Je '28/
Empire City Circus 08, 31 Jl 1871/
Enamel & Heating Co. Ltd. Summer '52/
Enheat Aircraft Summer '52/

Fairchild Aerial Surveys (of Canada) Ltd.
Jl '22/ Ag '23/ No '23/ 10 My '26/
Fe '27/
Fairchild Aircraft Ltd. Se '31/ 28 Ag '43/
Fairchild Air Transport Ltd. Je '26/ Fe '27/
Fairchild Aviation Ltd. Fe '27/ 27 Oc '27/
02, 16 Ja '29/
Fairey Aviation Co. of Canada 19 No '48/
Fast Air Service Transport Ltd. Jl '28/
First Saskatchewan Aviation Co. Ltd.
06 Mr '13/
Fleet Air Arm 08 No '42/
Fleet Manufacturing Ltd. 01 Fe '55/ 04 Je '55/
Franco-American Automobile Co. Mr '09/

Gatineau Gliding Club '49/
General Airways Ltd. 08 Mr '28/ 24 My '36/
Ginger Coote Airways Ltd. 27 Oc '38/
24 Mr '42/
Golden Hawks 16 My '59/ 07 Fe '64/
Great Western Airways Ltd. 20 Je '28/

Hamilton Aero Club 24 My '28/ 28 Ja '29/
Hoffar Bros. Jl '19/
Hoffar-Beeching Shipyards Je '29/

Imperial Airways 06 Ag '39/
Independent Force (RAF) 29 Ag '18/
Institute of Aeronautical Sciences, Toronto
Branch Ja '54/
Institute of Aerophysics, University of Toronto
26 Se '50/
Institute of Aircraft Technicians Ja '54/
Institute of Aviation Medicine '60/
International Aerial Transport Ltd. 24 My '19/
International Airways Ltd. Je '28/ 16 Ja '29/
International Civil Aviation Organization
06-28 My '47/
Interprovincial Airways Ltd. 02 Ja '29/
16 Ja '29/

J.V. Elliot Ltd. 27 Se '23/ 15 Fe '28/

Kingston Flying Club '35/ '36/ '38/ '51/

Laurentide Air Service Ltd. '22/ 05 Je '22/
Summer '23/ 22 Ap '24/ 23 My '24/
03 Se '24/ 21 Ja '25/
Laurentide Co. '20/ '22/
London Aero Club 28 Jl '28/

M and C Aviation Ltd. 15 Jl '31/
McConachie Air Transport Ltd. 16 Ja '37/
McCurdy Aeroplane Co. 20 Je '11/
Mackenzie Air Service Ltd. 30 Ja '32/
24 Mr '42/
Manitoba Government Air Services My '33/
Maritime Central Airways 11 Ag '57/ Oc '63/
May Airplanes Ltd. 16 My '19/
Ministry of National Defence for Air
23 My '40/
Montreal Light Aeroplane Club 12 My '28/
'32/ '33/ '34/ '39/
Museum of Science and Technology '54/

NATO 04 Jl '57/
National Aeronautical Collection 05 Ap '47/
06 Je '64/
National Aeroplane Co. 23 Jl '12/
National Air Races 29 Ag-07 Se '31/
National Air Photographic Library 29 Ja '25/
National Air Transport Ltd. 25 Jl '28/ Mr '29/
National Aviation Museum '37/ '54/
25 Oc '60/ 08 Fe '62/ 17 Se '62/
06 Je '64/
National Research Council Jl '29/ 01 Ja '30/
Je '31/ '31/ '32/ '37/ '42/ 22 Ap '46/
De '47/ 10-13 Se '48/ 06 Oc '55/
National Steel Car Corp. 13 Ap '38/
05 No '42/
Newfoundland Airways 19 No '30/
Newfoundland Skyways Ltd. Je '36/ 03 Jl '39/
Nickel Belt Airways My '41/
NORAD 12 My '58/ 13 My '63/ 31 Jl '64/
01 Ag '64/
Northern Aerial Minerals Exploration Ltd.
Mr '28/
Northern Air Service Ltd. Ap '25/
Northern Canada Traders Ltd. Ja '21/
Northern Skyways 23 Ja '35/
Northern Transportation Co. 04 Fe '35/

Ontario Motor League 08 Jl '10/
Ontario Provincial Air Service 22 Ap '24/
Oc '16/ '31/
Orenda Engines Ltd. 02 Ja '54/ 15 De '54/
Ottawa Flying Club 03 Je '29/

Pacific Airways Ltd. 10 Fe '25/ 01 My '28/
Pacific Western Airlines ltd. 30 My '53/
Pacific Western Airways Ltd. 09 Fe '56/
Pan-American Airways 02 Ap '35/
Patricia Airways & Exploration Co. Mr '26/
12, 14 Ap '26/
Penton, A.F. & Co. Mr '18/
Port Alberni Airways Ltd. 30 My '53/
Prairie Airways Ltd. 15 Mr '34/

Spanish River Pulp & Paper Co. 11 Jl '20/
Spilsbury & Hepburn Ltd. 06 No '43/
Starratt Airways & Transportation Ltd.
04 Fe '35/ 24 Mr '42/

Toronto Flying Club 01 My '28/ '37/
Transamerican Airlines Corp. 18 Ag '31/
Trans Canada Air Lines Ltd. 27 No '31/
06 Ap '37/ 01 Se '37/ 10 My '38/
01 Oc '38/ 01 De '38/ '38/ 01 Ap '39/
18 jl '39/ 01 Ja '40/ 01 Ap '40/
01 De '40/ 07 Ja '41/ 15 Ap '41/
10 My :41/ 01 My '42/ 06 Je '43/
22 Jl '43/ 01 Jl '44/ 22 Se '45/ 01 Jl '46/
15 Ap '47/ '47/ 01 My '48/ 01 De '48/
09 Ap '53/ 26 Fe '54/ 13 De '54/
01 Ap '55/ 02 My '55/ 09 De '56/
29 No '63/ Ja '65/
Turbo Research Ltd. 01 Jl '44/ My '46/

United Aircraft of Canada Limited 01 Fe '63/
United Air Services Ltd. 24 Mr '42/
United Air Transport Ltd. 30 Ag '34/
05 jl '37/ 14 Mr '39/
UN 18 Jl '60/
UNEF 20 No '56/
USAF 12-24 Se '48/ 01 Oc '61/ 20 Fe '62/
01 Jl '63/
U.S. Army 24 Ja '27/
U.S. Army Air Service 03 Se '20/
U.S. Navy 14 Jl '61/
U.S. Signal Corps 29 Ag '17/
University Air Training Corps 13 My '42/
University Air Training Squadrons 13 De '44/
University of Alberta 06-08 Jl '20/
University of Michigan '29/
University of Toronto 01 Jl '17/ Mr '19/
Jl '24/ Se '37/

Vickers Syndicate 16 Ja '29/ 19 Jl '29/
Victoria Aero Club 08 Jl-'28/
Victory Aircraft Ltd. 13 Ap '38/ 05 No '42/
25 Oc '45/ 01 De '45/

Western Canada Airways Ltd. 10, 27 De '26/
22 Mr '27/ 01 Je '27/ Ag-Se '27/
06 Oc '27/ '27/ 01 My '28/
12-20 Se '28/ 16 No '28/ 10-29 De '28/
23 Ja '29/ 01 Jl '29/ 27 Jl '29/
03 Mr '30/ 25 No '30/
Wicks Air Service My '41/
Willys-Overland of Canada Ltd. '18/
Wings Ltd. 11 Jl '34/ 23 Mr '42/
Winnipeg Flying Club 28 My '28/ '54/
Wright Co. 08 Jl '10/

Yukon Southern Air Transport Ltd.
16 Ja '37/ 14 Mr '39/ 24 Mr '42/


## ENGINES


Alvis Leonides engine Mr '53/
Alvis Leonides engine 06 Jl '56/
Avro Canada Chinook 17 Mr '48/
Canadian Pratt & Whitney PT-6 30 My '61/
14 Jl '61/
Orenda jet engine 10 Fe '49/ 13 Jl '50/
20 Je '51/ 30 Jl '53/
Orenda Iroquois engine 15 De '54/
Pratt & Whitney Wasp engine 30 De '52/
Sunbeam Arab engine 1918/


## EVENTS/MEETS


Battle of Britain 26 Ag '40/ 22 Oc '40/
British Commonwealth Lecture 15 Se '47/
06 Oc '55/ 09 Oc '58/
Canadian Air Pageant 05-06 Oc '29/
15-16 Ag '31/ 20-21 Ag '32/
19-20 Ag .33/
Canadian National Soaring Meet 20-27 Jl,
3-10 Ag '57/
Exercise "Carte Blanche" 20-28 Je '55/
Hudson Strait Expedition 17 Jl '27/
14 No '28/
Industrial Exhibition 13 Jl '11/
James Gordon Bennett Cup Race 17-19 Oc '10/
MacMillan Arctic Expedition 25 Ag '25/
Montreal Aircraft Exhibition 04-11 My '29/
Montreal Aviation Meet 05 Jl '10/
National (Ford) Air Tour 05 Oc '29/
14 Se '30/ 04 Jl '31/
National Defence Act passed 28 Je '22/
National Balloon Race 30 My '32/
National Elimination Balloon Race 04 My '29/
National Soaring Meet 28 Jl-5 Ag '56/
New York-to-Spokane Derby 21 Se '27/
New York-Toronto Air Race 25-29 Ag '19/
Owens Expedition Ag '19/
Operation Lookout Ja '60/
Round-the-world flights 06 Ap '24/ 3 Ag '24/
31 Ag '24/ 02 Ja-08 Fe '50/
04 Fe-17 Mr '54/
Schneider Trophy contest 10 Se '19/
2nd Western Canada General Air Show
01 Ag '36/
Thompson Trophy air race 04-06 Se '49/
Tinnerman Trophy air race 04-06 Se '49/
Tip Top Aerial Derby 08 Se '31/
Toronto Aviation Meet 08, 09, 11, 12, 14,
15, 16 Jl '10/
Trans-Canada Air Pageant 01 Jl '31/
United States National Air Races 04-06 Se '49/
18-19 Ag '51/
World Gliding Championships
29 My-13 Je '65/
World Soaring Meet 29 Je-13 Jl '56/


## FIRSTS


Earliest aeronautical experiment in Canada.
10 Ap 1837/
First aerial fatality in Canada 29 Se 1888/
First aerial passengers carried in Canada
08 Se 1856/
First aerial photography by the CAF
Sum '20/

First aerial stowaway in Canada 03 No '24/
First aerial survey in what is now Canada Ag '19/
First aerial voyage in what is now Canada. 10 Ag 1840/
First aeroplane built in Canada 05 Ap '10/
First aeroplane built in Canada to order and for export 05 Ap '10/
First aeroplane flight by a woman pilot in Canada 31 Jl '13/
First aeroplane flight in the Province of Alberta 28 Ap '11/
First aeroplane flight in the Province of British Columbia 25 Mr '10/
First aeroplane flight in the Province of New Brunswick 02 Se '12/
First aeroplane flight in the province of Prince Edward Island 25 Se '12/
First aeroplane flight over a Canadian city 26 Mr '10/
First aircraft constructed in Canada since WW1 26 Jl '23/
First aircraft manufactured by De Havilland Aircraft of Canada Ltd. 21 De '37/
First aircraft towed glider flight in Canada 31 Jl '30/
First aircraft type to go into series production in Canada 14 Jl '15/
First air mail in Newfoundland 28 Ma '21/
First air meet in western Canada 25 My '29/
First airplane to fly non-stop across the Atlantic east to west 13 Ap '28/ 25 Jl '28/
First Alaska Air Expedition of the USAS 25 Jl '20/
First all-Canadian designed bush aircraft 12 No '35/
First ambulance flight in Canada 09 Ag '20/
First ambulance flight in Northern Canada 28 Ag '20/
First amphibious aircraft in Canada 05 Je '22/
First ascent in Canada by a female aeronaut 29 Ag 1879/
First Atlantic crossing by commercial aircraft 03-06 Jl '37/
First attempt to sell aircraft in Canada Mr '09/
First aviation engine put into production in Canada '18/
First aviation meet in Canada opened 25 Je '10/
First Avro 683 Lancaster X arrived in England 15 Se '43/
First awards made to RCAF personnel 01 Ja '35/

First BCATP graduates arrived overseas 24 No '40/
First BCATP pupils reported for service flying training 22 Jl '40/

First Canadian Ace 04 Ja '17/
First Canadian air casulaty in World War 1 04 Fe '15/
First Canadian aircraft in U.S. National Air Races 01-06 Se '49/
First Canadian air engineer's license issued 20 Ap '20/
First Canadian Air Force flying fatality 11 Ap '21/
First Canadian Air Mail 24 Je '18/
First Canadian Aircraft engine is tested 08 Se '10/
First Canadian aircraft show 07-15 Jl '28/
First Canadian aviation company is formed Ap '09/
First Canadian aviation serial publication Mr '18/
First Canadian-born aeronaut to die in an aerial mishap 16 Jl 1899/
First Canadian commercial pilot's license issued 31 Jl '20/
First Canadian Company to provide year-round service in bush flying field No '23/
First Canadian designed fighter 17 De '38/
First Canadian glider pilot to earn "Silver C" badge '49/
First Canadian honeymoon by air 08 Je '27/
First Canadian international mail service started 15 Oc '20/
First Canadian jet aircraft, and world's second jet transport flight tested 10 Ag '49/
First Canadian jet engine 17 Mr '48/
First Canadian jet engine air-tested 13 Jl '50/
First Canadian military air service 16 Se '14/
First Canadian mining claim staked with the use of aircraft 22 Jl '20/
First Canadian private pilot's license issued 24 Jan '20/
First Canadian Public Transport Pilot's License issued 01 Ap '36/
First Canadian regular air mail service began 03 Se '24/
First Canadian scheduled air service began 23 My '24/
First Canadian technical paper on aeronautics published Mr '07/
First Canadian to be credited with bringing down an enemy aircraft 14 De '15/
First Canadian to be decorated for service in the air 11 Jl '15/
First Canadian to die piloting an aeroplane 15 Ag '11/
First Canadian to fly the Atlantic 09-10 Oc '30/
First Canadian to participate in the aerial exploration of the Antarctic 28 Se '29/
First Canadian to receive a pilot's license 23 Oc '10/
First Canadian to save his life by parachute 17 My '29/
First Canadian woman obtained a Master's Degree in Aeronautical Engineering '29/
First Canadian woman to become a licensed pilot 13 Mr '28/
First Canadian woman to parachute from an aeroplane 29 Je '27/
First change of aircraft in flight in Canada 28 Je-01 Jl '20/
First civil aircraft registered in Canada 20 Ap '20/
First civil demonstration in Canada by an aerial stuntman 31 My '19/

First commercial flight Canada-USA
05-06 My '19/
First commercial intercity flight 08 Oc .13/
First complete airport lighting system in
Canada 23 Ja '30/
First crash of a heavier-than-air machine in
Canada 31 Ag '07/
First crop dusting in Canada 13 Jl '27/
First cross-country flight in Canada to exceed
100 miles 10 Se '13/

First descent by parachute from a
balloon in the Yukon Territory
29 Ag 1899/
First direct flight from Canadian mainland to
Europe 08-09 Ag '34/
First direct transatlantic flight
14-15 Je '19/

First emergency parachute jump made by a
member of the RCAF 26 Ag '29/
First engine-powered, directed flight on a
lighter-than-air aircraft in Canada
13 Jl '06/
First exhibit of historic aircraft in Canada
09 Ag '19/
First eyewitness account of an aeronautical
event by a Canadian 16 Oc 1784/

First fatal aeroplane accident in Canada
06 Ag '13/
First flight by a Canadian aircraft in the high
Arctic 27 Jl '27/
First flight in Canada by a powered heavier-
than-air machine 23 Fe '09/
First flight in Canada by a powered heavier-
than-air machine carrying more than
one person 02 Ag '09/
First flight in Newfoundland 10 Ap '19/
First flight in the Province of Ontario
02 Ag '09/
First flight in the Province of Manitoba
15 Jl '10/
First flight of a powered heavier-than-air
machine built in Canada 12 Ag '09/
First flight of a powered heavier-than-air
machine piloted by a Canadian
12 Mr '08/
First flight of a heavier-than-air machine in
Canada Ag '07/
First flight over the Canadian Rocky Mountains
07 Ag '19/
First flight to St. Pierre and Miquelon
13 Je '27/
First flights of the Manuan air lift made
01 Ag '40/
First forest dusting in Canada
18 Je-27 Jl '27/
First four Elementary Flying Training Schools
officially opened 24 Je '40/
First four-engined civil aircraft registered in
Canada Je '43/
First freight by air in Manitoba 27 Jl '20/
First forest fire spotted from the air in
Canada 07 Jl '19/

First George Cross awarded to RCAF
10 No '41/

First inter-city aeroplane flights 02 Ag '11/
First international air mail from Canada
03 Mr '19/
First international air passenger by heavier-
than-air machine arrived in Canada
28 Fe '19/
First international air travellers arrive in Canada
22-23 Se 1859/
First interprovincial flight in Canada 08 Oc '13/
First jet aircraft brought down by RCAF
02 Oc '44/
First jet transport aircraft for the RCAF
delivered 20 My '53/

First landing in the Canadian Arctic
12 Ag '25/
First loop in an autogyro Se '31/

First Maritime Air Tour Ag '33/
First Maritime Provinces Air Pageant
01-02 Jl '29/
First member of RCAF flew over enemy
territory 29-30 Se '39/
First military flying fatality in Canada
08 Ap '17/
First military flying in Canada 27 Fe '17/
First modern air transport to be registered in
Canada 04 Ag '36/

First night aeroplane flight in Canada
23 Jl '13/
First night flight in Canada (dirigible)
09 Ag '09/
First non-stop flight Toronto-New York
29 Ag '19/
First non-stop trans-Canada flight
14-15 Ja '49/
First North American airline to use turbine-
powered aircraft (Trans-Canada Air
Lines) 01 Ap '55/

First overseas mail brought to Ottawa by air
27 Oc .27/

First parachute descents in Canada
04-06 Se 1888/
First parachute descent in Canada by a woman
02-03 Se 1891/
First parachute jump from an aeroplane by a
Canadian in Canada 05 Jl '19/
First parachute jump from an aeroplane in
flight over Canada 24 My '12/
First performance in Canada by an aerial
stuntman summer '17/
First paratroop training jumps carried out at
Camp Shilo 04 My '43/
First passenger service inaugurated over North
Atlantic 08-09 Jl '39/
First peacetime overseas deployment of an
RCAF squadron Ja '51/
First photograph taken from a heavier-than-air
machine Se '07/

First photographic survey operations in Canada Oc '19/
First photographs taken from a powered aircraft in flight in Canada 26 Se '12/
First pilots licensed in Canada 11 Jl '15/
First presentation of the J.A.D. McCurdy Award 25 My '54/
First publication in Canada completely devoted to an aeronautical subject Oc 1856/

First RCAF bomber attack carried out 12/13 Je '41/
First RCAF jet aircraft 28 Se '45/
First RCAF night fighter victory scored 01-02 Se '41/
First RCAF officer destroyed an enemy aircraft 25 My '40/
First RCAF offensive patrol over enemy territory 15 Ap '41/
First RCAF officer entered combat 23 My '40/
First RCAF squadron sailed for overseas 16 Fe '40/
First RCAF squadron went into action 26 Ag '40/
First RCAF victory in air combat over Korea 30 Mr '51/
First RCAF victory in the Battle of Britain 15 Ag '40/
First RCAF war casualties 14 Se '39/
First regular Atlantic air mail service over the northern route 26 Je '39/
First regular Canadian transatlantic air service inaugurated 22 Jl '43/

First seaplane flight in Canada 06 Jl '12/
First series production of aircraft in Canada summer '15/
First serving member of the Canadian Armed Forces to take an aeroplane flight in Canada 09 Mr '10/
First ski flying in Canada winter'17-'18/
First successful aeroplane flight in the Province of Quebec 25 Je '10/
First successful aeroplane flight in the Province of Saskatchewan 01 Je '11/
First successful radio communication between an aeroplane-in-flight and ground 27 Ag '10/
First successful voyage of a balloon constructed in Canada 08 Se 1856/

First technical paper on aeronautics delivered in Canada 20 Fe 1895/
First time an aeroplane did the "loop-the-loop" in Canada 27 Je '14/
First time Canada's western Arctic reached by air 01 Jl '29/
First time in history, pilots equipped with anti-G suits carried out combat operations 08 No '42/
First trans-Atlantic flight 16 My '19/
First transAtlantic glider flight 23 Je-01 Jl '43/
First trans-Canada flight from Halifax N.S. to Vancouver B.C. 07-17 Oc '20/
First transcontinental seaplane flight 11-19 Se '26/
First tri-motored aircraft registered in Canada 07 Ag '28/
First twin-engined aircraft in Canada 03 Se '15/
First twin-engined aircraft registered civilly in Canada 01 Je '22/

First use of ailerons in North America Se '07/
First use of aircraft by a Canadian police department 30 Ag '19/
First use of radio by Canadian civil aviation company summer '23/

First volume carriage of air mail in Canada 2 Se '20/

First Washington, D.C.-Ottawa, Ont. flight 15-16 Ap '20/
First Western Canada Annual Air Show 20 Jl '35/
First westward Atlantic flight 13 Ap '28/
First westward Atlantic solo flight 19 Ag '32/
First wind tunnel in Canada '02/
First wind tunnel tests in Canada of a complete model aircraft Jl '24/
First winter flights into Hudson Bay area Ja '29/
First woman aeroplane passenger in Canada 24 Ap '12/
First woman pilot to exceed Mach 1 18 My '53/
First woman to cross the Atlantic by air 05 Je '28/

Largest airlift of freight in Canada begins 22 Mr '27/

**MISCELLANEOUS**

**Alouette Satellite 28 Se '62/**
**H.M.C.S. "Bonaventure" 17 Ja '57/**
**Bomarc 28 De '61/**
**H.M.C.S. "Magnificent" 7 Ap '48/ 14 Je '57/**
**H.M.S. "Nabob" 12 Ja '44/**
**H.M.S. "Puncher" 12 Ja '44/**
**Thor-Agena B Rocket 28 Se '62/**
**H.M.C.S. "Warrior" 24 Ja '46/ 23 Ma '48/**

**PEOPLE**

Abercorn, Hugh von, Baron 17-19 Oc '10/
Absalom, George M. 26 No '12/
Acosta, Bertrand B. 01 Ja '17/
Adamowicz, Benjamin 08 Ag '33/ 28 Je '34/
Adamowicz, Joseph 08 Ag '33/ 28 Je '34/
Agar, Carl C. '50/
Alcock, John 14-15 Je '19/
Aldwinckle, R.M. 26 Oc '43/
Alexander, C.M. 24 My '60/

Alexander, Field Marshal Earl 05 Je '50/
Alexander, William Boyd 06 Je '11/
Allen, Stephen 30 Jl '13/
Alton, E.A. 01 Oc '24/
Anctel, Ernest 06, 18 Oc '12/
Anderson, C.M. 20 De '24/
Annis, R.H. 30 Ag '56/
Archibald, W.M. '35/
Armbruster, Paul 17-19 Oc '10/
Arnold, H.J. 11 J. '15/
Assmann, William F. 17-19 Oc '10/
Atkin, E.H. 15 Se '47/
Atkinson, Dr. 13 Jl '14/
Atkinson, D.S.E. 31 Oc '34/
Audet, R.J. 29 De '44/
Ayers, M. 19, 21 Ag 1862/ 22 Jl 1862/
11, 25 Se 1862/ 16 Oc 1862/
Ayers, Mrs. M. 22 Jl 1862/ 19 Ag 1862/
Ayling, James R. 08-09 Ag '34/

Bach, Morton Jl '21/
Backman, Carl 15 My '39/
Balbo, Italo 12, 28 Jl '33/
Balchen, Bernt 22 Mr '27/ 26 Ap '28/
Baldwin, Frederick Walker (Casey) 13 Ja '08/
12, 17 Mr '08/ 18 My '08/ 02 Ag '09/
07 Mr. 10/ 05 De '11/ 07 Ag '48/
Baldwin, Thomas Scott 26 Se '07/
Bales, Haden Herbert 19 Se '11/
Ballough, Ervin E. Sum. '17/ 05-06 My '19/
Banghart, F.I. 30 No '27/
Bannock, R. 13 Je '44/ 16 Ag '47/
Banting, Frederick, Sir 20 Fe '41/
Barker, William George 27 Oc '18/ 31 De '18/
09, 23 Ag-06 Se '19/ 04 Je '20/
12 Mr. '30/
Barker, Mrs. W.G. 06 Je '31/
Barlatier, Emile 19-20 Fe '11/ 03 Mr '11/
23-24 Je '11/
Barlatier, Simonne Riviere 19-20 Fe '11/
03 Mr '11/ 23-24 Je '11/
Barnes, Percy 15 Oc '20/
Barnes, W.R. 28 Jl '65/
Barnhill, Logan 29 Se '19/
Bateman, L.J. 04 My '44/
Bates, Louisa 21 Jl 1893/
Bath, C.L. 18 Je-27 Jl '27/
Battock, C.C. Mr '60/
Beach, Stanley Yale 26 Mr. '10/
Beachey, Hillery 22, 24 My '12/ 01 Jl '12/
Beachey, Lincoln 27 Je '14/ 11 Jl '14/
04 Se '07/ 20-22, 24, 26 Je '11/
27 Je '14/ 11 Jl '14/
Beal (mechanic) 11 Jl '20/
Beaudry, L. 15, 22 Se 1856/
Beemer, Alex 08 Je '27/
Beiler, Fritz 26 Ag '35/
Bell, Alexander Graham 28 De '05/ 05 Oc '07/
13 Jl '08/ 05 De '11/
Bellinger, P.N.L. 08 My '19/
Bennett, D.C.T. 21 Jl '38/ 25 Jl '38/
11 No '40/
Bennett, Floyd 12 Ag '25/ 25 Ap '28/
Bennett, V. Sidney Ja '21/
Benidickson, Mrs. W. 17 Se '62/
Bergin, Emil 08 Ag '33/
Berlyn, Martin 29 Se '28/
Berry, A.M. (Matt) 17 Ag-16 Se '36/ '36/
Beurling, G.F. 27 Jl '42/14 Oc '42/ 31 De '45/
20 My '48/
Biddlescombe, C.H. 17 Jl '19/
Bieler, Fritz 23 Je '28/
Billings, D.K. 17 My '14/
Bing, L.P.S. 01-02 Se '41/
Birchall, L.J. 04 Ap '42/
Bishop, A.A. 04 Ag '43/
Bishop, William Avery 02 Je '17/ 19 Je '18/
31 De '18/ 06 Je '31/ 11 Se '56/
Blackburn, J.H. '48/
Blakeley, Harold Wilton 15, 23 Jl '13/ 01, 06,
19, 22 Ag '13/ 06, 11, 12, 13, 15, 16,
18 Se '13/ 03 Oc '13/ 01 Jl '14/
07 Se '14/
Blakely, Tom 25 Je '14/
Blankertz, August 17-19 Oc '10/
Blank, P.E. 20 Fe '64/
Boal, E.W. 02 My '44/
Bochken, John 23 Ag '32/
Boeing, W.E. 28 Fe '19/
Boelcke, O. 28 Oc '16/
Bond, Harry 27 Jl '12/
Boomer, K.A. 25 Se '42/
Bouchier, B.J. '37/
Boudreault, Ovila '49/
Bowman, A. 16 Ja '56/
Boyd, J. Erroll 29 Je '30/ 08, 09-10,
22 Oc '30/ 11 Je '33/ 07 Jl '33/
22 Ag '33/
Bradley, Lorne 17 Jl '12/
Brame, Frank H. 04 Je '50/
Brancker, Sefton 22-24 Ja '24/
Breadner, L.S. 20 De '24/ 01 Ja '44/
Bready, (Aeronaut) 22-28 Se 1888/
Brintnell, W.L. 13-20 Se '28/27 Jl '29/
Brock, William 26 Ag '27/
Brodie, Capt. 08 Je '27/
Brookes, G.E. 29 Je '27/ 03 Je '35/ 01 Ja '43/
Brookins, Walter Richard 25, 26, 27, 28, 29,
30 Je '10/ 01, 02, 03, 04, 14 Jl '10/
17 Jl '12/
Brotman, Ben 08 Je '29/
Brown, Arthur Roy 21 Ap. '18/
Brown, Arthur Whitten 14-15 Je '19/
Brown E. 28 Je 1838/
Brown, Harry Bingham 05 No '12/ 04 Se '13/
Brown, John 02 Ag '30/
Browning, J.H. 23 Se 1880/
Bruce, R.R. 13 Je '44/
Bryant, Alys McKay 31 Jl '13/ 05 Ag '13/
Bryant, John Milton 31 Jl '13/ 06 Ag '13/
Buislay, Justin 24 My 1875/
Burbidge, Maurice '32/
Burke, E.J.A. 24 No '30/
Burnside, Frank H. 31 Ag '14/
Burrell, F.H. 24 Se '42/
Burridge, C.N. 01 Se- 14 Oc '47/
Burton, E.C. 15 Ag. '18/
Burton, John 18 My '09/
Buscombe, R.C. 29 My 1861/
Bush, R. 20 Jl '46/
Butler, Alan S. Ja '21/
Butler, S.W. 10 Mr '44/
Butterfield, F.E. 18 My 1835/
Byrd, Richard E. 19 Ag '18/12 Ag '25/

Cadbury, Egbert 05 Ag '18/
Caine, J.T. 02 My '44/
Caldwell, C.C. (Cy) My-Je '27/ 13 Je '27/
Caldwell, Colin Spencer (Jack) Se '24/
03 No '24/ Mr '28/ 17 My '29/
20 Je '29/
Campbell, D.M. 18 Jl '65/
Campbell, H.L. 01 Se '57/ 14 Se '62/
Campbell, J. 30 Ag '19/
Cannon, W.H. 09 Oc '29/
Capreol, E.L. 16 Ag '39/
Carleton, Cleo 01-03 Se 1897/
Carlincourt, M. see Lowe, Thaddeus Sobieski
Constantine
Carlstrom, Victor 16, 23 Je '13/ 13, 24,
28 Jl '13/ 12 Ag '13/ 28 Jl '15/
15 No '15/
Carr, W.K. 28 Oc-20 De '58/
Carr-Harris, B.G. 20 De '24/
Carruthers, William 25 Je '10/12 Jl '10/
Carson, Margaret M. 19 Ag '51/
Cass, R.W. 20 Fe '64/
Catton, W.E. 27 No-20 De '39/
Chalmers, R. 16 Ag '19/
Chapman, C.G.W. 13 Je '44/
Cheesman, Silas Alward 28 Se '29/ 19 Ag '37/
Chevalier, Henri-Emile Oc 1856/
Chevrolet, Gaston 06, 29 Jl '18/
Childerhose, R.J. 30 Ag '56/
Chilson, Mr. 04 Jl '19/
Christensen, F. 19 My '32/
Christie, R.G. 11 Ap '54/
Clark, Walter 08 Jl '08/
Clark, Wilson H. 24 My '36/
Clarke, J.M. Fe '27/
Claxton, B. 28 De '48/
Claxton, W.G. 31 De '18/
Clements, W.I. 29-30 Se '39/
Cleveland, H.D. 16 My '44/
Coakley, James 24 Je '11/
Cochran, Jacqueline 18 My '53/
Coe, Charles C. 04 Jl 1871/
Coffyn, Frank Trenholm 27, 28, 30 Je '10/
01, 02, 03, 15, 16 Jl '10/ 13, 22 Jl '11/
Coil, Emory W. 15 My '19/
Coli, F. 28 My-07 Je '27/ My-Je '27/
Colley, A.K. 28 My '20/
Collingnon, Robert H. 18 Ag '31/
Collins, Lydia 05 Ag '19/
Collishaw, R. 31 De '18/
Colman, S.W. 17 Ag-16 Se '36/
Connor, Harry P. 08 Oc '30/ 09-10 Oc '30/
Cook, Weldon B. 14 Jl '14/ 13 Ag '14/
Cooke, T.C. 17 Ap '44/
Cooper, E.J. 11 Ja '28/
Cottingham, Sherwin 22 Oc '30/
Cotton, Frederick Sidney 14 No '20/ Ja '21/
28 Mr '21/ 03 Mr '22/ My-Je '27/
13 Je '27/
Coursolles, M. 22 Se 1856/
Courtney, Frank T. 02 Ag '28/
Cowan, Richard W. 31 My 1878/ 28 My 1879/
31 Jl 1879/
Cowley, A.T.N. 28 Jl '15/
Cox, E.C. '32/ '33/ '34/
Cramer, Parker (Shorty) 16 Ag '28/ 28 Jl '31/
Creelman, J. 21 Je 1879/
Cross R. 01 Jl '06/
Curtiss, Glenn Hammond 01 Oc '07/ 20 Je '08/
Curtis, W.A. 01 Se '47/ 31 Ja '53/

Dallas, Jack see Benjamin Parker
Dallin, Capt. 23 Ag-06 Se '19/
D'Almeida, J.R. 11 Se '09/
Davis, Ethel 19 Je '12/
Davis, Harold P. 11 Je '33/
Day, F. 16 My '44/
Day, John Jacob 19 Se '11/
Dean, Godfrey, W. Se '31/
Dean, W.A. 15, 17 My '14/
Decker, Richard 11 Ag '39/
Delamere, R.G. 28 Jl '15/
De Lesseps, Jacques 25, 26, 27, 28, 29,
30 Je '10/ 01, 03, 04, 05, 08, 09, 11, 12,
13, 15, 16, 26 Jl '10/ 18 Oc '27/
de Mumm, Walter 17-19 Oc '10/
de Pinedo, Francesco 18 My '27/ 20 My '27/
DePries, Jack 14 Ap '11/
Desbarats, Mrs. C.G. 25 Jl '25/
De Vonda, Dorothy 18 Jl '12/ 12-14 Se '12/
Dickins, C.H. (Punch) 28 Ag '28/ 23 Ja '29/
01 Jl '29/ 01 Ja '35/
Diefenbaker, J. 28 Oc-20 De '58/ 25 Oc '60/
Diteman, Urban F. 09 Oc '29/
Dixon, Cromwell 25, 27 Je '10/ 04 Jl '10/
Doan, G.A. 17 Ag '20/
Doan, J.E. 14 Se '39/
Dobbin, E.C.W. 05 De '42/
Donahue, Robert 31 Ag '18/
Donaldson, Washington Harrison 17, 21, 22,
23, 26 Je 1875/
Donegani, Joseph 24 Ag 1835/
Doolittle, James Harold 20 Oc '31/
Doughty, Arthur 20 My '19/
Douglas, H.T. 15-16, 19 Ap '20/ 18 Je '20/
Dover, M.G. 27 Jl '20/
Drake, J.F. 19 Jl '47/
Drake, Stanley 28 Ja '13/
Drury, W.H.E. 12 Se '28/
Dugal, Hector 15-17 Oc '20/
Dunlap, C.R. 26 Je '43/ 22 No '43/ 14 Se '62/
31 Jl '64/
Dunstan, A. 15 Ag '18/
Dure, John 15 Se '49/
Durnin, W.J. 20 De '24/

Eagle, Y.T. Mid Jl '22/
Earhart, Amelia 05 Je '28/ 20 My '32/
Earlston, Prof. 23 My '01/
Eaton, Sir John 28 Jl '15/
Eckly, A. 13 My '19/
Edwards, C.H. 12 My '37/
Edwards, R.L. 26 Ag '40/
Edwards, Walter 24 Se '12/ 0
Eells, Fred G. 06 Jl '12/
Eielson, Carl Ben No '29/
Eliedon, Prof. Je 1875/
Elizabeth II, Queen of
05-13 Oc '64/
Elliot, J.V. 03 Mr
Ellis, Frank H. C
15-17 C

Henry, Hi 20 Jl '11/
Heron, P.W. 11 Fe '44/
Hersey, Henry Blanchard 21 Oc .07/
Hess, Charles Earl 13 Se '07/
Higgins, F.C. 20 De '24/
Hill, G.T.R. 22 Ap '46/
Hill, L. 16 Ja '56/
Hill, William R. 24 Mr '21/ 05 Ap '21/
Hillig, Otto 22 Je '31/
Hinkler, H.J.L. (Bert) 20 Oc '31/
Hinton, Walter 14 De '20/
Hiscocks, R.G. 11 Ap '54/
Hobbs, Basil D. 14, 28 Se '17/ 10 Se '19/
Hodgson, G. 29 My '17/
Hogan, Edward D. 04-06 Se 1888/ 16 Jl 1889/
Hogan, W. 19 Jl 1889/ 04 Se 1889
Hoiris, Holger 22 Je '31/ 28 Je '34/
Holden, L.L. 26-27 Se 1872/
Holley, J.H. 31 Jl '30/
Hollick-Kenyon, H. 19 Ag '37/
Honeywell, H.E. 05 Jl '08/
Hoover, Fred 21 Ag '12/
Hornell, D.E. 24 Je '44/
Horner, J.V. 02-03 Ja '29/
Horton, Clair G. 01, 13 Jl '14/
Horton, H.M. 27 Ag '10/
Hosmer, Elwood B. 02 Ag '28/
Howe, Clarence Decatur 29 Se '54/
Hoy, E.C. 31 My '19/ 07 Ag '19/
Hoyt, Ross G. 19, 21 Jl '29/
Hubbard, Edward 28 Fe '19/ 03 Mr '19/
15 Oc '20/
Hubbard, Gardiner Greene II 05 Ap '10/
04 Jl '10/
Hughes, Sam 16 Se '14/
Hunter, J.D. 01 Ag '37/
Hutchinson, E.R. 07-14 Se '12/ 25-29,
30 Ag '13/
Hutchinson, George R. 23 Ag '32/
Hyslop, Harvey N. 28 Je '21/

Ince, A. Strachan 11 Jl '15/ 14 De '15/
Irvine, Leslie 04 Jl '19/

Jaap, Alex 12 Ag '11/
Jackson, J.J. 02 Ag '11/
Jacques, D.R. '49/
James, Capt. 23 Ag-06 Se '19/
James, Mansell Richard 28, 29 My '19/
Janney, Ernest Lloyd 21 Se '14/ Ja '21/
29 Je '27/
Jannus, Antony H. Jl '15/ 14, 28 Jl '15/
03 Se '15/
Jarvis, William B. 16 Oc 1784/
Jellison, Joseph Earle 08, 29 Je '27/
13 Mr '28/
Jenkins, Gilbert Fe '27/
Johnson, Walter 24 Ma '21/ 05 Ap '21/
Johnstone, Ralph 25, 27, 28, 29, 30 Je '10/
01, 08, 09, 11, 14, 15, 16 Jl '10/
Johnstone, St. Croix 31 De '10/ 22 Mr '11/
03 Jl '11/ 09, 15 Ag '11/
Joliceur, J.A.F. 14-15 Ja '49/
Jones, C.S. (Casey) 12 Ap '26/
Jones, H.S. 22 De '41/
Joy, D.G. 09 Ag '20/ 01 Ap '36/
Juwel, May 06 Se 1899/

Kahre, W. 07 Jl '19/ Oc '19/
Keating, Edward 16 Se '09/
Kelsey, Earl H. 26 No '12/
Kent, J.A. 01 Oc '40/
Kenyon, Herbert Hollick 23 No-05 De '35/
Kerr, Mark 04 Jl '19/ 16 Ag '19/ 09 Oc '19/
Kierzkowski, Alexandre Edouard 08 Se 1856/
King, Charles G. 06-07-14-15 Oc '11/
06 Oc '11/
King, Samuel Archer 14 Oc 1863/
26-27 Se 1872/ 23 Se 1874/
Kirby, Jack 15 Oc '11/
Kloor, L.A. 14 De '20/
Knight, A.G. 28 Oc '16/
Koehl, Herman 13 Ap '28/
Koenemann, Ulrich ·28 Je '28/
Kokkinaki, Vladimir 28 Ap '39/
Kronfeld, R. 22 Ap '46/

Labatt, Dora 17 Jl '12/
LaChappelle, Duval 27, 28, 29, 30 Je '10/
01, 02, 03, 04, 09, 11 Jl '10/
Lamothe, G. 15 Se 1856/
Lamount, Nellie 02-03 Se 1891/
La Mountain, John 22-23 Se 1859/
Lamphier, T.G. 24 Ja '27/
Landry, Jean-Marie 30 My '14/ 13 Ag '14/
Lapham, Arthur C. 04 Se '13/
Laporte, Arthur E. 08-09 Jl '39/
Lariviere, P. 17 De '59/
Larsen, J.M. 09, 21 My '21
Lasley, L.E. Je '32/
Laur, Edgar L. 10 De '12/
Lauriat, Louis Anselm 10 Ag 1840/
Law, Ruth 06, 29 Jl '18/
Lawrence, T.A. 27 Jl '27/ 01 Je '44/
Leach, W.G. '60/
Leblanc, Alfred 17-19 Oc '10/
Leckie, Robert 14 My '17/ 05 Ag '18/
25 Mr '19/ 01 Ja '44/ 01 Se '47/
LeClaire, Prof. 09, 11 Je 1880/
Lee, Clyde Allen 23 Ag '32/
Lee, G.A. 10-13 Se '48/
Leigh, Z.L. '46/
Leitch, A.A. 27 Jl '27/
Leonard, John 29 Ag 1899/ 25 My '03/
Lesh, Lawrence Jerome Ag '07/ 20 or 21,
31 Ag '07/ Se '07/
Le Van, Howard 03 Jl '11/ 07-14 Se '12/
29 Jl-01 Ag '13/ 25 Jl '13/
Levanevsky, S. 19 Ag '37/
Levesque, J.A.O. 30 Mr '51/
Lewis, A. 17 Fe '28/
Light, Richard U. 21 Ag '34/ 06 Ja '35/
Lilly, A.J. 20 Jl '46/ 28 Mr '49/ 09 Ag '50/
Lindbergh, Charles Augustus 02 Jl '27/
25 Ap '28/ 30 Jl '31/ 11 Jl '33/
Lindbergh, Mrs. C.A. 30 Jl '31/ 11 Jl '33/
Littlejohn, G. 19 No '34/
Lizotte, Leonce 09 Oc '29/
Locklear, Ormer L. 28 Je-01 Jl '20/
05-08 Jl '20/
Loeb, Alexander 11 Ag '39/
Logan, M.B. 02 Se '09/
Logan, Robert Archibald 28 Jl '15/
18 Jl '22/
Lohner, George 22 Jl '10/

Longhurst, W.S. 23 Je-01 Jl '43/ 22 De '52/
30 Jl '53/ 28 Mr '57/ 18 No '60/
07 My '65/
Longman, T. 15 Ag '18/
Loudon, T.R. se '37/
Lowanda, Madame 26 Se 1884/
Lowe, Thaddeus Sobieski Constantine
17 Je 1858/ 01 Se 1858/
29 30 My 1861/
Luckey, William S. 03, 23 Je '13/
Lunardi, Vincent 16 Oc 1784/
Lymburner, J.H. 28 Ag '43/
Lynch, A.L. 28 Je '21/
Lyon, Robt. G. 11 Je '33/ 07 Jl '33/

McAlpine, C.D.H. 28 Ag '28/ 20 Se '29/
03 No '29/ 04 De '29/
McArthur, J.H.G. 04-06 Se '49/
McBride, R.E. 03, 30 Je '44/
MacBrien, J.H. 07-15 Jl '28/
McCanse, Betty 19 Ag '51/
Macaulay, Theodore C. 15, 17 25 My '14/
28 Jl '15/ 23 Se '15
McClintock, Lt. F.L. 15 Jl 1851/
McCombie, Robert 20 Ap '20/
McComiskey, B.J. 30 Ag '56/
McConachie, G.W.C. 05 Jl '37/ '45/
29 Je '65/
McConkey, Ben 27 Jl '12/
McCowan, Robert, Jr. 15 mr '11/
McCuen, Prof. W.W. 02-03 Se 1891/
McCurdy, John Alexander Douglas
01 Oc '07/ 23 My '08/ 06 De '08/
23 Fe '09/ 02, 12 Ag '09/ 07, 09 Mr '10/
24, 26, 27, 28, 29 Je '10/ 27 Ag '10/
23 Oc '10/ 30 Ja '11/ 20, 20-33,
24 Je '11/ 27 Jl '11/ 02, 03-05 Ag '11/
05 De '11/ 28 Jl '15/ 23 Fe '59/ '59/
25 Je '61
McDermid, Neil 28 De '05/
MacDonald, H.C. 17 Oc '28/
McDonough, W.J. 12 No '35/
McDougall, F.A. '63/
McGannon, W.H. 16 Ag '19/
MacGill, E.G. '29/
McGill, Frank S. 15 Jl '18/
McGinnis, G.L. '55/
MacGlashan, W.M. 15 Oc 1834/
McGrath, James 21 Se '12/
McGregor, F.M. 01 Se '37/
McGregor, G.R. '35/ '36/ '38/ 22 Oc '40/
15 Ap '41/
McKay, A.E. 28 Oc '16/
McKee, J. Dalzell 11-19 Se '26/
McKeever, Andrew Edward 30 No '17/
Mackenzie, A.M. 14 Je '46/ 06 Jl '56/
McKenzie, I.K. 08 Ap '62/
McKenzie, M.M. 28 Je '44/
McKillop, John A. 18 Ap '51/
McKnight, W.E. 31 De '45/
MacLaren, D.R. 31 De '18/ 10 Fe '25/
McLaren, F.G. 08 Ap '62/
MacLaren, Stuart 03 Ag '24/
McLarty, E.G. '53/
McLean, A.D. '41/
McLean, G.T. 18 No '60/
MacLean, J.A. 25 Oc '60/
McLeod, Alan A. 27 Mr '18/
McLeod, Alex 04 Se '11/
McLeod, H.W. 31 De '45/
McMullen, William 30 Ap-06 My '11/
McNaughton, A.G.L. Fall '32/
McNab, E.A. 15 Ag '40/ 22 Oc '40/
McNair, R.W. 31 De '45/
McNeal, J. 30 My '61/
McRae, D.G. 24 Ag '43/ 06 Se '43/ 18 No '43/
MacTavish, I. 13 Ja '60/
Mynarski, A.C. 12 Je '44/
Mackey, J. 20 Fe '41/
Madison, Nina 02-05 Se 1896/
Magar, Alexander (Sandor Wilczek) 13 Jl '31/
Magor, N.A. 22 Se '17/
Mann, E.O. '50/
Manning, Browne 18 Ap '11/
Marble, Charles 10 Oc 1894/
Markham, Beryl 05 Se '36/
Marks, J.W. 25 Jl '13/
Marquet, M. 28 Je '44/
Mars, James C. "Bud" 22 Se '09/
Marsh, W.J. 06 Ag '57/
Martin, Glen Luther 06 Ag '12/ 05 Ag '13/
Martin, James V. 27 Jl '11/ 10 Ag '12/
Massey, V., Governor General 20 Mr--5 Ap '56/
Masson, Didier 17 Oc '11/
Masson, J. 15 Se 1856/
Mathers, E.W. 24 Je '18/
Mattern, J. 05 Jl '32/
Maunsell, Major G.S. 09 Mr '10/
Maxwell, W.R. 17, 28 Ag '20/ 02 Se '20/
05 Fe '22/ 12 Ap '26
May, W.R. "Wop" 30 Ag '19/ 19 Ag '20/
se '20/ 02-03 Ja '29/ '29/ 01 Ja '35/
Mears, Henry 02 Ag '30/
Medcalf, James V. 28 Ag '27/ 06 Se '27/
Mee, N.A. Ltd. 03 Ja '29/
Meier, D.C. 06 Ag '57/
Menier, Prof. H. 27 My 1896/
Merklinger, B. 30 Ag '56/
Merrill, Harry T. (Dick) 14 Se '36/
Messner, E. 17-19 Oc '10/
Mestach, Georges 29 Ag '11/ 10 Jl '12/
26 Ag '12/ 02 Se '12/
Middleton, R.B. 15 De '43/
Miller, Frank 26 Ag 1896/ 07 Ag '02/
14 Se '02/
Miller, Mrs. J.M. 05 Fe '30/
Miller, John W. 15 Jl '22/
Miller, W.G.S. 30 Se-15 No '55/ 20 Mr '56/
05 Ap '56/
Miltgen, Paul 25 Je '10/
Mitchell, C.H. 20 Fe 1895/
Moffit, B.J. 04 My '43/
Millison, Amy 19-20 Ag '33/ 03 Oc '33/
Mollison, James A. 19 Ag '32/ 03 Oc '33/
28 Oc '36/
Moodie, Bob 08 Se 1859/
Moore, K.O. 08 Je '44/
Morgan, C.W.F. 18 My '19/
Morok, Charles 01, 08 Jl '12/
Morris, Raymond V. 02 Je '13/ 01 Jl '13/
Moulton, Hiram 28 Se 1878/

Mulock, Redford Henry 09 Mr '15/
29 Ag '18/
Musgrave, J. 13 My '43/
Myers, Carlotta 02 Jl 1883/

Nassr, Anthony M. 16 Se '09/
Neal, George A. Mr '53/ 30 Jl '58/
Nesbitt, Dr. & Mrs. James 08 Je '27/
Newbury, Abel T. 02 My '11/
Nichols, Ruth 22 Je '31/
Niles, Charles Frank 01 Jl '13/
Norcross, J.W. '20/
Noury, J.O. 04 Je '45/
Nungesser, C. 28 My-07 Je '27/ My-Je '27/

Oaks, H.A. (Doc) 14 Ap '26/ Oc '26/
27 De '26/ '27/ Ja '29/ 03 Ja '29/
Oates, Gordon 18 Ag '58/
O'Donnell, E.M. 07 Se '43/
Oliphant, M.E. 12 Se '28/
Onarheim, T.G. 06 Ag '57/
Orrell, J.H. 10 Ag '49/
Oscanyan, Paul 18 Jl '35/
Owens, Fred 27, 28, 30 Je '10/ 01, 02 Jl '10/

Pachero, Joaquin 23 Je '28/
Pacquette, Oliver Louis 28 Jl '31/
Page, Charles 31 My 1878/ 28 My 1879/
31 Jl 1879/
Page, Handley 16 Ag '19/
Palmer, L.T. Fe '27/
Parker, Benjamin 01 Jl '08/ 09 Ag '09/
Parker, D.F. 10 Ap '63/
Parkin, J.H. Jl '29/
Parkinson, J.D. 26 My '31/
Parmelee, Phil. O. 23, 24 My '12/
Parmer, O.S. 12 Jl '19/
Parvis, R.F. '54/
Pasmore, H.M. 27 Oc '27/
Patterson, Isabella 05 No '12/
Pearce 28 Ag '28/
Pearce, N.C. 17 My '14/
Pearkes, G.R. 11 Oc '60/
Pearson, Lester B. 02 Ja-08 Fe '50/
30 Se-15 No '55/
Peck, Brian 24 Je '18/
Peoli, Cecil Malcolm 15 Jl '12/ 02, 25,
26 Se '12/ 30 Je '13/ 04 Jl '13/
11 Se '13/ 06 De '13/
Pepper, George 01 Ag '11/
Perkins, Samuel F. 17-19 Oc '10/
Peterson, Carl 23 Ag '32/
Peterson, Edward C. 04 Se '11/
Philips, G.H.R. '31/
Phipps, W.W. '61/
Phripp, C.G. 10-13 Se '48/
Plenderleith, W.N. 04 Se '24/
Pollien, Gustave 06, 09, 18, 20 Oc '12/
06 Se '13/ 25 Je '14/
Post, Auguatus 17-19 Oc '10/
Post, Wiley 23, 30 Je '31/ 22 Jl '33/
Potocki, W.J. 16 My '61/
Pow, Al. 30 Jl-07 Ag '49/
Powell, L.A. 30 No '16/
Power, C.G. 23 My '40/
Power, W.C. 22 Jl '11/
Prest, Clarence Oliver Jl '21/ Mid Jl '22/
Preston, Edwin L. 18 Ag '31/
Prinz, Benny 25 Je '10/
Prosper, Louis 02 Ag '10/
Purcell, J. Stanley 02 Jl '14/

Quigley, Harry Stephen Se '22/ 9 Je '25/
16 Se '27/

Rabnett, Anthony Augustine 20 Jl '35/
Rae, John 10 Ap 1837/
Ralston, R.J. 23 Se '27/
Rambau, Alfred Xavier 08 Se 1856/
Ramsay, David S. 08 Se 1856/
Rankin, John G. (Tex) 12 Ag '29/
Rasche, Thea 28 Je '28/
Rawson, B.A. '47/
Ray, Lewis Hector 15 Jl '13/
Ray, R.B. 26-27 Ag '44/
Raymes, D.F. 30 Oc '42/
Raynham, F.P. 18 My '19/ 17 Jl '19/
Read, A.C. 14 My '19/
Ready, J.M. 26 Ag '29/
Reese, L. 08 Oc '21/
Reichers, Louis T. 13 My .32/ 28 Ag '32/
Reid, Leonard G. 08-09 Ag '34/
Reid, Percival Hall 28 De '11/ 19 Je '12/
23 Oc '12/
Reid, T.M. (Pat) Ja '29/ 03 Ja '29/ No '29/
'43-'43/ 09 Ap '53/
Reid, W.T. Fe '28/
Rennie, D.A. 14 Se '39/
Reno, Prof. 08, 12, 31 Jl 1871/
08, 17 Ag 1871/
Richardson, H.C. 08 My '19/
Richardson, James A. 10 De '26/ 26 Je '39/
Richardson, Mrs. J.A. 17 Se '62/
Richman, Harry 14 Se '36/
Richter, Joseph 08 Jl '11/
Riddell, W.G. Ja '40/
Robertson, F/O 22 Ap '46/
Robertson, William J. 15 Jl '09/
Robinson, Carl 29 Ag '07/
Robinson, E.L. 30 Oc '42/
Robinson, F.V. 28 My-07 Je '27/
Robinson, Hugh A. 28 Ap '11/
Robinson, William Curtis 08 Oc '13/
Rodgers, Capt (Possibly Capt B.D. Rodgers)
Jl '19/
Rogers, J.C. Kelly 06 Ag '39/
Ronald, Bruce (Reg) 08 Je '29/ 04 Jl '32/
Ross, A.D. 28 Je '44/
Ross, J.R. Oc '26/ 22 Mr '27/
Rossiter, Norman 24 Je '11/
Roth, G. 25 Jl '32/ 09 Ag '32/
Roy, A. 22 Se 1856/
Royer, J.A. 18 Je '20/
Russell, A.H. 08 Oc '43/
Russel, B.D. 22 Oc '40/
Russell, D. 04 Jl '19/
Russell, Robert B. 19 Je '12/ 28 Jl '14/

Sabourin 09 Ja '57/
St. Germain, J.R. 28 Je '44/
St. Henry, R.C. "Bob" 18 Ma '11/ 01 Je '11/
05 Ag '11/ 26 Jl '12/ 02 Se '12/
St. Laurent, Louis 04 Fe-07 Mr '54/
St. Martin, Hervé 05 Fe '22/

Ward, James J. 01, 10, 30 Jl '12/
Wasson, Everett 24 No '30/
Waterton, W.A. (Bill) 19 Ja '50/
Watkins, L.P. 17 Je '17/
Weaver, W.C. 20 De '24/
Webster, Clifford Lawrence 21 Se '14/
Webster, J. Clarence, Sr. 31 Ag '31/
Webster, John C. 25 Jl '31/ 10, 31 Ag '31/
Wedell, James Robert 01 De '31/
23 Oc '32/
Wells, E.P.H. (Billy) 01 Se '37/
Wells, T.A. '52/
Welsh, W.H. 15 Ag '19/
Wemp, B.S. 28 Jl '15/
Wensley, Tom 26 Se 1888/
West, R.B. '48/
Wilcockson, A.S. 05-08 Jl '37/
Wilkins, Hubert, Sir 28 Se '29/ 19 Ag '37/
Willard, Charles Foster 02 Se '09/ 27 Jl '11/
02, 03-05 Ag '11/
Williams, Charles W. 15, 26 Se 1888/
Williams, G. 28 Jl '15/
Williams, Prof. 11 Jl '06/
Williams, Roger Q. 29 Je '30/
Williams, T.F. 04 Je '45/
Wilshire, H.D. '22/ 22 Ap '24/
Wilson, A.H. 31 Jl '30/
Wilson, C.W. '47/
Wilson, H. Allan 26-28 Ag '20/
Wilson, J.A. '44/
Wilson, Robert F. 21 Ag '34/ 06 Ja '35/
Winfindale, A.F. 24 Se 1891/
Witmer, Charles C. 20-22, 24 Je '11/
Wolfe, R.R. 28 Je '44/
Wolcott, Charles W. 10 De '12/
Wood, Phillip S. 07 Se '27/ 21 Se '27/
Woodhill, Prof. 27 Jl 1891/
Woodward, Frank 29 Je-13 Jl '56/
Woodward, V.C. 31 De '45/
Workman, Wm H. 16 Ag '19/
Wright, J.G. '54/
Wynne-Eaton, C.S. 06 Jl '30/

Yorath, D.K. '49/
Young, F.I. 23 My '37/ '53/

Zebora, M. 28 Je '28/
Zimmers, Eduard 23 Ag '30/ 28 Ag '31/
Zimmerly, D.S. 07 Jl '29/
Zurakowski, Jan 18 De '52/ 25 Mr '58/
18 Ap '58/ '58/

**PLACES**

Abingdon, Eng. 05 Se '36/
Agadir, Mor. 05-07 Mr '60/
Agua Caliente, Mex. 12 Ag '29/ 19 Je '31/
01 De '31/ 23 Ja '32/
Aklavik, N.W.T. 01 Jl '29/ 30 Jl '31/
26 Ag '35/
Alaska Jl '21/ No '29/ 09 Ag '32/
02-08 Je '42/
Albany, N.Y. 01 Oc '28/
Alberta 01 Mr '38/
Almonte, Ont. 29 Ag 1879/
Amos, Que. 08 Mr '28/
Anchorage, Alas. 31 Jl '51/
Andover, Eng. 09 De '44/ Fe '45/ Mr '45/
Angliers, Que. 23 My '24/ 03 Se '24/
03 No '24/
Annette Island, Alas. 07 Jl '42/
Arctic Archipelago 30 Je '57/
Armstrong, B.C. 01 Jl '12/
Arnhem, Neth. 17-23 Ag '44/
Arnprior, Ont. 10-13 Se '48/
Ashcroft, B.C. 19 Se '11/
Atlantic City, N.J. 28 My '19/ 29 My '19/
Augusta, Maine 09 Ag '11/
Australia 08 Se '27/
Azores 16 My '19/ 20 My '27/ 02 Ag '28/
19 My '32/ 28 Jl '33/

Baddeck, N.S. 28 De '05/ 23 Fe '09/
25 Se '09/ 07, 09 Mr '10/ 18 Ag '56/
23 Fe '59/ 15 Je '59/
Baden Soellingen, Ger. 27Ag-04 Se '53/
Baffin Island, N.W.T. 27 Ag '34/
Bagington, Eng. 01 Mr '41/
Bagotville, Que. 01 My '42/ 01 Ag '51/
01 No '52/ 01 Oc '53/ 01 Oc '54/
11-12 My '57/ Jl '62/
Baker Lake, N.W.T. 30 Jl '31/
Bawlf, Alta. 26 No '12/
Bangor, Me. 14 Oc 1863/ 15 My '39/
Barre, Vt. 23 Ag '32/
Barrie, Ont. 30 Je .13/
Bath, N.Y. 31 Ag '14/
Battleford, Sask. 22 Ag '13/
Battle Harbour, Lab. 03 Ma '22/
Bay of Biscay 07 Se '43/ 04 My '44/
Beauchene, Que. 01 Ag '40/
Beausejour, Man. 01 Oc '61/
Bedlington, Eng. 01-02 Se '41/
Beloeil, Que. 24 Se 1891/
Belmont, Man. 12 Se '13/
Berck, Fr. 23 My '40/
Bering Island, Alas. 03 Ag '24/
Berlin, Ger. 29 Ag '18/ 07 Jl '29/
05 Jl '32/ 07 My '45/
Berlin, Ont. see Kitchener, Ont.
Bermuda 29 je .30/ 01 My '48/
Bienfait, Sas. 01 Oc '24/
Bieske, Hun. 13 Jl '31/
Billings, Mon. 21 Se '27/
Binghamton, N.Y. 15 No '15/
Birmingham, Ala. 20 Oc '31/
Bisset, Man. 06 Oc '27/
Boissevain, Man. 01 Ag '13/
Boston, Mass. 10 Ag 1840/ 08 Jl '08/
05 Ap '10/ 04 Jl '10/ 19 Je '12/
28 My '19/ 05 Je '28/
Botwood, Nfld. 28 Mr '21/ 03 Mr '22/
03-06 Jl '37/ 05-08 Jl '37/ 25 Jl '38/
15 My '39/ 26 Je '39/ 08-09 Jl '39/
06 Ag '39/
Boulogne, Fr. 15 Ap '41/
Boundary Bay, B.C. 01 Jl '42/
Bournemouth, Eng. 10 Se '19/
Bowesville, Ont. 15-16 Ap '20/
Brandon, Man. 23 Jl '12/ 15, 23, 25 Jl '13/
01 Ag '13/ 06, 15 Se '13/ 22 jl '16/
14 Se '30/

Brantford, Ont. 13 Jl '13/ 20-27 Jl '57/
03-10 Ag '57/ 18 Ag '58/
Breckenridge, Que. 15 Se '49/
Brest, Fr. 12 Fe '42/ 04-05 Ja '44/
Bridgeport, Conn. 04 Ag '33/
Brightwater, B.C. 27 Ag '12/
British Columbia 01 Mr '38/
Brockville, Ont. 01 Jl 1874/ 04 Se '12/
Brooklyn, N.Y. 16 Jl 1889/
Brownsville, Tex. 07 Jl '29/
Budapest, Hun. 13 Jl .31/
Buffalo, N.Y. 18 Je 1815/ 29 Ag '07/
26 Je '11/ 10 My '21/ 12 Ap '26/
29 Je '29/
Burgeo, Nfld. 23 Ag '32/
Burrard Inlet, B.C. 13 Je '14/

Cache Lake, Man. 22 Mr '27/
Caistor Centre, Ont. 26 No '12/
Calgary, Alta. 11 Jl '06/ 01 Jl '08/ 03 Jl '11/
12 Ag '11/ 17 Oc '11/ 01 Jl '12/
25 Je '14/ 02 Jl '14/ 30 Je-03 Jl '16/
09 Jl '18/ 07 Ag '19/ 28 Je-01 Jl '20/
20 Je '28/ 15 Se '28/ 10-29 De '28/
23 Ja '30/ 14 Se '30/ 01 Ja '37/
10 No '41/ 11 Ap '54/
Cambrai, Fr. 12 Je '44/
Cambridge Bay, N.W.T. 03 No '29/
Camp Borden, Ont. 02, 08 Ap '17/ 02 My '17/
05 Jl '20/ 09 Ag '20/ 01 Oc '20/
11 Ap '21/ 15 My '23/ Se '24/
20 De '24/ 29 Je '27/ 04 Jl '27/ Ap '30/
Ja '40/ 22 Jl '40/
Camp Shilo, Man. 04 My '43/
Canada Jl '21/
Canada East see Quebec
Canada West see Ontario
Cap de la Madeleine, Que. 28 Je '28/
28 Jl-05 Ag '56/
Cape Breton Island, N.S. 18 Je-27 Jl '27/
05 Se '36/ 11 Ag '39/
Cape Canaveral, Fla. 20 Fe '62/
Cape Sable, N.S. 31 Jl '42/
Capodichino, Naples, It. 20 No '56/
Cardington, Eng. 01 Ag .30/
Carp, Ont. '45/ 15 Se '49/
Carrington, N.Dak. 01 Je '11/
Cartierville, Que. 06, 09, 18, 20 Oc '12/
19 Je '12/ 06 Se '13/ 06 De '13/
29 Se '28/ Mr '29/ 23 Se '43/ Oc '44/
20 Jl '46/ 22 De '52/ 30 Jl '53/
28 Mr '57/ 17 De '59/ 13 Ja '60/
28 No '60/ 07 My '65/
Cartwright, Lab. 03 Ma '22/ 23 Ag '30/
25 Jl '32/ 11, 12 Jl '33/ 21 Ag '34/
18 Jl '35/
Casco Bay, Me. 31 Ag '24/
Ceylon 18 Mr-06 Ap '42/ 04 Ap '42/
Charlottetown, P.E.I. 17 Ag 1871/
07 Oc 1891/ 25, 26 Se '12/ 29 Se '19/
19 Fe '28/ 08 Oc '30/
Chatham, Mass. 14 My '19/
Chatham, N.B. 15 Se '49/ 06 Ag '57/
Chatham, Ont. 01 Jl '12/ 21 Ag '12/
23, 26 Je '13/
Chelsea, Que. 03 Jl 1877/
Chibougamou, Que. 09 Oc '29/
Chicago, Ill. 05 Jl '08/ 23 Oc '10/ 15 Ag '11/
04 Se '11/ 23 Jl '12/ 07 Jl '29/
28 Ag '31/ 25 Jl '32/ 12, 28 Jl '33/
12-14 Se '48/
Chicoutimi, Que. 17-19 Oc '10/
Chile 24 My '60/
Chilliwack, B.C. 01 Jl '14/
Churchill, Man. 22 Mr '27/ 17 Jl '27/ 30 Jl '31/
15 Fe-06 My '46/ 12-24 Se '48/
Cincinnati, Ohio 15 Se 1888/
Cleveland, Ohio 22-28 Se 1888/ 30 Je '31/
29 Ag-01 Se '31/
Clifden, Ire. 14-15 Je '19/
Cloncurry, Aust. 12 Oc-10 De '32/
Coalbranch, Alta. 30 Ag '19/
Cochrane, Ont. 16 Ag '28/ 03 Ja '29/
28 Jl '31/ 18 Ag '31/
Cold Lake, Alta. Ag-Se '27/ 15 No '54/
11 Oc '55/
Cologne, Ger. 30-31 My '42/
Comox, B.C. 01 Jl '52/ 01 No '54/
Copenhagen, Den. 18 Ag '31/
Cormorant Lake, Man. 09 Ag '32/ 26 Ag '35/
Cornwall, Ont. 19-20 Fe '11/ 05 Se '13/
Cornwallis Island, N.W.T. Ag-Se 1850/
15 Jl 1851/
Coronation Gulf 09 Ma '21/
Corpus Christi, Tex. 20 Oc '31/
Cranbrook, B.C. 07 Ag '19/
Crystal Beach, Ont. 11 Jl '14/ 04, 05 Jl '19/
Cyprus 12-23 Ma '64/

Dartmouth, N.S. 17 Je '40/ Ja '42/ 20 Ap '42/
28 Ag '42/ 01 Oc .42/ 01 De '45/
02 Se-14 oc '47/ 19 No '48/ 04 Jl '55/
16 Ja '56/ 30 Ag '56/
Dauphin, Man. 27 Jl '20/
Davidson, Sask. 01 Ag '11/
Dawson, Y.T. 29 Ag 1899/ 03 Se '20/
Dayton, Ohio 01 Je '22/ Se '24/
Dease Point, N.W.T. 09 Se '29/
Debert, N.B. 15 Ja '42/
Deer Lake, Nfld. 21 Ag '34/
Denmark 22 Je '31/ 28 Jl '31/
Deseronto, Ont. summer '17/
Detroit, Mich. 03 Jl '11/ 10 My '21/ se'24/
28 Jl '31/ 18 Ag '31/ 18-19 Ag '51/
Dieppe, Fr. 19 Ag '42/
Digby, Eng. 09 De '40/ 01 Mr '41/
Dildo Harbour, Nfld. 19 My '32/
Dortmund, Ger. 06-07 Oc '44/
Dorval, Que. 28 Mr '49/ 09 Ag '50/ 01 Ap '53/
13 De '54/ 19 De '58/
Downsview, Ont. 24 Se '42/ 22 My '46/
16 Ag '47/ 13 No '51/ 29 Se '54/
30 Jl '58/ 30 My '61/ 09 Ap '64/
Dublin, Ire. 13 My '32/ 11 Ag '39/
Dunnville, Ont. 28 Ja '13/

Eastmain, Que. 27 Ag '34/
East Portland, Que. 01 Jl 1878/
East Templeton, Que. 26 Se 1884/
Edmonton, Alta. 01 Jl '06/ 28 Ap '11/
18 Je .12/ 10 De '12/ 09, 09-13 Jl '18/
16 My '19/ 30 Ag '19/ 05-08, 06-08,
25 Jl '20/ 19 Ag '20/ Se '20/ 03 Se '20/
09, 21 My '21/ Jl '21/ 13 Je '28/ Ag '28/

10-28 De '28/ 02-03 Ja '29/ 19 Jl '29/
10 De '29/ '29/ 14, 17 Se '30/
15 My '31/ 30 Je '31/ 30 Ja '32/
22 Jl '33/ 30 Ag '34/ 05 Jl '37/
01 Ap '39/ 01 Je '44/ 15 Fe-06 My '46/
15 Ap '46/ Fe '47/ 01 Mr '47/
09 Fe '56/
Egypt 04 Je '42/
Eindhoven, Neth. 17-23 Se '44/
Elizabeth, N.J. 05-06 My '19/
Ellesmere Island, N.W.T. 12, 25 Ag '25/
England 23 Je '31/ 26 Ag '35/ 14 Se '36/
25 Jl '38/ 01 Oc '40/ 15, 23 Ap '41/
08, 10 My '41/ 16, 17, 24, 30 Je '41/
01 Jl '41/ 12, 20 Ag '41/ 15, 18,
27 No '41/ 07, 19 De '41/ 02,
01 Ap .42/ 18 My '42/ 25 Je '42/
15 Oc '42/ 07, 09 No '42/ 01 Ja '43/
01 My '43/ 15 Je '43/ 15 Se '43/
04 Se '44/ Oc '44/ 14 Jl '48/
English Channel 30 De '44/
Erie, Penn. 20 Fe '12/
Erie Beach, Ont. 30 Jl '13/
Esquimault, B.C. 27 Jl 1891/
Estevan, Sask. 01 Oc '24/

Fairbanks, Alas. 30 Je '31/
Fairfax, Vt. 23-24 Je '11/
Falaise, Fr. 17-20 Ag '44/
Fanning Is., (Line Is.) Fe '27/
Father Point, Que. 16 Se '27/ 27 Oc '27/
Fiji Is. Fe '27/
Fogo, Nfld. 28 Mr '21/
Fort Churchill, Man. 08 Je '29/ De '47/
Fort Erie, Ont. 20-22, 24, 26 Je '11/
22 Fe '38/ 01 Fe '55/ 04 Je '55/
Fort George, Que. 27 Ag '34/
Fort McMurray, Alta. 23 Ja '29/ 26 Ag '35/
Fort Norman, N.W.T. Ja '21/ 26 Ag '35/
Fort Simpson, N.W.T. 24 Mr '21/ 05 Ap '21/
23 Ja '29/
Fort Vermilion, Alta. 02-03 Ja '29/ '29/
Fort William, Ont. 04 Se '11/ Je '32/ Se '37/
17 De '38/ 24 Je '40/ 29 Jl '43/
16 Ja '56/
Foynes, Ire. 05-08 Jl '37/ 21 Jl '38/
26 Je '39/
Fredericton, N.B. 22 Jl 1839/ 26-28 Ag '2-/
09 Oc '29/ 14 se '39/
French Creek, N.Y. 25 Jl 1860/

Gander, Nfld. 04 Jl '42/
Gander Airport, Nfld. 17 Je '40/ 11 No '40/
Gasport, N.Y. 25 Se 1862/
Georgetown, Ont. 16 Fe '61/
Gimli, Man. De '50/ 30 Ag '56/
Goderich, Ont. 18 Ag '31/
Golden, B.C. 07 Ag '19/
Goose Bay, Lab. 15 Ap '47/ 14 Jl '48/
Grand Forks, B.C. 07 Ag '19/
Grand Junction, Cal. 03 Oc '13/
Grand'Mère, Que. 05-08 Je '19/
Grand Prairie, Alta. 19 Ag '20/
Grave, Neth. 17-23 Se '44/
Great Falls, Mon. 14 Se '30/
Great Whale River, Que. 28 Jl '31/
Greenland 16 Ag '28/ 08 Je '29/ 23 Ag '30/
28 Jl '31/ 28 Ag '31/ 23 Ag '32/
11 Jl '33/ 21, 27 Ag '34/ 18 Jl '35/
14 Jl '48/
Greenly Island, Lab. 13 Ap '28/ 15 Ap '28/
26 Ap '28/ 25 Jl '28/
Greenport, N.Y. 09 Oc '19/
Greenwood, N.S. 31 Mr '50/ 30 Ap '51/
Grenada, Cal. 01 De '31/
Griffith's Island, N.W.T. 15 Jl 1851/
Grostenquin, Fr. 28 Se-11 Oc '52/
12-16 Fe '57/
Guelph, Ont. 27 Jl '12/ 28 Jl '13/
Gulf of St. Lawrence 24 De '46/ 08 Fe '62/

Haileybury, Ont. 03 Se '24/ Ap '25/
Halifax, N.S. 28 Je 1838/ Se 1847/ 31 Jl 1871/
Ag 1883/ 02 Oc 1891/ 26 Se '07/
01 Oc '07/ 31 Ag '11/ 16 Se '12/
04 Se '13/ 05 Je '18/ 19 Ag '18/ 08,
14 My '19/ 05-08 Je '14/ 15 Ag '19/
26-28 Ag '20/ 07-17 Oc '20/ 17 Jl '27/
05 Je '28/ 23 Ag '30/ 11 Jl '33/
01 Ap '38/ 16 Fe '40/ 20 My '40/
08 Je '40/ 15 Ap '41/ 01 Mr '47/
14-15 Ja '49/
Halton, Eng. 22 Ag '18/
Hamburg, Ger. 28-29 Jl '43/ 28-29 Jl '44/
Hamilton, Ont. 10 Ap 1837/ 29 My 1861/
22 Jl 1862/ 21 Je 1875/ 18 My '09/
27 Jl '11/ 02 Ag '11/ 24 Jl '13/
12 Ag '13/ 15 My '14/ 23 Se '15/
28 My '20/ 27 Se '23/ 08 Je '27/
13 Mr '28/ 24 My '28/ 06 Je '29/
01 Jl '31/ 15 My '35/ 15 Ap '46/
Hammondsport, N.Y. 13 Ja '08/ 12,
17 Mr '08/ 18, 23 My '08/ 20 Je '08/
06 De '08/
Harbour Deep, Nfld. 30 mr '24/
Harbour Grace, Nfld. 04, Jl '19/ 26 Ag '27/
06, 07 Se '27/ 17 Oc '28/ 09 Oc '29/
25 Je '30/ 02 Ag '30/ 08, 09-10 Oc '30/
22, 23 Je '31/ 13 Jl '31/ 13, 20 My '32/
05 Jl '32/ 23 Ag '32/ 07 Ag '33/
28 Je '34/ 14 Se '36/ 28 Oc '36/
Hartford, Conn. 28 Ja '29/
Harwich, Eng. 17 Je '17/
Hatton, Sask. 30 My '32/
Hatt's Mills, N.B. 14 Oc 1863/
Havana, Cuba 30 Ja '11/ 22 Mr '11/
26 No '28/ 23 Fe '29/ 28 Ag '32/
Hawaii Oc '59/
Hawkes Bay, Nfld. 31 Ag '24/
Hazelton, B.C. 25 Jl '20/ 03 Se '20/ Jl '21/
Hendon, Eng. 31 De '10/
High River, Alta. 27 Jl '29/
Holyrood, Nfld. 19 My '32/
Honolulu, Haw. Fe '27/ 19 No '34/
Honeoye Falls, N.Y. 08 Fe '62/
Hopedale, Lab. 23 Ag '32/
Hudson, Ont. 03 Mr '26/ 27 De '26/
Humboldt, Sask. 28 Je '21/
Huntingdon, Que. 08 Se 1896/

Iceland 08 Je '29/ 17 Ap '44/ 14 Jl '48/
Icy Tickle, Lab. 31 Ag '24/

Ingersoll, Ont. 08 Jl '12/
Ireland 25 Je '30/ 20 My '32/ 24 Ap '44/
11 Se '44/
Irish Creek, Ont. 04 Jl 1871/
Issoundun, Que. 11 Ag '57/
Italy 28 Jl '33/
Ithaca, N.Y. 15-16 Ap '20/
Ivigtut, Gre. 31 Ag '24/
Jackson, Mich. 04-06 Se 1888/
James Bay 05 Fe '22/
Japan 07 De '41/
Jasper, Alta. 25 Jl '20/
Jean Baptiste, Man. 22 Oc '12/

Kamsack, Sask. 27 Jl '20/
Karachi, Pak. 03 Mr '53/
Kattegat 02 My '45/
Kelowna, B.C. 13 Ag '14/
Key West, Fla. 30 Ja '11/ 26 No '28/
Kingston, Ont. 18 My 1835/ 25 Jl 1860/
05 Se 1860/ 03 Je '12/ 02, 03 Je '13/
25-26 Ag '33/ 30 Jl-07 Ag '49/
04 Je '50/
Kiska, Alas. 25 Se '42/
Kiskisink, Que. 17-19 Oc '10/
Kingston, Jam. 01 De '48/
Kitchener, Ont. 15 Jl '12/ 28 Jl-05 Ag '51/
Korea 27 Jl '50/ 30 Mr '51/ 23 Ja '53/
Krefeld, Ger. 22 Je '31/
Krugerville, Alta. 10 Ag '07/

Labrador Ag '19/ 17 Fe '28/
Lac du Bonnet, Man. 01 je '27/ 06 Oc '27/
26 Ag '29/ 09 Ag '32/ My '33/
26 Ag '35/
Lac la Biche, Alta. 09 Ag '32/
Lake Fortune, Que. 23 My '24/
Lake Ontario 15 No '15/
Lake Puskatamika, Que. 24 My '36/
Lakeside, Que. see Pt. Claire, Que.
Lanark, Ont. 04 Jl '13/
Larder Lake, Ont. 21 Ja '25/
La Tuque, Que. 17-19 Oc '10/
Leamington, Ont. 30 No '27/
Leaside, Ont. 01 My '28/
Leksand, Swed. 15 My '39/
Lerwick, Shetland Isles 28 Jl '31/
Lethbridge, Alta. 14 Jl '11/ 01 Ag '19/ Jl '21/
14 Se .30/ 01 Ap '39/
Liard River, B.C. 24 No '30/
Liverpool, Eng. 16 Fe '40/ 20 My '40/
08 Je '40/ 24 No '40/
London, Eng. 16 Oc 1784/ 22 Se 1891/
16 Ag '19/ 04 Je '20/ 29 Je '27/
26, 28 Ag '27/ 06, 07 Se '27/ 17 Oc '28/
08 Je '29/ 09 Oc '29/ 20 Oc '31/
12 Oc-10 De '32/ 08-09 Ag '34/
28 Oc '36/ 28 My '39/ 01 Ja '40/
15 Se '47/ 06 Oc '55/ 09 Oc '58/
London, Ont. 21 Ag 1862/ 16 Oc 1862/
26 Je 1875/ 22-28 Se 1888/ 13 Se '07/
25 My '12/ 16 Je '13/ 08 Je '27/
28 Ag '27/ 06 Se '27/ 28 Jl '28/
01 Ap '38/ 24 Je '40/ 14 My '43/
Long Beach, Cal. 29 Je '65/
Long Branch, Ont. 14 Jl '15/ 03 Se '15/
Long Island, N.Y. 23 Oc '12/ 04 Jl '19/
09 Oc '19/ 14 De '20/ 11 Jl '33/
Long Lac, Ont. 28 Ag '31/
Long Lake, Man. 01 Je '27/
Long Point, Ont. 23 Je 1875/ 20 Fe '12/
Longueuil, Que. 28 Ja '29/ 27 No '31/
31 Oc '34/ 24 Ag '37/ 14 Je '46/
30 De '52/
Lorainville, Que. 17-19 Oc '10/
Los Angeles, Cal. 06 Ag '12/ 16 Se '14/
12 Se '28/

Magdalen Island, Que. 27 Ag '23/ 11 Ja '28/
Mr '28/
Malta 27 Jl '42/ 14 Oc '42/
Malton, Ont. 16 Ag '39/ 27 My '40/ 24 Je '40/
05 No '42/ 01 Ag '43/ 25 Oc '45/
01 De '45/ 17 Mr '48/ 10 Fe '49/
27 Je '49/ 10 Ag '49/ 19 Ja '50/
13 Jl '50/ 20 Je '51/ 04 Oc '57/
25 Mr '58/ 18 Ap '58/ 04 De '58/
11 Ag '60/ 16 My '61/ 12 Je '63/
Manila, P.I. 06 Ja '35/
Manitoba 01 Mr '38/
Manouane, Que. 01 Ag '40/
Marville, Fr. 01-04 No '54/ 01 Ja '62/
Medicine Hat, Alta. 24 Je '11/ 02 Se '12/
Melbourne, Aust. Fe '27/
Menin, Belg. 25 My '40/
Merrickville, Ont. 29 Ag 1879/
Metz, Fr. 29-30 Se '39/ 10 Ap '53/
Mexico Jl '21/ Mid Jl '22/ 16 Ja '54/
Mexico City, Mex. 23 Je '28/ 20 Oc '31/
23 Oc '32/
Mimico, Ont. 11 Se '09/
Minetto, N.Y. 24 Ag 1859/
Minnedosa, Man. 20 Jl '11/ 18 Jl '12/
Miscou Island, N.B. 28 Ap '39/
Mohawk, N.Y. 02 Jl 1883/
Moisie, Que. 12 Se '39/
Moncton, N.B. 11 Ja '28/ 19 Fe '28/
09 De '29/ 01-02 Jl '29/ 01 Ja '40/
01 My '42/
Montauk Point, N.Y. 15 My '19/
Montmedy, Fr. 10 Jl '56/
Montreal, Que. 15 Oc 1834/ 24 Ag 1835/
04, 08, 15, 22 Se 1856/ 04 Ag 1860/
11 Se 1862/ 31 My 1878/ 28 Se 1878/
21 Je 1879/ 31 Jl 1879/ 18 Se 1880/
22, 24 Se 1891/ 19 Se 1892/ 13 Jl '06/
Ag '07/ 20 or 21, 31 Ag '07/ Se '07/
Mr '09/ 26 Mr '10/ 16 My '10/
29 Je '10/, 12, 26 Jl '10/ 02 Ag '10/
22 Oc '10/ 03, 22 Mr '11/ 06,
23-24 Je '11/ 19 Se '11/ 06-07-14-
15 Oc '11/ 06, 09, 14, 15 Oc '11/
28 De '11/ 19 Je '12/ 14, 22 Se '12/
23 Oc '12/ 06 Se '13/ 08 Oc '13/
06 De '13/ 25, 27 Je '14/ 29 Ag '17/
24 Je '18/ 12 Jl '19/ 26-28 Ag '20/ '20/
10 My '21/ 05 Je '22/ 22-24 Ja '24/
04 No '24/ 25 Jl '25/ 10 My '26/
11-19 Se '26/24 Je '27/ 16 Se '27/
Fe '28/ 28 Ap '28/ 07-15 Jl '28/ 02,
10 Ag '28/ 01 Oc '28/ De '28/ 04-11,
17 My '29/ 20 Je '29/ Ag '29/
05 Oc '29/ 09 De '29/ 01 Ag '30/

26 My '31/ 03, 07 Jl '31/ 10,
15-16 Ag '31/ 04, 25 Jl '32/ 20-21,
28 Ag '32/ 12 Oc-10 De '32/ 12 Jl '33/
19-20, 25-26 Ag '33/ 01 Se '34/
19 No '34/ 23 Ja '35/ 18, 20 Jl '35/
20 Jl '36/ 23 My '37/ 05-08 Jl '37/
01, 28-29 Ag '37/ 21 Jl '38/ 01 De '38/
01 Ap '39/ 18 Jl '39/ 06 Ag '39/
20 My '40/ 16 Ag '40/ 01 De '40/
22 De '41/ 04 Ja '43/ 23 Je-01 Jl '43/
15 Ap '46/ 06-28 My '47/ 09 Jl '47/
01 My '48/ 01, 15 De '48/ 28 Mr '49/
Ja '54/ 14-15 Oc '54/ 19 De '58/
25 Je '61/
Moose Factory, Ont. 17, 28 Ag '20/ 02 Se '20/
14 De '20/ 30 Jl '31/
Moose Jaw, Sask. 15 Je '31/ 09 Ap '53/
Morden, Man. 10 Se '13/ 11 Se '13/ 12 Se '13/
13 Se '13/ 13 Jl '27/
Morrisburg, Ont. 16 Ag '19/
Moscow, USSR 19 ag '37/ 28 Ap '39/
Mt. Slesse, B.C. 09 De '56/
Munich, Ger. 28 Jl '65/
Munster, Ger. 19 Oc-16 No '45/
Murray Bay, Que. 26 Ap '28/
Musgrave Harbour, Nfld. 14 Se '36/
Muskoka, Ont. 18 Jl '39/ 01 De '40/

Namao, Alta. 22 Ap '46/ 10-13 Se '48/
20 No '56/ Jl '62/
Nanaimo, B.C. 9 Je 1880/
Napanee, Ont. 01 Jl '12/ 01 Jl '13/
Nassau, Bah. Is. 01 De '48/
Neareagh, N.S. 07 Ag '48/
Nelson, B.C. 24 Se '12/ 14 Jl '14/
Newark, N.J. 20 Jl '36/
New Britain, Conn. 13 Jl '06/
New Castle, Del. 17 oc '35/
Newfoundland 14 No '20/ My-Je '27/
13 Je '27/ 20 My '32/ 17 Je '40/
20 Fe '41/ 25 Oc '41/
New Glasgow, N.S. 08 Ag 1871/
Newport, Vt. 06 Se 1899/
New Westminister, B.C. 10 Oc 1894/
14 Oc .10/ 26 Mr '10/ 01 Se '51/
New York, N.Y. Se 1847/ 06, 07, 15 Oc '11/
09, 25 My '12/ 01, 08 Jl '12/ 02 Se '12/
03 Je '13/ 01 Jl '14/ 15 No '15/
29 Ag '19/ 04 Je '20/ '20/ 09, 10,
21 My '21/ 11 Se '24/ 12 Ap '26/
26 Ap '28/ 01 Oc '28/ 19, 21 Jl '29/
28 Se '29/ 05 Fe '30/ 25, 29 Je '30/
02, 23 Ag '30/ 22, 23 Je '31/ 07,
13 Jl '31/ 19 My '32/ 05 Jl '32/
19 Ag '32/ 11 Je '33/ 22, 25, 28 Jl '33/
19-20 Ag '33/ 27 Ag '34/ 18, 20 Jl '35/
26 Ag '35/ 14 Se '36/ 28 Oc '36/
05-08 Jl '37/ 10 My '41/
Niagara Falls, Ont. 08 Je .27/
Nome, Alas. 19, 21 Jl '29/ 26 Ag '35/
Normandy, Fr. 06 Je '44/ 07 Je '44/
North Adams, Mass. 20-21 My .10/
North Battleford, Sask. 26 Jl '12/ 19,
22 Ag '13/ 14 Se '30/
North Bay, Ont. 17ñ19 Oc '10/ 01 Ap '53/
15 Mr '54/ 11 Oc '55/ Oc '59/
28 De '61/ 13 My '63/ 28 Se '63/
North Luffenham, Eng. 01 No '51
30 My-15 Je '52/
North Haven, Me. 30 Jl '31/
Northolt, Eng. 17 Ag '40/
North Magnetic Pole 19 Jl '47/
North Sydney, N.S. 31 Ag '18/
North Vancouver, B.C. 14 Se '02/
North West River, Lab. 03 Jl '39/ 12 Se '39/
Norway 18 Jl '35/
Nottingham Island, N.W.T. 08 Je '29/

Oakland, Cal. 14 Jl '14/ 19 No '34/ 28 my '38/
Oakville, Ont. 13 Jl '13/
Ogdensburg, N.Y. 19-20 Fe '11/
Old Orchard Beach, Me. 26 Ag '27/ 06 Se '27/
28 My '39/
Onagawa Bay, Jap. 09 Ag '45/
Ontario 18 Je-27 Jl '34/
Oran, Alg. 08 No '42/
Orlando, Fla. 19 Ag '51/
Ortebello, Ita. 12 jl '33/
Oshawa, Ont. 04 Je '50/
Oslo, Nor. 23 Ag '32/
Oswego, N.Y. 04 Jl 1871/
Ottawa, Ont. 17 Je 1858/ 01 Se 1858/
22-23 Se 1859/ 03 Jl 1877/ 12 Se 1877/
01 Jl 1878/ 27 Ag 1878/ 01 Jl 1883/
26 Se 1884/ 16 Se '09/ 22 Jl '10/
11 Se '11/ 07-14 Se .12/ 15 Jl '13/
11 Se '13/ 08 Oc '13/ 06 Jl '18/
15 Ag '18/ 15-16, 19 Ap '20/
summer '20/ 26-28 Ag '20/
22-24 Ja '24/ 11 Se '24/ Se '24/
24 Ja '27/ 29 Je '27/ 02 Jl '27/
27 Oc '27/ 05-08 Se '28/ 03 Je '29/
Jl '29/ 05 Oc '29/ 01 Ja '30/ 12 My '30/
Je '31/ 03, 30 Jl '31/ 02 Oc '31/ '31/
23 Oc '32/ '32/ 27 Ag '34/ 20 Jl '36/
'37/ 18 Jl '39/ 17 De '39/ 05 Ag '40/
01 De '40/ '42/ Je '43/ 18 Oc '43/
05 Fe '45/ 01 Oc '45/ 15, 21, 22 Ap '46/
01 Mr '47/ 05 Ap '47/ 01 No '49/ '49/
05 Je '50/ Ja '54/ 11 Ap '54/ 25 My '54/
.54/ 06 Oc '55/ 15 My '57/ 01 Jl '59/
25 Oc '60/ 06 Je '64/

Palmdale, Cal. 26 My '61/
Paris, Fr. 02 Ja '52/ Ag '52/ 01 Oc '52/
10 Ap '53/
Parrsboro, N.S. 04 Jl '19/ 09 Oc '19/
Parr Town, N.B. see St. John, N.B.
Patricia Bay, B.C. 10 Ja '42/ 15 Je '42/
02 Se-14 Oc '47/
Peace River, Alta. Ja '21/
Peace River Crossing, Alta. Se '20/ 24 Ma '21/
Peelee Island, Ont. 30 No '27/
Peenemunde, Ger. 17-18 Ag '43/
Pelly, Sask. 27 Jl '20/
Pembina, N. Dak. 03 Fe '31/
Pennfield Ridge, N.B. 19 Ag '32/
Petawawa, Ont. 02, 12 Ag '09/
Peterborough, Ont. 12 Ag '12/ 12-14 Se '12/
21 Se '12/ 13 Se '18/
Philadelphia, Penn. 11 Oc 1856/ 24 Ag 1859/
15 Jl '18/
Pictou, N.S. 31 Ag '24/
Pilot Mound, Man. 10, 11 Se '13/ 12 Se '13/

Pittsburg, Penn. 20 Je '11/
Placentia Bay, Nfld. 23 Ag '32/
Pleasantville, Nfld. 18 My '19/
Plymouth, N.H. 26-27 Se 1872/
Point Barrow, Alas. 30 Jl '31/
Pointe aux Trembles, Que. 12 No '35/
Pointe Claire, Que. 24, 25, 26, 27, 28, 29, 30 Je '10/ 01, 02, 03, 04, 05 Jl '10/
Portage la Prairie, Man. 10 Jl '07/ 12 Jl '10/ 22 My '12/
Port Arthur, Ont. 04 Se '11/
Port au Prince, Haiti 07 Jl '33/
Port Burwell, Lab. 27 Jl '27/ 08 Je '29/ 07 Jl '29/
Port Colborne, Ont. 17 Je 1875/
Port Elgin, Ont. 01 Jl '13/
Port Harrison, Que. 18 Ag '31/ 28 Ag '31/
Port Hope, Ont. 01 Jl '14/
Portland, Me. 05 Oc '29/
Portland, Ore. 14, 18 Ap '11/ 24 Se '12/ 05 Se '13/
Portmarnock Strand, Ire. 19 Ag '32/
Port Menier, Que. 23 Ag '32/
Port of Spain, Trin. 01 De '48/
Port Stanley, Ont. 17 Jl '12/
Port Washington, N.Y. 03-06 Jl '37/ 26 Je '39/ 08-09 Jl '39/
Povungnituk, Que. 27 Ag '34/
Prestwick, Scot. 23 Je-01 Jl '43/ 15 Ap '47/
Prince Albert, Sask. 15 Jl '31/
Prince Edward Island 27 Ag '23/
Prince George, B.C. 25 Jl '20/
Prince Rupert, B.C. Jl '21/ 06 Ap '24/ 03 Ag '24/ 09 Ag '32/
Puget Sound, B.C. 25 Ag '28/

Quebec Jl '26/ 18 Je-27 Jl '34/
Quebec City, Que. 23 Ag 1892/ 29 Ag '11/ 26 Ag '12/ 25-29 Ag '13/ 30 My '14/ 13, 31 Ag '14/ 21 Se '14/ 26-28 Ag '20/ 18 Jl '22/ 25 De '27/ de '27/ 25 Ap '28/ 01 De '28/ 14 No '28/ 02, 03, 07 Jl '31/ 25-26 Ag '33/ 19 No '34/ 01 Ja '37/ 22 De '41/
Queensport, N.S. 23 Ag '30/
Quidi Vidi, Nfld. 10 Ap '19/ 18 Jl '19/

Rabat, Mor. 05-07 Mr '60/
Red Lake, Ont. Mr '26/ 03 Mr '26/ 12, 14 Ap '26/ Oc '26/ 27 De '26/
Regina, Sask. 05 Ag '11/ 30 Jl '12/ 29 Jl-01 Ag '13/ 20 Ap '20/ 31 Jl '20/ 08 Oc '21/ 29 My '28/ 10-29 De '28/ 04 Jl '32/ 25 Jl '33/ 04 Ag '33/ 01 Je '35/
Remi Lake, Ont. 17, 28 Ag '20/ 02 Se '20/
Reno, Nev. 01 De '31/
Republic of the Congo see Zaire
Repulse Bay, N.W.T. 27 No-20 De '39/
Resolute Bay, N.W.T. Ag-Se 1850/ 15 Jl 1851/
Reykjavik, Ice. 24 Ja '44/
Rheine, Ger. 29 De '44/
Richmond Gulf 03 Ja '29/
Ridgefield, N.J. 15 No '15/
Rimouski, Que. 28 Ap '28/
Rivière au Fortin, Qué. 09 Oc '29/
Rivers, Man. 09 Jl '45/ 09 Ja '57/ 23 Oc '65/
Rockcliffe, Ont. 01 Ja '42/ 15 De '43/
Rockcliffe Air Station 15 My '57/ 6 Ju '64/
Rockford, Ill. 16 Ag '28/
Rome, It. 20 My '48/
Rome, N.Y. 04 Jl 1871/
Rothesay, N.B. '02/ 28 Ja '09/ 21 Se '09/
Rouyn, Que. 23 My '24/ 03 Se '24/ 03 No '24/ 21 Ja '25/ Ap '25/ 23 My '37/
Ruhr, Ger. 16-17 My '43/
Rupert House, Que. 28 Jl '31/ 18 Ag '31/

Sackville, N.B. Summer '52/
St. Anns, Ont. 29 My 1861/ 30 My 1861/
St. Anthony, Nfld. 03 Mr '22/
St. Catharines, Ont. 30 My 1861/ 28 Jl '14/
Ste. Anne, Que. 31 Jl 1879/
St. Eugène, Ont. 29 Jl-06 Ag '50/
St. Felicien, P.Q. 09 Oc '29/
Ste. Felicite, Que. 18 Oc '27/
St. Hilaire, Minn. 01 Jl '12/
St Hubert, Que. 24 Je '27/ Ag '27/ 12 My .28/ 05-06 Oc '29/ 28 Ag '43/ 01 Se '48/ 01 No '49/ 01 Mr '51/ 01 Je '51/ 15 De '51/ 12 Fe '52/ 01 Ag '52/ 01 Mr '53/ 01 Je '53/ 01 Oc '54/ 30 Ag '56/ 12-16 Fe '57/ 13 My '63/
St. Hubert Airport, Que. 05 De '42/
Ste. Hyacinthe, Que. 20-21 My '10/
St. Jean, Que. 22 Se '64/
St. John, N.B. 16 Oc 1784/ 10 Ag 1840/ 04 Ag 1860/ 12 Jl 1871/ 19 Je '12/ 02 Se '12/ 14 Oc '13/ 22 Je '31/ 23 Ag '32/ 01 Ap '38/ 36 No '54/
St. Johns, Nfld. 18 Ma '19/ 10 Ap '19/ 15 My '19/ 14-15 Je '19/ 09 Oc '29/ 06 Jl '30/ 19 No '30/ 11 Jl '33/ 28 My '39/ 01 My '42/ 30 Oc '42/
St. Jude, Que. 21 Je 1879/
Ste. Julie de Verchères, Que. 03 Mr '11/
St. Lambert, Que. 15 Se 1856/
St. Leonard, Que. 11 Se 1862/
St. Louis, Miss. 21 Oc '07/ 17-19 Oc '10/ 22 My '12/
St. Marc, Haiti 11 Je '33/
St. Paul, Minn. 10 Jl '07/
St. Pierre, Que. 18 Jl '35/
St. Pierre & Miquelon 13 Je '27/
Ste. Thérèse, Que. 29 No '63/
St. Thomas, Ont. Je 1875/ 19 Jl 1889/
St. Yon, Fr. 29 Je-13 Jl '56/
San Diego, Cal. 30 My '11/ 19 Je '12/
San Francisco, Cal. 15 Jl '10/
Saskatchewan 01 Mr '38/ Je '61/
Saskatoon, Sask. 08 Ag '08/ 18 My .11/ 01 Je '11/ 06 Ag '12/ 06 Mr '13/ 16 Se '14/ 25 Jl '20/ 28 Je '21/ 04 My '28/ 08 Je '29/ 14 Se '30/
Sault Ste. Marie, Ont. 01 Jl '12/ 26 Ag '35/
Savage Harbour, P.E.I. 04 My '29/
Savona, N.Y. 24 Jl '13/
Sayabec, Que. 26-27 Se 1872/
Schwerte, Ger. 12-13 Je '41/
Scotland 14 Jl '48/

Seattle, Wash. 28 Fe '19/ 03 Mr '19/ 15 Oc '20/ 23, 25 Ag '28/ 04 Ag '36/ 01 Se '37/
Selfridge Field, Mich. 24 Ja '27/ 02 Jl '27/
Selkirk, Man. 13 Jl '14/
Seven Islands, Que. 03 Jl '39/
Shediac, N.B. 12 Jl '33/ 03-06 Jl '37/ 26 Je '39/ 08-09 Jl '39/
Sheepshead Bay, N.Y. 27 Ag '10/
Shelter Bay, Que. 15 Jl '22/
Sherbrooke, Que. 04-06 Se 1888/ 04 Se 1889/ 02-03 Se 1891/ 02-05 Se 1896/ 01-03 Se 1897/ 06 Se 1899/ 04 Se '07/ 02 Se '12/ 30 Ag '13/ 07 Se '14/
Shetland Isles 18 Mr-06 Ap '42/ 03, 11, 13, 24 Je '44/
Shippegan, N.B. 18, 20 My '27/
Shoal Harbour, Nfld. 28 Jl '33/
Siberia Jl '21/ Mid Jl '22/
Sicily 11-12 Jl '43/
Sioux Lookout, Ont. 14 Fe '39/
Sitka, Alas. 06 Ap '24/
Skagerrak 17 My '42/
Solsgirth, Man. 04 Se '11/
Southampton, Eng. 03-06 Jl '37/
South Cerney, Eng. 29 My-13 Je '65/
South Pond, Me. 11 Jl '33/
Spicer Islands, N.W.T. 31 De .46/
Staten Island, N.Y. 05 No '12/
Stockholm, Swed. 16 Ag '28/
Straits of Belle Isle 28 My-07 je '27/
Stratford, Ont. 03, 09 Je '13/
Sturgis, Mich. 11 Jl '06/
Sudbury, Ont. 17-19 Oc '10/ 11 Jl '20/ Sum '23/ 18 Ag '31/ 04 Jl '32/ My '41/
Summerside, P.E.I. 04 My .51/ 01 My '61/
Sydney, Aust. Fe '27/ 13 Jl '49/
Sydney, N.S. 15 Mr '11/ 05 Je '18/ 21 Ag '34/ 01 My '42/ 07 Je '42/

Tampa, Fla. 16 Ja '54/
Tampico, Mex. 23 Je '28/
Teheran, Iran Se '62/
Telegraph Creek, B.C. 03 Se '20/
The Pas, Man. 15-17 Oc '20/ Ag-Se '27/ 07 Je '32/ 12-24 Se '48/
Three Rivers, Que. Se '24/
Thunder Bay, Ont. see Fort William, Ont. and Port Arthur, Ont.
Todmorden, Ont. 15 Se 1888/ 03-05 Ag '11/
Tofino, B.C. 10 Ap '42/
Tokyo, Jap. 26 Ag '27/ 27 Jl '50/
Toledo, Ohio 13 Se '07/ 16 Se '09/
Torbay, Nfld. 18 My '42/ 16 My '59/
Toronto, Ont. 24 Ag 1859/ 08 Se 1859/ 25 Je 1860/ 19 Ag 1862/ 25 Se 1862/ 23 Se 1874/ 24 My 1875/ 22 Je 1875/ 20 Fe 1895/ 29 Ag '07/ 09 Ag '09/ 02 Se '09/ 07, 08, 09, 11, 12, 14, 14, 15, 16 Jl '10/ 03 Fe '11/ 08 Jl '11/ 02, 03-05 Ag '11/ 05 De '11/ 19 Je '12/ 06 Jl '12/ 10 De '12/ 13 Jl .13/ 15, 17 My '14/ 28 Jl '14/ Jl '15/ 11, 14 Jl '15/ 28 Jl '15/ Summer '15/ 03, 23 Se '15/ 15, No '15/ 29 Mr '16/ 15 My '16/ 01 Ja '17/ 22, 27 Fe '17/ Mr '18/ 24 Je '18/ 29 Jl '18/ 15 Ag '18/ Oc '18/ '18/ 05-06, 20, 24 My '19/ 05, 09 Ag '19/ 23 Ag-06 Se '19/ 29 Ag '19/ 19 Ap '20/ 28 My '20/ 04 Je '20/ 09 Ag '20/ '20/ 10 My '21/ 22 Ap '24/ 08, 29 Je '27/ Mr '28/ 08 Mr '28/ 25 Jl '28/ 01 Oc '28/ Mr '29/ Ap '29/ 29 Je '29/ 05 Oc '29/ 19 No '30/ 06 Je '31/ 03 Jl '31/ 08 Se '31/ 20 Oc '31/ 05 Oc '32/ 22 Ag '33/ My '34/ 26 Ag '35/ Se '37/ 13 Ap '38/ 15 Se '38/ 18 Jl '39/ 18 Se '39/ 15 Ap '40/ 01 De '40/ 15 Ap '41/ 10 My '41/01 Ag '43/ Ag '44/ 15 Ap '46/ No '47/ 01 My '48/ 10-13 Se '48/ 01 De '48/ 26 Se '50/ 01 Oc '50/ '53/ Ja '54/ 16 Ja '54/ 29 Je-13 Jl '56/ '60/ Je '61/
Trenton, Ont. 23 Je '13/ 15 Ap '40/ 24 No '40/ 16 Ja '45/ 01 Mr '47/ 01 Ja '62/
Trepassey, Nfld. 20 My '27/ 05 Je '28/
Trepassey Bay, Nfld. 08, 14, 16 My '19/
Trois Rivières, Que; 16 Ag 1892/
Truro, N.S. 29 Se '19/
Tunisia 26 Je '43/
Tyneside, Ont. 21 Oc '07/
Tyringham, Mass. 28, 29 My '19/

United States Jl '21/
Upper Heyford, Eng. 20 No '18/
Uplands, Ont. 08 Ja '51/ 01 Se '51/ 30 My-15 Je '52/ 01 Jl '52/ 01 Ja '53/ 21 Je '54/ 01-04 No '54/
Uplands Air Station, 15 My '57/ 25 Oc '60/
Ushant (Ouessant), Fr. 08 Je '44/

Vaagso, Nor. 27 De '41/
Valemount, B.C. 21 Jl '29/
Vancouver, B.C. 25, 26, 28 Mr '10/ 14, 18 Ap '11/ 30 Ap-06 My '11/ 11 Jl '11/ 10, 13, 24 Ap '12/ 04, 23, 24 My '12/ 01 Jl '12/ 10 Ag '12/ 05 No '12/ 31 Jl '13/ 13 Je '14/ 01 Jl '14/ 28 Fe '19/ 03 Mr '19/ 13, 31 My '19/ Jl '19/ 07 Ag '19/ 07-17 Oc '20/ 11-19 Se '26/ Fe '27/ 08 Se '27/ 23, 25 Ag '28/ 05-08 Se '28/ Je '29/ 27 Jl '29/ 12 Ag '29/ 31 Jl '30/ 19 Je '31/ 01 De '31/ 23 Ja '32/ 04 Jl '32/ 05 Oc '32/ 25-26 Ag '33/ 06 Ja '35/ 20 Jl '35/ 01, 04 Ag '36/ 01 Ag '37/ 01 Se '37/ 01 Mr '38/ 28 My '38/ 01, 27 Oc '38/ 01 De '38/ 17 Fe '39/ 01 Ap '39/ 02 Ja '42/ 15 Je '42/ 06 Je '43/ 06 No '43/ 15 Ap '46/ 01 Mr '47/ 14-15 Ja '49/ 13 Jl '49/ 15 Oc '50/ 31 Jl '51/ 11 Ap '54/ 01 Se '55/ 16 Ja '56/ 06 Jl '56/ 30 Ag '56/
Vandenberg, Cal. 28 Se '62/
Vega Harbour, Spain 06 Se '43/
Vermilion, Alta. 02 My '11/
Vernon, B.C. 07 Ag '19/

Victoria, B.C. 20 Jl 1871/ 26 Ag 1896/ 23 My '01/ 07 Ag '02/ 22 Se '09/ 08 Se '10/ 30 My '11/ 24 My '12/ 06 Ag '13/ 13 My '19/ 15 Oc '20/ 08 Jl '28/ 07, 23, 25 Ag '28/ 06 Je '43/
Victoria Island, N.W.T. 15 Fe-06 My '46/
Victoria Land, N.W.T. 09 Mr '21/
Virden, Man. 06 Ag '13/

Wadhope, Man. 06 Oc '27/
Wakeham Bay, Que. 28 Jl '31/
Wales 05 Je '28/
Walkerville, Que. 08 Jl '08/
Wangerooge Island, Ger. 25 Ap '45/
Warsaw, Pol. 08 Ag '33/ 28 Je '34/
Wasaga Beach, Ont. 03 Oc '33/ 08-09 Ag '34/
Washington, D.C. 15-16, 19 Ap '20/ 02 Jl '27/ 20 Oc '31/ 07 Jl '33/ 12 My '58/
Washington State 10 Oc 1894/
Watertown, N.Y. 22-23 Se 1859/ 5-6 My '19/
Watford, Ont. 28, 29 My '19/
Wawanesa, Man. 06, 10, 12, 13, 15 Se '13/
Webbwood, Ont. 11 Jl '20/
Wellington, B.C. 11 Je 1880/
West Germany 18 Oc '58/
Weston, Ont. 08 Jl '10/
West Palm Beach, Fla. 11 Se '56/
West Shefford, Que. 05 Jl '08/
Weyburn, Sask. 16, 18 Se '13/
Whitecourt, Alta. 19 Ag '20/
White Haven, Penn. 26 Se 1884/
White horse, Y.T. 25 My '03/ 18 Je '20/ 03 Se '20/ 19, 21 Jl '29/ 02 Ap '35/ 05 Jl '37/
Willow Grove, Pa. Se '31/
Windsor, Ont. 27 Se '10/ 03 Jl '11/ 23 Je '28/ 12 Se '28/ 26 No '28/ 23 Fe '29/ Mr '29/ 05 Oc '29/ 04, 13 Jl '31/ 19 Ag '51/ 16 My '59/
Windsor, N.S. 02 Jl '14/
Windsor Mills, Que. 24 Je .40/
Winnipeg, Man. 21 Jl 1893/ 27 My 1896/ 02, 16 Je '01/ 31 My '09/ 15 Jl '09/ 15 Jl '10/ 13, 22 Jl '11/ 09, 24 My '12/ 10 Jl '12/ 11 Jl '14/ 4-5 Ag '16/ 27 Jl '20/ 15-17 Oc '20/ 01 Oc '24/ 10 De '26/ 01 Je '27/ 24, 28 My '28/ 28 Ag '28/ 10-29 De '28/ 25 My '29/ 07 Jl '29/ 27 Jl '29/ 14 Se '30/ 03 Fe '31/ 15 Je '31/ 05 Oc '32/ 20 Oc '36/ 01 Oc '38/ 26 Je '39/ 27 No-20 De '39/ 01 Oc '40/ 01 Mr '44/ 01 De '44/ 15 Ap '46/ 01 Mr '47/ 10-13 Se '48/ 11 Ap '54/
Winnipeg Beach, Man. 01, 13 Jl '14/
Woodstock, N.B. 08 Jl 1871/
Woodstock, Ont. 28 Oc '12/ 24 Jl '13/
Wrangell, Alas. 25 Jl '20/

Yarmouth, N.S. 15 Fe '42/ 19 My '42/

Zaire 18 Jl '60/
Zweibrucken, Ger. 7 Mr '53/ 11-12 My '57/

## ERRATA

Page 21, 1 Oc '07: read Frederick for Fredrick
Page 56, 6 Au '12: read Glenn for Glen
Page 122 caption: read Laurentide for Laurentian
Page 189, 23 No '35: read Herbert for Heber
Page 248, caption: read trial for trail
Page 311, 04 Ja '17: read ace for Ace
Page 313, 16 Ma '19: read transatlantic for trans Atlantic
Page 314, 06, 18 Oc '12: read Anctil for Anctel
Page 316, 03, Jl 1877: read Grimly for Grimely
Page 317, 23 No '35: Read Hollick-Kenyon for Kenyon, Herbert
Page 324, 01 Ag '40: read Manuan for Manouane